Communications
in Computer and Information Science 171

Jim James Yonazi Eliamani Sedoyeka
Ezendu Ariwa Eyas El-Qawasmeh (Eds.)

e-Technologies and Networks for Development

First International Conference, ICeND 2011
Dar Es Salaam, Tanzania, August 3-5, 2011
Proceedings

Springer

Volume Editors

Jim James Yonazi
The Institute of Finance and Management
P.O. Box 3918, Dar Es Salaam, Tanzania
E-mail: yonazijim@gmail.com

Eliamani Sedoyeka
The Institute of Finance and Management
Faculty of Computing, Information Systems, and Mathematics
P.O. Box 3918, Dar Es Salaam, Tanzania
E-mail: sedoyeka@gmail.com

Ezendu Ariwa
London Metropolitan Business School
London Metropolitan University
Eden Grove - EG4.06, 2-16 Eden Grove, London N7 8EA, UK
E-mail: e.ariwa@londonmet.ac.uk

Eyas El-Qawasmeh
King Saud University
Information Systems Department
Riyadh 11543, Saudi Arabia
E-mail: eyasa@usa.net

ISSN 1865-0929
e-ISSN 1865-0937
ISBN 978-3-642-22728-8
ISBN 978-3-642-22729-5 (eBook)
DOI 10.1007/978-3-642-22729-5
Springer Heidelberg Dordrecht London New York

Library of Congress Control Number: 2011932357

CR Subject Classification (1998): H.4, C.2, H.3, I.2, D.2, H.5

Typesetting: Camera-ready by author, data conversion by Scientific Publishing Services, Chennai, India

Printed on acid-free paper

Springer is part of Springer Science+Business Media (www.springer.com)

Message from the Chairs

The First International Conference on e-Technologies and Networks for Development (ICeND 2011), co-sponsored by Springer, was organized and hosted by The Institute of Finance Management (IFM), Dar-es-Salaam, Tanzania, during August 3-5, 2011 in association with the Society of Digital Information and wireless communications. The ICeND 2011 was planned as a major event in the area of Internet technologies and serves as a forum for scientists and engineers to meet and present their latest research results, ideas, and papers in the diverse areas of web applications, data communications, networks, mobile communications, and information technology.

The conference include guest lectures and 29 research papers for presentation in the technical session. This meeting was a great opportunity to exchange knowledge and experiences for all the participants who joined us from around the world to discuss new ideas in the areas of the internet and its technologies as well as other applications related to the Web and networking. We are grateful to The Institute of Finance Management (IFM), Tanzania, for hosting this conference. We use this occasion to express our thanks to the technical committee and to all the external reviewers. We are grateful to Springer for co-sponsoring the event. Finally, we would like to thank all the participants and sponsors.

Faraja Igira
Jim James Yonazi
Zanifa Omary

Preface

On behalf of the ICeND 2011 Program Committee and The Institute of Finance Management (IFM), Tanzania, welcomed the participants to The First International Conference on e-Technologies and Networks for Development (ICeND 2011) held at The Institute of Finance Management (IFM).

ICeND 2011 explored new advances in internet technologies, networking, e-learning, software applications, computer systems, digital information and data communications technologies. It brought together researchers from various areas of software engineering, information sciences, and networking to address both theoretical and applied aspects of web technologies and networking. We hope that the discussions and exchange of ideas will contribute to advancements in the technology in the near future.

The conference received 90 papers, out of which 29 were accepted, resulting in an acceptance rate of 32%. The accepted papers are authored by researchers from 12 countries covering many significant areas of web applications and wireless communications. Each paper was evaluated by a minimum of two reviewers.

Finally, we believe that the conference proceedings document the best research in the studied areas. We express our thanks to The Institute of Finance Management (IFM), Tanzania, Springer, the authors, and the organizers of the conference.

Organization

General Chair

Faraja Igira	The Institute of Finance Management, Tanzania

Program Chairs

Jim James Yonazi	The Institute of Finance and Management, Tanzania
Zanifa Omary	Dublin Institute of Technology, Ireland

Program Committee

Noraziah Ahmad	University Malaysia Pahang, Malaysia
Yoshiro Imai	Kagawa University, Japan
Jan Platos	VSB-Technical University of Ostrava, Czech Republic

Publicity Chairs

Maitham Safar	Kuwait University, Kuwait
Larry Stapleton	Waterford Institute of Technology, Ireland
Zuqing Zhu	University of Science and Technology of China, China

Table of Contents

Web Ontology

Biometrics Technologies

Networks

Information and Data Management

Computational Intelligence

Network Security

Artificial Intelligence

Security

Sensor Network

Web Applications

Web Services

Wireless Communications

Others

A Generic Model for a Multidimensional Temporal Social Network

Przemysław Kazienko[1,2], Elżbieta Kukla[1], Katarzyna Musial[3], Tomasz Kajdanowicz[1,4], Piotr Bródka[1,4], and Jarosław Gaworecki[1,2]

[1] Wrocław University of Technology, Wyb.Wyspianskiego 27, 50-370 Wrocław, Poland
[2] Research & Engineering Center Sp. z o.o., ul. Strzegomska 46B, 53-611 Wrocław, Poland
[3] Bournemouth University, Fern Barrow, Poole, Dorset BH12 5BB, UK.
[4] Telnet S.K.A., ul. Obrońców Poczty Gdańskiej 13A 52-204 Wrocław, Poland
{kazienko,elzbieta.kukla,tomasz.kajdanowicz,piotr.brodka, jaroslaw.gaworecki}@pwr.wroc.pl, kmusial@bournemouth.ac.uk

Abstract. A comprehensive generic model for a multidimensional, temporal social network is proposed in the paper. It covers three main dimensions: layers, time windows and social groups. All the dimensions share the same set of nodes corresponding to social entities, usually individuals. Layers correspond to different types of relationships between humans, e.g. social and semantic, that can be derived from different human activities in IT systems; time windows reflect the temporal profile of the social network, whereas groups (social communities) are sets of similar humans. The intersection of all dimensions is called a view; it represents the statement of a single social cluster (group) with connections of only one type (from a single layer) and with the snapshot for a given period. Views can be aggregated by one, two or even all three dimensions simultaneously using filtering of dimension instances. Apart from description of the multidimensional model, its applicability is also considered in the paper.

Keywords: social network, multidimensional social network, multi-layered social network, temporal social network, network model, social groups modeling.

1 Introduction

Representation and analysis of the social interactions and activities of people have recently become a very important area of research which attracts people from many fields. Social network analysis is a set of tools that enable investigation of static and dynamic characteristics of both vertices and edges of networks. Although many of these techniques and methods have been developed for the last few decades, the research in this area was limited to small datasets about people and their interactions gathered by sociologists through surveys and questionnaires. Nowadays we have experienced rapid growth of social structures supported by communication technologies and the variety of Internet- and Web-based services. This results in an opportunity to process data (gathered in computer systems) about interactions and activities of millions of individuals.

J.J. Yonazi et al. (Eds.): ICeND 2011, CCIS 171, pp. 1–14, 2011.

Due to scale, complexity and dynamics, social networks built based on gathered information from the Internet, World Wide Web and other sources are very difficult to analyse in terms of traditional social network analysis methods that are at our disposal. Each of those social networked systems are a source of different information about people and their activities, which are the source of different types of relations – layers – within a single network. This change has triggered new techniques which enable analysis of large datasets as well as methods that support the investigation of different types of data. All the extracted networks can be viewed as multidimensional structures, however what should be emphasized is the lack of research published with respect to multidimensional social networks models.

From the data gathered in different systems supported by communication technologies, the information about both nodes and relations between them together with their characteristics can be extracted. This knowledge is the base to create a social network. Nodes in such social networks are digital representations of people who use various services such as electronic mail, telecommunication systems, social networking sites, multimedia sharing systems, etc. Based on peoples activities the relationships of different types existing within a given service communication channel are extracted. The diversity of communication channels results in networks that are multidimensional, i.e. these are networks that consist of more than one type of relationship. Based on each communication channel, a separate relation that can be also called a layer of a network is created. Each social network also features the high clustering coefficient which indicates that many communities exist. This results in yet another dimension of each network. Moreover, there is one more element that needs to be considered – time. The behaviour of all nodes in a social network is time-dependent, i.e. time factor cannot be neglected during analysis. Time factor in an analogous way, as it is in physics, can be treated as an additional dimension.

As it was pointed out earlier, although the social structures were extensively investigated in the past, there is no intense research in the area of modelling the multidimensional temporal social networks. The goal of this article is to build a model for multidimensional social networks that will also be able to present the dynamics of this structure. The concept of multidimensionality needs to cover both different types of relations between nodes and communities existing within each relational layer.

The rest of the paper is structured in the following way: Section 2 outlines the research that has already been conducted in the field of social networks and their multidimensional aspect. In Section 3 the model of multidimensional temporal social network, together with three dimensions (layer, time window and group), is described. Section 4 presents possible applications of a developed model and finally Section 5, the conclusions are provided.

2 Related Work

Social networks and their analysis is one of the main streams in the complex networks research field and has its origins in 1950s. A general concept of social networks is very simple and can be defined as the finite set of actors and relationships that link these actors. Different researchers developed their own variations of this concept as they analysed it from different perspectives [14], [26], [28], [29]. Each application domain of this concept has resulted in separate branch of research. The well-known networks that were analysed in the past are: scientist collaboration networks [24], movie-actor networks, student friendship networks [2], sexual contact networks [22], labour market [21], public health [5] and psychology [25]. Data for the enumerated cases were mainly gathered based on surveys and questionnaires.

Nowadays, based on data gathered in computer systems, a new type of social network can be extracted and analysed. These networks are usually automatically extracted from such data sources as: bibliographic data [12], blogs [1], photos sharing systems like Flickr [16], e-mail systems [18], telecommunication data [3], [19], social services like Twitter [15] or Facebook [9], video sharing systems like YouTube [7], Wikipedia [6] and many more. Networks created based on these types of data are called online social networks [8], [11], web-based social networks [13] or computer-supported social networks [30].

Scientists focus their research efforts on investigating the structure and function of these networks; however they usually take into account only one type of relation between people. It should be emphasized that in most real-world social networks, there exist many different relationships as described in Section 1 and will be further described in more detail. So far only a few scientists have focused their research interests at multi-layer social networks.

The problem of multiple relations was investigated in [28] where the graphical, algebraic and sociometric notations for multiple relations are proposed. Wasserman and Faust proposed to use Image Matrices for Multiple Relations. This notation is a theoretical concept that has been found hard to implement in the environment with several different layers. Furthermore, authors emphasized interpreting each image separately seems to be ad hoc. They suggest comparing pairs of images and investigating multi-relational patterns such as multiplexity or exchange. This solution does not solve the problem with large-scale networks where many types of relation exist.

In another approach, Kazienko *et al.* investigated the Flickr photo sharing system and have distinguished eleven types of relationships between users [16]. A special type of social network that allows the presentation of many different activities is called a multi-layered social network [4], [17]. It can be represented in a multi-graph [10], [28]. The network layers were created based on communication channels and there was no implementation of either a time factor or communities concept, which authors of this article find to be crucial for the generic nature of the network concept. However, this research was an inspiration for the authors to propose a formal model that encompasses different network's dimensions under the umbrella of a single framework.

Overall, due to their complexity, such networks are more difficult to analyse than simple one-layered social networks and no established methods have been developed.

In this paper, authors focus on developing a conceptual, generic model for a multidimensional temporal social network that enables the capture of information about different types of activities and interactions between users, the communities existing within each relation type, as well as represent the dynamics of user's behaviour.

3 A Model of a Multidimensional, Temporal Social Network

3.1 General Concept

The general idea behind the model for a multidimensional temporal social network endeavours to provide a framework allowing the description of all social interactions that exist between network actors. As the social network represents interaction between users, it needs to be modelled in respect of the type of relationship, its strength and relation dynamicity. Moreover, it is expected that the model also allows the gathering of additional customized description of all relations that may be easily concluded, in order to provide an informative presentation of networks and individuals characteristics.

The proposed model for a multidimensional temporal social network is based on the principal profile of multidimensional and dynamic social networks. The basis of each social network is a structure made up of individuals, which are tied by one or more specific types of interdependency, such as friendship, kinship, common interest, financial exchange, likes and dislike, etc. In order to represent such entities, the model assumes the representation of nodes and edges, where nodes represent individuals (social entities) and edges – interconnections between them. Obviously, as multiple numbers of interconnection types exist, the edges may represent distinct meanings of the relation. Therefore, the model assumes they are contained in some semantic layer of relations of the same meaning.

Usually, social networks are not a static structure and may comprise relations that change over time. Therefore, the set of network actors may vary over time. The dynamics of relations and nodes needs expressing and is modelled by time windows – a set of static pictures (snapshots) representing the state of the network obtained in certain time interval.

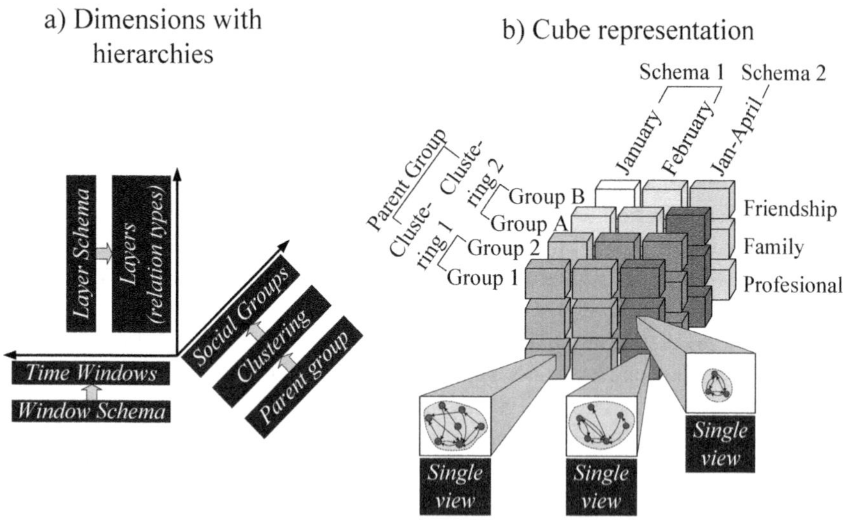

Fig. 1. Three dimensions with hierarchies (a) and the cube representation of multidimensional social network (b)

Additionally, the proposed model encompasses information not only about dynamicity and different kind of relations but also the groups that exist within a given relation layer and in a specific time window. It provides the opportunity to distinguish distinct sets of nodes with a high density of internal edges and low density of edges between those sets.

Summarizing, the general concept of the model considers three distinct dimensions of social networks: layer dimension, time-window dimension and group dimension, see Fig. 1a.

All the dimensions share the same set of nodes that correspond to social entities: single humans or groups of people.

3.2 Layer Dimension

Layer dimension describes all the relationships between the users of a system. The relations may represent direct communication between users via e-mail or phone. However they may also result from human activities in an IT system, e.g. sharing and co-editing documents in a business intranet.

In general, three categories of relations are distinguished: direct relation, pseudo-direct relation and indirect relation.

- Direct relation (Fig. 2) is a relation that directly connects two different users. Both participants are conscious of being in relation, e.g. in e-mail communication a sender as well as a receiver know that a process of information exchange takes place.

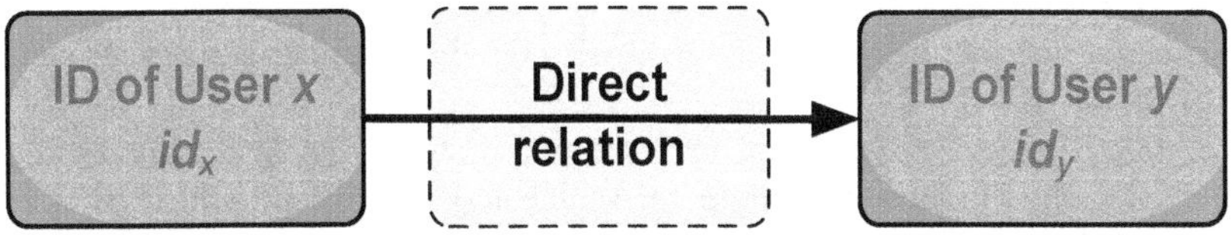

Fig. 2. Direct relation between users x and y

- Pseudo-direct relation (Fig. 3) connects two different users via an intermediary object. The object is subjected to the activities of both users x and y. Activities of x and y may be the same or different. Reference to this pseudo-direct relation may occur in two forms: a pseudo-direct relation with the same roles and a pseudo-direct relation with different roles. The first of them refers to a situation when both of the users play the same role with respect to the object, e.g. commentator of a photo. The second type of pseudo-direct relation occurs when acting on the object, one of the users plays a different role than the other, e.g. user y reviews a paper written by user x. Note that in the case of pseudo-direct relations users do not need to be directly engaged in creating and maintaining the relation, moreover one or both of them may not be conscious of its existence.

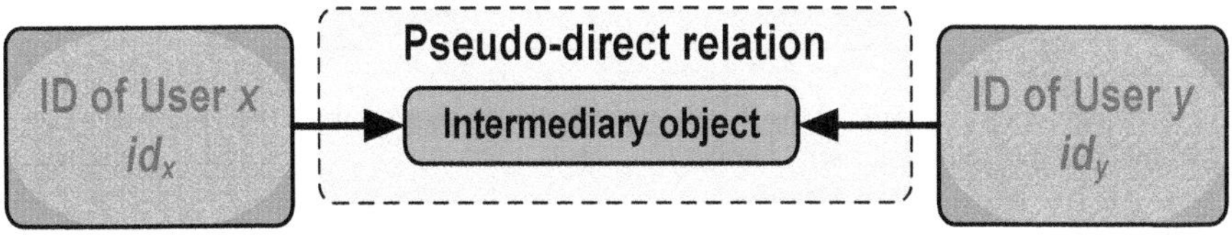

Fig. 3. Pseudo-direct relation between users x and y

- Indirect relation (Fig. 4) occurs between two users whose profiles are similar. It is a kind of a demographic filtering that retrieves all the users with the same or similar profiles. None of users is conscious of the existence of the indirect relation.

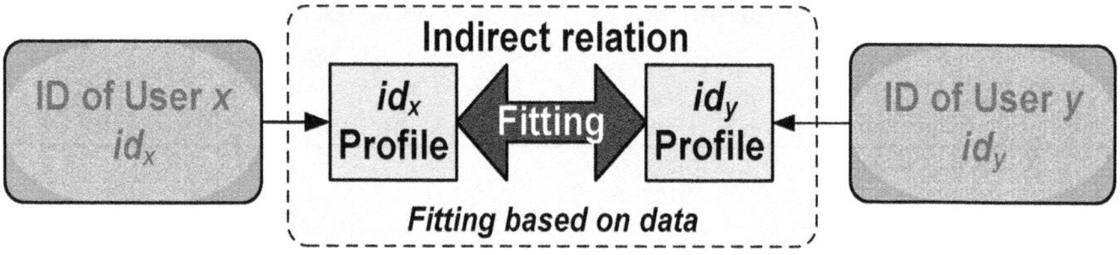

Fig. 4. Indirect relation between user *x* and *y*

A relationship between the users may be directed, when it takes place from one user to another, or undirected if a direction of the relation is not determined.

The relationships occurring between people have different natures. Going to the same school, shopping in the same e-magazines, being a friend of somebody, writing an SMS to somebody, attending e-lectures are only a few examples of the relation types. Based on the data available in a given system it is possible to extract all the types of relationships that occur between its users, defining in this way a set $= \{R_1, R_2, \ldots, R_n\}$, where $R_i, i = 1, 2, \ldots, n$ is a type of relation. In turn, every $R_i, i = 1, 2, \ldots, n$ is a set of pairs $R_i = \{\langle user_x, user_y \rangle | user_x \in Users, user_y \in Users,\ user_x \neq user_y\}$.

Let *IDU* define a finite set of users of one system. The layer dimension in the model of a multidimensional, temporal social network is represented by a set $L = \{l_1, l_2, \ldots, l_n\}$, where n is a number of all the relationships that can be derived from data available in the system and $l_1, l_2, \ldots, l_n$ are the layers corresponding to the relations. Particular layers $l_1, l_2, \ldots, l_n$ consist of the same *IDU* set (nodes in graph representation) connected by relations (edges) of the types: R_1 in layer l_1, R_2 in layer l_2, and R_n in layer l_n respectively (Fig. 5).

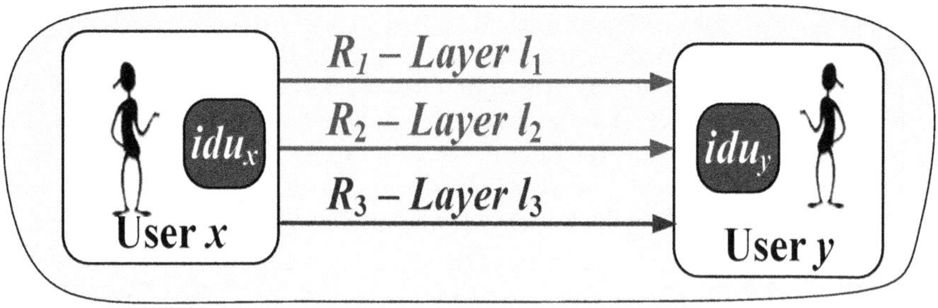

Fig. 5. Three types of relationships R_1, R_2 and R_3 between users *x* and *y* that form three layers of multidimensional, temporal social network

Note that single layer l_i represents a simple social network including all the users of the system connected to each other by relationship R_i, whereas two or more layers gives a multi-layered social network with the same set of nodes connected by more than one relationship.

Layer dimensions could be created according to one or another Layer Schema, e.g. Schema A: layer1 – *friendship*, layer2 – *business*, or Schema B: layer1 – *email exchange*, layer2 – *phone calls*. Schemas form an additional upper level in the layer dimension hierarchy. As a result, the social network may be analyzed with respect to any simple (single relation) or different complex (multi-relation) layer schemas.

3.3 Time-Window Dimension

Temporal analysis of social networks is possible thanks to time-window dimensions. A time-window is a period of time with well-matched width. It may be a snapshot at a given time stamp, i.e. relation existing at that time, but also relations extracted for a given period, i.e. based on human activities within that time window.

Time-window limits social network analysis to those users (nodes) and relationships (edges) that have existed in a period defined by time-window size. Resulting social networks may be simple (one-layered) or multi-layered. Comparing networks obtained in successive time-windows make it possible to complete missing information or predict changes that may occur in the future.

A fundamental problem of temporal SNA is time-window resolution, i.e. its width. If a time-window is too narrow, structural parameters of the social network are not correlated. Besides, too narrow a window introduces relatively big noise in parameter values. On the other hand, too wide a time-window causes loss of information about temporal dependencies that occur between relations and nodes in the social network. Moreover, the dimensions of time-windows for different structural parameters of the social network may vary. So, for temporal analysis, it is necessary to apply a method - like presented in [27] - that enables a choice of time-window optimal size.

Similar to layer dimension, time-window dimension comprises time-windows with different sizes, moving windows, etc. that correspond to various Window Schemas, see Fig. 1.

3.4 Group Dimension

The concept of a group is not precisely defined in a social network environment. In general, it is considered that a group comprises of similar people. Frequently, instead of definition we find conditions (criteria) that should be fulfilled for the group to exist. Most of these conditions derive from an idea, that a group is a social community whose members cooperate more often within the group than outside it. So, in a social network context, a group may be defined as a subset of users who are strongly connected with the other members of the group and loosely with members of other groups.

In the model of a multilayered, temporal social network, group dimension is supposed to contain all the social groups it is possible to obtain in the clustering processes. However, different clustering algorithms may be applied. Clustering creates the second level in the hierarchy of group dimension. In addition, a *Parent*

Group concept is introduced. It is a virtual object - a root of a group hierarchy, which preserves information about inter-group relations used further in the aggregation process. A single social group may include a subset of social network users connected by single relation or more than one relation in a given period of time. Thus it may be considered a multi-layered structure in a time-window. A group may also evolve in time. Its temporal changes and their dynamics give valuable information.

3.5 Views

The above mentioned dimensionality of the model for multidimensional temporal social networks is utilized to conclude the state of the network providing its static picture. The concept of views as a core of the model is introduced. Single view is a sub-network consisting only of nodes and edges that belong to particular layer, time window and group. It means that the single view describes the state of the sub-network composed of nodes tied by edges representing the same type or relation between nodes, from the same time, and that are in the same group of nodes.

Thus, the concept of the model for multidimensional temporal social networks may be compared with principal assumptions of the logical architecture of data warehouses. As seen in Fig. 1b, a single cube is representing the view that encapsulates relations existing within a given layer, group and time-window simultaneously.

3.6 Aggregations by Dimensions

As the concept of views provides the atomic insight on the sub-network, there arises the natural expectation to provide possibilities to operate on multiple views in order to consider not only a single view but more compounded patterns from the entire network. Therefore, some aggregation operators working on dimensions are required. Aggregations should offer the ability to analyze such sub-network structures as accumulated network activity from particular layers, time-windows or groups. For instance, one can perform an analysis of the network, considering activity from selected time-windows aggregating a given single hour of the day for all the days in the week only.

Moreover, views can be aggregated by one, two or even all three dimensions at the same time. The aggregation creates a new social network object composed of nodes and edges from the considered views but with recalculated relation strengths. This recalculation is accomplished by taking into account only those relationships that occur in the selected views.

There exist several approaches of views' aggregation. Among others, typically, the relation strengths may be aggregated by:

- sum of relation strengths,
- mean of relation strengths,
- weighted sum of relation strengths,
- weighted mean of relation strengths.

Obviously, all the above mentioned aggregations are performed on edges existing between the same pair of nodes but in distinct views. Additionally, another aggregation for a set of nodes appearing in distinct views may be performed by a union of sets of nodes.

Moreover, aggregation operations may consider an additional profile of relations – timeliness. As a result, older relations can be treated as less significant while strength is calculated.

4 Model Applicability

4.1 Aggregations by Dimensions

The first step in data pre-processing is data cleaning and validation, similar to the next step, the way data is treated depends on data type. In this step, all data that does not contain essential information is deleted. These are essentially information such as message timestamp, message id, sender or recipient id/mail address in case of mails data, and in the case of billing data, phone call timestamp and duration or dialler and receiver id/phone number are important. Cleaned data is validated to ensure the integrity of the data is preserved. For example, if a user email address is invalid, it is removed during the cleaning phase, and all messages from or to this person must be removed to preserve integrity. The next step is a transfer of the cleaned and validated data into a unified structure: hierarchical pre social network. In data describing communication such as billings or mail logs, where two or more peoples communicate with each other via an object (billings: phone call, teleconference; mail logs: mail, thread), each person can have a different role towards this object, through which they communicate (mail: sender, receiver; mail thread: thread creator, thread participant; phone call: dialler, receiver) [23]. Objects may even have a hierarchical relationship. For example, in mail logs, a thread contains one or more mails. Thus, a hierarchical pre-social network can be created by gathering all object-based relations between people and grouping those objects into a hierarchy. The third step is flattening the hierarchy of objects to one selected level, see [20] for details. During this phase, all object based relations are identified on different levels. Then the selected ones are copied to the object, taking into consideration what they are directly or indirectly connected to and which level they belong to. The network layers detection is started after the flattening process. During layer detection the permutations of all role pairs are created and these pairs (*role a*, *role b*) are treated as layers. For each layer all connections between two people x and y are counted. Those connections must meet the two conditions described below:

- The first person x has the first role a and another user y has the second role b,
- Users x and y are not the same person.

The last phase of data pre-processing is the multi-layered social network creation. In this step, layers which should be added, are selected and time windows are defined. The whole process is described in [20]. An additional unclassified group called *Parent group,* which covers all layers and windows is created in order to preserve intergroup edges. *Parent group* is at the top of the group dimension hierarchy.

4.2 Internal Structures

The data structure for a three-dimensional social network is presented in Fig. 7. The main element of this representation is a network object that describes the social network name and start and end date. The network object aggregates all nodes that belong to the social network. The first dimension is based on layers, the second are time windows, whereas the third one is social groups. Additionally, all groups, except the top one (*Parent Group*), have information about the top group – *Parent Group* aggregating the entire network. Each of three dimensions have information/description about how the dimension hierarchy was created (Window - window_scheme, Layer - layer_scheme, Group - group_clustering - Parent Group) and name of the object. In addition, the time dimension has information about the period: when it starts and ends. Those three dimensions are related to a single view object (corresponding to a fact in the data warehouses model). A view object aggregates edge objects that describe relations between two nodes in one layer, window and group.

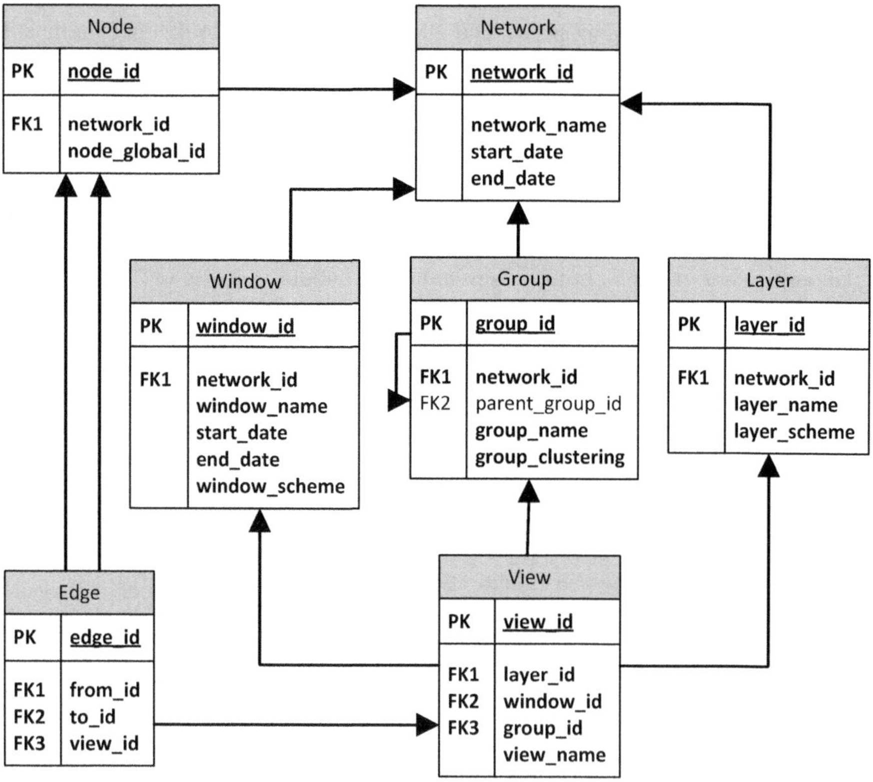

Fig. 6. Data structures for the multidimensional social network

All elements mentioned above can have their own attributes which describe them in more detail. One exception is the node element, whose attributes are grouped depending on how the element attribute was calculated, e.g. the node can have separate attributes calculated for the entire network, for single layer, window, group or view element.

4.3 Model Usage

The model and the representation of the multidimensional temporal social network described above, can be utilized for analysing a large social networking system and big organizations (Fig. 7).

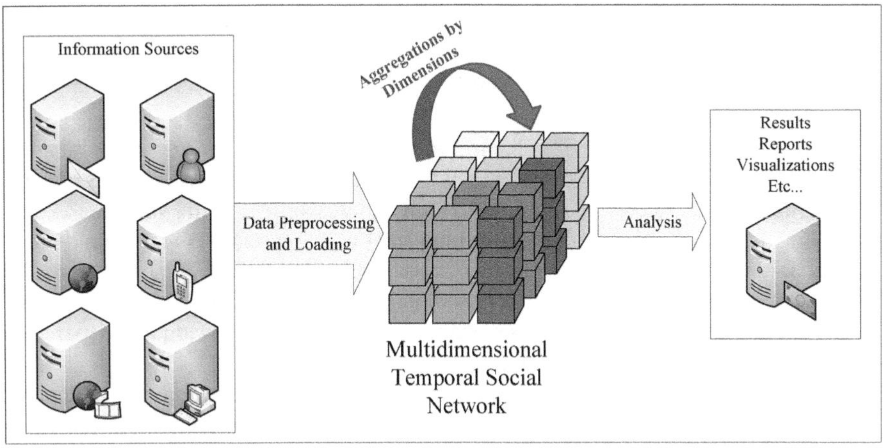

Fig. 7. Example of the system which utilize Multidimensional Temporal Social Network

Layer dimension allows analysis of systems where people are connected by many different relationships such as complex social networking sites (e.g. Facebook), where people are linked as friends, via common games, "like it", etc. or in regular companies: department colleagues, best friends, colleagues from the company football team, etc. Multidimensionality provides an opportunity to analyse each layer separately and in the same time investigate different aggregations of layer dimension as well as compare them. For example, we have a network consisting of four layers, two from the real word: family ties, work colleagues and two from the virtual world, i.e. friends from Facebook and friends from an MMORPG game. Now, one can analyse each layer separately, aggregate layers from the real world and compare it to the virtual world layers aggregation, and finally, aggregate all layers together.

Time dimension allows investigation of the network dynamics and evolution over time. For example, the analysis of adding or removing one network member affects the network over a longer period of time, how a particular group (e.g department or project team) changes over time, or how each network layer changes and how it affects the whole network.

Finally, the group dimension enables the study of groups existing within the social network. Using the presented model not only usual social groups can be analysed (friend family, school, work, etc.) but also groups created upon various member features like gender, age, location etc. Additionally, one can compare the different methods of grouping, e.g by means of a social community extraction or typical data mining clustering.

Summarizing, the described model facilitates an analysis of all three dimensions simultaneously, e.g. how interaction on different layers of two social groups changes over time. Moreover, any measure can be calculated separately for view, layer, window, group, or any aggregation of the above, or compared to each other to find the specific characteristics of each dimension, or the network can be analysed as a whole. Thus, the network multidimensionality presents new possibilities for social network analysis.

5 Conclusions and Future Work

As it was pointed out in the introduction to this paper, the multidimensional analysis of social networks is a new research field. This means that in order to facilitate its development one needs a framework for representing such structures. Such multidimensional analysis is especially important as the researchers try to understand the cause and effects of different phenomena such as information or the spread of diseases and these cannot be inferred based on a single user activity.

The model proposed in this paper enables the combination of data and perceives human interactions and activities in a broader view.

Layer dimension supports the investigation of different communication channels and peoples activities within each of them. Group dimension enables the detection and analysis of communities within different layers of a network. This provides information about which relation type (activities) groups are more likely to form.

A combination of layer, group and time-window dimension in a form of view supports an analysis of many types of relationships and groups that additionally change over time. This allows observation of what kind of relations form what types of groups and if these communities overlap between different relation layers. Such an approach can be crucial, for example when a company tries to introduce a new offer for its customers. What communication channel should the company use? Who is the person to whom the offer should be sent? Answers to these questions can be found using multidimensional network analysis.

The developed model also enables an analysis of the behaviour of groups, nodes and relations in time. This provides additional insight that helps to understand the dynamics of social structures. Due to the time-window dimension it is possible to find out which groups and relation layers are stable and which dynamically change over time.

The proposed model for multidimensional temporal social networks is an original idea that enables investigation of complex social networks from many different perspectives.

Acknowledgments. This work was supported by The Polish Ministry of Science and Higher Education, the development project, 2009-11, the research project, 2010-2013, and the fellowship co-financed by the European Union within the European Social Fund.

The research leading to these results has received funding from the European Union Seventh Framework Programme (FP7/2007-2013) under grant agreement no. 251617.

The research results were also obtained during the training in the "Green Transfer" project co-financed by the European Union from the European Social Fund.

References

1. Agarwal, N., Galan, M., Liu, H., Subramanya, S.: WisColl: Collective Wisdom based Blog Clustering. Information Sciences 180(1), 39–61 (2010)
2. Amaral, L.A.N., Scala, A., Barthelemy, M., Stanley, H.E.: Classes of small–world networks. Proc. the National Academy of Sciences 97, 11149–11152 (2000)
3. Blondel, V.D., Guillaume, J.-L., Lambiotte, R., Lefebvre, E.: Fast unfolding of communities in large networks. J. Stat. Mech., P10008 (2008)
4. Bródka, P., Musial, K., Kazienko, P.: A Method for Group Extraction in Complex Social Networks. In: Proc. the 3rd World Summit on the Knowledge Society. Communications in Computer and Information Science, CCIS, vol. 111, pp. 238–247. Springer, Heidelberg (2010)
5. Cattell, V.: Poor people, poor places, and poor health: the mediating role of social networks and social capital. Social Science and Medicine 52(10), 1501–1516 (2001)
6. Capocci, A., Servedio, V., Colaiori, F., Buriol, L., Donato, D., Leonardi, S., Caldarelli, G.: Preferential attachment in the growth of social networks: The internet encyclopedia Wikipedia. Physical Review E 74(3), id. 036116 (2006)
7. Cheng, X., Dale, C., Liu, J.: Statistics and social networking of YouTube videos. In: Proc. the 16th International Workshop on Quality of Service, pp. 229–238. IEEE, Los Alamitos (2008)
8. Chiu, P.Y., Cheung, C.M.K., Lee, M.K.O.: Online Social Networks: Why Do "We" Use Facebook? In: Proc. the First World Summit on the Knowledge Society. CCIS, vol. 19, pp. 67–74. Springer, Heidelberg (2008)
9. Ellison, N.B., Steinfield, C., Lampe, C.: The benefits of Facebook "friends:" Social capital and college students' use of online social network sites. Journal of Computer-Mediated Communication 12(4), article 1 (2007), `http://jcmc.indiana.edu/vol12/issue4/ellison.html`
10. Flament, C.: Application of graph Theory to Group Structure. Prentice-Hall, Englewood Cliffs (1963)
11. Garton, L., Haythorntwaite, C., Wellman, B.: Studying Online Social Networks. Journal of Computer-Mediated Communication 3(1), 75–105 (1997), `http://jcmc.indiana.edu/vol3/issue1/garton.html`
12. Girvan, M., Newman, M.E.J.: Community structure in social and biological networks. Proc. the National Academy of Sciences 99(12), 7821–7826 (2002)
13. Golbeck, J., Hendler, J.: FilmTrust: movie recommendations using trust in web-based social networks. In: Proc. Consumer Communications and Networking Conference, IEEE Conference Proceedings, vol. 1, pp. 282–286 (2006)

14. Hanneman, R., Riddle, M.: Introduction to social network methods, online textbook. University of California, Riverside (2005), http://faculty.ucr.edu/~hanneman/nettext/
15. Huberman, B., Romero, D., Wu, F.: Social networks that matter: Twitter under the microscope, First Monday, pp. 1–5 (2009)
16. Kazienko, P., Musial, K., Kajdanowicz, T.: Multidimensional Social Network and Its Application to the Social Recommender System. IEEE Transactions on Systems, Man and Cybernetics - Part A: Systems and Humans 41(4) (2011) (in press)
17. Kazienko, P., Musial, K., Kajdanowicz, T.: Profile of the Social Network in Photo Sharing Systems. Proc. 14th Americas Conference on Information Systems. Association for Information Systems, AIS (2008) ISBN: 978-0-615-23693-3
18. Kazienko, P., Musiał, K., Zgrzywa, A.: Evaluation of Node Position Based on Email Communication. Control and Cybernetics 38(1), 67–86 (2009)
19. Kazienko, P., Ruta, D., Bródka, P.: The Impact of Customer Churn on Social Value Dynamics. International Journal of Virtual Communities and Social Networking 1(3), 60–72 (2009)
20. Kazienko, P., Bródka, P., Musial, K., Gaworecki, J.: Multi-layered Social Network Creation Based on Bibliographic Data. In: SocialCom-10, The Second IEEE International Conference on Social Computing, SIN-10 Symposium on Social Intelligence and Networking, August 20-22, pp. 407–412. IEEE Computer Society Press, Minneapolis (2010)
21. Montgomery, J.: Social Networks and Labor-Market Outcomes: Toward an Economic Analysis. American Economic Review 81 5, 1407–1418 (1991)
22. Morris, M.: Sexual network and HIV. AIDS 11, 209–216 (1997)
23. Musial, K., Bródka, P., Kazienko, P., Gaworecki, J.: Extraction of Multi-layered Social Networks from Activity Data. Journal of Global Information Management (accepted, 2011)
24. Newman, M.E.J.: The structure of scientific collaboration networks. Proc. of the National Academy of Sciences 98, 404–409 (2001)
25. Pagel, M., Erdly, W., Becker, J.: Social networks: we get by with (and in spite of) a little help from our friends. Journal of Personality and Social Psychology 53(4), 793–804 (1987)
26. Scott, J.: Social Network Analysis: A Handbook. SAGE Publications, London (2000)
27. Sulo, R., Berger-Wolf, T., Grossman, R.: Meaningful Selection of Temporal Resolution for Dynamic Networks. In: Proceedings of the Eighth Workshop on Mining and Learning with Graphs, MLG 2010, pp. 127–136. ACM, New York (2010)
28. Wasserman, S., Faust, K.: Social network analysis: Methods and applications. Cambridge University Press, New York (1994)
29. Watts, D.J., Strogatz, S.: Collective dynamics of 'small-world' networks. Nature 393, 440–444 (1998)
30. Wellman, B., Salaff, J., Dimitrova, D., Garton, L., Gulia, M., Haythornthwaite, C.: Computer Networks as Social Networks: Collaborative Work, Telework, and Virtual Community. Annual Review of Sociology 22(1), 213–238 (1996)

An Adaptive Learning Approach for Fault-Tolerant Routing in Ad Hoc Networks

Sudip Misra[1], P. Venkata Krishna[2], Akhil Bhiwal[2], Amardeep Singh Chawla[2], and Bernd E. Wolfinger[3]

[1] Indian Institute of Technology, Kharagpur, West Bengal, India
[2] VIT University, Vellore, Tamil Nadu, India
[3] University of Hamburg, Hamburg, Germany

{smisra.editor,parimalavk,bhiwalakhil, amardeepchawla}@gmail.com, wolfinger@informatik.uni-hamburg.de

Abstract. Reliable routing of packets in a Mobile Ad Hoc Network (MANET) has always been a major concern. The open medium and the susceptibility of the nodes of being fault-prone make the design of protocols for these networks a challenging task. Faults in these networks may occur either due to the failure of nodes or due to their reorganisation in the network. These faults can eventuate to packet loss, which degrades the performance of any routing protocol. In this paper, we propose a routing algorithm, named as *learning automata based fault-tolerant routing algorithm (LAFTRA)*, which is capable of routing in the presence of faulty nodes in MANETs using multi-path algorithm. In this work, we have used Learning Automata (LA) for optimizing the selection of paths from multipath routing. The results of simulation of our protocol using network simulator 2 (NS-2) shows the increase in packet delivery ratio and decrease in overhead compared to the existing protocols.

Keywords: MANET; Fault tolerant routing; Learning Automata; Optimization.

1 Introduction

MANETs are dynamic and continuously changing networks, having groups of nodes which are not centrally administered [1-4]. Designing a routing protocol for such an environment is a challenging task. The situation gets worse when there are faulty nodes in the network, as they increase the data loss and degrade the performance of protocols [5]. Xue and Nahrstedt [5-6] confirmed that designing a fault-tolerant routing protocol is NP-hard because of the unavailability of accurate path information in adversarial environments [5]. As MANETs are inherently decentralized, there exists multiple, but in general not sufficiently stable routes, between any two nodes. In order to set an efficient communication mechanism between the nodes, strong routing fabrics between the intermediate nodes are required, and if the intermediate nodes misbehave, then the efficiency and performance of the network is significantly affected [15-17]. To a great extent, the current available ad hoc network routing

J.J. Yonazi et al. (Eds.): ICeND 2011, CCIS 171, pp. 15–25, 2011.

protocols [7] suppose that every node in the network provides a guaranteed packet delivery rate to the destination, but such an assumption usually does not hold in realistic environments [6]. The positions of the nodes in MANETs change over time. Also, a node functioning properly at one point in time may become faulty at a later point. Therefore, a fault-tolerant routing protocol is needed for transferring data with some specific data delivery rate.

In the proposed solution, we have used Learning Automata (LA) [8-9, 10, 12, 14] to design a fault-tolerant routing protocol. LA has been traditionally used to model biological learning systems [8-9]. The theory of LA can be applied in problems aiming at finding the optimal action, taking the random environment into account. The learning cycle involves two components, the Random Environment (RE) and a Learning Automaton. The process of learning is performed by interacting with the RE, and computing its responses to choose the best (closest to optimum) action.

In our solution, more priority is given to nodes with higher "goodness value" (defined in Section 3) and in turn increasing the packet flow through the shortest path, which contains the highest number of healthy nodes. This ensures a higher packet delivery rate than on any other path. We have established this by giving more priority to nodes which respond well, i.e., those that forward more packets. Therefore, while the sender sends packets, more packets will pass through a node that responds well over time and faulty nodes will be gradually isolated in a seamless manner. As a result, at the end of a learning cycle, most of the packets pass through those edges which have the nodes with higher goodness value. A self-learning machine is placed at each node, which, based on the feedback from the network, takes appropriate actions. This is done by allowing the intermediate nodes to learn about the network and, thus, become fault-tolerant, thereby providing a high packet delivery ratio for the network. This is done through the collaboration of the LA with the neighbour nodes. The current node can then decide which next hop to be chosen by following the suitable edge based on the goodness value of the path and then suitably forwarding the packets to the destination. The calculation for goodness value of a path is done on the basis of LA probability updating scheme model. During the learning process, the goodness value of a node is calculated based on the response for each packet by the destination, it receives from the sender. Using this, the goodness value of a path is calculated and updated in the goodness value table of a node.

We carried out a literature survey on works relating to fault-tolerant routing in MANETs and also on works that have integrated LA model in networking problems. End-to-End Fault-tolerant (E^2FT) routing algorithm [6] is a state-of-the-art algorithm proposed by Xue and Nahrstedt in which routing is based on end-to-end computation using a route estimation and route selection process. Route selection is done via two procedures: Confirmation and Dropping. Confirmation is a procedure which selects a path from a given set of paths with specific packet delivery ratio. Dropping is a procedure which drops a given path if the packet delivery ratio of that path falls below a given threshold value. In this manner, using the route estimation process, the path probability estimation for the available paths is done, and, thereafter, using the route selection process, a reduced set of paths can be selected within a very small time interval, based on the constraint. Misra and Oommen [11, 18] improved the performance of the algorithm presented by Xue and Nahrstedt [6] using the concepts of weak estimation learning.

The primary contribution of the work is the development of a fault-tolerant routing algorithm using the concepts of LA. Besides, the proposed algorithm is designed for scalability. Therefore, dense distribution of nodes in a given terrain is feasible by minimally affecting the performance of the network. Also, the proposed algorithm can be implemented on top of any MANET routing protocol, though we have used AODV for our simulation study and analysis. Whereas with a learning system in place, the network can quickly respond to the fault. Besides, the whole network does not have to be probed again for the optimal path after every packet delivery failure. The network chooses the next most optimal path whenever a fault occurs in the existing routing path. Also, with the help of simulations performed, we can say the proposed algorithm is scalable and there is no significant loss in packet delivery ratio which was not the case with any of the existing fault-tolerant routing algorithms for MANETs.

2 Learning Automata

2.1 Introduction

Learning Automata (LA) [12] is a self-operating learning model, where "learning" refers to the process of gaining knowledge during the execution of a simple machine/code (automaton), and using the gained knowledge to decide on actions to be taken in the future. This model has three main components – the *Automaton*, the *Environment* and the *Reward/Penalty* structure.

The Automaton refers to the self-learning system. The medium in which this machine functions is called the Environment. The Automaton continuously performs actions on the Environment, the Environment responds to these actions. This response may be either positive or negative and it serves as the feedback to the Automaton, which, in effect, leads to the Automaton either getting rewarded or penalized. Over a period of time, the Automaton learns the characteristics of the Environment and identifies "optimal" actions that can be performed on the Environment. A comprehensive overview of LA can be found in the classic text by Narendra and Thathachar [10]. It can also be found in the book pertaining to the advances in the field related to the properties of network and games of automata by Thathachar and Sastry [14].

2.2 Automaton

The Learning Automaton can be represented as a quintuple represented as {Q, A, B, F, H}, where [11]:

- Q: is the finite set of Internal States Q = $\{q_1, q_2, q_3 \ldots q_n\}$ where q_n is the state of the automaton at instant n.
- A: is a finite set of actions performed by the automaton. A = $\{\alpha_1, \alpha_2 \ldots \alpha_n\}$ where α_n is the action performed by the automaton at instant n.
- B: is a finite set of responses from the environment. B = $\{\beta_1, \beta_2, \beta_3 \ldots \beta_n\}$ where β_n is the response from the environment at an instant n.

- F: is a mapping function. Maps the current state and input to the next state of the automaton.
- H: is a mapping function. Maps the current state and response from the environment to determine the next action to be performed.

2.3 Environment

The Environment corresponds to the medium in which the Automaton functions. Mathematically, an Environment can be abstracted by a triple {A, B, C}. A, B, and C are defined as follows [10].

- $A = \{\alpha_1, \alpha_2, \ldots, \alpha_r\}$ represents a finite input set
- $B = \{\beta_1, \beta_2, \ldots, \beta_r\}$ is the output set of the environment, and
- $C = \{c_1, c_2, \ldots, c_r\}$ is a set of penalty probabilities, where element $c_i \in C$ corresponds to an input action α_i.

We now provide a few important definitions used in the field of LA. Given an action probability vector **P** (t) at time 't', the *average penalty* is defined as [10]:

$$\begin{aligned} M(t) &= E[\beta(t)|P(t)] = Pr[\beta(t)=1|P(t)] \\ &= \sum_{i=1}^{r} Pr[\beta(t)=1|\alpha(t)=\alpha_i] \times Pr[\alpha(t)=\alpha_i] \\ &= \sum_{i=1}^{r} c_i p_i(t). \end{aligned} \tag{1}$$

The average penalty for the "pure-chance" automaton is given by [10]:

$$M_0 = \frac{1}{r}\sum_{i=1}^{r} c_i. \tag{2}$$

As $t \to \infty$, if the average penalty $M(t) < M_0$, at least asymptotically, the automaton is generally considered to be better than the pure-chance automaton. E [M (t)] is given by [10]:

$$E[M(t)] = E\{E[\beta(t)|P(t)]\} = E[\beta(t)]. \tag{3}$$

3 System Model

3.1 Network Model

We represent an ad hoc network using a graph W = (V, E), where V represents the set of vertices and E the set of edges. The vertices are the nodes in the network and the edges are the links in between the nodes. A path is a set of vertices connected to each other from a vertex (which can also be source) to destination. Faults can appear in any node in the network independent of its path, and faults can occur unpredictably. We

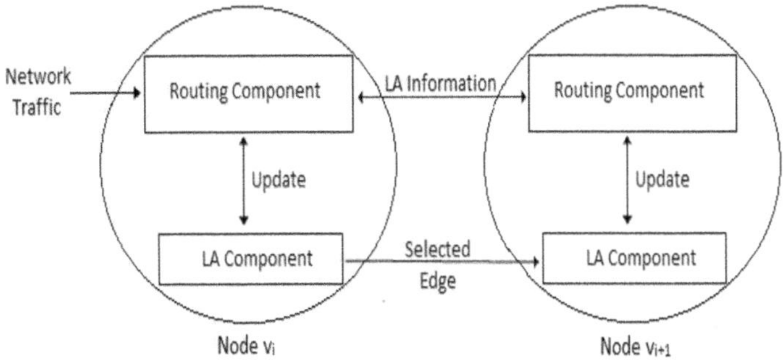

Fig. 1. LAFTRA system

assume all links in the network to be bidirectional, i.e., if $(v_i, v_{i+1}) \rightarrow E$, then $(v_{i+1}, v_i) \rightarrow E$ also exists. Each node 'v' has two components: a routing component and an LA component. Each node's LA component functions independently of others and shares updates through an update table maintained at the routing component which shares LA information through the neighbour nodes. As shown in Fig. 1, the LA component shares the information across the neighbouring node to learn about the network.

3.2 Learning Automata Model

In the proposed model, an LA is associated to each node in the MANET. Each LA component has the parameters described in Table 1.

Table 1. LA parameters

Parameter	Description
A	Set of paths available between two nodes in the network. A = $\{\alpha_1, \alpha_2 \ldots. \alpha_n\}$, where α_i is the path selected by a node at instant i.
B	Success/failure of packet delivery. $B_i \in \{0, 1\}$, $1 \le i \le n$, where β_i is the response from the environment at an instant i.
G	Goodness value of a node determines its packet delivery capability. If the goodness value of a particular node is high, the packet delivery ratio via that node will also be high.
Y	Goodness value of a path determines the packet delivery capability of a path. Goodness value of a path is cumulative average of goodness value of all the nodes available in the path. Y_n is the goodness value of path at an instant n.
R	Reward Constant ($0 < R < 1$). Used in the rewarding scheme.
P	Penalty Constant ($0 < P < 1$). Used in the penalizing scheme.
T	Threshold goodness value for a path.

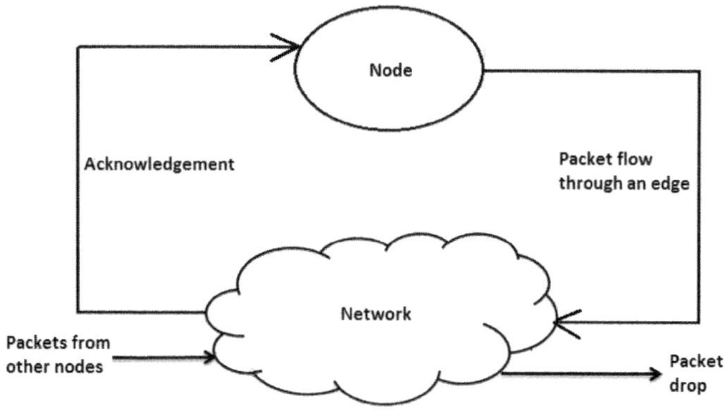

Fig. 2. Learning automata model for fault-tolerant routing protocol

Fig. 2 shows the LA model for our protocol. The node, which through itself, has forwarded the packets coming from the network gets an acknowledgement message from the destination and accordingly the updation scheme is applied to the path from where the acknowledgement has arrived to the current node.

4 LAFTRA – Learning Automata-Based Fault-Tolerant Routing Algorithm

4.1 Reward/Penalty Scheme

The LA at each node will apply a rewarding scheme on successful packet delivery and a penalty scheme on packet delivery failure. Higher value of R would lead to quick convergence of multiple paths to a single path but the path thus selected will not be robust enough whereas a lower value of R will lead to slow convergence rate but the path thus selected will be more robust. This is due to the fact that with low value of R, the path selected for routing will go through rigorous selection process and hence would be better.

Similarly, value of P should be around 0.3-0.5 which decreases the goodness value to half on every packet delivery failure. If the value of P is too low, then source will continue to use the path till long after a fault occurs in the network. If value of P is too high, the network will not tolerate even the accidental packet failure.

4.2 LA Based Fault Tolerant Routing Algorithm

The LAFTRA algorithm will take the set of available paths between source and destination as input and will produce the most optimal path as output. Along with this, it will also store goodness value of other paths from itself to its destination in goodness table maintained at each node. The algorithm will begin by initializing the appropriate value of reward constant, penalty constant and threshold goodness value of the path.

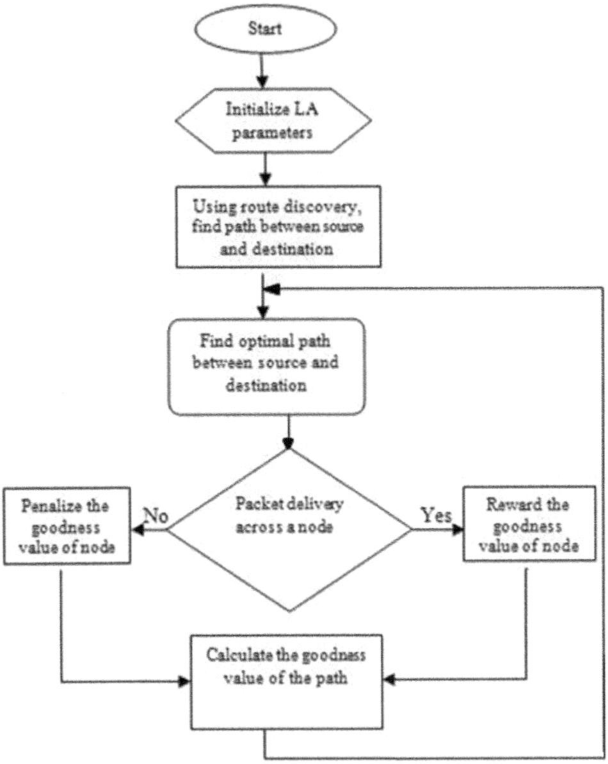

Fig. 3. System strategy

Once the route discovery phase is completed, source will send the packet to destination via multiple paths. On receiving the packet destination acknowledges the source by sending ACK packets. LA at each node will use these ACK packets to calculate the goodness value of the path from itself to destination and store it in the goodness value table. Once a path crosses the threshold goodness value, then that particular path will be used for routing instead of multiple paths.

Each node's goodness table will be updated as packets keep passing through that node. This will reflect the current network condition between source and destination.

In case of packet delivery failure, the LA stationed at node will penalize the path through which failure occurred. This way, any fault that occurs in the network will be detected quickly. If the goodness value of the path reduces below the threshold value, the path will be discarded and the alternate path which has highest goodness value among other paths will be used. A flowchart of the given algorithm is shown in Fig. 3.

5 Simulations

In order to evaluate the performance of the proposed protocol, we have conducted extensive simulation studies using the ns-2 [19]. We compared the performance of the proposed protocol with that of AODV [13], E^2FT [6] and FTAR [16]. The simulation parameters used in our experiments are shown in Table 2.

Table 2. Simulation parameters

Number of Nodes	20-1200
Simulation time	900s
Speed of the mobile nodes	0 – 20 m/s
Underlying MAC protocol	IEEE 802.11
Channel Type	Wireless Channel
Mobility model	Random waypoint
Traffic-Type	CBR (TCP)
Terrain Dimensions	1200mx1000m
Routing Protocol	LAFTRA

5.1 Simulation Environment

The following experiments (a) and (b) were carried out with 50 nodes which contains both well behaved and faulty nodes.

5.2 Simulation Results

(a) *Variation in packet delivery ratio with respect to the percentage of faulty nodes*:

This experiment was conducted to study the performance of LAFTRA in the presence of faulty nodes. We have taken the percentage of faulty nodes to indicate the number of faulty nodes in a given environment. We have conducted the experiment by varying the number of faulty nodes against packet delivery ratio. All our simulation results are presented with 95% confidence intervals.

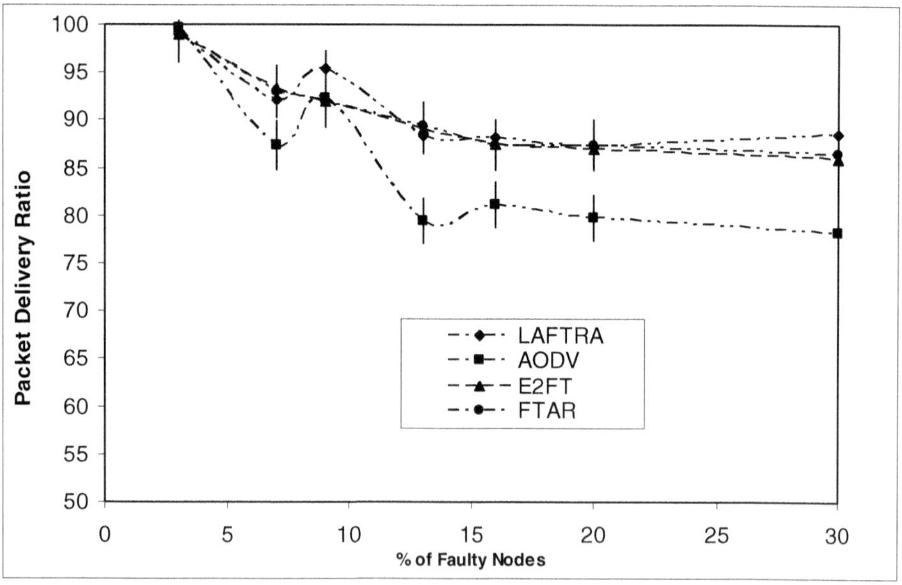

Fig. 4. Graph for packet delivery versus the percentage of faulty nodes

Fig. 4 shows the variation in packet delivery ratio with respect to the percentage of faulty nodes in the network. In our conducted experiments, we have introduced up to 30 % faulty nodes and estimated the packet delivery ratio and overhead. We observe from Fig. 4 that as the percentage of faulty nodes increases, LAFTRA performs better in terms of packet delivery ratio when compared to AODV, E2FT and FTAR due to the learning process incorporated by it. Initially, LAFTRA shows a lower packet delivery ratio than AODV because of the learning phase incorporated by it in which it calculates the goodness value of a path and of the nodes by using control packets. But as the percentage of faulty node increases in the network, the performance of AODV decreases. We also observe that when faulty nodes are more than 25%, then the packet delivery ratio of LAFTRA is much more as compared to AODV, E2FT and FTAR. LAFTRA gets an alternative optimal path using the goodness table present at each node being part of the network. Hence its performance is better than the other approaches.

(b) *Variation of packet delivery ratio versus number of nodes:* LAFTRA is a scalable fault-tolerant routing algorithm. We have analyzed the scalability by comparing the packet delivery ratio while increasing the number of nodes as shown in Fig. 5. We have compared our result with AODV and DSR among which AODV is said to be more scalable and gives a consistent packet delivery ratio when the number of nodes is very large. As the number of nodes increases, the performance of DSR drops down drastically – this can be explained by its source routing nature. As the number of nodes increases LAFTRA performs better than AODV due to its learning and fault-tolerant nature. When the number of nodes is 200, then the packet delivery ratios of AODV and LAFTRA are nearly the same, as can be seen in Fig 5. As the number of nodes increases, LAFTRA has a better packet delivery ratio than both AODV and DSR.

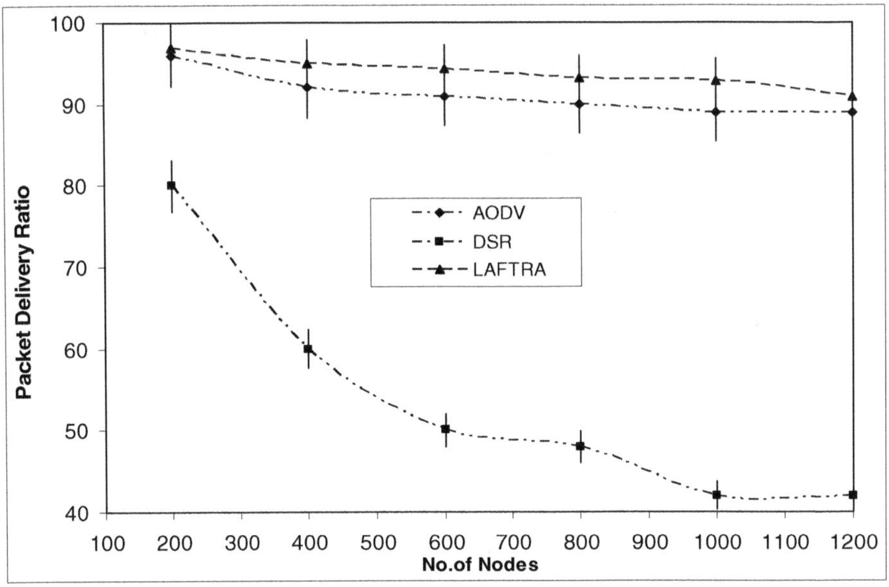

Fig. 5. Packet delivery ratio versus the number of nodes

6 Conclusions

In this paper, we proposed an LA–based fault-tolerant routing algorithm for MANETs incorporating a learning process which gets executed at each node and the collective orchestration of the process at all the nodes determines the performance of the overall system. The advantage of the proposed approach is that if an existing link fails, alternative routes can be determined based on the goodness values calculated by LA. Hence, the node can again be successfully restored back in the network, once the link gets established or an alternative route is found.

The results of simulation experiments carried out for LAFTRA against the benchmark algorithms are found to be satisfactory. In particular, LAFTRA achieves a high packet delivery ratio and during the increase in the number of faulty nodes in a network. Also, the proposed algorithm is scalable due to the learning process incorporated by it.

Acknowledgements. The work of the first author was supported in part by a grant from the Council of Scientific and Industrial Research (CSIR), Grant Ref. No. 22/477/09-EMR-II.

References

1. Salem, N., Hubaux, J.-P.: Securing wireless mesh networks. IEEE Wireless Communications 13(2), 50–55 (2006), doi:10.1109/MWC.2006.1632480
2. Akyildiz, I., Wang, X., Wang, W.: Wireless mesh networks: a survey. Computer Networks 47(4), 445–487 (2005), doi:10.1016/j.comnet.2004.12.001
3. Yi, P., Tong, T., Liu, N., Wu, Y., Ma, J.: Security in Wireless Mesh Networks: Challenges and Solutions. In: Sixth International Conference on Information Technology New Generations, ITNG 2009, pp. 423–428, 27–29 (April 2009), doi:10.1109/ITNG.2009.20
4. Glass, S., Portmann, M., Muthukkumarasamy, V.: Securing Wireless Mesh Networks. IEEE Internet Computing 12(4), 30–36 (2008), doi:10.1109/MIC.2008.85
5. Xue, Y., Nahrstedt, K.: Providing fault-tolerant ad hoc routing service in adversarial environments. Wireless Personal Communications 29(3-4), 367–388 (2004)
6. Xue, Y., Nahrstedt, K.: Fault-tolerant routing in mobile ad hoc networks. In: Proceedings of the Wireless Communications and Networking Conference (WCNC 2003), vol. 2, pp. 1174–1179 (March 20, 2003), doi:10.1109/WCNC.2003.1200537
7. Royer, E.M., Toh, C.-K.: A review of current routing protocols for ad hoc mobile wireless networks. IEEE Personal Communications 6(2), 46–55 (1999), doi:10.1109/98.760423
8. Narendra, K.S., Thathachar, M.A.L.: Learning Automata: A Survey. IEEE Transactions on Systems, Man and Cybernetics SMC-4(4), 323–334 (1974), doi:10.1109/TSMC.1974.5408453
9. Tsetlin, M.L.: Automaton Theory and the Modelling of Biological Systems. Academic Press, New York (1973)
10. Narendra, K.S., Thathachar, M.A.L.: Learning Automata. Prentice-Hall, Englewood Cliffs (1989)
11. Oommen, B.J., Misra, S.: A Fault-Tolerant Routing Algorithm for Mobile Ad Hoc Networks Using a Stochastic Learning-Based Weak Estimation Procedure. In: IEEE International Conference on Wireless and Mobile Computing, Networking and Communications, 2006 (WiMob 2006), pp. 31–37 (June 2006), doi:10.1109/WIMOB.2006.1696374

12. Lakshmivarahan, S.: Learning Algorithms: Theory and Applications. Springer, New York (1981)
13. Perkins, C., Belding-Royer, E., Das, S.: Ad hoc On-Demand Distance Vector (AODV) Routing. IETF, RFC 3561 (July 2003)
14. Thathachar, M.A.L., Sastry, P.S.: Networks of Learning Automata. Kluwer Academic, Dordrecht (2003)
15. Misra, S., Krishna, P.V., Abraham, K.I.: Adaptive Link State Routing and Intrusion Detection in Wireless Mesh Networks. IET Information Security 4(4), 374–389 (2010), doi:10.1049/iet-ifs.2009.0196
16. Misra, S., Dhurandher, S.K., Obaidat, M.S., Verma, K., Gupta, P.: A Low Overhead Fault-Tolerant Routing Algorithm for Mobile Ad-Hoc Networks Based on Ant Swarm Intelligence. Simulation Modelling Practice and Theory 18(5), 637–649 (2010)
17. Misra, S., Krishna, P.V., Abraham, K.I., Sasikumar, N., Fredun, S.: An Adaptive Learning Routing Protocol for the Prevention of Distributed Denial of Service Attacks in Wireless Mesh Networks. Computers and Mathematics with Applications 60(2), 294–306 (2010), doi:10.1016/j.camwa.2009.12.035
18. Oommen, B.J., Misra, S.: Fault-Tolerant Routing in Adversarial Mobile Ad Hoc Networks: An Efficient Route Estimation Scheme for Non-Stationary Environments. Telecommunication Systems 44(1-2), 159–169 (2010), doi:10.1007/s11235-009-9215-4
19. ns-2: Network Simulator 2, `http://www.nsnam.org`

Challenges in Sustaining Municipal Broadband Networks in the Developing World

Amos Nungu*, Terrence Brown, and Bjorn Pehrson

KTH Royal Institute of Technology, Forum 120, 164 40 Kista, Sweden
{amnungu,terrence,bpehrson}@kth.se

Abstract. Municipal or community networks seem to be a constructive first step in the process of establishing sustainable broadband networks in areas where the demand for broadband communication services is larger than the supply. Besides meeting the acute demand, one purpose is to stimulate the market by demonstrating connectivity feasibility, to reduce the risks involved for commercial actors. One of the keys to the sustainability and scalability of such networks is a well designed and managed institutional framework based on the local prerequisites.

In this paper, we report on our experience from the establishment of the Serengeti Broadband Network in Northern Tanzania. We have been using a public-private partnership approach to create a not-for-profit organization to manage and operate a network first deployed as a research and education effort. We present and discuss our approach, comparing and contrasting to other approaches found in the literature. We conclude that success requires local ownership. Thus, the institutional framework should aim at creating local commitment and leadership.

Keywords: community networks, developing world, management, operational sustainability, ownership, public-private-partnerships.

1 Introduction

In recent years, we have observed an increasing trend to build community broadband networks supporting socio-economic development, especially in under-served areas. The lack of supply is often due to high perceived risks caused by underdeveloped policies and regulatory frameworks, lack of basic infrastructure leading to high costs, and uncertain revenues due to sparse populations with weak payment capability. The purpose of the community network is to reduce these risks by demonstrating feasibility. A common strategy is to involve public sector entities involved in providing basic public services, such as education, health-care and local administration, as anchor customers. This motivates public infrastructure investments and establishes the long term commitment required for sustainability [1]. To also attract private investments and leverage the expertise available in the private sector, it has been proposed that community networks should be created and managed in a private-public-partnership (PPP) model [2], [3].

* Corresponding author.

J.J. Yonazi et al. (Eds.): ICeND 2011, CCIS 171, pp. 26–40, 2011.

There are challenging needs for innovation from most aspects to build sustainable community networks in under-served areas. The goal of this paper is to discuss and analyze the management challenges. The analysis is based on experiences from the implementation of a broadband community network in Tanzania where the institutional framework formed naturally in the implementation process. The first author coordinated the design and implementation of this network.

Management is discussed in relation to ownership and leadership. We use the terms "community" and "municipal" interchangeably. The term broadband refers to high speed connectivity within the local network while the upstream connection may or may not be broadband.

2 Background

While voice networks increasingly penetrate rural and remote areas in the developing world, this does not apply to broadband networks. Phone networks, mobile or fixed, target individual subscriptions, in the case of mobile networks defined by the SIM-card and the phone. The penetration is measured in teledensity, essentially the percent of subscriptions in relation to the total population. Broadband networks require more competent users, a more complex supply chain and larger user investments. The target is thus to a larger degree organizations rather than individuals. To measure the penetration in terms of how many citizens have access is thus more complex. The access may come via telecentres, public institutions, employers, etc, rather than individual subscriptions.

The challenges involved in providing broadband access to break the communication isolation of the under-served areas are several:

Policy and regulation: The political awareness and will to provide inclusive affordable broadband access yet needs to be established and consolidated and the regulatory frameworks needs to be developed to fit the needs of the knowledge society. The public, consumer and producer interests need to be balanced and the market liberalized and transformed from high-price/low-volume to low-price/high-volume. Competition regulations need to be enforced to make producers focus on user-value rather than limitation of choice.

Consumers: The core of the consumer base in under-served areas consists of the communities themselves and their local administrations, the municipalities. While individuals may be poorly educated and caught in poverty, basic public services, such as education, health-care and local administration, are national public concerns and responsibilities.

Producers: The potential producers of communication services in remote areas only see low revenues, high costs and high risks. They may have the competence, skills and resources but will not take the lead until they see profitable business with manageable risks. The local communities need to assist in the development of innovative business models focusing on and enforcing provision of user values.

To speed up the development, there is a need not to wait for last mile solutions from the producer side but to also deploy first mile solutions from the consumer end: to establish local broadband communication networks between end-users on a community level. Learning from history, this is how the global telephone network was built in the 19th and 20th century.

The technical challenges include unreliable power supply and lack of communication infrastructure, adequate and affordable network equipment and complete supply chains. In other contexts, we have demonstrated that it is possible to meet these challenges by using innovative technical solutions, including locally available renewable energy sources [4] and network equipment based on selected standard PC hardware and open source software components [5].

However, until we also have innovative management and business models meeting the local market and business challenges, the operation of the network will not be sustainable. Thus, there is a need for an institutional framework designed to accommodate the local factors affecting the revenue model and operations of the network.

3 Related Implementations

In this section, we discuss three related deployments looking into the context, motivation, and management.

3.1 Macha Works

Macha is an isolated rural community situated in the Southern province of Zambia, 380 km by car from capital Lusaka (a one hour direct flight). Approximately 128,000 people live in traditional rural houses within a radius of 35km of Macha, more than 20,000 families (households).

A communication network has been implemented in Macha community since 2004 [7]. The network was initiated by a Dutch telecommunications engineer who moved to Macha to join his wife working as a doctor at a malaria institute. The institute is a result of a partnership of the Zambian government, Johns Hopkins University of Baltimore and the Macha Mission Hospital.[1] The initial infrastructure was setup with $50,000 in seed money from the malaria institute.

The main users of the Internet in Macha include the hospital, the research institute, an Internet café, the Community Centres and the primary school.[2]

To operate this communications network, "Macha Works", a non-profit cooperative company was set up. Macha Works has an ICT unit, LinkNet, which is owned by Macha community [8]. Macha Works itself is an international organization launched and registered in the Netherlands.

3.2 Jokkmokk

Jokkmok is one of the fourteen municipalities in the county of Norrbotten, northern Sweden, with a population of 5,000 inhabitants, and an area of 20,000[3] km^2.

[1] http://www.ieee.org/portal/site/tionline/index.jsp?pageID=institute_level1_article&TheCat=1016&article=tionline/legacy/inst2009/jun09/profile.xml.

[2] http://www.machaworks.org/en/history_linknet.asp, May 2011.

[3] http://www.scb.se/Pages/TableAndChart____159278.aspx, May 2011.

This translates to 0.3 persons per square kilometre, which is too sparse a population for traditional communications service providers to identify a market potential.

In 1998, the municipality itself initiated the roll-out of a broadband network within Jokkmokk, known as City Net, using *regional development funds* from the government as a grant, with the condition attached that they were not supposed to operate it.

However, as there were no commercial actors interested in providing ICT services in the area, the municipality decided to initially be responsible, creating an IT unit, Jokknet[4] that was tasked to operate the network until a commercial operator should come forward. Finally, after twelve years, OpenNet,[5] an operator of apartment husing networks in the City of Stockholm, took over the operations starting from 1st November, 2010.[6]

3.3 Nepal Wireless

Nepal wireless is a community-based network built around technical volunteerism and donations of funds and equipment. Their objective is to link the community around the Himalayan mountains in Nepal to the world, with a goal of providing better education, healthcare, communications, means for weather and climate change monitoring, and to stimulate job creation.

The project started as a single man's (Mahabir Pun) dream to connect a single high school, which was achieved in 2003. It has grown to connect more than ten villages. *NepalWireless* was registered in 24th July, 2009 as non-profit company.[7]

4 ICT4RD Municipal Broadband Networks

The Information and Communication Technology (ICT) for Rural Development (ICT4RD) project in Tanzania [6] was designed with a goal of creating a model for building and sustaining broadband communication networks in rural areas. The project is funded by the Swedish International Development Agency (SIDA)[8] and executed through a partnership between the Tanzania Commission of Science and Technology (COSTECH);[9] Dar es Salaam Institute of Technology (DIT),[10] Tanzania; and the Royal Institute of Technology (KTH),[11] Sweden. ICT4RD strategy is to build local broadband communication networks that will create awareness among users to stimulate the development of local markets.

4 `http://www.jokknet.se/`, May 2011.
5 `http://www.norrbotten.opennet.se/`, May 2011.
6 `http://www.jokknet.se/extdefault.aspx?id=2062`, May 2011.
7 `http://www.nepalwireless.net/index.php`, May 2011.
8 `www.sida.se`, May 2011.
9 `www.costech.or.tz`, May 2011.
10 `www.dit.ac.tz`, May 2011.
11 `www.kth.se`, May 2011.

In order to attract the necessary investments to establish the network, the primary focus chosen on the user side is on facilitating basic public services, including education, health and local government. This made it possible to attract funds from the donor community and to get access to government infrastructure resources. The funds necessary to operate and maintain the network is provided through connecting all sorts of users willing to pay for connectivity. Additional services and applications have been implemented to develop the local market and increase the revenue stream. To reduce costs, we advocate sharing of resources and buy in to existing communication infrastructure wherever possible. Another important part of the strategy to achieve sustainability is to establish and maintain strong ties with education and training institutions for capacity building and access to pools of technical students going for their practical work and thesis projects. ICT4RD project is running two pilot sites in Tanzania, the Serengeti and Wami Broadband Networks, to help testing and validating its rural connectivity model. Both pilots are community-owned broadband networks based on publicly owned optic fiber, affordable routers, switches and wireless technologies as presented in [9]. Due to space limitations, the paper will focus on the Serengeti pilot; only making reference to Wami when necessary.

Serengeti and Bunda are two districts in the Mara region, northern Tanzania with a total population about 500,000 people [10]. In the 2005 Poverty and Human Development Report [11], they were ranked among the poorest districts in the country, positioned at 116th and 119th respectively out of 119 districts. In 2006, a baseline study was carried out in both districts to benchmark the need/use of ICT, focusing on education, health and local government [12]. The study revealed that: agriculture and livestock are carried out by 90% of the population; both districts rely on the central government for about 95% of their budgets; anda few organizations, public and private, have Internet via VSATs or dial-up, purchased using donor funds, usually via a project. The baseline study further noted that:

- Local government authorities (LGA) require reliable communication both to the central government and to the citizens, thus broadband connectivity would improve their efficiency.
- The education sector has a shortage both of teachers and textbooks. The use of broadband connectivity would facilitate e-learning to compensate for the deficits and improve the quality of education offered.
- There was a lack of trained staff in the healthcare sector, poor communication channels and insufficient facilities. Broadband connectivity could facilitate tele-medicine where the few available medical doctors could provide consultations to primary health centers via video conferences.

4.1 Stakeholders Identification

In this subsection, we highlight stakeholders of broadband communication in rural areas, grouped into anchor customers and partners.

Anchor Customers. The community is the target group where the communication network will enhance information access and efficient delivery of services. Public institutions, including, local government offices, schools and health-care units serve as anchor customers. Examples of value proposition to these institutions are:

- *Education:* ICT resources made available via the network can to some extent compensate for the lack of teachers and textbooks. Using the communication network, a few competent teachers can train students in several schools at the same time using a video conferencing service. Hence, the connectivity will improve service delivery. The network can also be used to make teacher training more efficient, including in-service training.
- *Health:* ICT resources made available via the network can to some extent compensate for the lack of trained health-care workers, especially doctors, shortage of hospital facilities and poor communication channels. The communication network can be used to disseminate health information and for remote consultation via a video conference service, using the same few qualified doctors and nurses to treat more people. Hence, the connectivity will improve service delivery while reducing the cost. The network can also be used for continuing education and training of health workers to improve the situation.
- *Entrepreneurs:* Access to market information can create business opportunities and provide access to micro-finance institutions such as KIVA[12] and MYC4.[13] This group also includes potential service providers that can strengthen the local ICT supply chain by providing maintenance and repair, creating local content as well as training.
- *Local Government Administration:* The communication network will improve internal communications and facilitate rationalization of the internal work processes by taking advantage of information systems. The network will also enhance the delivery of public services to the citizens, and has the potential to make them interactive, via the web. The public services can thus be made more available at lower cost.

Partners. The partners discussed here include government at all levels and their development partners, as well as private and public organizations that can provide access to infrastructure resources or human resources with adequate skills.

- *Central government and development partners*: Among the goals of these organizations is to improve the quality of life of the citizens, especially those in dire poverty. The organizations run and/or fund various outreach programs in all sectors. The connectivity provides a platform through which they can reach the citizens and the local communities to disseminate various content, such as HIV awareness.

---

[12] `www.kiva.org`, May 2011.

[13] `www.myc4.com`, May 2011.

- *Local governments*: The local district councils accepted to become partners when they saw the potential of the project. It was agreed that they were to take ownership and leadership of the development project, initially by participating and providing various resources (such as land) during the implementation, and then to provide management and continue to operate the network also when the project comes to an end.
- *Telecommunication Infrastructure Owners*: This group includes various infrastructure owners, public as well as private, such as the Ministry of Water, the power utility company, and incumbent telecommunications company and commercial wireless operators. These organizations are providing services and benefit from the market development resulting in more users interested in their services. They also benefit from community networks as a new customer segment interested in excess capacity in their infrastructures.
- *Training Institutions*: These institutions need to offer their students apprenticeship opportunities to get of experience working life.
- *Local Service Providers*: There are a few small local service provider companies that benefit from the emerging broadband markets, as well as from the increase in human resources having relevant technical skills.

4.2 Community Engagement

In late 2006, a technical survey to determine how to build the network and who should be connected at this pilot phase was conducted. This information was discussed with the district officials, where decision was based on technical merits related to availability of power supply and reachability. A coordinator from the local government was appointed at this stage to start working with the project.

A national workshop involving all stakeholders including representatives from both districts, respective ministries and the academia was held in January 2007. In this workshop, the need to have ICT departments at district levels to spearhead ICT issues was discussed. Another issue discussed was the modalities on how to transfer the leadership of the project from the consortium to the local government representing the local community.

ICT Awareness-raising. A series of awareness-raising and training events on the district/community level followed, including: an ICT-awareness-raising workshop targeting local governments; basic computer usage training events to all interested; and training in ICT entrepreneurship and management issues to prospective ICT entrepreneurs.

Local Focus Groups. Focus groups were created with the primary objective of pioneering ICT4RD initiatives and internalising the effort within community level [13]. Thus members were individuals from government (health, education), and business community. The coordination of these groups was left under the local government since it was already decided that they would take over the management of the project.

In-house Trainings. The training was focused on basic use of ICT services such as email and web-browsing. Open training sessions were organized in the districts as well as in-house training subject to the availability and knowledge differences between participants. Since staff members move between locations, recurrent training events were required.

4.3 Network Implementation

The Serengeti network was implemented and inaugurated by the President of Tanzania in June 2007. The technical implementation details have been summarized in [14]. At the pilot phase, the following users were connected:

- Local Government Administration: To stimulate the usage, both district councils connected to the Serengeti Broadband network were supported to deploy internal local area networks before being connected to the broadband backbone.
- Health Sector: Two district hospitals and two primary health centers, one from each district, are connected. The objective is to facilitate collaboration between the hospitals and consultations between primary health centres and hospitals.
- Education: Seven secondary schools are connected. The goal is to facilitate sharing of scarce resources, such as the best teachers, to provided courses via the network. Lectures and other material can be recorded and shared via the local server.
- Community: One public access point is provided in each district.

Each connected user was given an Internet phone (VoIP), a computer and a power backup system (UPS). A full-fledged local server is running where basic communication services include web hosting, emails, and Voice over IP (VoIP) are installed. It is the responsibility of all other remaining groups (private individuals, NGOs, Business, etc) to request connections, purchasing their own equipment, paying for the connection charges and the monthly contribution.

5 Searching for Sustainability

Apart from participation in the ICT awareness and training efforts, there was initially no commitment made from the local governments in Bunda and Serengeti Districts to take responsibility for the future operation of the network. They were also reluctant to contribute to the running costs. We believe that this is due to the dependency on the central government. Municipalities are accustomed to a top down approach where funds and execution plans come from the central government. The local government role is to execute and report back only.

5.1 Testing Market for Readiness in Wami

Due to lack of readiness to take over leadership observed in the Serengeti pilot and the fact that the Bagamoyo local government council was far from the pilot area to be part of the network, it was decided to separate "ownership" from "management and operation" in Wami pilot. A request for proposal (RFP) was issued in August 2007 [15] to ask established ICT service providers to bid so that they could use the existing infrastructure to provide broadband services in the community. The response to the RFP was mixed. Some individuals requested that infrastructure should be established in their respective areas while the the big players responded that the market was too small and risky. One big company (Simbanet)[14] sent in their bid with a condition that another entity should be on the ground acting as a reseller of their services gaining 10% for every purchase made.

Observing the challenges from the Serengeti pilot and the response to the RFP, it was decided to conduct a sustainability study in August 2008 to explore mechanisms empowering the community to take ownership and leadership.

5.2 Community Ownership and Sustainability Study

A study was commissioned in August 2008, looking into how ICT can stimulate economic growth and development in the Bunda and Serengeti districts by identifying opportunities and constraints for community engagement in ICT4RD project [16]. The study methodology included literature review, observations in field and face-to-face semi-structured interviews to all stakeholders.

The study reported that the Bunda and Serengeti districts are engaged in agriculture, mining and fisheries, and, as neighbors to the biggest national park in the country, also are prime areas for tourism. The study further grouped potential ICT users (anchor customers) as follows:

1. Local Government Authority (LGA) - Each department in the district council had computers. They needed local area networks to interconnect their computers to facilitate document sharing. They also needed to connect with health facilities and schools in their districts to disseminate information and get reports.
2. Non-Governmental Organizations (NGOs) - There was a concentration of NGOs in both districts, some of them with head offices in the capital city. Their need was mainly Internet access to support communication with their head offices and sponsoring donor.
3. Business Community - Both districts are dominated by small and medium size traders that could benefit from better communications with financial institutions and potential customers.

This study also found that there was no sense of ownership in the local government. The recommendation was to build an institutional framework securing local ownership and leadership.

There is already financial and operational sustainability as discussed in next section under current status.

[14] www.simbanet.co.tz, May 2011.

6 The Institutional Framework

After the sustainability study, a series of consultative meetings about what kind of entity to put in place started immediately with all identified stakeholders in the community.

An ICT Board was created as a not-for-profit, public-private-partnership (PPP) to create a sense of inclusiveness and responsibility to the community. It was registered as an NGO to avoid government bureaucracy, secure autonomy in its operations, make it possible to apply for development funds from the government and other sources, and most importantly, make it possible to sell services to cover the costs for its operations.. The board members are representatives from various community entities, including central government, local government, locally active NGOs, Community Based Organizations (CBOs), Faith Based Organizations (FBOs) and Small and Medium Enterprises (SMEs)). The board members are serving on voluntary basis, members of the sub-committees are sourced within the community based on skills. There are six major functions of the board as follows:

1. Promoting, developing, supporting, and coordinating all ICT activities within the district.
2. Formulating district level ICT development policies (within the framework of broader national ICT policy) and to foresee its implementation.
3. To ensure a wider ICT adoption in the community in the district. To provide platform for deliberations, networking and experience-sharing among all stakeholders involved in ICT development within and outside the district.
4. To oversee the implementation of the district ICT policy, the direction and plans of the entity.
5. Collaborating with ICT experts in the provision of ICT services to district level ICT users.
6. Coordinating the provision of ICT services and connectivity to different ICT user groups e.g. NGO, Government, CBOs, FBOs, including designing of sectoral ICT programs such as catering for education, health, fisheries, agriculture and business sectors.

Alternative Structures Considered: Instead of a PPP, NGO, not-for-profit ICT Board, other options could have been:

- *A pure community owned without involvement from the local government.* This option works best if there is a local champion in the community to undertake the challenge and associated risks.
- *A pure local government-owned not-for-profit company.* This option was not considered since the local government did not show interest in taking full responsibility.
- *Trusteeship* The project could have been handed over to a private company with an understanding that the ownership would be handed over to the community, once it was ready. This was not considered since there was none that could have taken over the operations and management.

6.1 Organizational Structure

In addition to the secretariat, three committees were formed: finance; advocacy and awareness-raising; and research and development. For political and economic reasons, the secretariat of the Board was designed as follows:

1. The chairperson is the District Commissioner (DC), a representative from the central government: to diffuse any political issues from the councilors when it comes to the use of ICT for developmental issues in the district.
2. Vice chair is from the private sector or civil society to balance the PPP model.
3. The technical advisor is the District Executive Director (DED), a representative from the local government who is responsible for all development activities in the district. DED has the budget, manpower, other resources as well as knows government developmental priorities.
4. The Manager (responsible for coordination of day to day activities of the board) should be an employed person from the local government. This was more economical than political choice for two reasons: 1) At this initial stage, the Board could save money allowing the council to pay salary to its manager. 2) The manager will have access to inside information from the local government through DED and the DC.
5. The treasurer should be from the community.

There was a trade-off in the proposed organizational structure above. On one hand, the board risked being turned into a department of the local government, due to the general cultural attitude that government is in charge and the difficulty in regarding other stakeholders as equals. On the other hand, government could make important contributions in terms of human resources, land and funds, since the focus was entirely on the ability to create sustainable broadband markets.

The ICT4RD project paid for Internet access during one year (2009), giving the boards time to plan and adjust themselves before meeting that expense. It should be mentioned that the project also recruited a technician for each district and employed them for one year (2009) with a possibility for the boards to employ them permanently. The funds to pay their salaries were transferred to the board's bank account to enhance ownership. The board and the ICT4RD management committee worked in parallel until June 2009 when the network was officially handed over. The ICT4RD project management committee remained as advisors.

6.2 Challenges Observed in the ICT Board

After the creation and implementation of the institutional framework, new challenges were observed as follows:

- *Lack of confidence* from community members This is partly due to a long time culture where people working in government offices are perceived as the most knowledgeable. It is also partly due to the fact that most government

officers are not accustomed to involving ordinary people in frank and open consultations on matters affecting the society. Traditionally most decisions in the community are made at higher levels and simply passed down to ordinary people for endorsement. In this way, people (even community leaders) outside the government systems does not have confidence to work as equals with their counterparts from government offices.
- We observed another cultural challenge on *consultant dependency.* Most stakeholders resisted the participatory approach to creating ownership during the institutional framework creation process. They demanded that the consultant, the expert, was paid to deliver final outcomes and should know the best practice.
- *Donor mentality:* When discussing how to raise funds, board members from local government and civil society organizations expected involved donors or the central government to provide the funds necessary for the continuation of the project.

To overcome these challenges, a community specialist was employed to provide technical support for one year (June 2009 - June 2010), providing capacity building to all board members and the individual committees as follows: Using a participatory process approach to assist the board to create a three year strategic plan; Provide management training to individual secretariat members on their roles and responsibilities; Assist the finance committee to develop an implementation plan and modalities for billing and collecting money from users and for writing new proposals to other financing sources; Assist the advocacy and awareness committee on how to report the impact they bring as a result of the use of ICT; and Assist the research and development committee to develop a plan for connecting new customers and follow up those already connected.

6.3 Current Status

In a recent survey conducted in March 2011, it has been observed that the local government departments are the main users of the network for various reasons: 1) They have most educated staff in the whole districts who need Internet for work-related as well as private communication; 2) Education and health services are a responsibility of the local government, thus, connecting them in a local area network makes it easier to facilitate communication and other broadband services. Thus, the local governments are taking lead to making sure the network is functioning properly by contributing heavily to the running costs.

More than 45 customers (equivalent to more than 100 computers) have been connected. This number includes four private Internet cafes used as community access points. There is financial and operational sustainability. The observations indicate the ICT Board has achieved its goals in having a strong customer base.

The ICT Board has now matured. To grow beyond the current stage, it requires a management with business skills. Feedback from community board members reveals that the chair and manager, being government employees, make the board feel like a government entity, thus, they cannot run it in a more business like environment.

7 Discussions

In an effort to discuss the challenges in creating local ownership to provide leadership and sustain community broadband networks in rural areas of the developing world, this paper presented the genesis of an institutional framework of a community network in Tanzania.

7.1 Comparison to Other Implementations

A general institutional framework proposed in the literature [17] and implemented in Serengeti communication network is the PPP. The institutional mechanism and the organization structure in the reference pilot were influenced by the local community context as well as the funding sources. PPP is a common practice in ICT projects in developing countries [18]; Tanzania has been using a PPP model at the local government level for provisioning other services as well [19]. When compared to similar implementations discussed in section III, we observe that there is no standard management method. However, PPP seems to prevail at different levels, either at funding, management, or operations.

The Jokkmokk implementation is from Sweden (a developed country), with established communication policy, regulatory framework, easy access to funding, and skilled labor. The Jokkmokk network was initiated by the local government itself as a way of fulfilling their obligations in improving service delivery and access to information for their citizens.

Macha Works and Nepal Wireless, on the other hand, are from the developing world, where telecommunication coverage does not reach everywhere, the communication policy and regulatory framework is not comprehensive, and access to funding as well as skilled labor is very challenging, a similar situation to Serengeti network. The difference between these networks and Serengeti is that both were initiated by individuals who live in the local environment, they needed communication (Internet) and they know the power of ICT while Serengeti was initiated from academia. Hence, there was a need to create local champions or some sort of ownership.

7.2 Challenges and Limitations

The authors believe that the challenges observed during the implementation, including the donor mentality, consultant dependency and lack of confidence from community members, are common to most developing countries as they have similar governance structures. Both challenges are a result of the top-down approach as central governments are used to send directives for execution.

Having the manager from the local government saved costs (salary) to the ICT Board and created a direct link with the council, which was good in gaining inside knowledge on LG priorities and convincing them to fund the board. However, this arrangement could also be a limitation to the growth of the board, as the appointed personnel might lack management and business skills required to run and expand the board. There is another danger of turning the ICT Board into another department at the council, killing the sense of community. Thus, the position as board manager should be employable based on merits as the initial arrangement has accomplished its purpose.

8 Conclusions and Recommendations

The goal of this paper was to discuss and analyze an institutional framework for building and sustaining community broadband networks in rural areas of developing regions. With a reference to a pilot implementation in Tanzania, the paper presented and discussed an institutional framework, mechanisms and organization structure for such networks. This was then compared to other implementations and the literature. Following are the recommendations for the management of the ICT Board to take it to the next level:

- Select chair from the community, based on merits not position
- Advertise the manager position; make it an employable position with a strategy of half salary and half bonus-based payment, with respect to how many customers connected (have performance targets). Someone who has managerial and entrepreneurial skills who can run the Board as an enterprise.
- The District Commissioner should be a member of honor of the Board.

The challenges observed affecting both management and sustainability of community broadband networks include: *dependence* on central government or consultants; *donor mentality*; and *lack of confidence* where community members not active in contributing during discussions if placed together with local government officers.

Generally, we can conclude that until we also have innovative management and business models meeting the local market and business challenges, the operation of the network will not be sustainable. Thus, there is a need for an institutional framework designed to accommodate the local factors affecting the revenue model and operations of the network.

References

1. Gillett, S., Lehr, W., Osorio, C.: Local Government Broadband Initiatives. J. Telecommunications Policy 28(7-8), 537–558 (2004)
2. Csaba, S., Károly, F., Zoltán, H.: Motivations, Design and Business models of wireless community networks. J. Mob. Netw. Appl. 13, 147–159 (2008)
3. Mandviwalla, M., Jain, A., Fesenmaier, J., Smith, J., Weinberg, P., Meyers, G.: Municipal Broadband Wireless Networks. J. Commun. ACM 51(2), 72–80 (2008)
4. Nungu, A., Olsson, R., Pehrson, B.: On Powering Communication Networks in Developing Regions. In: Proceedings of the 16th IEEE Symposium on Computers and Communications (IEEE ISCC), Kerkyra (Corfu), Greece (2011)
5. Nungu, A., Olsson, R., Pehrson, B.: On the Design of Inclusive Ubiquitous Access. In: Proceedings of the Third International Conference on Ubiquitous and Future Networks (IEEE ICUFN), Dalian, China (2011)

6. Information and Communication Technology for Rural Development (ICT4RD), Tanzania, http://www.ict4rd.ne.tz/
7. Matthee, K.W., Mweemba, G., Pais, A.V., Stam, G., Rijken. M.: Bringing Internet Connectivity to Rural Zambia Using a Collaborative Approach. In: 1st ACM/IEEE International Conference on Information and Communication Technologies and Development, India, pp. 1–12 (2007)
8. Stam, G., Oortmerssen, G.: Macha works! In: Proceedings of the WebSci 2010: Extending the Frontiers of Society On-Line, Raleigh, NC, USA (2010)
9. Nungu, A., Pehrson, B.: Interconnection of Broadband Islands in Developing Regions. In: IEEE 3rd International Conference on Testbeds and Research Infrastructures for the Development of Networks and Communities, Orlando, pp. 1–6 (2007)
10. Tanzania National Bureau of Statistics (NBS), http://www.nbs.go.tz/
11. National Strategy for Growth and Reduction of Poverty Report. Tanzania (2005)
12. Mascarenhas, O.: Serengeti Baseline Study. Bunda and Serengeti Districts. ICT4RD, Tanzania (2006)
13. Bwamkuu, A.J.: ICT Demand Creation Report. Bunda and Serengeti Districts. ICT4RD, Tanzania (2007)
14. Nungu, A., Genes, N., Pehrson, B.: Serengeti Broadband. In: Proceedings of the 2nd ACM SIGCOMM Workshop on Networked Systems for Developing Regions (NSDR), Seattle (August 2008)
15. Bwamkuu, A.J.: Commercializing the Broadband Services Provisioning in Rural Tanzania; a Case Study of Wami Broadband Project. Masters Thesis, KTH Royal Institute of Technology (2009)
16. Mlongetcha, M.: Towards Community Ownership and Sustainability of ICT4RD Projects in Tanzania Study Report. ICT4RD, Tanzania (2008)
17. Bar, F., Namkee, P.: Municipal Wi-Fi Networks: The Goals, Practices, and Policy Implications of the U.S. Case. Communications & Strategies 61, 107–125 (2006)
18. Hosman, L., Fife, E.: Public Private Partnerships and the Prospects for Sustainable ICT Projects in the Developing World. J. Bus. Sys., Gov. and Eth. 2, 55–66 (2007)
19. Ngowi, H.P.: Public-Private-Partnership (PPP) in the Management of Municipalities in Tanzania Issues and Lessons of Experience. African Journal of Public Administration and Management, XVII, 1–18 (2006)

Corporate Green Technology and Grid-Driven e-Learning Framework in Developing Economy

Ezendu Ariwa[1], Ejiofor Virginia .E.[2], Ibeabuchi Emeka[2], and Chiaha Jude Chukwudi[2]

[1] London Metropolitan University, UK
[2] Department of Computer Science,
Nnamdi Azikiwe University, P.M.B 5025, Awka – Nigeria
e.ariwa@londonmet.ac.uk, e.ariwa@ieee.org

Abstract. Grid computing is a new paradigm of distributed computing that facilitates virtual collaboration and interaction through the sharing of both hardware and software resources within a virtual organisation. A grid is indeed an aggregate of software and hardware resources that are available for one another for the rendering of mutual non-trivial services. Grid computing has enormous capability that makes it an ideal complement for enhancing the capability of existing e-learning frameworks. The ordinary e-learning framework offers functionalities that are limited only to the exchange of data (i.e. both textual and multimedia) and as such the nature of interaction do not include academic collaboration and sharing of hardware resources. In this research, we developed a model of Grid Enabled E-learning framework for institutions of higher learning in Nigeria that will facilitate quality and complete knowledge delivery on the e-learning platform and multi- institutional resource sharing and collaboration. This definitely provides greater capabilities for ordinary e-learning frameworks. Structured Systems Analysis and Design Methodology (SSADM) was used in the analysis and design stage of this research. The design of the system has a front-end Graphical User Interface (GUI) web-based application and a back-end Relational Database Management System (RDBMS). The front-end was designed using ASP.NET, using C# as a programming language while the back-end is designed using Microsoft Structured Query Language (SQL) Server 2005.

Keywords: e-learning, Grid computing, Graphical User Interface, virtual collaboration, Green Technology.

1 Introduction

E-learning has increased in importance as people realize that the use of technology can improve learning. E-learning essentially entails the transfer of skills and knowledge via electronic media (Zaheer et al). It is a set of applications and processes that use the available electronic media and tools to deliver vocational education and training. This could be via Internet (Web), local area network (Intranet) or stand alone personal computers. Consequently, many e-learning environments have been proposed and developed. However, in general they are oriented to address a specific e-learning functionality and in most cases are not developed to interoperate with other

J.J. Yonazi et al. (Eds.): ICeND 2011, CCIS 171, pp. 41–51, 2011.

e-learning tools or environments. This fact excludes the possibility of harnessing learning resources from multiple platforms for the creation of a hyper e-learning environment. Most of the existing e-learning framework offers functionalities that are limited only to the exchange of data (i.e. both textual and multimedia) and as such the nature of interaction and collaboration on the existing E-learning platform does not include the sharing of hardware resources that grid computing engenders. Zaheer et al gave a list of enablers for effective e-learning infrastructure where it was discovered that the various enablers are not catered for in the current Internet-based architecture for e-learning.

This research describes a Grid-Enabled E-learning Framework for institutions of higher learning in Nigeria that will facilitate quality and complete knowledge delivery on the e-learning platform. The Grid-Enabled E-learning Framework will enhance the functionalities of existing models of e-learning architecture by facilitating:

1) Inter-institution sharing of resources;
2) The aggregation of available resources in the grid for collaborative problem solving;
3) The engagement of remotely located specialized resources;
4) Research collaboration among institutions through virtual research libraries; and
5) Utilization of scarce software licenses available on remotely located media on the grid.

A Computational grid is a hardware and software infrastructure that provides dependable, consistent, pervasive and inexpensive access to high-end computational capabilities. It is concerned with the coordinated resource sharing and problem solving in dynamic, multi-institutional virtual organization according to Foster, I, Kesselman, C. and Tuecke, S. (et al, 2001). According to Foster(et al, 2001), grid computing was defined as flexible, secure, coordinated resource sharing among dynamic collections of individuals, institutions, and resources. Daramola and Ayo (et al 2005) defined grid computing as a computing paradigm for collaborative problem solving within a virtual organization facilitated through coordinated resource sharing and the rendering of mutual non-trivial services.

The core characteristics of a grid computing include:

i. Ability to negotiate resource-sharing arrangements among a set of participating providers and consumers and to use the resulting resource pool for some purpose.
ii. Availability of a resource sharing scheme that allows direct access to computer, software, data and other resources as required by a range of collaborative problem solving and resource-brokering strategies emerging in industry, science and engineering.
iii. A resource sharing scheme that is highly controlled with resource providers and consumers defining clearly and carefully just what is shared, who is allowed to share, and the conditions under which sharing occurs.
iv. Existing virtual organizations within which all grid transactions occur i.e. a group of individuals and/or institutions whose interaction are defined by a set of protocols.

1.1 E-Enabled and Grid-Enabled e-Learning Concepts

The emergence of Internet brought about the term eLearning. The e-learning is widely used in most of the developed countries to promote distance education (DE) and life long learning. It can be defined as an innovative approach for delivering electronically mediated, well designed, learner-centered, and interactive learning environments to anyone, anyplace, anytime by utilizing the internet and digital technologies in concern with instructional design principles (Anonymous 2003, Hedge and Hayward, 2004). The European Union e-learning Action Plan defined e-learning as "the use of new multimedia technologies and the Internet to improve the quality of learning by facilitating access to resources and services as well as remote exchanges and collaboration. Further steps have also been taken to take learning to mobile device users in order to make learning ubiquitous (m-Learning & u-Learning). According to Akintola and Ojokoh (2005) e-learning can be defined as teaching and learning activities over the internet just like we have e-Commerce, e-Government and e-Banking. Internet connects millions of computers worldwide providing a means of reaching learners on a global level.

Applications and processes of e-learning include web based learning, computer-based learning, virtual classrooms, and digital collaboration, where content is delivered via the internet, intranet/extranet, audio and/or video tape, satellite TV, CD-ROM (Islam, 1997) and mobile devices. E-learning is now a multi-billion dollar activity worldwide. The rapid and intensive use of ICTs in education in the developed countries facilitated the establishment of 100% ICT based Universities called 'virtual universities'. In addition, many world-leading conventional universities are now also offering some of their academic courses through various ICTs for their distant learners and established themselves as the 'dual mode universities'.

The historic launching of 700 courses from 33 academic disciplines as 'Open courseware' by http://ocw.mit.edu/OcwWeb/Global/all-courses.htm Massachusetts Institute of Technology (MIT) offers a tremendous resource for faculties, students and self-learners around the world. In contrast, the infrastructure of ICTs in the developing or the least developed countries is very weak and thus, intensive use of e-learning in DE is still a dream for their universities and institutes. Recently, ICTs are rapidly expanding in some of the developing countries, and hence, it offers an opportunity to consider its use in the promotion of DE. It offers students considerable benefits including increase access to learning, life-long learning opportunities, and convenience of time and place (Pierre 1998).

Basically e-Learning can be synchronous or asynchronous. In synchronous e-Learning, the instructors and learners are required to simultaneously participate in teaching and learning programmes at their respective locations. This refers to delivering lectures in real-time to remote learners at the same me, this makes use of videoconferencing facilities and internet chats.

In asynchronous e-learning, however the Instructors and learners are not required to simultaneously participate in learning programmes. Learners have more control over learning time, process and content. This refers to on-demand delivering of lectures. This makes use of websites, e-mails, and bulletin boards mode of learning and is the predominant system due to ease of development and implementation.

E-Learning has several advantages for potential learners. Some of the advantages are:

a. E-Learning facilitates self-paced learning. In the CAI mode, for example, computers individualize learning, while giving immediate reinforcement and feedback.
b. Multimedia e-Learning tools with integrated graphic, print, audio, and video capabilities, can effectively link various technologies. Interactive video and CD-ROM technologies can be incorporated into computer-based instructional units, lessons, and learning environments.
c. E-Learning is interactive. Microcomputer systems incorporating various software packages are extremely flexible and maximize learner control.
d. E-Learning increases access to Education. Local, regional, and national networks link resources and individuals, wherever they might be. In fact, many institutions now offer complete undergraduate and graduate programs relying almost exclusively on computer-based resources.
e. E-Learning provides collaborative learning environments by linking students with the instructors and co-learners in other geographical locations.
f. It also allows for easy maintenance of instructional materials.

Despite all the enumerated benefits however e-Learning has some limitations among which are the following:

a. Computer networks, which are the backbone of e-Learning system are costly to develop. Although individual computers are relatively inexpensive and the computer hardware and software market is very competitive, it is still costly to develop instructional networks and purchase the system software to run them.
b. The technology is changing rapidly. Computer technology evolves so quickly that the distant educator focusing solely on innovation "not meeting tangible needs" will constantly change equipment in an effort to keep pace with the "latest" technical advancements.
c. Widespread computer illiteracy still exists. While computers have been widely used since the 1960's, there are many who do not have access to computers or computer networks.
d. Students must be highly motivated and proficient in computer operation before they can successfully function in an e-learning environment.

The concept of grid computing support for e-learning has been criticized from various quarters. Critics hold the view that the modern Internet-based architectures, tools, and technology support nearly every feature required by e-learning and thus incorporating the grid is largely unnecessary. However, most of the existing e-learning frameworks offer functionalities that are limited only to the exchange of textual and multimedia data, and as such, the nature of interaction and collaboration on the existing e-learning platform does not include the sharing of hardware resources which grid computing provides. Zaheer et al ,2004 gave a list of enablers for effective e-learning infrastructure where it was discovered that the various enablers are not catered for in the current Internet-based architectures. This provides sufficient basis for the implementation of grid-enabled e-learning platforms.

1.2 An Inter Grid-Enabled e-Learning Model for Multi-institutional Collaboration

Grid computing offers enormous positive potentials for virtual collaborations among Nigerian institutions. This is because it offers the opportunity for different institutions to leverage on one another's resources, especially those resources that are scarce and very expensive. Also, it provides a platform for students both at the undergraduate and graduate levels to benefit from the expertise base of personnel and diversity of knowledge available in several institutions apart from the one where they have direct studentship. Some other anticipated benefits include:

- Increased capacity for collaborative research and problem solving;
- Improvement in overall computational throughput;
- The opportunity of leveraging available learning resources in all units and departments of several institutions being underutilized;
- Coordinated sharing of resources for mutual benefits for improved pedagogy and curriculum development; and
- Optimal usage of available hardware resources.

1.3 Enabling Technologies for Inter Grid Collaboration

Some of the essential components that must be included in the Intergrid architecture to ensure healthy multi-institutional interaction include:

- **Grid Resource Provider (RP):** This is responsible for providing resources to users within a particular local grid (Intragrid) and to users from other grids.
- **IntraGrid Resource Manager (IRM):** This is responsible for the allocation and management of resources in a local grid and uses local protocols in order to communicate with resources provided by resource providers to an Intragrid. Different IRMs can use different policies to allocate grid resources. Examples of technology to enable such IRMs include Shirako, Virtual Grids, VioCluster and Virtual Workspaces.
- **Grid Resource Broker (GRB):** Clients wanting to allocate grid resources can utilize a GRB to do so. The GRB uses resources from the Grid and Intergrid when demand surpasses the resources its grid can offer. Examples of existing brokers that can be adapted to such a scenario include Gridbus Resource Broker and Service Manager of Shirako.
- **Client** (**CL**) A Client or Service Creator interacts with the IRM via a Grid Resource Broker to allocate resources to deploy a service. When a Client requires more resources than what their internal resource broker can provide, the IRM can contact the Grid Gateway or InterGrid Gateway, which then redirects resource requests to other grids where there is supply. An IRM can contact the InterGrid Gateway when the client requires more resources that its grid is able to provide or when it is more cost-effective to allocate resources from other grids.
- **Inter Grid Gateway (IGG):** An IGG is aware of agreements with other InterGrid Gateways and thus acts as a grid selector taking into account policies defined in the grid to which it belongs and making the necessary conversions. An IGG can also be in charge of allocating inter-grid resources and establishing new

peering agreements when there is a need for users from a grid to gather resources from another grid.

- **Grid Gateway (GG):** A GG is responsible for similar functions as an IGG, but within a single Grid. A Grid Gateway provides functions similar to those of Virtual Organization Membership Services (VOMS), such as managing the membership of Intra-grids.

2 Results and Discussions

2.1 Methodology

The structured system analysis and design methodology (SSADM) was employed in the analysis and design stages of this research. SSADM takes a modular approach to this Grid e-Learning System initiative using a best practice guide to ensure the successful implementation of one part of the project at a time; this makes the project more scalable. The Relational Database Management (RDBM) of the application was executed first and tested to make sure that it conforms to all requirements (specifications, business rules and constraints). After which the front-end GUI (Graphical User Interface) application was integrated. This methodology allows the system to start small and break down the implementation process into modules that are attainable, based on the requirement and resource availability. SSADM accepts the waterfall model of the system development. In this model each phase is completed and signed off before the next phase can start. This approach is employed in this project because it sets up a comfortable dialogue between the user, analyst, designer and programmer. The design of the proposed system has a front-end Graphical User Interface (GUI) web-based application and a back-end Relational Database Management System (RDBMS). The front-end is designed with ASP.NET, using C# as a programming language while the back-end is designed using Microsoft Structured Query Language (SQL) Server 2005. The database is developed based on the Entity-Relationship Model.

2.2 Use Case Model for the Proposed System

Use cases are the different tasks that a system user can perform using the system. It describes the system functions from the perspective of external users. It describes a whole process of interaction between a system and its users; it captures the goal of the users and the responsibility of the system to its users.
System Actors:

1. Students
2. Administrator
3. Institution

Use Cases are:

- Search Books
- Download Books
- Navigate Libraries

- Join Framework
- Manage Books
- Manage library
- Oversee Admin

Use Case Description

1. Search Books: Students and other researchers can log on to the site and search for books and research materials available on the site or navigate to other university libraries within the framework.
2. Download Books: All books available within the framework are open for download by students and other researchers with a variety of downloadable formats: pdf, xls, doc, e.t.c
3. Navigate Libraries: Students can access other university libraries within the framework through hyperlinks navigation.
4. Join Framework: A university administrator can join the Grid eLearning System via the Join Framework Portal. Such university is automatically added to the Grid's database upon the Join Framework process.
5. Manage Books: An Administrator uploads new books to the Grid's database.
6. Manage Library: A system administrator updates the library from time to time.
7. Oversee Admin: The institution selects the system administrators.

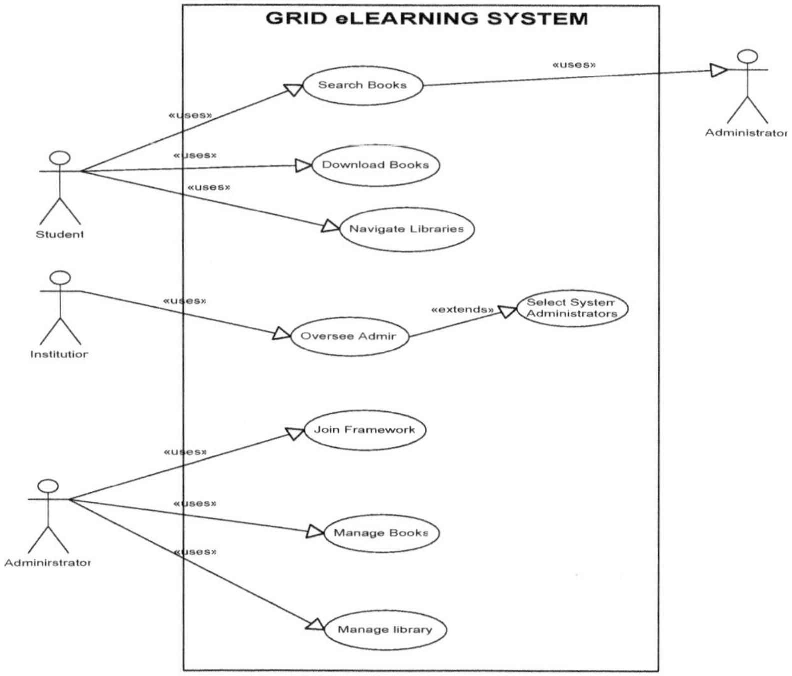

Fig. 1. Grid e-learning system

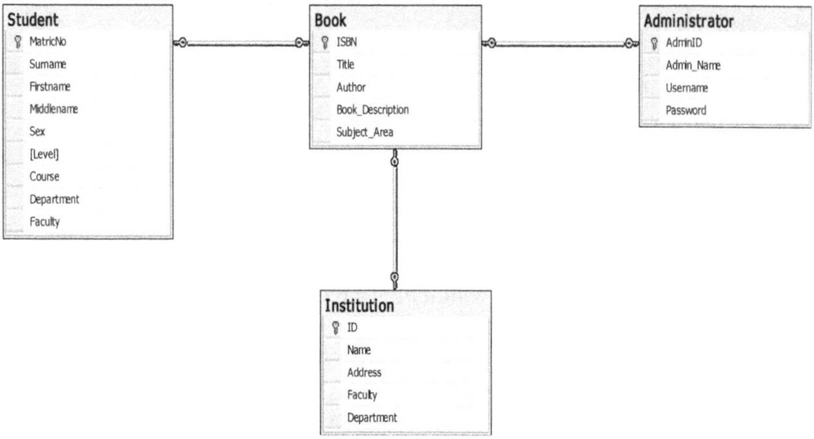

Fig. 2. Database Schemas

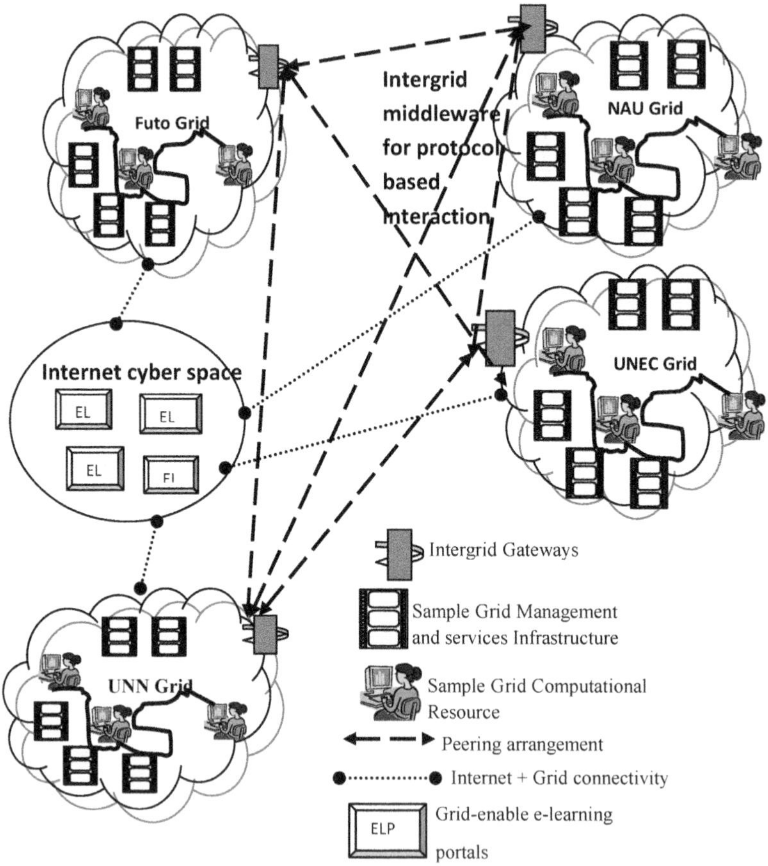

Fig. 3. The Architecture for Intergrid Enabled E-learning framework

3 Implementation

The system input is designed to receive data from the user (Students, Administrator and Other Researchers). The first set of input to the system is a pair of Username and Password for the system administrators. After the pair has been entered, the system authenticates the administrator by validating the username and password. This is done

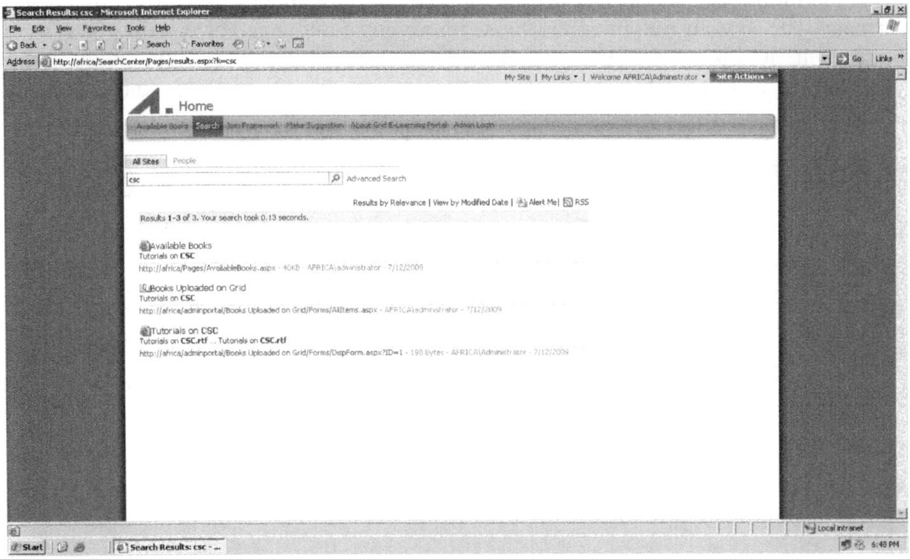

Search result page

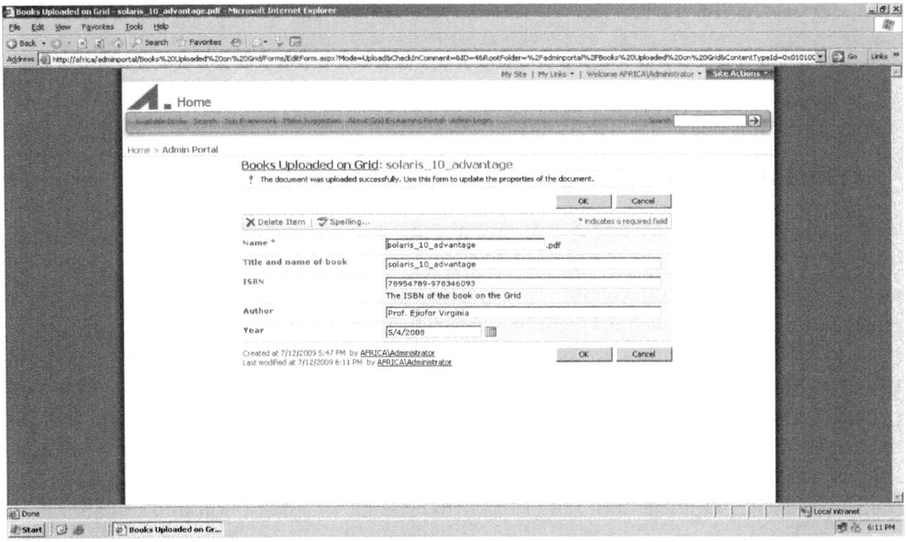

Upload book page

calling the login stored procedure which in turn checks the database by verifying if both the Username and Password supplied exist in the database. If true, the system authenticates the administrator else, the admin is denied access. The other input is if the administrator is just joining the framework. He/she is prompted to enter his/her institution's details, which will then be stored in the database.

The system output presents information to the user either as detailed information or in form of a report. The major output of this system is the live research materials available on the framework for download and can be seamlessly exported in various formats. The system output is the most important component of a working system because the interactivity of the system depends on its output. This is the main reason why the output of an information system determines the effectiveness and efficiency of the system.

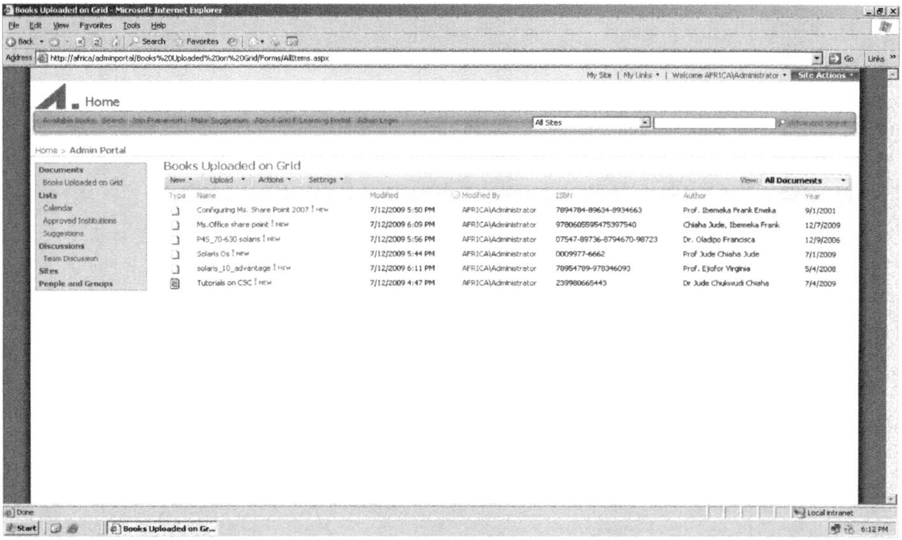

View available books page

4 Conclusion

A framework for ensuring research collaboration among institutions through virtual research libraries has been developed. During the analysis phase, it was found out that most existing e-learning systems were limited to transfer of skills and knowledge via electronic media to deliver vocational education and training. However, in general they are oriented to address a specific e-learning functionality and in most cases are not developed to interoperate with other e-learning tools or environments. This fact excludes the possibility of harnessing learning resources from multiple platforms for the creation of a hyper e-learning environment. Most of the existing e-learning framework offers functionalities that are limited only to the exchange of data (i.e. both textual and multimedia) and as such the nature of interaction and collaboration on the existing e-learning platform does not include the sharing of hardware resources which grid computing engenders.

The developed Grid-Enabled E-learning Framework for institutions of higher learning in Nigeria will facilitate quality and complete knowledge delivery on the e-learning platform. The Grid-Enabled E-learning Framework will enhance the functionalities of existing models of e-learning architecture by facilitating: Inter-institution sharing of resources; the aggregation of available resources in the grid for collaborative problem solving; the engagement of remotely located specialized resources; research collaboration among institutions through virtual research libraries; and utilization of scarce software licenses available on remotely located mediums on the grid.

References

Britton, C., Doake, J.: Software System development: A Gentle Introduction, 2nd edn.

Principle of information systems for management, 2nd edn. Williams C. Brown Company, Dubuque, IA

Stoecker, M.A., Steve, J.: Stein with Tony Northrup. Microsoft .NET FRAMEWORK 2.0 Windows Based Development Training Kit

Coreware solutions by Remote Lecturing System. Microsoft SQL SERVER 2005 Database Design and Implementation (2005)

Calway, B.A.: System Approach for Virtual Learning Development. Swinburne University of Technology, Lilydale

Glenn, J.A.: Broad View of Systems Analysis and Design. Implication for Research for University of San Francisco

Sommervile, L.: Software Development Life Cycle (SDLC), 3rd edn.

Pressman, R.S.: Software Engineering – A practitioner's Approach, 5th edn. McGraw Hill, New York

Pfleeger, S.L.: Engineering – Theory and Practice. Prentice Hall, Englewood Cliffs

Low Cost Wireless Technology and Digital Board for Education in Rural Kenya

F. Bertarelli[1], S. Padoa[1], G. Guaraldi[1], E. Genovese[1], M. Corradini[1], B. Mayeku[2], and J. Kilwake[2]

[1] Università degli Studi di Modena e Reggio Emilia, Via Vignolese 905/b, 41125 Modena, Italy
{fabio.bertarelli,stefania.padoa,giacomo.guaraldi, elisabetta.genovese,matteo.corradini}@unimore.it
[2] Masinde Muliro University of Science and Technology, P.O.Box 190, 50100 Kakamega, Kenya
mayekub@yahoo.com
jkilwake@mmust.ac.ke

Abstract. The application of wireless technologies in education is having a big development, but contrary to what we think the tools are not overly expensive. Thanks to the spread of wireless coverage, it's possible to reach the most remote corners and rural areas with simple mobile phone connected to a central system of information dissemination. This paper explores the use of wireless technology in combination with low-cost tools that have enabled access to education in rural areas of Kenya: this is a work in progress that will surely give you amazing results in the coming years.

Keywords: Mobile technology; wireless communication; education; rural area.

1 Introduction

Information technology and communication today allows to send and receive information in detail, even in rural areas. Schooling in regions poorly served by road networks, such as Kenya rural areas, can be spread effectively by technological tools not too expensive. For example, a digital board in combination with bluetooth microphones and iphones becomes a powerful tool for the diffusion of information and education through wireless technology. The digital board, introduced in schools as a tool for students with disabilities, can become an instrument for facilitating access to education by those who live in areas poorly served by infrastructure. This paper explores the possibility to connect to each other very distant areas through the use of a low-cost technology combined with the digital whiteboard, a tool of enormous potential yet in widespread use.

2 Wireless Communication Technology for Educational Purposes

The mobile revolution is here with us. The whole world is going mobile. Phones, PDAs (personal digital assistants), computers and media devices now fit in our pockets

J.J. Yonazi et al. (Eds.): ICeND 2011, CCIS 171, pp. 52–60, 2011.

and can connect us to a variety of information sources and enable communication nearly everywhere we go. People are increasingly connected and are digitally communicating with each other in ways that would have been impossible to imagine only a few years ago. Mobile devices are becoming increasingly powerful and accessible as wireless networks cover most of our daily environment and a variety of software frameworks makes the task of building mobile applications simpler.[1] In Kenya, mobile phones are having an amazing impact every where especially in marginalized communities like rural areas and pastoralist communities. Once disconnected from the rest of the country and so marginalized, since the emergence of mobile phone technology these communities have at least now become part of the country's journey to progress. There has never been any technology in Kenya that has rapidly cut across the entire country reaching out all classes of people like mobile phones. More than 54% Adult Kenyans have a mobile phone or have access to one. There was a time when majority of Kenyans especially from marginalized communities could walk miles to reach a banking facility so that they can make any transactions like withdrawing, depositing or sending money to their loved ones far from them. With the introduction of mobile banking facilities by major mobile service providers in the country, money transfer and banking has never been easier as it is today. There are many more areas in which mobile technologies, especially the mobile phone, have had a great influence not only in Kenya but all over the world not forgetting how it has changed the face of communication.

3 Mobile Technology in Education

One important field where mobile technology is causing much transformation is education. The combination of wireless technology and mobile computing is resulting in rapid transformations of the educational world. The emerging of mobile technologies that can support a broad range of learning activities on a variety of mobile devices, a concept referred to as mobile-learning (m-learning) has come a long with transformations in the learning environment. M-learning is conceptualized as the acquisition of knowledge and skills by using mobile technology, anywhere, anytime.[2]

There are a wide range of considerable appeals that has led to the massive embrace of mobile technology for there educational use. Some of the unique properties of mobile devices that make them appealing for education use among others include: Portability, social interactivity, availability, context sensitivity, connectivity and individuality. There portability permits the learners' mobility and makes information access more convenient for the learners and teachers. The affordability and availability of the devices like mobile phones by learners can offer students more opportunities to work on academic projects individually, to support group projects or even explore class work with fellow students. Further more, Mobile devices can support social interactivity in that they can allow data exchange and collaboration with other learners. Mobile devices can both gather and respond to real or simulated data unique to the current location, environment and time [3] thus context sensitive. They can also allow a shared network to be created by connecting mobile devices to data collection devices, other devices or to a common network. With mobile devices, scaffolding for difficult activities can be customized for individual learners hence supporting individuality.

Generally, m-learning can be said to be capable of offering many benefits in education field. The impact of using mobile learning technology may lead to achieving the main objectives of reaching more people at the same time, providing access using a ubiquitous technology such as mobile phones, which require a very low learning curve, and in ensuring equity to the disadvantaged. However it requires proper integration of several components. The major ones are technology, pedagogy and the organizational components. Integrating these components can be challenging. A part from the challenges, m-learning faces some constraints caused by the use of its mobile technologies such as the limited screen size, reduced energy, resolution capacity and location change during an activity. One important and very crucial aspect to any m-learning initiative is the appropriate design and development of its learning environment. As emergent trends and transformation arise in educational set up as a result of these mobile technologies, it is vital to explore best we might use these resources to support learning.

4 Learning Community

One of the vital aspects of an effective learning environment is the presence of a learning community. Establishing appropriate interactive online communication environments empowered by mobile learning technologies is essential and complex.[4] A learning community comprises of timely, meaningful interaction among the community, thus bringing a normal class room situation in place. This may include the aspects of class discussions, group discussions, question - answer sessions with the teacher or among student with real time response/feedback, involving voice conversation, face-to-face, feedback etc. A learning community exhibits the presence of a rich, collaborative and conversational experience.

The backbone for a rich, collaborative and conversational experience is interaction. Just like face to face learning, m-learning must support interaction between tutor and the learner, among the learners, and the learning materials. However in a normal school or campus scenario, not all these interactions may be necessarily computer mediated. There are occasion where some face-to-face elements is retained. This may not be the case in an ideal distance learning environment. Distance learning is not always location-and-time agnostic, factors that may lead to lack of a learning community. Lack of a learning community may pose dangers on the quality of education offered in a distance learning environment. Distance-learning programs often encounter problems with student motivation and performance[5]. These problems stem partly from lack of learning community[5].

5 Teacher Effectiveness

Another measure to effective learning is gained in student achievements. Research into teacher effectiveness has shown that the teachers who produced the most gains in student achievement were those who were "well organized, managed student disruptions by monitoring behavior and enforced rules in a consistent manner".[6] Successful self-management of learning comes as a result of developing competence and skill in learning how to learn, and this developing independence needs to be supported by teachers. [6] Therefore, to promote effective learning, the teacher should be in control of the learning community with all outside interventions being carefully regulated by the teacher.

6 Learning Environment

However, as many trends are emerging with the new digital technologies becoming increasingly personalized, learning has become more individualized and learner centered. These new trends have the potential to change the learning environment. Education has already started to move away from classroom-based teaching towards creating managed spaces for conversational learning that build on the students' own technologies, activities and resources.[6] As learning becomes more situated, individualized and learner centered, more control is given to the learner than to the teacher. Learners whether children or adults can manage their own knowledge and learning across a lifetime of educational needs and experiences. Placing much control to the learner may present challenges in promoting effective learning. Due to the fact that the students own the device, they will want to control their personal technology and also, due to the mobility of the device, the ability to link to activities in the outside world provides students with the capability to 'escape' the classroom and engage in activities that do not correspond with either the teacher's agenda or the curriculum. This also poses deep challenges and disruptions to the traditional system of education with the precepts of teacher-led instruction, the sealed classroom, a common curriculum, and individual assessment. A mobile learning device may become a zone of conflict between teachers and learners, with both trying to wrest control especially the opportunities it affords for managing and monitoring learning. However, it is important to remember that an ideal learning community that promotes effective learning should have the teacher in control.

As learning moves more outside of the classroom and into learner's environment hence becoming more situated and personal, where is the place of a learning community with the teacher being in control?

Furthermore, though mobile learning technologies have been the subject of serious academic research, there has been little attention paid to the impact of the latest technological developments on distance education. Mobile learning technologies in distance learning have been modeled and influenced by a variety of new communication technologies. Past and future developments must be considered in order to devise a unique, open and interactive system of distance learning which supports a cohesive learning community through technology in the higher education system. Therefore, how best can mobile technology support an effective and efficient learning community which supports all interactions (Thus interaction between tutor and the learner, among the learners, and the learning materials) in a distance learning environment?

7 The Cmplete e-Learning System

The project was launched successfully using low-cost technologies already in the country, combined with wireless modems and digital whiteboards. The initial phase was facilitated by the fact that in Kenya the mobile phone companies have extended

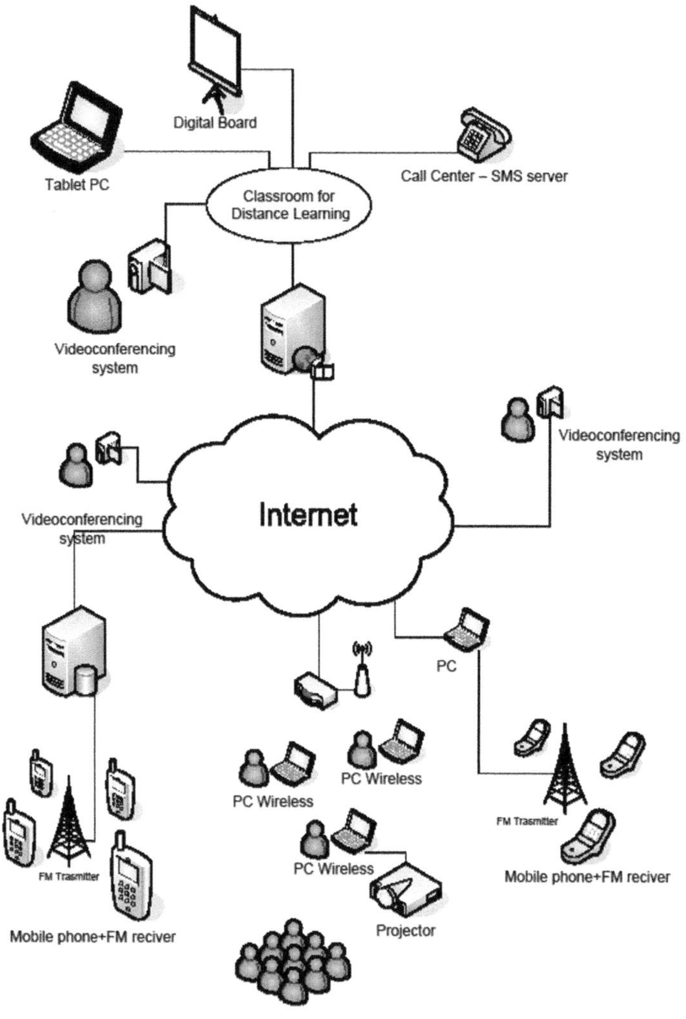

Fig. 1. The complete scenario

their network coverage in rural areas even more inaccessibile, thus allowing us to use an already existing network in the region. The system consists of a digital whiteboard, PCs and videoconferencing devices. The digital whiteboard is a tool used at the University of Modena and Reggio Emilia: initially introduced as an aid for students with disabilities, it has shown its potential in the involvement and inclusion of all students to academic lessons. The work in progress in Kenya aims to spread education and information, including areas poorly served by infrastructure, thanks to distance learning and simple low-cost technologies. The videoconferencing devices allow you to see and listen to the lessons anywhere there is a PC connected to the board, but the added value of this system is that the material produced during the lesson is recorded and stored by the board and deposited in a repository, by where it can be consulted again. Applications are not limited to education, because through e-learning we can send information of all kind. Now let's examine briefly the possible stations that could be created in those areas.

Fig. 2. Wireless USB modems in Kenya

The first possibility is the creation of a station with a wireless modem and laptop PCs.

Thanks to the wireless network coverage is most often the case, because the costs of access are limited. The major difficulty, namely the lack of electricity in rural areas, can be adequately substituted through the use of solar panels. In this way, and with the help of laptop computers, you can create classes and aggregation areas where students can meet each other: the lesson becomes more interesting and effective, and you also create social situations of encounter and relationship between students and teachers. The technology that often hampers the concrete relations in this case becomes a mean for communication in remote and disadvantaged areas, allowing the spread of culture and information in a widespread and persistent way. At a later stage, to improve this aspect, it could conceivably be an implementation of the video channels or websites dedicated, which allow you to connect webcam to enhance the educational experience of learners. What you have is actually much less than would be expected to have. In this sense there are two other possibilities:

The first one lets we take advantage of e-learning simply using a phone with an integrated FM receiver. The station has an FM transmitter capable of transmitting the audio signal around a few meters. The advantages of this type of transmitter are many: it costs very little, insignificant size (you can put it in your pocket) and very low consumption, so that you can use solar batteries at low cost. This is an even simpler solution than the first one, with lower costs and greater ability to geographic spread. The second possibility is to use a server that acts as a repository for lessons that have already taken place. In this way you can enjoy not only the lesson in progress, but also those already carried out, as well as materials from other working groups. This creates e-learning stations on which to implement a data warehouse for management and exchange of material.

Fig. 3. Netbook in rural area

8 Interactiviy

In stations B and D communication focuses on low-cost solutions, namely the SMS or short calls. In this perspective should be developed services Instant Messaging Server and Call Center station of type A. This makes it possible to request submission of a lesson or clarification on the issues discussed from a server or from a station of type B. The station type B, once implemented, can not depend on the main station, as the GSM network is now extended to remote areas.

With these considerations, the station B can also be seen as a type A station in "germinal" phase which then, depending on use and on the funds available, you can add more advanced services and equipment (probably using later tools of type A stations still working that time and technology and the increase of users may have rendered inadequate, but that is well suited for low-tech stations).

The activity of videoconferencing is certainly the most desired and most expensive services that the outline contains. The devices are stations operating on H.323 protocol TCP / UDP [8] as the one in fig. 6, which has been tested for operation and effectiveness in contexts other than the scenario given (and therefore should be tested in these contexts, but for scarcity of resources will be implemented at the end of the project), can be used both for end users, and for the continuous training of teachers to understand how to update content on their topics of teaching, training and adjustments to the rules and functions that a teacher should relate to better carry out their work. The activity of video conferencing for these purposes cut down costs significantly, or in some cases is the only way to implement strategies for staff who not withstanding being in rural areas are loaded with heavy work commitments and end up delaying (sometimes too ....) training activities[9].

It would be good establishing training sessions for teachers, not only to maintain the quality of the topics covered, but also to ensure the satisfaction of operators. Information technology enables great opportunities for cultural exchange and in fact reduces the physical distance, gathering thoughts and ideas.

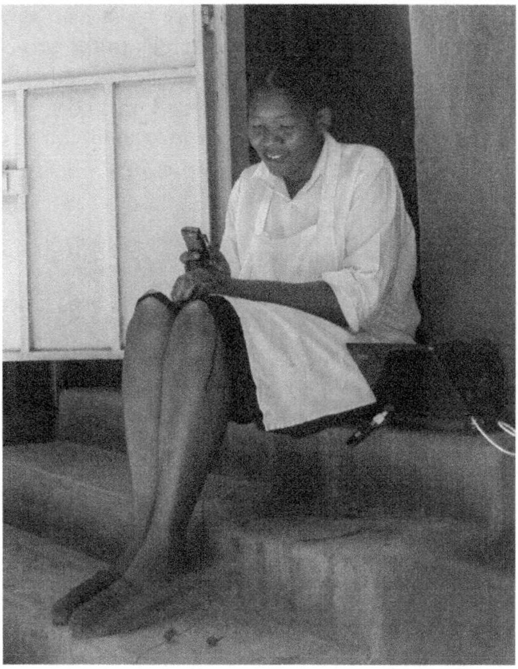

Fig. 4. Mobile phone with FM reciver in rural area

Fig. 5. Solar cell and bananas

9 Significance of the Application System

As we have seen, the use of low-cost technology for distance learning allows you to extend the opportunity to give higher education to many people, especially those coming from rural and backward areas. The e-learning in fact, as we have seen also at the University of Modena and Reggio Emilia, thanks to the project of digital boards, facilitates the approach and the inclusion even in the most disadvantaged situations, such as disability or lack of infrastructure, roads and transport. In rural areas of Kenya can be so much food for thought and research to students of distance education, as well as for designers and for those who develop effective learning environments for e-learning.

Fig. 6. Videoconferencing station

References

[1] Mulliah, A., Stroulia, E.: Mobile devices for collaborative learning in practicum courses. International Journal of Mobile Learning and Organisation 3(1), 44–59 (2009)

[2] Geddes, S.J.: Mobile learning in the 21st century: benefit for learners (2004), http://www.flexiblelearning.net.au/knowledgetree/edition06/download/geddes.doc

[3] Naismith, L., Lonsdale, P., Vavoula, G., Sharples, M.: Literature Review in Mobile Technologies and Learning (2007)

[4] Kurubacak, G.: Identifying Research Priorities and Needs in Mobile Learning Technologies for Distance Education: A Delphi Study. International Journal of Teaching and Learning in Higher Education 19(3), 216–227 (2007)

[5] Laine, T.H., Suhonen, J.: Establishing a mobile blog system in a distance education environment. International Journal of Mobile Learning and Organisation 2(2), 149–165 (2008)

[6] Guaraldi, G., Genovese, E., Bertarelli, F., Corradini, M., Kilwake, J., Mayeku, B.: Ict and university education: enhanced didactic tools for person with special needs. Submitted Eng. Schi. And Tech. MMUST (2010)

[7] Bertarelli, F., Corradini, M., Guaraldi, G., Genovese, E., Kilwake, J., Mutua, S.: The Digital Board in a University Setting: Two Real Cases in Europe and East Africa. In: Lytras, M.D., Ordonez De Pablos, P., Avison, D., Sipior, J., Jin, Q., Leal, W., Uden, L., Thomas, M., Cervai, S., Horner, D. (eds.) TECH-EDUCATION 2010. Communications in Computer and Information Science, vol. 73, pp. 259–264. Springer, Heidelberg (2010)

[8] H. 323 Protocol, http://www.iec.org

[9] Sharples, M.: Disruptive Devices: Mobile Technology for Conversational Learning (2007)

Utilization of C# Neural Networks Library in Industry Applications

Ondrej Krejcar[1,2]

[1] University of Hradec Kralove, FIM, Department of Information Technologies, Rokitanskeho 62, Hradec Kralove, 500 03, Czech Republic
Ondrej.Krejcar@ASJournal.eu
[2] VSB Technical University of Ostrava, Department of Measurement and Control, 17. Listopadu 15, 70833 Ostrava Poruba, Czech Republic
Ondrej.Krejcar@remoteworld.net

Abstract. Paper deal with a problems related to design and realization of application with the help of neural networks library, which is developed in object orientated programming language C#. This application classifies data that are obtained within industrial processes. Data used in this project was received during measurement of material diagnostics and its structural defects. Core of developed application is based on neural networks design, which is capable to classify whether the material has defect or not. Before classification itself it is necessary to set structural parameters of the neural network to obtain a good quality results. Afterwards application outputs are compared with outputs from Statistica programme, which is also used for classification purposes. Statistica uses for classification of the measured data algorithms of the artificial intelligence as well. Basically this project's aim is to substitute Statistica programme by application developed in C#.

Keywords: artificial neural networks, supervised learning, AForge.Neuro, material diagnostics, Statistica programme.

1 Introduction

Many artificial neural networks architectures were developed since the first moments of their introduction. Practical usage of these various architectures is very broad and many tasks may be solved by them. Neural networks as part of artificial intelligence issue, is quickly evolving branch of computer engineering, which allows solving tasks that would have (when used conventional computing algorithms) high performance requirements on computing power because of the complex mathematical description. Generally many real tasks can be solved by linear models described by complicated mathematics, usually systems of inhomogeneous differential equations. Realization of this kind of solutions is often time consuming, sometimes even impossible because of too complex mathematical description.[3] To design solution even for this complicated tasks, neural networks were developed during 20th century. Neural networks are a non-linear models that allows to solve specific tasks from almost all areas of engineering.

J.J. Yonazi et al. (Eds.): ICeND 2011, CCIS 171, pp. 61–72, 2011.

1.1 Basic Elements of the Neural Networks

Each of these neural networks architectures has in principle basically one element in common. This element is called neuron. Neuron in computer environment is very similar to its biological pattern. It can be imagined as object with many inputs and only one output. Every input has its own weight value which is important for defining of the priority during neural processing. Another basic element of the neuron is its threshold which determines input values needed to activate neuron processing so that it can work as designated [3].

Last basic element of the neuron is its transfer function which determines the way of neuron processing. Output value of the neuron is computed by this transfer function which transfers input values combined by threshold. There are many kinds of transfer functions used in application based on neural networks. The most common transfer function is threshold function or sigmoid. Details of this transfer function will be provided in other chapters of this project.

Architecture of the artificial neural network which uses only one neuron is called perceptron. This architecture can classify only to two classes, that's why it is used rarely in practical applications [1]. For the real purposes the architecture composed of more neurons is used. These neurons are set in layers. In principle there are three layers: input layer, hidden layer and output layer. Input layer's task is to adjust raw input data so that it can be computed by the rest of the neural network afterwards. Hidden and output layers are computing power of the application [4]. Details of this kind of neural network architecture will be provided hereinafter.

1.2 C# Neural Networks Library

Support for the solution of this project in .NET framework is C# neural network library which was introduced by the British programmer Andrew Kirillov in 2006. Kirillov won the prize of the Codeproject.com server [5].

This library contains a huge amount of classes and objects that can be used for design of the various architectures of the artificial neural networks. Programmer also attached some demonstrative application developed in library which shows the principles of neural networks design.

2 Industry Domains Definition

Many methods and algorithms are applied in material diagnostics issue nowadays. Some of them are very precise and are able to diagnose materials correctly, some are less efficient when determining required material properties. An important subset of diagnostics is material defects diagnostics. Researchers from VSB Technical University of Ostrava came up with a defect diagnostics method which uses the emission of pulses which are fetching to the diagnosed body. Accelerometers then measure the body's response to these pulses. Obtained data is transformed by Fast Fourier Transformation and modified by filters in MATLAB afterwards [2].

Adjusted data is needed to be computed by an instrument, which allow researchers to classify the material as convenient or inconvenient. Statistica programme developed by Statsoft company has been this classification instrument so far. This commercial software contains neural network's design and can be used for classification purposes.

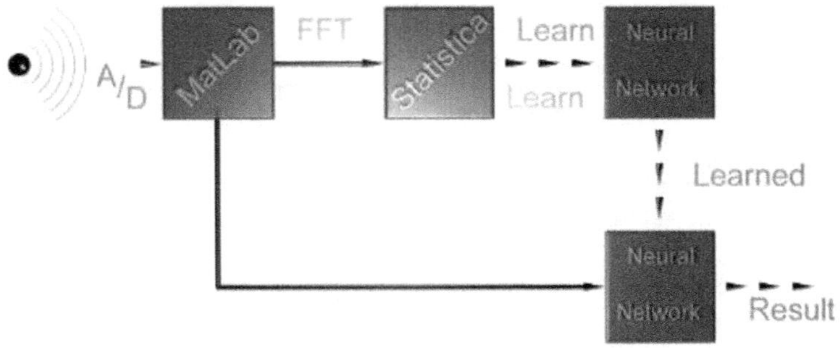

Fig. 1. Measurement network scheme [2]

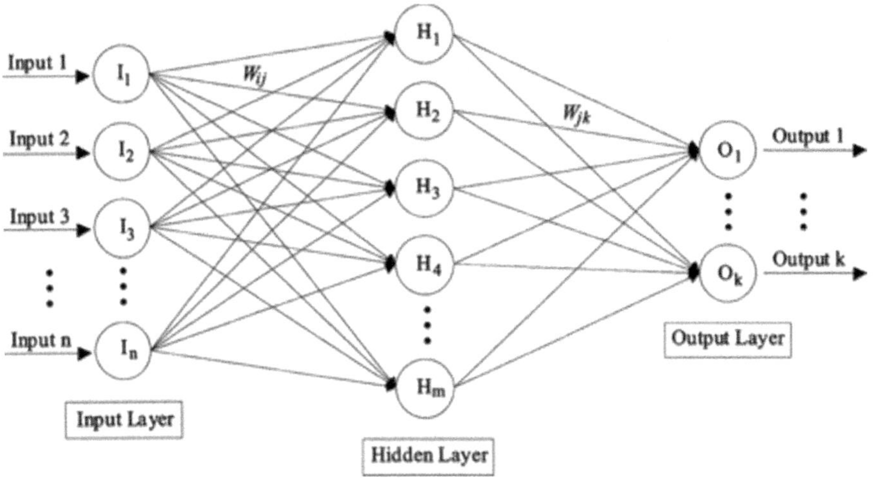

Fig. 2. Three-layer neural network

Aim of this project is to substitute this commercial software by application that works in .NET framework as less expensive possibility of classification of the measured, adjusted and modified data.

Essence of the whole problem is classification of the material diagnostics. It is required that from the programme outputs is possible to assess whether the material has defects and if so, what kind of defect that would be.

When designing the architecture of the neural network it is necessary to take into consideration, that there has to be as many neurons in input layer as the count of the classes of input samples. The neurons count in the hidden layer is needed to find out empirically. The neurons count in the output layer is equal to count of classes in which the input data is classified.

Architectures with so called supervised learning algorithms are implemented for the classification purposes. In these architectures it is necessary to learn designed neural network for the first time with some reference data (samples of measurement materials with no defects), so that the neural network can recognize whether the other samples are obtained from materials with defects of without defects.

2.1 Supervised Learning Process

In principle the supervised learning process of the multi-layer neural networks runs method of setting the neurons input's weights to random values, usually in the range from 0.1 to 0.3. As transfer functions the threshold functions are usually applied for the first time learning. Number of iterations is set. This count determines the length learning process. The reference data is then submitted to the neural network's inputs. In these data the correct output values are known.

After that the learning process begins. During this process the input's weights, thresholds and transfer functions of neurons in all layers are set. The first settings usually take place in input layer.

The aim of this part of the learning process is to set the neural network's parameters so that the errors in comparison to required values in output values are minimalised. A certain count of iterations runs through. After that it is necessary to check whether the error's values are in range of tolerance which depends on the chosen type of the neural network or on type of the application.

If there are still too high errors, the learning process runs through again until the required range of tolerance is achieved. It is possible that after running through the all preset iterations the neural network is not learned in a good quality.[4] In such cases it is necessary to take into consideration of reset the values of weights and transfer functions before the learning process begins.

As soon as the neural network is learned in sufficient quality, the process of validation and testing takes place.

The learning set of samples serves for searching the neural network model, the validation set for model validating and testing set for testing usability of model.[8]

For the purposes of diagnostics the three-layer neural network architecture is implemented in Statistica programme. This architecture is based on perceptron learning process, however there are more neuron in this architecture (in comparison to typical perceptron architecture), neurons are spread into three layers.

2.2 Perceptron Learning Algorithm

- Values of the weights are randomized
- If the output is correct, the weights don't change
- If the output value is supposed to be equal to 1, but it's 0, weights of the active inputs are incremented.
- If the output value is supposed to be equal to 0, but it's 2, weights of the active inputs are decremented.

Inputs are active when its value on inputs above threshold has non-zero value. Quantity of weight's values change (when incrementing or decrementing) depends on the chosen option:

- Solid additions are applied when incrementing or decrementing
- Addition's values change depends on error values. It is convenient the increase them when the error is higher and conversely. This speed-up convergence can lead to learning inability.
- Variables and non-variables are combined depending on error.[1]

Although the network is based on perceptron learning system, it acts like a multi-layer network.

2.3 Elementary Properties of Multilayer Neural Networks

Let φ: RM (input) => RN (output) be a continuous mapping, then hidden layers and weights (thresholds) values can be found in such way that φ is realised by this network with arbitrary precision.[3]

If some network (its weights) exists to such arbitrary continuous mapping φ, it is possible to find x to approximate value y ≅ φ(x) by this algorithm:

- to the inputs of neurons in input layer values of all all elements of vector x are submitted. Outputs of neurons in input layer obtain values yi = xi, i = 1,..., m, and are transferred along the lines with weights, which are marked wji to the inputs of all k-neurons of hidden layer (j = 1, ..., k)
- these values are computed by neurons from the hidden layer to its response and proceed them to inputs of the neurons in higher layer
- this activity is continuously spread until
- from the output layer neuron the response vector x of the entire network y is created.

3 Proposed Solution

This chapter is devoted to detailed description of the C# neural network library, which, as aforesaid, is possible to use for design of application that classifies outputs of spectral analysis of material diagnostics.

Library AForge.Neuro.dll is based on Microsoft Visual Studio Solution called AForge, which contains elementary classes, methods, components and other elements that can be used not only for design of neural networks, but even for design genetic algorithms, fuzzy systems, image processing, robotics and many other practical applications. AForge.Neuro.dll namespace contains interface and classes for computing purposes of neural networks. Following description of all classes that are contained in the library helps for better insight of neural network architectures design.

3.1 Classes in AForge.Neuro Library

Neuron class is elementary class of the whole library. Method Neuron has only one input parameter in its argument which is count of neuron's inputs. This class also contains vector of all neuron inputs weights and one output variable. After neuron is created, all its input weight values are set by Randomize method. The range of these randomized values is from 0 to 1. Weight value are during following learning process changed, so that the results and its errors are minimalised.

Layer class is basically similar to Neuron Class and summarizes common functions of all neural layers. In this class particular parameters of the whole layer are determined, that means count of neurons in layer, overall count of layer inputs. Resulting vector of layer outputs is generated by using method Compute.

In standard practice is Network class the most popular class. If some specific kind of neural network architecture ought to be implemented, it is necessary to include this class and extend it with required parameters of given architecture, e.g. Kohonen self-organizing maps that are capable to recognize colors.

Network class contains declaration of overall number of inputs to neural network, number of layer in network and number of neurons in each layer. From this generally designed class inherits classes ActivationNetwork and DistanceNetwork, which can be used for particular design of applications.

3.2 Design of Application

Design of application which substitutes Statistica programme is possible by using ActivationNetwork class.

This class differs from its parent in input parameter of method ActivationNetwork. It is necessary to set type of activation function which, after calculation of the weighted sum of inputs and threshold values of neuron, transfers potential of each neuron and eventually generate output signal.

Description of most common non-linear transfer functions that are used for classification purposes follows.

ActivationNetwork class is generally used for design of multi-layer neural network architectures, which is also this project's case.

DistanceNetwork class differs from ActivationNetwork class in way of calculation of output values.

Output of each neuron is defined as the difference (distance) between values of weights and values of inputs. DistanceNetwork is composed of one layer and is usually used for solving elastic networks or self-organizing maps tasks.

As Network class have Neuron and Layer classes its Activation and Distance variations which also differs in input parameters of its methods. However these classes are rarely used in practical applications. Nevertheless for design of specific kinds of neural network architectures library AForge.Neuro.dll contains these classes.

IActivationFunction interface forms the basis of transfer functions of all neurons. Among method defined in this interface is mathematical definition, then first and second differentiation of defined function.

From this interface come out three activation functions that can be used for programming of neural networks:

- ThresholdFunction
- SigmoidFunction
- BipolarSigmoidFunction

ThresholdFunction class implements this simple mathematical function into neural network architecture. This function acquires zero ouput values in negative domain and value 1 in positive domain. However this function can only be used for the simpliest applications.

3.3 SigmoidFunction Class

SigmoidFunction class which implements non-linear sigmoid with 0 to 1 range is much more common. Presicion of neural network learning depends on its steepness that is defined as $\lambda = \text{tg}\ \alpha$. In this class default setting of λ value is 2. It is possible to change this value if the neural network is not trained in a good quality.

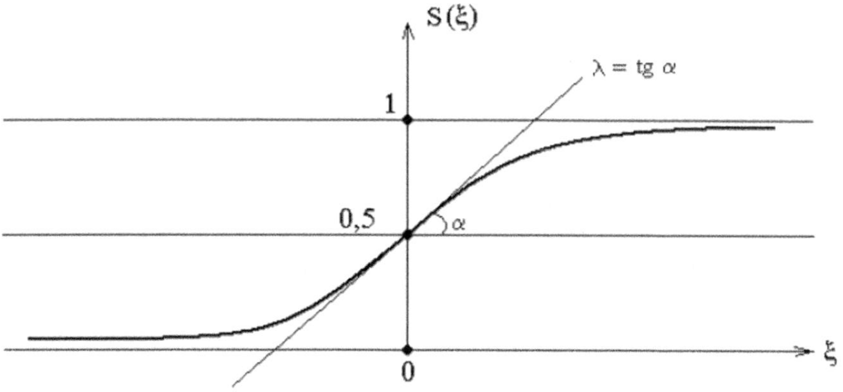

Fig. 3. Sigmoid progression [7]

Bipolar sigmoid differs from common sigmoid only in range of output value which is from -0.5 to 0.5. During neural network training it is recommended to try both non-linear transfer functions and depending on errors in the outputs choose the one that achieves better results.

3.4 Neural Network Learning Algorithms

AForge.Neuro.Learning namespace contains classes and interfaces, in which user defines types of learning algorithms that is used in required application.
There are two basic interfaces in the library:

- ISupervisedLearning (supervised learning algorithms), from which BackPropagationLearning class, DeltaRuleLearning class and PerceptronLearning class inherits.
- IUnsupervisedLearning (unsupervised learning algorithms), from which ElasticNetworkLearning class and SOMLearning class inherits.

During unsupervised learning no required output values are submitted to neural network model. Training process is based on finding similarities among samples that are submitted to network. This kind of learning is often used in applications implementing self-organizing map when colorful samples are sorted by RGB values. However unsupervised learning is not issue of this project.

For classification purposes it is necessary to use supervised learning algorithms. Samples of adjusted data obtained from spectral analysis of material diagnostics (material without defects) is submitted to neural network.

It is possible to use PerceptronLearning class for design and development of application that classifies spectral analysis data.

Principles of supervised learning are described in second chapter of this project. The only input argument of PerceptronLearning method is name of neural network.

Library also provides supervised learning algorithm called Delta Rule, which in one-layer neural networks runs method of determining addition of gradient of error function and following minimalisation of this error. Library then provides Back

Propagation algorithm, which is basically an extension of Delta Rule learning. Back Propagation is nowadays the most popular algorithm used for training of neural networks.

Other information relevant to AForge.Neuro.dll library is provided in well-arranged help in HTML format, which is attached to the library.

4 Implementation of Proposed Solution

Application which is able to classify data obtained from spectral analysis of diagnostics of internal material defects can be programmed in object orientated language C#. Support for this design is AForge.Neuro.dll library which is described in previous chapters. Project is designed in Microsoft Visual Studio 2008. This chapter is devoted to development of source code of entire application.

First of all it is necessary to include beside common libraries also AForge, AForge.Neuro and AForge.Neuro.Learning libraries and also Threading which enables usage of thread in the project.

At the beginning all needed variables are declared, memory array allocated and delegation for thread is created. Memory buffer which may contain previous data is cleaned by Dispose method. All buttons and check boxes are disabled before the input data is loaded.

User loads reference data by using button LOAD. Data is then loaded by File.OpenText(openFileDialog.FileName) method to allocated array, which server as training set for the neural network model.

If data is in wrong format, it has to be parsed (it depends on particular input data – outputs of MATLAB spectral analysis). It is necessary to adjust parse algorithm to specific task to achieve compatibility with submitted input data. All imported data is shown in the table so that used can check whether the import process ran through without any problems. This can be performed by using ShowTrainingData method. In this method date arrays are allocated and filled with imported data. If there is too much data, used can save them to file, so that i will be easier to check import correction. After importing data all buttons and control components are enabled.

User sets required parameters of neural network in GUI before training process starts:

- learning rate – this parameter determines the sensitivity of finding the global minimum of the error function, in other words how precisely will be model of neural network trained. If value of learning rate is too high, it is possible that neural network will not be trained in a sufficient quality because of not finding the global minimum, but only local minimum of error function. If value of learning rate is too low, it can overload computer, so that the model of neural network will not be trained at all. Default setting of learning rate is usually 0.1.
- lambda value – this value influences steepness of transfer function, which determines how vector of neuron's output signal is generated, default setting of lambda value in AForge.Neuro library is 2.
- hidden layer neurons count
- iterations count
- transfer function

User changes these parameters to achieve best results when training the neural network.

SearchSolution method is the heart of the application. Input and output data arrays are declared and initialized. Output array has as many elements as the number of classified classes.

After that it is necessary to create the neural network architecture itself. For classification purposes it is convenient to use ActivationNetwork method, which is described in previous chapter. In the method's argument is chosen transfer function and numbers of neurons in each layer. User can only set number of neurons in hidden layer. ActivationLayer method creates layers of the network (command ActivationLayer layer[i]=network[i], where i is layer of the network).

For supervised learning purpose PerceptronLearning method is used. In its argument there is name of trained neural network. Command teacher.LearningRate = learningRate sets sensitivity of global minimum of error function finding to the teacher.

Statistical data is saved by using StreamWriter method (creates two files: Error function file and Weight set file). Command error = teacher.RunEpoch (input, output) starts learning process of the neural network. Variable Error is saved into array. As soon as it reaches value within range of tolerance, command break terminated training process. Current iteration is shown in textbox, so that user can change network parameter or number of iterations if training process lasts for too long time.

After training process is finished, progression of error function is shown in graph.

After training phase can validation and testing phases be performed. By pressing button SOLVE all submitted input sample runs through the trained network and output values are calculated. Difference between training and testing is in substitution of command teacher.RunEpoch by Compute method. All buttons of output graphs, from which user interprets achieved results, are now enabled. Graphs are shown by using of ZedGraph library afterwards.

5 Testing of Developed Application

Testing of the outputs of the neural networks is generally quite complicated procedure, because it's important to interpret the results correctly. Before the beginning of the learning process it's convenient to remove irrelevant data from the input set. Irrelevant data can be e.g. non-numerical or nominal variables. Nominal variables (two-position – e.g. man and woman or multiple-position) have to be transformed to numerical variables by vectors, for example man=(0,1), woman=(1,0) [4]. When input data is adjusted to designated shape, it's divided into three sets – learning set, validating set and testing set. Default setting of the ratio in Statistica programme is following: 70% of the input data is learning set, 15% validating set and 15% testing set. To achieve better results when modeling the neural network it is possible to reset the percentage ratio.

User sets all required settings of the neural network before the learning process (chapter IV.) When the neural network is learned for the first time, user checks values of the error function (the difference between required values submitted by the teacher and outputs of the network), which determines the quality of the learning process. If the network is learned insufficiently, there are many possibilities of achieving better results:

- change counts of the neurons in hidden layer – this count has a great influence on the learning
- change of the transfer function of the neurons – in case of achieving insufficient results try to change sigmoid to bipolar sigmoid of the simple threshold function (threshold fcn. is used only when simple input data is provided)
- change steepness of the transfer function (lambda value) – steepness influences computed transferred potential (output signal) of each neuron
- change of the iterations count
- change learning rate value – this value determines the size of the step when searching the global minimum of the error function
- another adjustment of the input data – scaling of input data (usually linear scaling). To achieve better results it is recommended to transfer submitted data to a certain range of values that fits better to the not learned network.

If these structural changes of the neural network don't help to achieve better outputs, it is recommended to think about using another neural network architecture or changing the learning method. It is impossible to get no errors of the output in the practical applications.

Statistica programme uses for the classification tasks three layer perceptron architecture, nevertheless it is necessary to take into account that Statsoft company who develops this software for many years has its own Know-How, that can definitely help to improve the quality of the learning process as far as empirical changes of the network structural parameters are concerned, as so as the learning algorithms and adjustment of the output data.

As soon as the error function of learned neural network achieves range of tolerance, validation phases starts. Validation phase validates the quality of learning. Validating set of data is submitted to the neural network and processed by the network without the learning again. After output set of data is computed, it is compared whether the error function achieves tolerated values.

When the neural network is ready, it is possible to submit data obtained during industrial process and interpret outputs of the classification afterwards.

In case of diagnostics of the material defects the network classifies whether the material has a defect or not. If there is a defect, it classifies which kind of defect it is.

When designing the neural network, it's necessary to keep in mind, that neuron count of the output layer determines the number of classes in which the input data will be classified.

6 Conclusions

In this project we provided support for the design and realisation of application developed in object orientated programming language C#, which will classify data obtained on basis of the material defects diagnostics.

The application implements three layer perceptron architecture that was so far used pro classification purposes in commercial programme Statistica. After realization of this application it will be possible to substitute Statistica programme. Support for programming of the application is C# neural network library called AForge.Neuro.dll, which was introduced on codeproject.com server by programmer Andrew Kirillov in 2006.

Author of this library reserves rights to its usage and it is forbidden to use it for the commercial purposes without his agreement.

When compiling the theoretical part of this work, we used particularly expert materials focused on neural networks and we understood the basic principles of their design.

As far as my opinion is concerned, we think that the future of neural network is very perspective, because very complicated and complex tasks can be solving by these algorithms.

Acknowledgement. This work was supported in part by (1) „Centre for Applied Cybernetics", Ministry of Education of the Czech Republic under project 1M0567, (2) „SMEW – Smart Environments at Workplaces", Grant Agency of the Czech Republic, GACR P403/10/1310, (3) „SCADA system for control and monitoring of processes in Real Time", Technology Agency of the Czech Republic, TACR, TA01010632 and (4) "User Adaptive Systems", VSB - Technical University of Ostrava under project SP/2011/22. We also acknowledge support from student Jakub Hlavica.

References

1. Jirsik, V., Horacek, P.: Neural networks, expert systems and speech recognition. Study Support FEKT VUT, 7–46
2. Krejcar, O., Frischer, R.: Detection of the Internal Defects of Material on the Basis of the Performance Spectral Density Analysis, pp. 3–11
3. Krejcar, O.: Problem Solving of Low Data Throughput on Mobile Devices by Artefacts Prebuffering. EURASIP Journal on Wireless Communications and Networking, Article ID 802523, 8 pages (2009), doi:10.1155/2009/802523
4. Neural Networks in Statistica program (2010), `http://www.statsoft.com/textbook/neural-networks/` (Quoted November 3, 2010)
5. Neural Networks on C# - The Code Project (November 19 , 2006), `http://www.codeproject.com/KB/recipes/aforge_neuro.aspx` (Quoted October 25, 2010)
6. Krejcar, O., Janckulik, D., Motalova, L.: Complex Biomedical System with Biotelemetric Monitoring of Life Functions. In: Proceedings of the IEEE Eurocon 2009, St. Petersburg, Russia, May 18-23, pp. 138–141 (2009), doi:10.1109/EURCON.2009.5167618
7. Mikulecky, P.: Remarks on Ubiquitous Intelligent Supportive Spaces. In: 15th American Conference on Applied Mathematics/International Conference on Computational and Information Science, pp. 523–528. Univ. Houston, Houston (2009)
8. Krejcar, O., Frischer, R.: Non Destructive Defects Detection by Performance Spectral Density Analysis. Journal Sensors, MDPI Basel 11(3), 2334–2346 (2011)
9. Brida, P., Machaj, J., Duha, J.: A Novel Optimizing Algorithm for DV based Positioning Methods in ad hoc Networks. Elektronika Ir Elektrotechnika (Electronics and Electrical Engineering) 1(97), 33–38 (2010) ISSN 1392-1215
10. Augustynek, M., Penhaker, M., Korpas, D.: Controlling Peacemakers by Accelerometers. In: 2010 The 2nd International Conference on Telecom Technology and Applications, ICTTA 2010, Bali Island, Indonesia, March 19-21, vol. 2, pp. 161–163. IEEE Conference Publishing Services, NJ (2010), doi:10.1109/ICCEA.2010.288, ISBN 978-0-7695-3982-9

11. Pindor, J., Penhaker, M., Augustynek, M., Korpas, D.: Detection of ECG Significant Waves for Biventricular Pacing Treatment. In: 2010 The 2nd International Conference on Telecom Technology and Applications, ICTTA 2010, Bali Island, Indonesia, March 19-21, vol. 2, pp. 164–167. IEEE Conference Publishing Services, NJ (2010), doi:10.1109/ICCEA.2010.186, ISBN 978-0-7695-3982-9
12. Tucnik, P.: Optimization of Automated Trading System's Interaction with Market Environment. In: 9th International Conference on Business Informatics Research. Lecture Notes in Business Information Processing, vol. 64, pp. 55–61. Univ. Rostock, Rostock (2010)
13. Labza, Z., Penhaker, M., Augustynek, M., Korpas, D.: Verification of Set Up Dual-Chamber Pacemaker Electrical Parameters. In: 2010 The 2nd International Conference on Telecom Technology and Applications, ICTTA 2010, Bali Island, Indonesia, March 19-21, vol. 2, pp. 168–172. IEEE Conference Publishing Services, NJ (2010), doi:10.1109/ICCEA.2010.187, ISBN 978-0-7695-3982-9

Preliminary Analysis of 4G-LTE Mobile Network Sharing for Improving Resiliency and Operator Differentiation

Venmani Daniel Philip[1], Yvon Gourhant[1], and Djamal Zeghlache[2]

[1] Orange Labs, France Telecom R&D, Lannion, France
[2] TELECOM & Management SudParis, Evry, France
{danielphilip.venmani,yvon.gourhant}@orange-ftgroup.com,
djamal.zeghlache@it-sudparis.eu

Abstract. An aim of our ongoing research is to take pragmatic approach to the "last mile" issue and provide a solution to improve resiliency and look at traffic prioritization primarily for 4G-LTE mobile networks. Hence, this paper proposes a solution to the same considering two schemes. The first solution is based on exploring OpenFlow as an architecture for e-Node B virtualization where resource sharing takes place in the access network part and the second solution is based on infrastructure sharing considering sharing the backhaul network infrastructure to improve resiliency among the operators. The paper discusses about the resiliency mechanisms that are adapted in the backhaul network of the operators and henceforth concludes that despite the resiliency mechanisms, there are occasions when the network resources are not available for the end users which necessitates the need for sharing another operator's backhaul, thus decreasing the overall unavailability time.

Keywords: Backhaul Networks, e-Node B Virtualization, Infrastructure Sharing, 4G-LTE, Resiliency mechanisms.

1 Introduction

Mobile Network operators have been adapting to a classical approach such as to have an exclusive use of the wireless network resources such as spectrum, sites, transmission lines, backhaul network infrastructure, core networks, etc [1]. However, cell site sharing which was mostly due to the lack of site locations and environmental aspects has been widely adopted as form of passive sharing especially in rural areas. Recent developments show further expansion towards the concept of 'resource sharing' i.e. wider network infrastructure sharing and, as expected, spectrum sharing. Active sharing (e.g., Radio Access Network (RAN) sharing but not limited to this) has been already set up by operators in different ways (mostly in Europe due to the ease of political and regulatory issues) which includes 3G RAN sharing between T-Mobile & Hutchison 3 UK, Vodafone & Hutchison 3 Sweden, Orange & Vodafone Spain. It is considered seriously for the 3G deployments even in urban areas such as the small towns in Spain with a population range of 1000 and 25000 people, since it achieves, in addition to the passive sharing, roughly 43% saving in Capital Expenditure (CAPEX) and 49% in

J.J. Yonazi et al. (Eds.): ICeND 2011, CCIS 171, pp. 73–93, 2011.

Operating Expenditure (OPEX) [2]. Besides, infrastructure sharing has a good impact on energy consumption which is primordial in emerging countries. Africa as a whole is characterized by a very low penetration rate of fixed networks (e.g. 0.7% in Senegal, 3% in Cameroon). By contrast, a significant and rising part of the population owns a mobile phone: 25% on average [3]. Both the rurality of the population and its insolvency acts as a brake upon prospective deployment of fixed infrastructures taking into account the huge investments necessary to install wired solutions. While satellite-based access solutions (VSAT) are too expensive to be deployed widely, a growing set of alternative technologies have emerged that raise hope for ambitious broadband access roll-outs through contained capital expenditure.

Now within this context, focusing towards emerging countries where operators are newly deploying their mobile network infrastructure, enhancing reach through the creation of infrastructure is the need of the hour. To maintain increased growth levels, the service providers need to push out to rural and remote areas. However, the capital costs for this are very formidable and are simply not addressable through the revenues currently generated. The ever falling tariffs and the resultant decline in Average Revenue Per User (ARPU) has become a serious area of concern for service providers in emerging countries. Declining ARPU leaves the service provider with lesser amount of re-investible funds for expansion of service, which otherwise could have been far more widespread by now. Hence, it is becoming an accepted practice for operators to share site locations and masts. There are also examples of sharing complete network operations. However, with a high degree of shared resources using today's technologies, the stimulation for competition is gradually reducing.

In emerging countries such as the sub-Saharan African countries like Kenya, Uganda, Nigeria as well as the Eastern European countries, where the backhaul network connectivity is mostly based on microwave, it is undesirable for each cellular operator even if they were able to afford it, to replicate expensive telecom infrastructure to reach the subscribers in remote rural areas. Hence, they go for access network sharing where the same e-Node B is shared between operators. From the existing network sharing policies, it is possible that a User Equipment (UE) may switch from operator A e-Node B to operator B e-Node B in case of failure in network A. But we do not consider to retain this option as a preference of choice inorder to provide network differentiation that will highly be based on limited radio access frequencies when access network sharing is just a temporary solution for launching 3G or 4G-LTE more rapidly. This can have an impact on the inability of the operators to differentiate themselves over a long duration of time, where every operator becomes unique in terms of QoS. This solution will not be valid when all operators will have enough clients to fill their resource. Hence, from a research perspective, we emphasize the way to evolve infrastructure sharing where the policies could enable "Service Differentiation", ex. service priorities, dynamic sharing policies between operators. This is proposed as our first solution which could be carried out by virtualization of e-Node Bs of operators. This would apply to remote areas, where more dynamicity and differentiation in access network sharing could be incorporated by OpenFlow [48], [50], [51] mechanisms, especially when the Telecom regulator imposes it. Our second solution is based on backhaul network infrastructure sharing between operators. This allows mobile network operators to leverage on existing infrastructure to provide affordable and reliable services to urban as well as rural and remote consumers, especially to support the increasing data traffic due to broadband services. Infrastructure sharing is nevertheless equally important in the urban areas where the presence of 2 or 3 operators and a rapidly increasing mobile subscriber base for data and broadband services, is resulting in more and more investments for infrastructures being put up by each operator to cater to higher traffic requirements. This ultimately leads to the need for additional backhaul links. Traditionally backhaul networks have been acquainted with Ethernet cables, fiber, copper wires, microwave and other means of limited and expensive cabled infrastructures - each with its own advantages and disadvantages. Apart from sharing the equipments to reduce cost between operators and increasing coverage for customers, infrastructure sharing can be exploited to the next level of using it for resiliency purpose in which the backhaul network of the operators are shared. Our current proposed solution takes into account infrastructure sharing between microwave backhaul connectivity only taking into account the huge investments necessary to install wired solutions in emerging countries. The concept of backhaul network infrastructure sharing among the operators during peak traffic conditions or network failure situations is provided as an alternative for resiliency mechanisms. Current resiliency mechanisms are based on over-dimensioning and re-routing mechanisms that are mainly deployed on core networks but they cost too much for being largely deployed till the last-mile backhaul network compared to the probability of outage. Our solution paves a way for seamless connectivity even till the last mile without additional links. In order to provide a low cost alternative, the basic consideration for our solution requires prerequisites that do not exist today in LTE e-Node B implementations. Typically e-Node B should have atleast minimal IP support, which gives the ability to route the traffic via another operator backhaul network. With our solution, e-Node Bs are expected to behave as Provider Edge routers with minimal IP capabilities or a routing node, with full IP capabilities. In addition to having the basic IP capabilities, the operators also must agree upon the resource allocation in the Service Level Agreements (SLAs) clearly. Hence, in this paper, the state of the art dealing with the problem characterization associated with the set backs of the existing routing protocols and the use of resiliency mechanisms already adapted by the operators in order to backup their networks is clearly detailed.

The rest of the paper is structured as follows. Section II describes the state of the art covering business model, regulation and standardization issues in network sharing and gives a brief overview of the various virtualization projects carried out and its stand in today's communication world. It can be noted that the existing state of the art for network sharing deals mostly with the access network sharing. Section III details about the existing resiliency mechanisms, the limitations of them and will go deeper in the backhaul network problem characterization by looking at topology issues. This is followed by the last section where we will present two schemes, one that deals with virtualization of e-Node Bs for access networks sharing in rural and remote areas and the other scenarios that illustrate backhaul network infrastructure sharing as a way for achieving resiliency which concludes the paper.

2 State of the Art

2.1 Business Models

The mobile backhaul network infrastructure is the critical link between the broadband subscribers and the core network. Mobile backhaul networks connect the remote base stations towards to the mobile operator's core networks and provide access to customers. Mobile operators increasingly are focused on mobile backhaul network transport. Sharing the infrastructure as such can lead to obvious benefits and is in fact already done to some degree [4]. It is useful to distinguish capacity driven network deployment from coverage driven network deployment when determining success criteria or targets for cost and energy reduction [1]. These factors have a much higher impact especially in emerging countries. The capacity driven scenario is characterized by a high traffic density, a dense network, and usage of all available spectrums due to the huge impact of the increase in the broadband traffic. In this scenario, the conventional manner to further increase capacity is to add sites. With sites increasing, backhaul network links capacity also has to be increased to support the traffic density.

2.2 Fundamental Limits and Regulatory Framework

Promoting network sharing is a useful tool for regulators and policy makers to encourage mobile network deployment and coverage improvement in the un-served less populated areas. There are several instruments that can be used to promote network sharing. National roaming arrangements are probably the most simple and effective arrangement. While national roaming leads to a certain level of uniformity between operators, it is important to analyze to what extent this uniformity leads to a significant restriction of competition. National authorities that have anti-competitive concerns may allow network sharing for a limited period (e.g. for a period of five years) of time in order to promote roll out in an initial phase of network deployment. From high level perspectives, the regulation policies regarding the infrastructure sharing are basically the same in the world. Basically, the passive infrastructure sharing is allowed and highly encouraged. As with regard of the active sharing, it is also authorized in particular the e-Node B, the antennas and the transmission system. However, depending on the country, some limitations have to be considered regarding the level of sharing in particular for the spectrum, the RNC. This limitation is explained by the fact that sharing of active mobile equipment may raise concerns about restricting competition between the sharing operators. Sharing active network infrastructure usually leads to mobile operators offering similar network coverage, quality and transmission speeds. Henceforth, it requires strong co-ordination between operators.

A fundamental objective of resource sharing is to find a stable operating point based on certain fairness and efficiency criteria [5]. Many well-known concepts, like proportional fairness [6] and bargaining theory [7], were derived in a context other than wireless communication. The used utility models do not typically explicitly model resource or infrastructure sharing [8]. The concept of collaborative networks is gaining momentum and it is also closely related to the idea of infrastructure sharing [9]. From the past researches, infrastructure sharing solutions have proven to be a critical lever contributing to the growth of the telecommunication sector and are very promising in emerging countries where the market is growing fast. In this context, there are a wide variety of technological approaches that appear from today's perspective, considering current technologies have already reached its maturity state and there have been a number of best practices that have been identified in order to promote passive and active mobile infrastructure sharing [10].

2.3 Existing Standardizations and Literatures for Network Sharing

As per [11], there are two architectures for network sharing that have been standardized. Hence, according to it, a network sharing architecture shall allow different core network operators to connect to a shared radio access network. The operators not only share the radio network elements, but may also share the radio resources themselves. As a result of this, the Multi-Operator Core Network (MOCN) configuration, in which multiple Core Networks (CN) nodes, operated by different operators, connected to the RAN is only shared, in other words the e-Node B is only shared by the operators. Another sharing configuration called the Gateway Core Network (GWCN) in which Mobility Management Entity (MME) is shared in addition to the RAN. Less equipments (e-Node B and MME) are shared in LTE when compared to the former 3G-UMTS (Node B, Radio Network Controller (RNC), Mobile Switching Centre (MSC), Serving GPRS Support Node (SGSN)) in this case. In addition to the above two described network sharing scenarios of [11], there are also few other scenarios that are proposed in [12]. They are Multiple Core Networks Sharing common radio access network as per the 3GPP Release 99 architectural standards, Geographically Split Networks Sharing, Common Network Sharing, Common Spectrum Network sharing, Multiple Radio Access Networks sharing common core network. Again in [11], exclusive details of Network sharing for UMTS Terrestrial Radio Access Network (UMTS) and E-UTRAN are covered. According to [13], E-UTRAN shall support for multi relationship E-UTRAN nodes and Evolved Packet Core (EPC) nodes by the establishment of S1-flex. However, the above mentioned network sharing standardizations deal only with RAN sharing. It also gives very little insight on core network sharing but does not give any specification for backhaul network infrastructure sharing while it is always possible for the operators to share the backhaul in some models (e.g. Geographical Split model) with and without access network sharing. The preliminary pre-requisite for backhaul network sharing is the ability of the e-Node B to route the traffic via another operator backhaul network, thus sharing of backhaul network infrastructure. It is a non-negotiable concern that until now, there are only limited research results that show the way for dynamically routing resources between operators when they share their network. i.e. when two operators share their network including sharing their backhaul network infrastructure and when either one of the operator's link fail, there is no mechanism that defines how the traffic density has to be re-routed via the other operators available link based on transmission metrics, yet with meaningful energy savings.

Our scenarios for backhaul network sharing essentially require that the e-Node B is capable of detecting fault in a link on its own network and automatically routing the traffic towards another operator backhaul network with whom the sharing agreement is signed. To do this, the need to consider several routing protocols for the backhaul of LTE-EPC architecture arose. Therefore, it becomes self-explanatory that the choice of protocol here is either a connection–oriented or connection-less protocol.

Cooperative wireless access networks [14] employing connection-less packet forwarding techniques is a burgeoning field of research. As opposed to the approach in which each terminal autonomously transmits to the access point or base station, cooperative communications assume that multiple terminals or relays collaborate to improve the overall effectiveness of the network. Cooperative access networks, when combined with appropriate coding techniques [15], can be used improve the robustness of communications thanks to the increased diversity [16], [17]. The cooperation can take different forms. It can bee among peers, such as in [18], [19], or using fixed dedicated relays [20], [21]. In both cases, it is necessary that the two devices willing to cooperate are in each other's transmission range. If the nodes, relays and base stations belong to several different access networks (operated by different providers), the opportunities for collaboration are greatly diminished.

Nevertheless, mobile operators are reluctant to base their mobile backhaul network on connection-less packet networks. The concern is that connection-less networks will not be capable of providing the levels of quality and reliability necessary to support voice services. Connection-less packet networks also demand new operational procedures and re-training of staff. Hence the dilemma facing mobile operators: the demands of future services are best met using a packet-based network, but connection-less packet networks could affect existing revenue-generating voice services. However with the introduction of connection-oriented packet networks, there is a possibility of solving this dilemma. In this paper, we present a migration plan using connection-oriented packet transport IP/MPLS [22] solution, which provides a path to a fully packet based network with the levels of quality and reliability that can support both existing and future services. However, it has to be noted that the routing protocol that is decided to be adapted on the backhaul network infrastructure has to be compatible with the rest of the operators who agreed to share the infrastructure, since we are dealing with protocols that has to handle network sharing scenarios, i.e. both the operators must agree upon the same protocol (IP/MPLS) to be used on their backhaul network.

2.4 Wireless Network Virtualization

The concept of virtualization itself is not completely new; it is a well known technique that has existed for years, especially in the computer world like the use of virtual memory and virtual operating systems. Network virtualization will allow operators to share the same physical infrastructure and have networks coexisting in a flexible, dynamic manner utilizing the available resources more efficiently. This implies that the physical infrastructure needs to be virtualized into a number of virtual resources being offered to the different virtual networks. While virtualization for servers, routers and wire line links has been extensively studied in the literature [23-28], the wireless part has not yet received major consideration within today's research. The new idea is to use virtualization to create complete virtual networks. This involves applying the current operating system virtualization experience for network components, leading to virtual network resources like virtual routers, virtual links, and virtual base stations. A number of research initiatives and projects all over the globe have started focusing on Network Virtualization, e.g. GENI [29] [30], PLANETLAB [31],

VINI [32], CABO [33], Cabernet [34] in the United States; 4WARD [35] [36] in Europe, AKARI [37], AsiaFI [38] in Asia and many others. This shows that the current direction in designing the Future Internet is going in favor of having multiple coexisting architectures, instead of only one, where each architecture is designed and customized to fit and satisfy a specific type of network requirements rather than trying to come up with one global architecture that fits all. That is why Network Virtualization will play a vital role as it helps diversifying the Future Internet into separate Virtual Networks (VNets) that are isolated and can run different architectures within. Taking these into account, we emphasize our idea to virtualize the e-Node Bs and to provide to each operator a virtual machine on the routers in the backhaul network, which paves the way for operator differentiation and resource sharing.

3 Problem Characterization

3.1 Resiliency Mechanisms

Networks can be impacted by failures, which cause network downtime and thus decrease the availability (or increase the unavailability, usually measured in number of minutes per year during which the network is not fully available). Therefore, the reliability of each network functional block (e.g. a link, a node, a linecard within a node, Small Form-factor Pluggable (SFP) module on a linecard, etc.) is characterized by a parameter called Mean Time Between Failures (MTBF). MTBF values for network equipment are usually provided by equipment vendors. MTBF for links can be assessed based on statistical data (e.g. the chance of a microwave link failure calculated by taking into account all microwave failures that affected a certain network in a certain period of time). When a failure occurs and the network becomes unavailable, a repair action is required to bring the network back to a fully functional state. The repair process takes some time, during which the network remains unavailable. Depending on the type of the failed functional block, repair times may vary (e.g. a fiber cut is much more difficult to repair than a failed linecard). Therefore, each type of failure can be assigned with a Mean Time To Repair (MTTR) value, based e.g. on statistics gathered during the actual network operation. Availability of a network segment or a whole network can be evaluated using different models, which usually take into account MTBF and MTTR of each functional block in the network. As described above, the MTTR is the average time necessary to restore a signal, to repair a cable, to change a card, to reboot a system. The table below points out some standard MTTR based on French Networks.

Table 1. List of MTTR for hardware and infrastructure

Elements	MTTR (in hours)
Optical fibre/ Copper Cable	14
ODF/CDF	2
DU/Node B	6
Hardware/ IDU	4

They are dependent of the maintenance logistics applied to the local network context conditions (geography, location of the spares) and can vary in function of the local network context specificities, consequently. Moreover, MTTR for urban and rural area can be also dissociated. As a matter of fact, every operator establishes their own set of different resiliency mechanism at every relevant layer (namely datalink, transport, logical IP) of the network to protect the network from failures. However, all of these prove that the existing resiliency mechanisms adapted by operators still prove to have their own downtimes and hence this led to the primary consideration to propose to share the backhaul network infrastructure with other operators under network failure conditions. The availability of the network can be increased by sharing or using the backhaul network infrastructure of the other operator with whom the sharing policy is concluded. Such mechanisms allow for quick network failover.

3.2 Backhaul Network Topologies

With the consideration of backhaul network infrastructure sharing among operators, it is equally important to select the right topology for wireless backhaul networks to support the additional backhaul capacity requirements due to sharing another operator traffic with minimum infrastructure investments. This means that despite the current existing topology of the backhaul of mobile network operators, the resulting topology that arises when backhaul network infrastructure is shared between operators should result in minimum number of links than the number of links usually required for resiliency.

There are many parameters to be considered when selecting a network topology, and even more when it comes to radio networks, where Line-Of-Sight (LOS), rain zone and other propagation factors are taken into account, as well as infrastructural considerations such as antenna sites and towers. The common topology choices for radio networks are trees or rings, or a combination of both. The tree topology in itself is a combination of two other basic topologies – the chain and the star, as shown below in fig. 1.

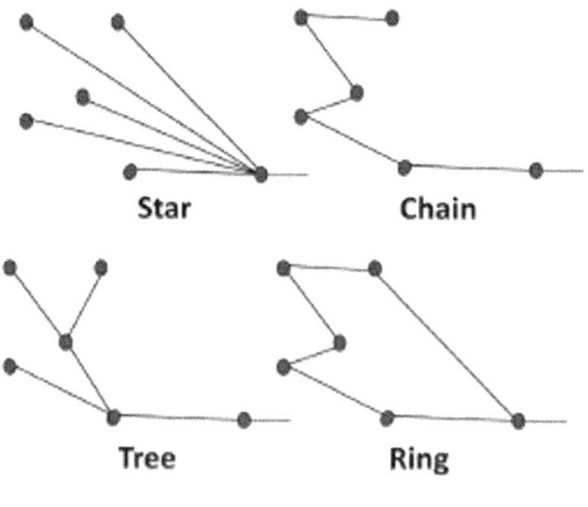

Fig. 1. Common Backhaul Network Topologies

Star topologies use a separate link from a hub to each site. This is very simple, but inefficient for microwave systems, as it requires longer radio links and a Line Of Sight (LOS) for each link (which may be impossible). The star topology also makes for very poor frequency reuse, since all the links originate at the same point, and interference is more likely to occur between links using the same frequency. In chain topologies, all sites reside on a single path, solving the problems inherent to star topologies, but resulting in a very sensitive topology in which the first link malfunction can cause a complete network failure. Therefore, most of the links should be protected. Combining the chain and the star yields a tree topology, in which fewer links can cause major network failures, and only those links require protection schemes. Alternatively connecting the chain yields the ring topology, which is considered to be the most efficient topology in terms of protection with least number of links, hence resiliency and therefore availability as well are better than the rest of the topologies.

3.3 Topology Modeling

To choose the best topology from the existing microwave topologies, we considered two systems models - one with a tree topology and the other with star topology depicted as below in fig. 2. These system models do not represent any live topology models but our own assumption based on internal studies on existing models within Orange Labs.

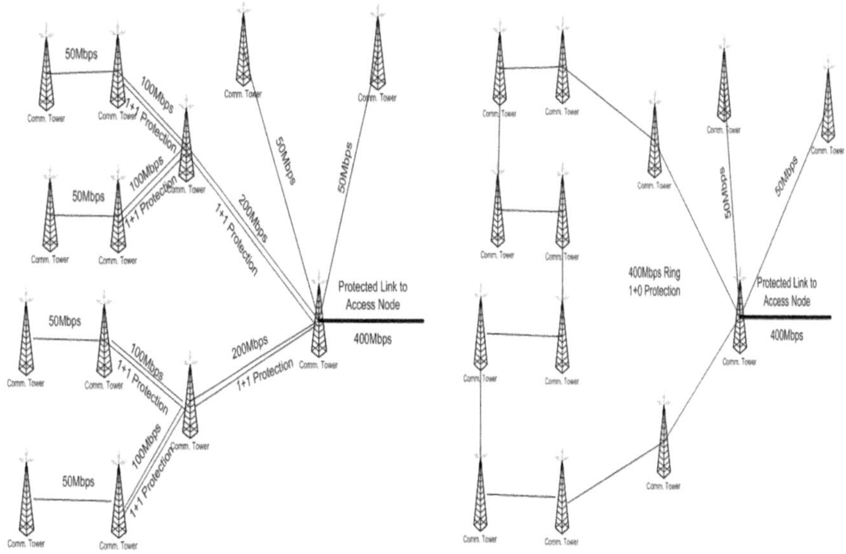

Fig. 2. Chain and Ring based Backhaul Network Topologies

Table 2. Physical inventory for topology modeling

	Tree Topology	**Ring Topology**
Number of Terminal Pairs	18	13
Number of antenna	24	26
Maximum number of hops during failure	3	10

The tree topology takes into account a typical radio cluster with one fiber site and 10 cell sites requiring 50Mbps each and aggregated to a total of 400Mbps all connected in a chain fashion and two separate cell sites each requiring 50Mbps connected to the main hub. The tree uses protected links wherever a link failure affects more than a single site. Hence, it assumes that every link that supports more than one site has a double link, i.e. 1+1 protection, thus counted as 2 links. This is not the case of ring topology. The ring topology requires fewer microwave links. On the other hand, rings require higher-capacity links, i.e. the entire ring is a 400Mbps ring with no additional link protection needed. The table below gives a brief description about the physical inventory for the topology modeling for our system.

From the table, it can be concluded that the cost comparison is not straight forward and can vary depending on the particular case. Another factor influencing cost is spectrum reuse. Since rings have no more than two links at every node, better frequency reuse is usually achieved and rings are often implemented using only a single pair of frequency channels. A clear cut advantage of ring topology is its superior resiliency. The protected tree is indeed protected against equipment failures, but does not provide any path redundancy. Thus it is more vulnerable to heavy fade conditions, as well as to complete site failure (due to an electricity outage, or weather-related disturbances). The ring also provides superior availability, due to the ring's inherent path diversity. In a ring topology, service failures occur only when both paths fail. Thus, in order to achieve the same end-to-end target availability within a tree and a ring, the ring links can be designed for lower availability than the tree links. Operators can therefore reduce expenses by deploying smaller antennas, and by reducing power at the ring link sites.

Therefore, from the table above and from the above discussions, it is convincing to come to a conclusion that the ring topology is the best suitable topology for obtaining maximum efficiency in terms of cost and protection. Hence we conclude that the resulting topology arising out of backhaul network infrastructure sharing between two operators has to result in a ring topology that will result in minimum CAPEX, thus providing superior availability and resiliency. This is illustrated more detailed in the section below with the proposed scenarios.

4 Proposed Solution

There are a wide variety of options that might have to be considered when accessing the viability of infrastructure sharing. Mobile network sharing is a very complex process that involves the complete commitment from parties participating in the sharing scenario based on certain rules before getting started. Hence, under most situations, the agreements and sharing policies are based on the possession of controlling influence of the respective parties. For example, this can be a 50-50 or 75-25 or 80-20 percentage based sharing policy for two operators who are beginning the operations completely from scratch and have decided to join hands to deploy their network under a shared basis.

Our solution is based upon two schemes. The first scheme is based on e-Node B virtualization, where virtual machines are built upon e-Node B and the resources of physical e-Node B owned by another operator is controlled remotely by the sharing operator. This can be realized by the implementation of OpenFlow protocol. The second scheme consists of two possible scenarios (but not limited to) with backhaul network infrastructure sharing which could pave the way for network availability under network failure conditions as well as solve bandwidth aggregation problems under peak traffic conditions within the context of 3GPP-LTE/EPC. Also, detailed here, is the service level agreement that operators who share their network/backhaul have to agree upon for the best benefit of each one of them. From our previous conclusions, the choice of the routing protocol for the backhaul network infrastructure is decided to be IP/ MPLS. Hence, every e-Node B and every router within the backhaul architecture has to be implemented with IP/MPLS capability, thus capable of detecting the failure of delivery of packets by Time to Leave (TTL) value defined in the MPLS packet format and thereby forwarding the packets to the adjacent e-Node B of another operator. Here, the e-Node B does not choose to forward the packet to another neighboring e-Node B of its own operator. This is to minimize and avoid the peer-to-peer links between e-Node Bs of the same operator and thus reducing the number of additional links for resiliency. Thus, the operators who agree to share the network infrastructure must also agree upon deploying the same routing protocol, i.e. IP/MPLS in their networks. However, the discovery of e-Node B belonging to another operator, with whom the sharing agreement is signed, should result in the formation of ring topology, since the ring having the maximum advantages over all other topologies described in the previous section. Also, it has to be taken care that the resulting topology that is arising out of establishment of links for backhaul network infrastructure sharing between operators should not result in more number of links than the number of links that were required for setting up resiliency. In order to do this, the network topology design of the operators' backhaul network has to be transparent to every operator.

Scheme 1: OpenFlow as an architecture for e-Node B virtualization.

This solution deals primarily with the access network sharing where the resources of e-Node Bs are shared and controlled by operators who have concluded on a sharing agreement. Although, access network sharing has already been standardized in 3GPP [52], there are no solutions proposed to control the resources of e-Node B by another operator other than the one who owns it physically. The idea is to have a dedicated OpenFlow network which implements flowvisor based virtualization [39]. Flowvisor based virtualization gives the possibility to slice or virtualize bandwidth, traffic, topology of any given network to give each slice its own fraction on a link to the sharing operator. This requires a basic primitive to divide link bandwidth or to associate a specific set of traffic to one or more virtual networks so that one set of traffic can be cleanly isolated from another. There are well-known ways to do this, and the hardware abstraction can provide some choice as to how it is implemented [40-44]. This is done by deploying OpenFlow protocol within the network architecture. VLANs [45] are widely used for segmentation and isolation in networks today. VLANs virtualize standard Ethernet L2 broadcast domains by decoupling the virtual links from the physical ports. This allows multiple virtual links to be multiplexed over a single virtual port, and it allows a single switch to be segmented into multiple, L2 broadcast networks. However, VLANs differ from FlowVisor in that rather than virtualizing the network control layer generally, they virtualize a specific forwarding algorithm (L2 learning). FlowVisor, on the other hand, not only supports a much more flexible method of defining networks over flow space, it provides a model for virtualizing any forwarding logic which conforms to the basic flow model. With OpenFlow, it is possible to run virtual machines on e-Node Bs. Then, OpenFlow controllers on each mobile operator network equipments are configured. Each controller implements per-operator custom forwarding logic. Then per-operator topology restricted to subset of real topology, traffic queuing requirements are configured and thus all packets to/from a set of addresses belonging to a certain operator or all traffic belonging to a group of users (e.g. Platinum, Gold, Silver customers) or quite specific kind of traffic can be controlled and managed. Thus, operators will be able to control and monitor the resources of a physical e-Node B without really having to take control over it. This would enable service differentiation within the access network in far remote areas where the Telecom regulator imposes access network sharing.

Scheme 2: Backhaul network Infrastructure Sharing.

Scenario A: Static Bandwidth Allocation for each operator in the backhaul network.

Infrastructure sharing in the backhaul network should enable the operators to be able to share the network resources that are available for the backhaul networks without having to invest any further. Now, according to this scheme, each operator has to be able to allocate sufficient amount of its own resource for the other operator who is sharing the infrastructure for the purpose of load sharing and to tackle network failure situations. Considering this scenario, each operator can agree to reserve a certain amount of its own resource for the other operator who is sharing the backhaul network. This has to be defined in the service level agreement. Each operator chooses to allocate a certain percentage of their network bandwidth to the other. This allocation is fixed and the sharing operator is allowed to use this part of the resource anytime and irrespective of any traffic priority, i.e. voice, video etc. and the charging policy are based on a fixed basis irrespective of how much resource is used.

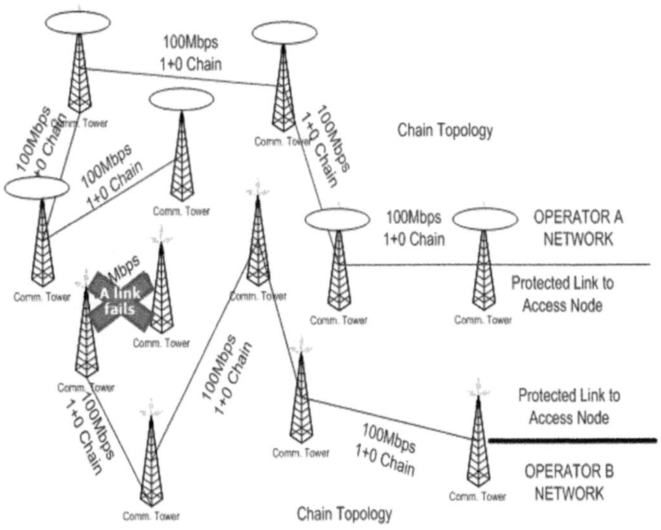

Fig. 3. Link Failure in Operator B last mile backhaul network which is a chain topology by default

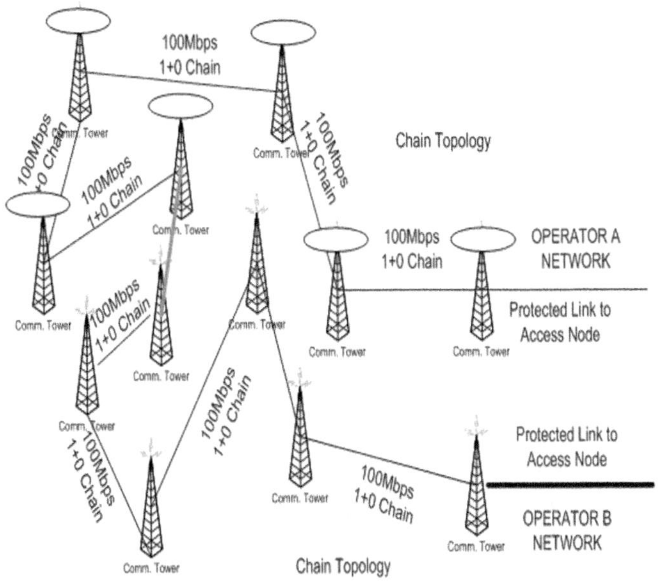

Fig. 4. Backhaul Network sharing between operators resulting in a ring topology (Thanks to e-Node B's forwarding capability)

Let us consider two Greenfield mobile network operators, (since it is within the context focusing towards emerging countries) an operator A, who has provisioned its backhaul network, i.e. from e-Node B to Cell Site Gateway (CSG) and from Cell Site Gateway (CSG) to Mobile Aggregation Site Gateway (MASG) by microwave connectivity with a bandwidth of 100Mbps. Similarly, another operator B has also provisioned the backhaul network with a bandwidth of 100Mbps. Now, let us consider that both operators agree to share the backhaul network on a 80-20 basis. As per our solution, they agree to reserve 20% of their own available bandwidth resource to each other. This means that each operator would occupy 80Mbps bandwidth for its own customers and its own purpose and 20Mbps is allocated for the other operator with whom the backhaul network is shared, i.e. the provisioning for the mobile backhaul is done in a way that only 80Mbps is reserved for the own purpose and the remaining 20Mbps is reserved for the sharing operator. This way, the operator B could use the reserved 20Mbps bandwidth of operator A at times when there is a failure encountered in its backhaul or at times when the traffic load is peak in its network. At such times, it would be better for the operator B to prioritize the traffic flowing through the backhaul of operator A. The same holds good for operator A too. This is depicted in the figure below. Inorder to pictorially differentiate between operators, the communication towers with a circle on top refers to the operator A and the communication towers without a circle refers to operator B. Fig. 4 represents a scenario when the last-mile link in operator A fails.

Our conclusion for the implementation of the above proposed scenario is based upon IP/MPLS. As per the LTE network architecture specification [46], the e-Node B establishes S1 and X2 interfaces. The S1 interface terminates on the anchor point Gateway (aGW). The X2 interface runs between e-Node Bs and is used for neighbor discovery, handovers and cell optimization. Each e-Node B needs to be able to communicate with its direct neighbors. Based on LTE ongoing standardization and implementation, the S1 and X2 interfaces will be based on IP over Ethernet [47]. Taking advantage of this IP capability, we establish the two fundamental connections in the mobile backhaul network. One is the point-to-point connection between the transport equipment connecting the cell sites and the transport equipment connecting the central sites for transporting S1. Also, S1 interface of the operator A has a point-to-point connection with the transport equipment connecting the central sites of operator B and vice versa for the other operator as a result of the backhaul network sharing agreement. The other one is the point-to-point connection between the transport equipments/interfaces connecting two e-Node Bs for transporting X2. Now incorporating IP/MPLS protocol within the backhaul network of the LTE architecture, the Label Switched Paths (LSP) and Pseudo Wire (PW) are established using static provisioning. The e-Node Bs serve as Provider Edges (PEs). LSPs are established by the network operator here in this scenario for backhaul network sharing purpose between them, such as to create network-based IP virtual private networks and also to route traffic along specified paths through the network inorder to differentiate between the operators. When a labeled packet from operator B is received by an MPLS router of operator A, the topmost label is examined. Based on the contents of the label, the packet is routed along the specified path designated for operator B. Routers can have prebuilt lookup tables that tell them which path to take based on the topmost label of the incoming packet so they can process the packet very quickly. This is shown in the figures 3 and 4. Since the path is setup statically, it is much easier to plan the network, because at any given time, operator can view the overall network usage and based on this information can expand the network in much more predictable and efficient manner. In addition, every LSP/PW connection is bi-directional, which means both forward and return path will traverse through the same set of MPLS-TP nodes. This function is also referred to as deterministic data plane. This function allows operators to not only troubleshoot the network with confidence but also that the operators can identify the troublesome parts of the network before the actual problem really happens.

Once IP/MPLS is implemented for packet routing, inorder for the operators to prioritize their own traffic in other operator's backhaul network, we propose a solution based on OpenFlow [48]. This prioritization is necessary at times when the operator does not have access to its own backhaul network due to a failure and limited with the allocated bandwidth of the sharing operator. On such occasions, the operator must decide the type of traffic that has to be re-routed via another operator backhaul network. We take advantage of OpenFlow's flexibility for dynamic definition of flow granularity [49]. With this, traffic can be aggregated based on a set of flows with common characteristics by which the operator has the liberty to differentiate the traffic that flows over the backhaul network.

The advantages of adapting to a solution based on this scenario 1 are

- The main advantage being that the solution is simple technically.
- The user traffic coming to e-Node B effectively utilizes the capacity on both the operators' backhaul network resource, i.e. network resource of its own backhaul and network resource of the sharing operator.
- The operators do not have to take care or even pay attention to the traffic of the sharing operator that flows through their own backhaul network infrastructure after the provisioning.
- Since, they only "share" their available bandwidth with the other operator and not really provision with any additional links, this kind of sharing does not incur any additional cost to operators.
- The operators have the liberty to choose to prioritize the type of traffic that he would want to flow in the sharing backhaul bandwidth. Even better is, the operator can nonetheless care about the traffic priorities and just re-route a part of its own traffic in the shared bandwidth even at times when there is no failure in its own network.
- Traffic prioritization and service differentiation is not necessary (at times when there is no failure in their own network) considering this situation since the operators are given complete liberty with the additional bandwidth they are allocated by the sharing operator.

However, the drawbacks are

- Ratio needs to be defined effectively because it may be difficult to ensure contracts on quality (e.g., delay, jitter, loss rate, availability) and availability.
- An operator may pay for a backhaul network having good quality and another operator may benefit of that without needing to invest in a backhaul network having the same quality for the benefit of the other operator. But, this situation already exists in the traditional active infrastructure sharing, which is always considered a "Contract or SLA issue"
- The operators still could monitor the traffic flows of each other, if they wanted to. But, this could be forfended strictly by mentioning in the SLA.

Scenario B: Dynamic resource sharing in the backhaul network between each operator.

Considering this scenario where the operators do not have any prior reservation of network resources of the other operator at any point of time, the resource sharing on the backhaul network takes place dynamically. Dynamically allocating the available network resources means that each operator requests for network resource as and when needed from the shared operator. Our approach on this scenario is a layer-3 based implementation. The reason to choose the same is this implementation is transparent to MME and therefore reduces the complexity on MME. Typically when there is a failure in one operators' network, it necessitates the need for additional resources from the other operator. To support this additional need, a shared controller allocates on-demand LSP in each operator network, thanks to interface with operator owned controllers that reserve resources in each operator network. This shared controller reserves resources related to shared links between both operator e-Node Bs (e.g. X_A interface). The on-demand LSP crossing the operators' networks have to be monitored in order to account resources borrowed between operators. The advantage of this implementation, as mentioned before, is that the implementation is transparent to the MME. The disadvantage of this solution is, since it is transparent to the MME, the MME might have granted more capacity than the network can have at time T. However, this mechanism allows service providers to engineer the MPLS tunnel LSPs to optimize network bandwidth, directing traffic flow over specific core tunnels to maximize throughput, reduce congestion, and better utilize the resources in the backhaul network. The paths of the MPLS tunnel LSPs can be calculated and provisioned with a control plane or an OSS-based solution using MPLS standard MIBs. The control plane includes tools such as OSPF-TE and ISIS-TE to distribute the information on the network topology and the actual utilization of the resources providing information such as link bandwidth, link utilization, and priority. The control plane also includes tools such as RSVP-TE to signal the tunnel LSP and reserve resources and states along the paths according to the service specifications. Again, inorder to prioritize traffic in each operators' network, we considered OpenFlow for this scenario, it allows for more flexibility in terms of traffic prioritization mechanisms and thus allowing the mobile network operators having more control of the resources as described before.

Furthermore, in such a design, where resources are allocated on-demand, when a single MW link fails, it does not result in the interruption of the entire traffic on a given e-Node B, rather the total available bandwidth is only decreased. It means that packets are still forwarded towards the destination e-Node B, but the data rate is reduced. However, the advantage here is dynamic load sharing mode can be used to increase available bandwidth inorder to support heavy data traffic under peak hours. The drawback of this solution is that they may require a significant amount of network resources (control plane resources, such as established PWs or LSPs, and forwarding plane resources, i.e. the actual use of network bandwidth) for the traffic prioritization purposes.

5 Economic Analysis

As mentioned previously, the underlying motivation for this research is to provide a solution to improve resiliency till the "last mile" of the 4G-LTE mobile network backhaul without any extra costs on additional links and also to show that better performance can be achieved by network virtualization in LTE systems based on the contract configurations and the traffic load of each operator when the backhaul network resources are shared among them, especially within the context of emerging countries. Hence, as a first step towards this, we evaluated the cost that is required for microwave connectivity at the last mile by considering Kampala zone of Uganda based on the current traffic tendencies. The first step is to realize the cost for a microwave transport solution to connect all e-Node Bs of the area to the access site. The table below summarizes our geographical considerations for Kampala region which considered as a dense area of Uganda.

Table 3. Geographical modeling for backhaul network transport

Kampala study	
Dense area	177km²
e-Node B	78
Cells	234
Radius of 1 cell	540m
Distance between e-Node B	935m

Table 4. Economic evaluation

First mile All Microwave	CAPEX cost (in Euros)	Annualized cost (Assumption 8 years, in Euros)	ASSUMPTION (License cost/per year, in Euros)	Annual cost (in Euros)
60M	499297	87849	227136	314985

With this in mind, we evaluated the economic results with microwave backhaul network connectivity at the last mile considering 60Mega bandwidth per e-Node B (high traffic condition). We obtained the following results summarized in table 4.

Here the CAPEX costs takes into account the cost of the equipment, software license, instrumentation and control services and accessories and software network management services. The license cost of microwave is assumed to be an estimation of 2912 euros/link. From the table above, it is conclusive that an operator has to invest Euros 3,14,985 per annum simply to provide backhaul network transport, if the operator decides to invest solely, besides the CAPEX. Hence from our proposal, it is evident that the performance of backhaul network transport can be improved without any extra investment for additional investment by sharing the backhaul network and thus routing the traffic through another operator backhaul transport networks.

Also, to evaluate the performance of OpenFlow for our proposal, we referred to the experimental tests of [53], from which we can conclude that OpenFlow is an alternative to IP Routing because it does the same layer-2 and layer-3 functions with a high performance and scalability. OpenFlow does not just do layer-2 and layer-3 forwarding, but also can do port forwarding and layer-4 forwarding, so we can consider it more flexible and configurable considering operator differentiation. If we observe the obtained results of the experimental tests, we can see that OpenFlow has similar performance results as IP Routing in terms of Throughput and processing with large forwarding tables. Switching technology has obtained no good results with small packets and large forwarding tables compared with the layer-2 Ethernet Switching technology and with layer-3 IP Routing technology. Also classic software switching and routing techniques have bad forwarding performance when the system is overloaded due to high-rate flows. Hence we can affirm that OpenFlow code has been well-implemented and optimized for forwarding tasks.

6 Conclusion

As the mobile communications sector continues its relentless expansion with more subscribers and more advanced services generating ever-greater volumes of traffic, operators must invest in their infrastructure to provide the bandwidth to meet demand. Network congestion or mobbing and traffic overloading is resource-sharing problem, which will upswing whenever resources are not enough to meet users demands. The LTE/EPC evolution is an evolution towards an all-IP architecture and will fundamentally change how mobile backhaul networks are built in the future. The availability of ethernet-enabled e-Node Bs and the evolution towards LTE/EPC pushes IP awareness further into the edge of the mobile network. Mobile operators are beginning to view these backhaul networks like carrier ethernet environments offering multiple concurrent services. As discussed in the paper, there are lots of other factors involved too, which may cause network congestion including failure of network equipments and list goes on. There may be some particular preliminary steps from network service providers that require to be completed by cell site installers before installing cell sites. With all these factors leading to the consideration of maintaining QoS, which essentially has become an important aspect in the networks mostly by the increased usage of real-time communications in many production networks. The level of recovery directly affects the service level (data loss and recovery time) provided to end users in the event of a network failure. There is a correlation between the level of recovery provided and the cost to the network.

With backhaul network infrastructure sharing, the cost reductions will lead to a reduction of business risk for the involved operators. The cost and energy reduction in this scenario is of a similar magnitude, since more traffic can be served with the same equipment before additional sites are needed. With all these in mind, backhaul network infrastructure sharing could be one of the problem solvers to tackle the issue of restoring network failures or undermining peak traffic problems. The next step of this work will consist to validate the solutions proposed here by implementing a prototype and measuring performance.

Acknowledgment. The authors would like to thank Isabelle BOYER-HEARD, Christian COLLET, Pierre-Luc François, Orange Labs, France Telecom R&D, Lannion, France, for their valuable inputs towards evaluating the available resiliency mechanisms and for the MTTR values of the French network.

References

1. Jorswieck, E.A., Badia, L., Fahldieck, T., Gesbert, D., Gustafsson, S., Haardt, M., Ho, K.M., Karipidis, E., Kortke, A., Larsson, E.G., Mark, H., Nawrocki, M., Piesiewicz, R., Romer, F., Schubert, M., Sykora, J., Trommelen, F., Van den Ende, B., Zorzi, M.: Resource Sharing in Wireless Networks: The SAPHYRE Approach. In: Cunningham, P., Cunningham, M. (eds.) Future Network and Mobile Summit 2010 Conference Proceedings, IIMC International Information Management Corporation, vol. 8, pp. 978–971 (2010), ISBN: 978-1-905824-16-8
2. Frisanco, T., Tafertshofer, P., Lurin, P., Ang, R.: Infrastructure Sharing for Mobile Network Operators From a Deployment and Operations View. In: Network IEEE Operations and Management Symposium, NOMS 2008 (2008)
3. Digital World Forum, Low cost broadband access and infrastructure, `http://digitalworld.ercim.eu/wp3.html`
4. Radio Spectrum Policy Group: Opinion on wireless access policy for electronic communications services (WAPECS): A more flexible spectrum management approach (2005)
5. Boudec, J.Y.L.: Rate adaptation, congestion control and fairness: A tutorial. Technical report, Tutorial, Ecole Polytechnique Federale de Lausanne, EPFL (2003)
6. Kelly, F., Maulloo, A., Tan, D.: Rate control for communication networks: Shadow prices, proportional fairness and stability. Journal of Operations Research Society 49, 237–252 (1998)
7. Peters, H.J.M.: Axiomatic Bargaining Game Theory. Kluwer Academic Publishers, Boston (1992)
8. Busi, N., Manfredini, C., Montresor, A., Zavattaro, G.: Towards Data driven coordination Infrastructure for Peer-Peer systems. Department of Science and technology, University of Bologne
9. Barcelo, J., Infante, J., Oliver, M.: Department of Information and Communication Technologies. In: Wireless Open Access Networks: State-of-the-art and Technological Opportunities, Universitat Pompeu Fabra, Carrer Tanger 122-140, 08018 Barcelona, Catalunya, Spain
10. Meddour, D.E., Rasheed, T., Gourhant, Y.: On the role of infrastructure sharing for mobile network operators in emerging markets. Computer Networks, Recent Advances in Network Convergence 55(7), 1576–1591 (2011), `http://www.sciencedirect.com/science/article/B6VRG-528P8FF-1/2/0c4d37bd3af22ca654537ade6eebc362`, doi:10.1016/j.comnet.2011.01.023
11. 3GPP Release 6 Technical Specification Group: Network sharing; Architecture and functional description (TS 23.251)
12. 3GPP Techincal Report (TR 22.951): Service aspects and requirements for network sharing
13. 3GPP Technical Specification (TS 36.300): Evolved Universal Terrestrial Radio Access (E-UTRA) and Evolved Universal Terrestrial Radio Access Network (E-UTRAN); Overall description; Stage 2
14. Battiti, R., Cigno, R., Sabel, M., Orava, F., Pehrson, B.: Wireless LANs: from War Chalking to Open Access Networks. Mobile Networks and Applications 10(3), 275–287 (2005)
15. Hunter, T., Nosratinia, A.: Cooperation diversity through coding. In: Proceedings of IEEE International Symposium on Information Theory (2002)
16. Sendonaris, A., Erkip, E., Aazhang, B., Inc, Q., Campbell, C.: User cooperation diversity. Part I. System description. IEEE Trans. Commun. 51(11), 1927–1938 (2003)

17. Sendonaris, A., Erkip, E., Aazhang, B.: User cooperation diversity. Part II. Implementation aspects and performance analysis. IEEE Trans. Commun. 51(11), 1939–1948 (2003)
18. Cui, S., Goldsmith, A., Bahai, A.: Energy-efficiency of MIMO and cooperative MIMO techniques in sensor networks. IEEE J. Sel. Areas Commun. 22(6), 1089–1098 (2004)
19. Jayaweera, S.: Virtual MIMO-based cooperative communication for energy-constrained wireless sensor networks. IEEE Trans. Wireless Commun. 5(5), 984–989 (2006)
20. Pabst, R., Walke, B., Schultz, D., Herhold, P., Yanikomeroglu, H., Mukherjee, S., Viswanathan, H., Lott, M., Zirwas, W., Dohler, M., et al.: Relay-based deployment concepts for wireless and mobile broadband radio. IEEE Commun. Mag. 42(9), 80–89 (2004)
21. Soldani, D., Dixit, S.: Wireless relays for broadband access (radio communications series). IEEE Commun. Mag. 46(3), 58–66 (2008)
22. RFC 5462: Multiprotocol Label Switching (MPLS) Label Stack Entry: "EXP" Field Renamed to "Traffic Class" Field
23. Williams, D.E., Garcia, J.: Virtualization with Xen: Including Xenenterprise, Xenserver, and Xenexpress. Syngress Publishing, Inc. (May 2007) ISBN-13: 9781597491679
24. Bhatia, S., Motiwala, M., Muhlbauer, W., Valancius, V., Bavier, A., Feamster, N., Peterson, L., Rexford, J.: Hosting virtual networks on commodity hardware. Georgia Tech. University, Tech. Rep. GT-CS-07-10 (January 2008)
25. Kohler, E., Morris, R., Chen, B., Jahnotti, J., Kasshoek, M.F.: The Click Modular Router. ACM Transaction on Computer Systems 18(3), 263–297 (2000)
26. VROUT: http://nrg.cs.ucl.ac.uk/vrouter
27. VMware Server, http://www.vmware.com/products/server/
28. Cisco VN-Link: Virtualization-Aware Networking, white paper, http://www.cisco.com/en/US/solutions/collateral/ns340/ns517/ns224/ns892/ns894/white_paper_c11-525307_ps9902_Products_White_Paper.html
29. GENI Planning Group: GENI: Conceptual Design, Project Execution Plan. In: GENI Design Document 2006-2007 (January 2006), http://www.geni.net/GDD/GDD-06-07.pdf
30. GENI: Global Environment for Network Innovations, http://www.geni.net/
31. Bavier, A., Bowman, M., Culler, D., Chun, B., Karlin, S., Muir, S., Peterson, L., Roscoe, T., Spalink, T., Wawrzoniak, M.: Operating System Support for Planetary-Scale Network Services (March 2004)
32. Bavier, A., Feamster, N., Huang, M., Peterson, L., Rexford, J.: In VINI Veritas: Realistic and Controlled Network Experimentation. In: ACM SIGCOMM 2006 (September 2006)
33. Feamster, N., Gao, L., Rexford, J.: How to lease the Internet in your spare time. ACM SIGCOMM Computer Communications Review 37(1) (January 2007)
34. Zhu, Y., Zhang-Shen, R., Rangarajan, S., Rexford, J.: Cabernet: Connectivity architecture for better network services. In: Workshop on Rearchitecting the Internet (December 2008)
35. Niebert, N., Baucke, S., El-Khayat, I., et al.: The way 4WARD to the creation of a Future Internet. In: ICT Mobile Summit, Stockholm (June 2008)
36. 4WARD project page, http://www.4ward-project.eu
37. AKARI Architecture Conceptual Design for New Generation Network (translated version 1.1), http://akari-project.nict.go.jp/eng/conceptdesign/AKARI_fulltext_e_translated_version_1_1.pdf
38. Asia Future Internet (AsiaFI), http://www.asiafi.net

39. Sherwood, R., Gibb, G., Yap, K.K., Appenzeller, G., McKeown, N., Parulkar, G., Casado, M.: FlowVisor: A Network Virtualization Layer. Deutsche Telekom Inc., R&D Lab, Palo Alto, CA
40. Turner, J.S., Crowley, P., DeHart, J., Freestone, A., Heller, B., Kuhns, F., Kumar, S., Lockwood, J., Lu, J., Wilson, M., Wiseman, C., Zar, D.: Supercharging PlanetLab: A high performance, multi-application, overlay network platform. In: SIGCOMM 2007, Proceedings of the 2007 Conference on Applications, Technologies, Architectures, and Protocols for Computer Communications, pp. 85–96. ACM, New York (2007)
41. A virtual network infrastructure, `http://www.vini-veritas.net`
42. `http://www.virtualbox.org`
43. VMware, `http://www.vmware.com`
44. White, B., Lepreau, J., Stoller, L., Ricci, R., Guruprasad, S., Newbold, M., Hibler, M., Barb, C., Joglekar, A.: An integrated experimental environment for distributed systems and networks. In: Proceedings of the Fifth Symposium on Operating Systems Design and Implementation, pp. 255–270. USENIX Association, Boston (2002)
45. L. S. Committee. IEEE802.1q: IEEE standard for local and metropolitan area networks virtual bridged local area networks. IEEE Computer Society, Los Alamitos (2005)
46. 3GPP Technical Specification (TS 36.3xx Series): Evolved Universal Terrestrial Radio Access (E-UTRA) and Evolved Universal Terrestrial Radio Access Network (E-UTRAN); Overall description
47. MMBI White Paper on Use of MPLS in LTE, MR-238, Issue: 1, Issue Date (February 2010)
48. `http://www.openflow.org/`
49. `http://www.openflow.org/wk/index.php/Aggregation`
50. Heller, B.: OpenFlow Switch Specification v0.8.9 (brandonh@stanford.edu), `http://www.OpenFlowswitch.org/documents/OpenFlow-spec-v0.8.9.pdf`
51. OpenFlow: Enabling Innovation in Campus Networks, `http://www.OpenFlowswitch.org/documents/OpenFlow-wp-latest.pdf`
52. 3GPP Release 9 Technical Specification (TS 23.251 version 9.2.0): Universal Mobile Telecommunications System (UMTS); LTE; Network sharing; Architecture and functional description
53. Mateo, M.P.: OpenFlow Switching Performance, Masters Thesis, Politecnico Di Torino (July 2009)

Ontology Matching for Web Services Composition

Pavel Tyl*

Technical University of Liberec
Hálkova 6
461 17 Liberec 1
Czech Republic
pavel.tyl@tul.cz
http://www.cs.cas.cz/~tyl

Abstract. Web services became one of the best means for web application interoperability. There is a need to have a scalable and extensible model to deliver distributed information and functionality integrated as independently provided, interoperable services in a distributed environment. Several distributed services can be dynamically composed (chained) as a new service to accomplish specific tasks. Such a model of service composition (chaining) is one of the most important research topics of next generation web services.

This paper discusses possibilities of using ontology matching techniques for web services interoperability and composition, describes such processes, explain their difficulties and propose a model for web service composition based on suitable ontology matching techniques.

Keywords: ontology matching, web services composition.

1 Motivation

Let's suppose this motivation scenario [10]:
We want to deliver some electronic product from a web shop to some address by a shipping service. Online electronic shop service provides its output description in some ontology. Shipping service uses a second ontology for its input description. Then the matching of these ontologies could be used for:

- checking that what is delivered by the first service, e. g., a `DVD_Recorder`, matches what is expected by the second one, e. g., some `Object` (shipping service does not accept life animals),
- verifying preconditions of the second service, e. g., `Size` in centimeters, etc.
- generating a mediator for transforming the output of the first service to the second one's input.

* This project is supported by grant GAP202/10/0761 and cofinanced from the student grant SGS 2010/7821 "Interactive Mechatronics Systems Using the Cybernetics Principles".

J.J. Yonazi et al. (Eds.): ICeND 2011, CCIS 171, pp. 94–103, 2011.

We can see only two parts of a chain in this short example, but there could be many more. For example there are web services able to compare products (e. g., `DVD_Recorders`) from different data sources (catalogues), some web services do it even more sophisticated using user preferences, etc.

2 Introduction

2.1 Ontology Matching

Ontology matching is the process of finding "correspondences" (also called relationships [3]) between elements within different ontologies which have to be (semantically) compared and, eventually, joined. The output of the matching process is a set of such correspondences between two (or, in general, more ontologies) called an *ontology alignment*. The "oriented" version of an ontology alignment is an *ontology mapping*.

Given two source ontologies o and o', an input ("preliminary") alignment A, a set of *parameters* (e. g., threshold) and *resources* (e. g., provenance metadata), the **matching process** (see Fig. 1) can be described by function f returning a *new alignment* A' between ontologies o and o':

$$A' = f(o, o', A, p, r).$$

Ontology matching is in most cases performed *manually* or *semiautomatically*, often with support of some *graphical user interface*. Manual specification of ontology parts for matching is *time consuming* and moreover *error prone process*. It results in a strong need for development of faster and/or less laborious methods, which can process ontologies at least semiautomatically.

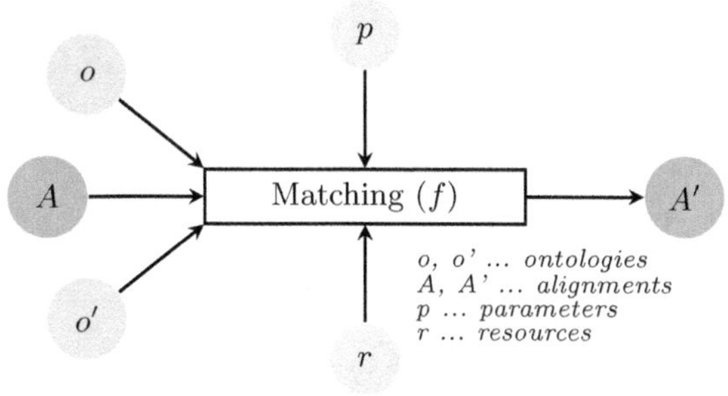

Fig. 1. Schema of a matching process [3]

2.2 Web Services

A web service is a network accessible interface to web application functionality. It is described in machine-readable format, most often in standardized web service description language, WSDL [16]. Way of communication between other computers and web service is specified in the web service's description with the help of Simple Object Access Protocol, SOAP [13]. SOAP messages are transfered by well-established protocols[1]. SOAP and WSDL protocols have easy machine-readable XML [18] syntax. Both SOAP and WSDL were designed to be independent on selected version of XML language, but obligated to be XML compatible.

The W3C [14] defines a web service as "a software system designed to support interoperable machine-to-machine interaction over a network. It has an interface described in a machine-processable format (specifically Web Services Description Language WSDL). Other systems interact with the web service in a manner prescribed by its description using SOAP messages, typically conveyed using HTTP with an XML serialization in conjunction with other web-related standards" [15].

Web services expose their interfaces to the web so that users (agents) can invoke them. **Semantic web services** provide a richer and more precise way to describe services through the use of knowledge representation languages and ontologies [4], e. g., OWL-S [12] or WSDL-S [17].

2.3 Web Service Composition

Web service discovery and integration is the process of finding web service able to deliver a particular service and composing several services in order to achieve a particular goal [8].

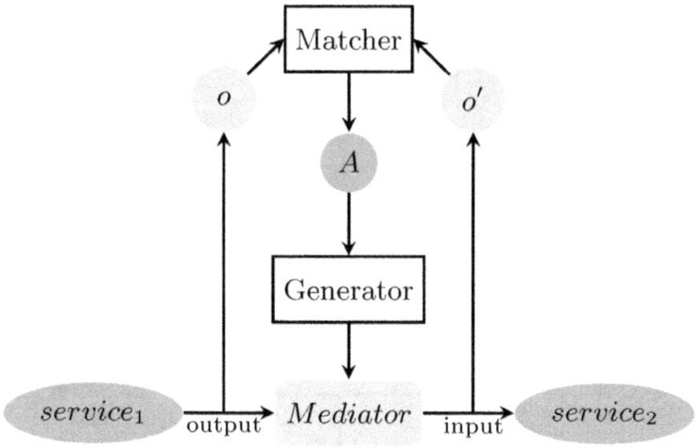

Fig. 2. Web service composition – in this case it is useful to (1) match relevant parts of ontologies o and o', thus resulting in alignment A and (2) *generate* a *mediator* between $service_1$ and $service_2$ in order to enable transformation of actual data [3]

Web services are often designed to be independent and replaceable and, therefore, web service processors are able to incorporate new services in their workflows and customers can dynamically choose other and more promising reliable services. For this reason, they must be able to compare the descriptions (model)

[1] Reason for SOAP messages "encapsulation" is an absence of trust from existing systems.

of these services (in order to know if they are really relevant) and to route the knowledge they process (in order to chain different services) by directing the output of some service to the input of another service [3].

Both for finding the appropriate service and for interfacing services, some data "mediator" is important as a bridge between different vocabularies [9]. Based on the correspondences between the terms of the descriptions, mediators must be able to translate the output of one service into a suitable input for another service (see Fig. 2).

The headstone of a mediator definition is an alignment between two ontologies. And this can be provided through matching the corresponding ontologies either offline when someone is designing a preliminary service composition, or online (dynamically) [5], when new services are searched for completing a request.

3 Web Service Composition by Ontology Matching

There are two possibilities one could use ontology matching techniques for web service composition:

1. Entire web service is described by the service ontology (WSMO[2]).
2. Web service is described by the traditional means and only its inputs and outputs are described by the ontologies.

Ontologies classifying and describing services are called service ontologies. According to our opinion it is not necessary to describe web services by ontologies (i. e., using WSML[3] [5]), because inner behavior of a web service *need not* (sometimes rather *must not*) be always transparent or accessible. But at least web services' outputs and inputs have to be described using ontologies for successful application of ontology matching techniques.

Every web service has its input(s) and output(s), in our case described as input ontologies $o(in\_s_1)$ and $o(in\_s_2)$ and output ontologies $o(out\_s_1)$ and $o(out\_s_2)$ (see Fig. 3). They can be part of the *web service I/O interface* or can be stored outside the web service itself.

Web service in our model is divided into two main parts – its *internal structure* and a *repository*. The *internal structure* is responsible for functional achievment of the exposed service, finding direct or intermediate answers. If the web service is able to provide a direct answer (reply to the *primary request*), the input ontology $o(in\_s_1)$ is processed in the *internal structure* and results are transferred to the output ontology $o(out\_s_1)$. In the case of intermediate answer, if the *web service 1* is compliant to be a part of a chain, $o(out\_s_1)$ is produced and devolved upon a *web service chain repository* with a goal of searching for the best available web service for the chain, so that its appropriate alignment (e. g., A_{12}) is in the *alignments repository*. There are following web service chains in the *WS1 Chain Repository* (see Fig. 3) and for example the last point says us that the output of

[2] Web Service Modelling Ontology – `http://www.wsmo.org`.
[3] Web Service Modelling Language.

web service 4 can be used as an input for *web service 1* and in such case we are able to match $o(out\_s_4)$ and $o(in\_s_1)$ and we know alignment A_{41}):

- *WS1–WS2*,
- *WS1–WS3*,
- *WS4–WS1*.

When a preliminary alignment A_{12} exists (provided manually or by some (semi) automatic means), it should be stored in the *alignments repository* for simple identification of reuse opportunities (see Sec. 3.1). Input/output ontologies $o(out\_s_1)$ and $o(in\_s_2)$, alignments $A_{12}, A_{13}, \ldots, A_{1n}$ and saved readymade *web service chains* are in the web service repository identified by their URIs[4]. It allows interaction with other services in order to negotiate operations the current service just cannot provide (e. g., when the current service is not available). Therefore at least the alignments (or the whole repository) should be always exposed in the same way as the inputs and the outputs of the web service.

If the suitable service (e. g., *web service 2*) is found and preliminary alignment exists, $o(out\_s_1)$ and $o(in\_s_2)$ are checked for their compatibility in a *compatibility checker* and if they pass, $o(out\_s_1)$ is easily converted in an *I/O converter* by using stored alignment A_{12} into $o(in\_s_2)$ and the request is passed on. Successful conversion and checks should be stored and cached.

If there is no alignment related to *web service 2* in our *alignments repository*, traditional matching methods (*Matcher* in Fig. 3) or manual matching have to be used. If related alignment exists, we can successfully apply an alignment reuse methods (see Sec. 3.1). According to [7] there are four matchmaking functions based on which web services can be chained: *Exact*, *PlugIn*, *Subsume* and *Intersection*. Otherwise (*Disjoint*), services are incompatible:

- **Exact** – if the output parameter out_s_y of s_y and the input parameter in_s_x of s_x are equivalent concepts (e. g., `DVD_Recorder` from our motivation example could be certainly delivered, because it is an `Object` and its `Size` is less than maximal allowed),
- **PlugIn** – if out_s_y is a subconcept of in_s_x (e. g., `DVD_Recorder` will be be delivered, if a shipping service is able to deliver whatever we want, any `owl:Thing`),
- **Subsume** – if out_s_y is a superconcept of in_s_x,
- **Intersection** – if the intersection of out_s_y and in_s_x is satisfiable,
- **Disjoint** – if the out_s_y and in_s_x are incompatible.

With *Exact* and *PlugIn* functions we are always able to match required web services, the matcher can fail in case of *Subsume* and *Intersection*.

3.1 Candidate Matching Techniques for Web Service Composition

It would be nice if we could always automatically create input and output ontology alignments at runtime. But it is not an easy task in the case of heterogenous

[4] Uniform Resource Identifier.

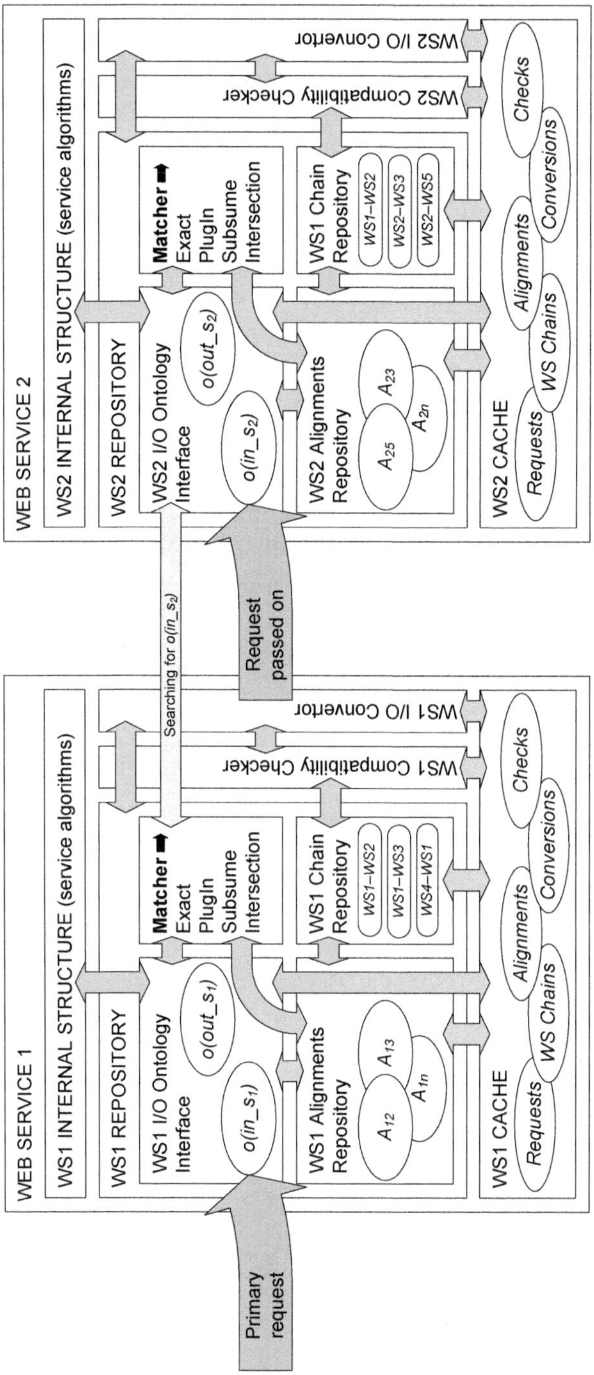

Fig. 3. Proposed model for the web service composition with using of an ontology matching

web service compositions. In addition such algorithms should be fast enough, there is no time for tuning parameters, manual corrections, etc. Therefore in our model we suppose at least preliminary ontology alignments of $o(out\_s_y)$ and $o(in\_s_x)$ at design time. Consequently we can always take an advantage of them. And at this moment an alignment reuse can come on scene.

Alignment reuse is motivated by an idea that many ontologies that should be matched are similar to already matched ones, especially if they describe the same domain(s). Ontologies from the same application domain usually contain many similar elements, typical for this domain. Therefore their mappings can provide good reusable candidates.

At first, matching problems are decomposed, then a set of ontology fragments is generated and finally previous match results can be applied at the level of ontology fragments rather than at the level of the whole ontologies [3]. According to [2] alignments of ontologies (e. g., o_y and o_x) can be saved in a repository in three possible forms:

- **Direct mappings** ($o_y \leftrightarrow o_x$) – ideal for reuse, one or multiple mappings are already available for the given match problem. Such mappings represent the shortest possible mapping paths, which do not involve any intermediary ontologies.
- **Complete mapping paths** ($o_y \leftrightarrow o_i$, $o_i \leftrightarrow o_x$ or $o_j \leftrightarrow o_y$, $o_x \leftrightarrow o_j$) – such mapping paths consist only of existing mappings.
- **Incomplete mapping paths** (same as complete, but i. e., $o_i \leftrightarrow o_x$ and $o_j \leftrightarrow o_y$ are to be matched) – the default match operation is first applied and missing alignments can be computed with less effort than directly matching the input ontologies.

All match results are compared (e. g., average similarity in the path, expected computational effort expressed by the path length, etc.) and ontologies composed.

Although alignment reuse seems to be the most important technique in the proposed model (more than technique we could call it matching strategy), there are some other basic techniques that cannot be omitted in the web service composition. In the following we list some of them together with the reason for their use:

- **Internal structure (constraint) based techniques** – before creating an ontology alignment, but much more for later use, we can do a verification of criteria as the set of the entity properties (e. g., their multiplicity), the range and the domain of the properties, cardinality, datatypes, etc. These techniques are easy to implement and if the ontologies ($o(out\_s_y)$ versus $o(in\_s_x)$) pass them, it will provide a basis on which other parts of an application can rely.
- **External ontologies based techniques** – external reference ontology (o_{ext}) can provide a common ground on which an alignment can be based. It can help in the case of disambiguity of multiple possible meanings of terms in given domain of interest. For example an alignment between $o(out\_s_y)$ and $o(in\_s_x)$ can be derived from two other alignments with external ontology

$(A(o(out\_s_y), o_{ext}$ and $A(o(in\_s_x), o_{ext})$[5]. External ontology is in the most cases a general reputable upper-level ontology (e. g., FMA[6] in medicine)
- Further we can use **relational structure techniques** (e. g., taxonomy relations), **propositional** and **description logic techniques** (these techniques cannot find an alignment alone, but when alignment is generated, we can ensure its completeness and consistency), etc.

4 Potential Problems of Web Services Composition

Issues worth mentioning to deal with when composing web services are:

Third-party sources – Two things remain unchanged with the web services in general:

- they use third-party sources and
- they have questionable reliability.

This is not to say that web services are unreliable, but it simply means that we have not a primary control of the source for our web application. When our sources are offline, our web service or web application is also offline. One way to avoid this problem is to keep an actual cache of all queries issued to our data sources in case of a service failure.
Caching is a good idea in general because it will definitely speedup repeated requests.

Rate limiting – Many public service interfaces may have to limit the number of requests an application or user can make within certain period of time. (This can be done by tracking the number of requests made by a single IP address or the system may require authentication.) This is another issue that could be partially or fully solved by request caching. Fig. 4 shows the position of web services among other web applications. As can be seen, they are supposed to be dynamic, but in contrast to P2P or B2B systems they should stay always correct, because we could obtain error chain instead of web service chain.

Reliability – Keeping the current cache of recent requests can help keeping our service online until our sources are back online. If more than one public service interface is available to provide the information, our composite web service requires then a fallback mechanism to be implemented. It allows our web service to switch to another source until our primary source has been reestablished or to find another reliable (data) source forever.

Vendor locking – This could be a huge problem in the future as more and more web service compositions will be created. What to do if a public application interface that serves alignments to thousands of web services and web applications suddenly goes offline for one day or forever or starts charging for their service? It is therefore necessary to share accessible sources or prepare mechanisms for rapid finding of other appropriate services.

---

[5] Here we can omit the input alignment, the resource and the parameters.

[6] Foundational Model of Anatomy – `http://sig.biostr.washington.edu/projects/fm`.

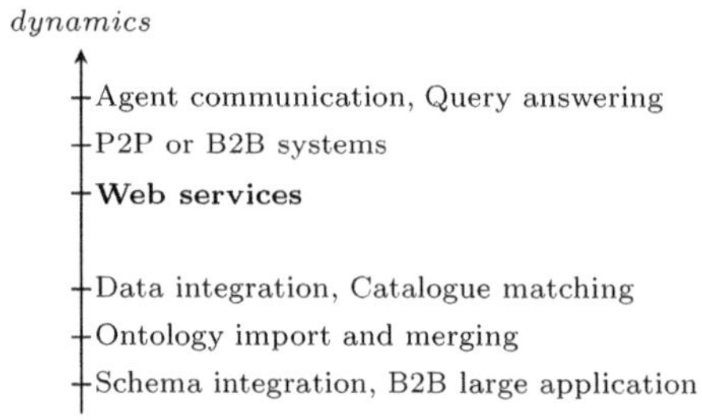

Fig. 4. Example applications ordered by their *dynamics*. Space under semantic web services shows that three top applications are considered to be dynamic.

Licensing restrictions – Some public web services restrict for what we can use them and sometimes which web services can we use together with them. We have to thoroughly read restrictions which may apply before adopting them to our web service chain[7]. This problem is similar to the above one and has the same possible solutions.

5 Conclusion and Future Work

In this paper the possibility of using ontology matching techniques in web service composition is presented and a complex model for such composition is proposed. There are many different applications which require or could take an advantage of ontology matching. But in the comparison with traditional applications such as information or schema integration, web service composition has its specific requirements – after preliminary steps (creating and processing alignments) it should be automatic and dynamic enough. Therefore we have to store these alignments and find the way how to replace them if necessary.

The next step we would like to work on is a design and implementation of an application according to the proposed model that will be able to compose e-learning systems for advanced testing (could be seen as web services) with the help of ontology matching (or, in general, ontology integration) techniques.

References

1. Alonso, G., Casati, F., Kuno, H., Machiraju, V.: Web Services. Concepts, Architectures and Applications. Springer, Berlin (2004) ISBN 3-540-44008-9
2. Do, H.: Schema matching and mapping-based data integration. PhD thesis. University of Leipzig, Leipzig, DE (2005)
3. Euzenat, J., Shvaiko, P.: Ontology Matching. Springer, Heidelberg (2007) ISBN 978-3-540-49611-3

[7] One more disadvantage is that these restrictions or rules can be time invariant and practically stochastic.

4. Fensel, D., Lausen, H., Polleres, A., De Bruijn, J., Stollberg, M., Roman, D., Domingue, J.: Enabling semantic web services: the web service modelling ontology. Springer, Heidelberg (2004) ISBN 978-3-540-34519-0
5. Guinchiglia, F., Mcneil, F., Yatskevich, M.: Web service composition via semantic matching of interaction specifications. Technical Report DIT-06-080. University of Trento (2006)
6. Mccandless, D., Obrst, L., Hawthorne, S.: Dynamic Web Service Assembly Using OWL and a Theorem Prover. In: Proc. 3rd IEEE International Conference on Semantic Computing, Berkeley, USA (2009)
7. Lécué, F., Delteil, A., Léger, A.: Applying Abduction in Semantic Web Service Composition. In: Proc. 2007 IEEE International Conference on Web Services, pp. 94–101. IEEE CS, Los Alamitos (2007)
8. Paolucci, M., Kawamura, T., Payne, T., Sycara, K.: Semantic Matching of Web Services Capabilities. In: Horrocks, I., Hendler, J. (eds.) ISWC 2002. LNCS, vol. 2342, pp. 333–347. Springer, Heidelberg (2002)
9. Roman, D., Lausen, H., Keller, U.: Web service modeling ontology standard (WSMO standard). Working Draft D2v0.2, WSMO (2004)
10. Cuel, R., et al.: D 1.4.1v2 Technology RoadMap (2005), `http://www.sti-innsbruck.at/fileadmin/documents/deliverables/Knowledge_Web/D1.4.1v2..pdf`
11. OWL – Web Ontology Language / W3C Semantic Web Activity, `http://www.w3.org/2004/OWL`
12. OWL-S – Semantic Markup for Web Services, `http://www.w3.org/Submission/OWL-S`
13. SOAP – Simple Object Access Protocol, `http://www.w3.org/TR/soap`
14. W3C – World Wide Web Consortium, `http://www.w3.org`
15. W3C – Web Services Glossary, `http://www.w3.org/TR/ws-gloss`
16. WSDL – Web Services Description Language, `http://www.w3.org/TR/wsdl`
17. WSDL-S – Web Service Semantics, `http://www.w3.org/Submission/WSDL-S`
18. XML – Extensible Markup Language / W3C XML Activity, `http://www.w3.org/XML`

A Preview Study on UWB Imaging System to Detect Early Breast Tumor

A. Naveena Lakshmi[1], S. Khatun[1,*], and S.A. AlShehri[2]

[1] Faculty of Computer Systems and Software Engineering
University Malaysia Pahang (UMP), 26300 Gambang, Kuantan, Pahang, Malaysia
[2] Department of Computer and Communication Systems Engineering
Faculty of Engineering, Universiti Putra Malaysia
Serdang, Selangor 43400, Malaysia
sabira@ump.edu.my,
{anapa.naveena,saaas101}@gmail.com

Abstract. Breast cancer is the second leading cause of cancer death after lung cancer among the women. In this paper we reviewed some breast cancer detection techniques like Mammography, Magnetic Resonance Imaging (MRI), ultra Sound and Ultra Wide Band (UWB) and its performances. Current UWB systems having some limitations including they are not able to detect the tumor at early stages, a multiple antenna array in terms of complex system and in all systems no pictorial 3D representation of tumor size. To overcome this limitation, a thorough investigation is done here, to find out the limitations of existing and proposed systems followed by the open issues which need to be resolved.

Keywords: Ultra Wide band, Breast Cancer, Tumor Detection.

1 Introduction

Currently cancer is one of the leading causes of mortality, with more deaths per year than heart disease among those under 85 years of old [1]. Breast Cancer is one of main causes for women's death in all over the world [2]. Around 50% of breast cancer cases in all over the world end up with death. The percentage is high because the detection of the cancer is typically very late. The early detection of tumor could help reduce the higher percentages of death cases. It could thus save a lot of lives [3].

Female breast consists of two main tissue types. (i) Adipose tissue stores fat in adiposities, large lipid-filled cells, and makes up the vast majority of the breast (Fig.1). (ii) The glandular tissue comprises a connection of lobules and branching epithelial ducts, which connect the network that allows for milk delivery. In addition, systems of vascular, connective, and neural tissues reside among the glandular and fat structures. The connective tissues are often referred to as the breast stoma.

Breast cancer, the most frequently is occurring cancer with an estimated 182,460 new cases reported in 2008 around the world among which approximately 26% in

* Corresponding author.

J.J. Yonazi et al. (Eds.): ICeND 2011, CCIS 171, pp. 104–115, 2011.

2008 in America [1]. Although statistics from the US mortality data project, breast cancer deaths to be decreased for the past decade, in 2004 they still accounted for 15.5% of all female cancer deaths. A graphical comparison of the cancer death rates is presented in Fig 2. In 2002, 103.7 per 100,000 persons were diagnosed with breast cancer in the more developed countries. In Canada, this rate was 124.0 per 100,000 persons, with 33.7 deaths due to the disease [4]. In Malaysia the breast cancer is most common in the Chinese, followed by the Indians and then, Malays. Here, every woman within 20 has chance of getting breast cancer in her lifetime. The cumulative life time risk of developing breast cancer for Chinese, Indian and Malay women are 1 in 16, 1 in 17 and 1 in 28 respectively [5].

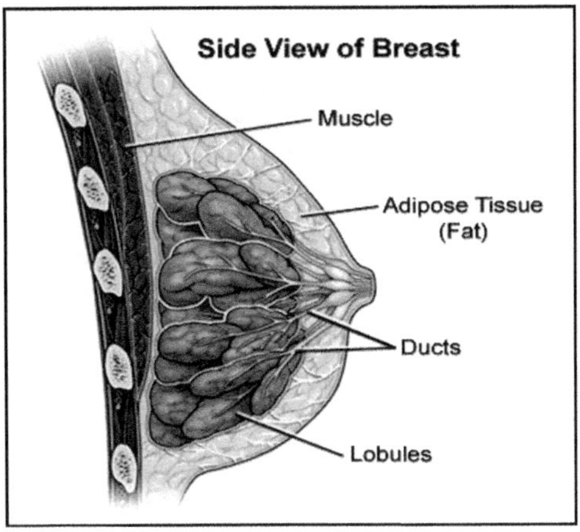

Fig. 1. Side view of the breast

The present standard screening method for detecting non palpable early-stage breast cancer is X-ray mammography. Despite the fact that X-ray mammography provides high resolution images using relatively low radiation doses, its limitations are well documented, especially in radiological dense glandular tissue [6]. As such, a number of research works examining the capabilities of emerging imaging modalities for breast cancer detection has been conducted. The investigation for new imaging techniques is motivated by the need for increased sensitivity and specificity; in younger women, in particular, breast tissue typically presents a higher dense-to-fatty tissue ratio, and suspicious lesions occurring in dense tissue breasts are statistically more likely to be missed by X-ray mammography [7]. In U.S. approximately 15% of all breast cancers are missed by conventional mammography, while 75% of all malignancies identified are found to be benign after biopsies [8]. In addition to this, it has been shown that traditional mammography results in a high rate of false positives, resulting in unnecessary biopsies and considerable distress to the patient [9, 10]. Issues also exist with the obvious alternatives to X-ray mammography of MRI and ultrasound imaging. Although MRI has a negative predictive value of 99% [11], the cost and sensitivity of these alternative imaging modalities are well documented, and preclude their widespread use [11–14].

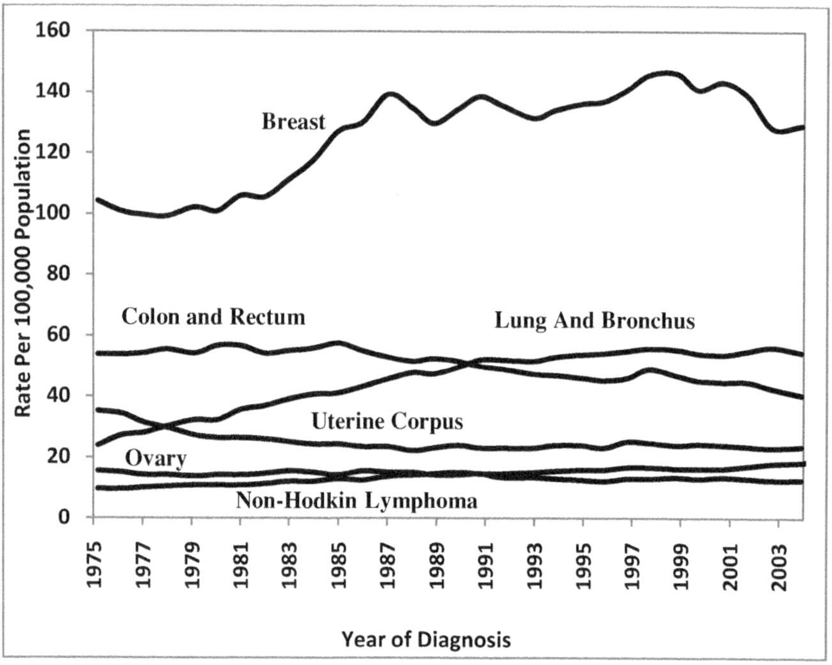

Fig. 2. Annual Age-adjusted Cancer Death Rates. (Source: US Mortality Data, 1960 to 2004, US Mortality Volumes 1930 to 1959, National Center for Health Statistics, Centers for Disease Control and Prevention, 2006.)

One of the most promising alternative imaging modalities is UWB microwave imaging. The physical basis for microwave imaging is the significant dielectric contrast between normal and malignant breast tissues that exists at microwave frequencies. This dielectric contrast between normal and malignant tissues ensures that any tumor present in the breast will provide backscattered energy that may be used to detect of the presence of the tumor when illuminated by microwave radiation, UWB radar imaging uses the reflected signals to determine the location of significant microwave scatterers. Microwave imaging is non-ionizing, does not require breast compression, is less invasive than x-rays, and is low cost.

2 Breast Tumor Detection Techniques

2.1 Mammography

Mammography as the standard imaging method for breast cancer screening [15] has resulted in reduced breast cancer mortality. However, the number of cancers escaping detection with mammography is substantial, particularly in dense breasted women, with sensitivity as low as 30–48% [16]. Computer-aided detection (CAD) improves sensitivity but does not identify all cancers [17, 18]. The Digital Mammographic Imaging Screen Trail (DMIST) trial found an improvement from 55% to 70% in cancer detection compared to film mammography [19], suggesting that substantial numbers of cancers are missed even with digital technology. Mammographically missed cancer is a particular problem for women with dense breasts [20]; Boyd *et al.* showed that the odd for interval cancers was 17.8% fold higher in extremely dense breasts compared to fatty breasts [20]. The performance of mammography is reduced for cancer detection in dense breasted women as mammograms are summation images, with all breast tissue overlapping in each view. Cancers may not be visualized because of overlying dense breast tissue [21]. Mammography can miss far posterior cancers in the retro-mammary space because of inadequate positioning of deep tissue. Although this method is very popular, it has some disadvantages [22]. One of the main drawbacks is the high miss detection which can reach 30% [23]. It also shows high positive and high negative detection. In some cases, it cannot detect if the tumor size is too small. It also can't detect malignant and benign tumors. Also it is very painful for the patients harmful for human tissue and cannot be used on patients under 40 years old [24].

2.2 Magnetic Resonance Imaging

Magnetic resonance imaging (MRI) has recently been recommended by the American Cancer Society (ACS) to screen women at very high risk of breast cancer [25]. Though highly sensitive, MRI is costly and may carry risks from the required contrast media [26]. MRI for breast cancer screening has also been characterized by lower specificity compared to mammography with a higher rate of false positives, misdetection leading to further follow up MRI and image guided biopsy costs [27]. A study done by Leach *et al.* reported MRI specificity is about 81%, compared to 93% specificity in mammography [28]. Griebsch *et al.* [27] reported MRI a almost four times more recalls than mammography for women with high familial breast cancer risk, and 70% of the recalls did not involve cancer. Because of lower specificity and higher cost, compared to mammography, MRI may not be optimal for breast cancer screening. In a study performed on women with a high risk factor for cancer, over 15%, the sensitivity of MRI was estimated to be 71.1%, compared to 40% for mammography and 17.8% for clinical breast examination [19]. The problem with MRI, however, is its associated cost and relative low amount of units globally.

2.3 Ultrasound

Ultrasound is an attractive supplement to mammography because it is widely available, relatively inexpensive and well-tolerated by patients [30]. Early reports using high-resolution ultrasound for breast cancer detection have shown promising results [31-34], but to detect non palpable tumors by this technique required high skill and longer time and that is why the technique is not used [35,36]. Berg *et al.* [37] also noted that the lack of uniformity and shortage of qualified personnel limit wide implementation of hand held imaging. Previous studies have shown that 3D Automated Whole Breast Ultrasound (AWBU) is feasible [38]. Wenkel E *et al.* has shown that 3D AWBU has excellent inter observer variability with 2D benign and malignant lesions [39]. However, the main disadvantage is its disability to produce high resolution for deep and condensed tissue structure such as fatty tissues [40]

2.4 Full UWB Imaging

Microwave Imaging is an emerging technique for several biomedical imaging applications. Microwave signals are non-ionizing form of electromagnetic waves and thus do not incur health hazard when used at low levels. The main question regarding the efficiency of UWB microwave imaging for breast cancer detection is its accuracy. In recent years, there have been developed some technique include, confocal [41], beam forming [42], time reversal [43], and Distorted Born Iterative Method (DBIM) [44]. Microwave detection is less expensive and safer than other forms of detection and also noninvasive. For these reasons, this method has been increasingly recommended as a regular examination and detection tool for early breast cancer detection.

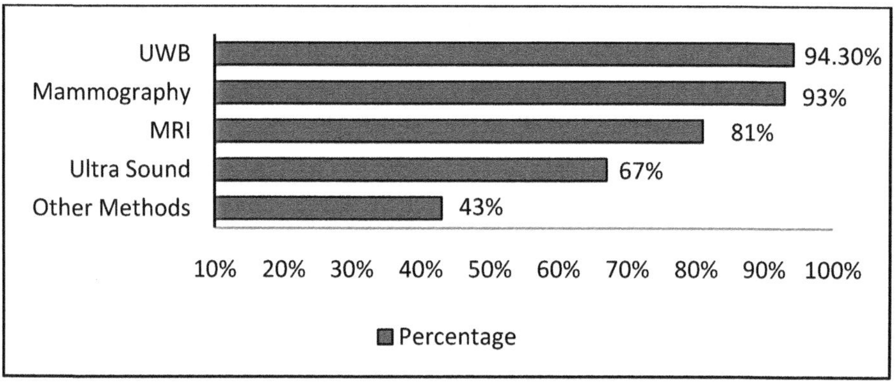

Fig. 3. Performance of Techniques

In Fig.3. comparison of the detection performance along various techniques is presented. Although UWB shows better results than the other techniques but it required clinical trials to prove its specificity as so far it is only under research and investigation stage.

3 Major Role of UWB Imaging to Detect Early Breast Tumor

Over the past few years, several research groups have been working on both hardware and software aspects of microwave breast imaging to take advantage of the high contrast of healthy and malignant tissue at microwave frequencies. The reason for the high contrast between malignant and normal tissue can be better understood through a brief examination of the frequency dependant electrical properties of biological tissue [45-47]. Several microwave imaging techniques have been suggested, including microwave tomography and confocal imaging.

The original mono static Delay-And-Sum (DAS) beam former is based on the confocal microwave imaging approach. In a Monostatic beam former, a UWB microwave signal illuminates the breast and microwave energy scattered by potential tumor sites are recorded by the transmitting antenna array element. R. H. T. Bates *et al.* [48] by applied the CLEAN algorithm [49] to process the received signals at each sensor, to resolve the Impulse Response (IR) components can be successfully resolved. The locations and scattering strengths of dominant scatters are then estimated based on the Time Of Arrival (TOA) data fusion concept. Simulation results have indicated the feasibility of detecting a tumor of 2 mm at depth of 2 cm. The DAS beam former involves time-shifting and summing the backscattered signals from the breast to create a synthetic focus. If a tumor exists at a specific focal point, then the returns from the tumor site will add coherently. Returns from clutter due to variations in tissue types will add incoherently, and therefore will be suppressed [50]. The first Multistatic DAS beamformer, where the breast is illuminated by each antenna sequentially and the backscatter energy is recorded at all antenna array elements developed [51]. The increased number of recorded channels reflected outwards via various propagation paths through the tissue, acquires more information about scatterers in the breast. The Traditional DAS (TDAS) beamformer by introducing an additional weighting factor, called the Quality Factor (QF), which is a measure of the coherence of UWB backscattering at a particular focal point within the breast [52]. Another variant of the DAS beamformer is the Delay-Multiply-and-Sum (DMAS) beamformer developed in [53]. Multiple antennas and focusing algorithm were used to form a spatial image of reflectivity, and to identify the presence and location of malignant lesions from their scattering signatures. The method was demonstrated by successful detection of a 2 mm diameter tumor in a 3-D numerical breast model. Three homogeneous and seven heterogeneous breast phantoms are designed with a series of dielectric permittivity and variability has been demonstrated, where soy bean oil [54] and flour-oil-saline mixture [55] had been used to simulate breast tissue in UWB imaging experiments. Successful detection of tumor simulants of 4 mm and 10 mm diameter are reported in the respective experiments [56]. The TSAR algorithm uses simple clutter reduction methods; however, tumors of 4 mm can be detected in a 3-D cylindrical breast model [57]. S. Kubota *et.al*, reported the Gaussian monocycle pulse with 15 GHz centre frequency, emitted from bow-tie antenna array which was fabricated on a Si chip (SC), and reflected back to the antenna array is presented [58]. Salvador and Vecchi [59] presented experiments using high dielectric homogeneous breast phantom made of flour-water mixture and coupling medium of alcohol. The Perfect Matched Layer Absorption Boundary Condition (PML ABC) is adopted by Xia Xiao *et al.* [60], where the author had investigated influence of dielectric properties from the skin, breast gland and the chest wall for breast cancer detection by UWB imaging. A simple breast phantom formed by a circular plastic container filled with a vegetable oil and plastic straws filled with water taken as an example to reduce the effect of the air-imaged body interface [61]. A Flexible UWB (FUWB) pulse generator is capable of generating a large set of pulses which is useful in screening systems for the detection of small size anomalies in breasts. UWB microwave signals can theoretically be used to detect breast tumors as small as 2 mm [62]. Recently, AlShehri *et al.* proposed a simple feed-forward back-propagation Neural Network (NN) model which successfully detected up to 0.25cm tumor [63]. In 2011 they used frequency 4.7 GHz and detected tumor size 100 μm in CST simulation and 1 mm in experiment [64]. In 2009, Yusoff *et al.* proposed absorption loss model of UWB signal by the body (Breast) tissue, which is very useful to determine the propagation range of UWB signal through the breast tissue [65].

Current UWB imaging using NN has some limitations. UWB imaging technique is unable to detect and locate very small sized tumor and it need more dimensionality [63]. Extracting useful information from the received signal is also another challenging task. Pattern Recognition tool like NN may turn to a solution but still choosing the right feature vector is important. Also, a variety of UWB antenna and antenna arrays had also been extensively studied to improve the collection of backscattered signals [51]. These algorithms provided good results under certain conditions, but most are not efficient in terms of computation time. Similarly, more complex antenna structures (and arrays) increase cost and complexity of the system. Hence to achieve accurate detection of tumor size and location using a simple antenna and Discrete Cosine Transformer (DCT) is a challenge in recent years. Research has to be done to make a better system which use UWB signal to detect early breast cancer efficiently. In all the systems there are no pictorial 3D representations of the tumor size. The work needed to be conducted in real time with real patients in terms of clinical test.

4 Comparison between Various Methods

Table 1. Comparison with Frequency and Tumor size

Techniques	Used Frequency Band (GHz)	Tumor Size Detected in diameter (mm)
X. Li (2001) (52)	1 Hz	2.5 mm
J.M. Sill (2005) (57)	4 GHz	20 mm
Yifan Chen (2006) (48)	6 GHz	2 mm
Bond (2006) (67)	11 GHz	2 mm
X. Zhuge (2007) (66)	5.5 GHz	2 mm
S. Kubota (2008) (58)	15 GHz	20 mm
M. Klemm (2008) (51)	9 GHz	2 mm
Xia Xiao (2009) (60)	6 GHz	6 mm
Wee Chang Khor (2009) (68)	3.1 GHz	5 mm
S. A. AlShehri (2009)(63)	4 GHz 8 GHz	2.5 mm 3 mm
S. A. AlShehri (2011) (64)	4.7 GHz	100 μm in simulation and 1 mm in experiment

A comparison between the techniques in terms of frequency and tumor size is presented in Table 1. It can be seen the UWB technique which used 4.7 GHz [64] can detect the tumor size up to 1 mm. The tumor detection delay among different methods [41, 49, 53, 59, 63, 64, 66, 67, 68] shown in Fig.4 reviles that Lim *et al* (2008) by using beam forming algorithm could detect the tumor in the shortest time (0.025 ns). However, reducing the number of antennas to detect the tumor is also one of the important task in the breast cancer.

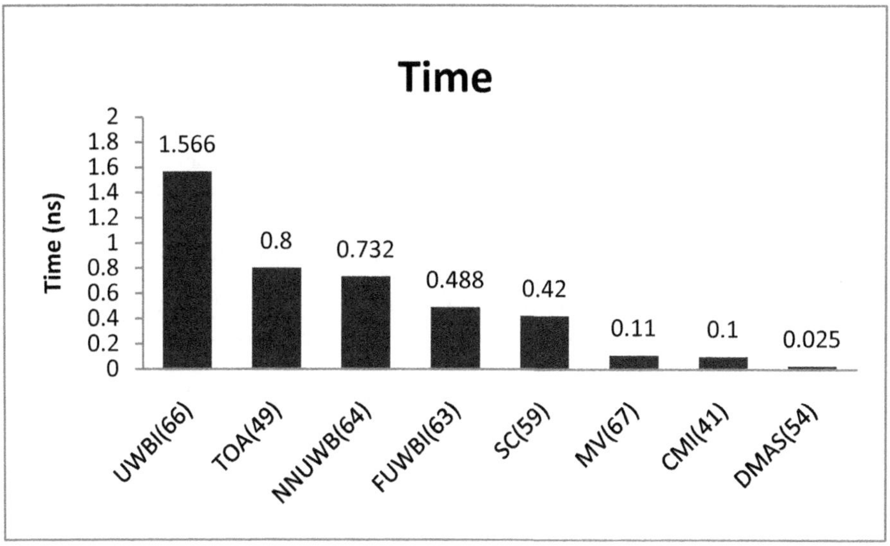

Fig. 4. Comparison of detection Time

5 Conclusion

An investigation details on early breast tumor detection and related techniques is presented in this paper with open issues. Advantages and disadvantages have been described. The result of the different author's has been shown in perspective of detection time, frequency and tumor size. To overcome the limitations of the above mentioned short comings, it was found that UWB technique is the appropriate for the detection because it is non ionizing, does not require breast compression, is less invasive than x-rays, and is low cost. The open issues are to investigate a new UWB imaging technique for early breast cancer detection to reduce dimensionality and enhance the NN system through a real time experiment.

References

1. Globocan 2002: Cancer Incidence, Mortality and Prevalence Worldwide. IARC Cancer Base No. 5. version 2.0. IARC Press, Lyon (2004)
2. Gail, M.H., Brinton, L.A., Byar, D.P.: Projecting individualized probabilities of developing breast cancer for white females who are being examined annually. J Natl. Cancer Inst. 81, 1879–1886 (1989)

3. Seidman, H., Stellman, S.D., Mushinski, M.H.: A different perspective on breast cancer risk factors: some implications of the non attributable risk. CA Cancer J. Clin. 32, 301–313 (1982)
4. Jemal, A., Siegel, R., Ward, E., Hao, Y., Xu, J., Murray, T., Thun, M.J.: Cancer Statistics. CA Cancer J. Clin. 58, 71–96 (2008)
5. Breast Health Information Center, `http://www.radiologymalaysia.org/breasthealth/about/FactsNStats.html`
6. Nass, S.L., Henderson, I.C., Lashof, J.C.: Mammography and Beyond: Developing Technologies for the Early Detection of Breast Cancer. Institute of Medicine, National Academy Press, Washington, DC (2001)
7. Bird, R.E., Wallace, T.W., Yankaskas, B.C.: Analysis of cancers missed at screening mammograph. Radiology 184, 613–617 (1992)
8. Hall, F.M., Storella, J.M., Silverstone, D.Z., Wyshak, G.: Non-palpable breast lesions: Recommendations for biopsy based on suspicion of carcinoma at mammography. Radiology 167, 353–358 (1988)
9. Bird, R.E., Wallace, T.W., Yankaskas, B.C.: Analysis of cancers missed at screening mammograph. Radiology 184, 613–617 (1988)
10. Elmore, J.G., Barton, M.B., Moceri, V.M., Polk, S., Arena, P.J., Fletche, S.W.: Ten-year risk of false positive screening mammograms and clinical breast examinations. New Eng. J. Med. 338, 1089–1096 (1998)
11. Lehman, C.D., Gatsonis, C., Kuhl, C.K., Hendrick, R.E.: MRI evaluation of the contra lateral breast in women with recently diagnosed breast cancer. New Eng. J. Med. 356, 1295–1303 (2007)
12. Viehweg, P., Paprosch, I., Strassinopoulou, M., Heywang Kobrunner, S.H.: Contrast enhanced magnetic resonance imaging of the breast: Interpretation guidelines. Top. Magn. Reson. Imag. 9, 17–43 (1998)
13. Kacl, G.M., Liu, P.F., Debatin, J.F., Garzoli, E., Caduff, R.F., Krestin, G.P.: Detection of breast cancer with conventional mammography and contrast-enhanced MR imaging. Eur. Radiol. 8, 194–200 (1998)
14. Staren, E.D., O'Neill, T.P.: Breast ultrasound. Surg. Clin. North Amer. 78, 219–235 (1998)
15. Shapiro, S., Venet, W., Strax, P., Venet, L., Roeser, R.: Ten to 14-year effect of screening on breast cancer mortality. J. Natl. Cancer Inst. 69, 349–355 (1982)
16. Mandelson, M.T., Oestreicher, N., Porter, P.L., et al.: Breast density as a predictor of mammographic detection: comparison of interval- and screen detected cancers. J. Natl. Cancer Inst. 92, 1081–1087 (2000)
17. Dean, J.C., Ilvento, C.C.: Improved cancer detection using computer-aided detection with diagnostic and screening mammography: Prospective study of 104 cancers. Am. J. Roentgenol. 187, 20–28 (2006)
18. Ho, W.T., Lam, P.W.T.: Clinical performance of computer-assisted detection (CAD) system in detecting carcinoma in breasts of different densities. Clin. Rad. 58, 133–136 (2003)
19. Pisano, E.D., Gastonis, C., Hendrick, E., et al.: Diagnostic performance of digital versus film mammography for breast cancer screening. N. Engl. J. Med. 353, 1–11 (2005)
20. Boyd, N.F., Guo, H., Martin, L.J., et al.: Mammographic density and the risk and detection of breast cancer. N. Engl. J. Med. 356, 227–236 (2007)
21. Bird, R.E., Wallace, T.W., Yankaskas, B.C.: Analysis of cancers missed at screening mammography. Radiology 184, 613–617 (2007)

22. Birdwell, R.L., Ikeda, D.M., O'Shaughnessy, K.F., Sickles, E.A.: Mammographic characteristics of 115 missed cancers later detected with screening mammography and the potential utility of computer-aided detection. Radiology 219, 192–202 (2001)
23. Huynh, P.T., Jarolimek, A.M., Daye, S.: The false-negative mammogram. Radiograph 18, 1137–1154 (1998)
24. Saslow, D., Boetes, C., Burke, W., et al.: American Cancer Society guidelines for breast screening with MRI as an adjunct to mammography. CA Cancer J. Clin. 57, 75–89 (2007)
25. Lin, S.P., Brown, J.J.: MR contrast agents: physical and pharmacologic basics. J. Magn. Reson. Imaging 25, 884–899 (2007)
26. Griebsh, I., Brown, J., Boggis, C., et al.: Cost-effectiveness of screening with contrast enhanced magnetic resonance imaging vs X-ray mammography of women at a high familial risk of breast cancer. Br. J. Cancer 95, 801–810 (2006)
27. Leach, M.O., Boggis, C.R., Dixon, A.K., et al.: Screening with magnetic imaging and mammography of a UK population at high familial risk of breast cancer: A prospective mluticentre cohort study (MARIBS). Lancet 365, 1769–1778 (2006)
28. Kriege, M., Brekelmans, C.T., Boetes, C., et al.: Efficacy of MRI and mammography for breast cancer screening in women with a familial or genetic predisposition. N. Engl. J. Med. 351, 427–500 (2004)
29. Liberman, L., Feng, T.L., Dershaw, D.D., Morris, E.A., Abramson, A.F.: US guided core breast biopsy: use and cost effectiveness. Radiology 208, 717–723 (1998)
30. Parker, S.H., Jobe, W.E., Dennis, M.A., et al.: US guided automated large core breast biopsy. Radiology 187, 507–511 (1993)
31. Benson, S.R., Blue, J., Judd, K., Harman, J.E.: Ultrasound is now better than mammography for the detection of invasive breast cancer. Am. J. Surg. 188, 381–385 (2004)
32. Berg, W.A., Gutierrez, L., Nessaiver, M.S., et al.: Diagnostic accuracy of mammography, clinical examination, US, and MR imaging in preoperative assessment of breast cancer. Radiology 233, 830–849 (2004)
33. Crystal, P., Strano, S.D., Shcharynski, S., Koretz, M.J.: Using sonography to screen women with mammographically dense breasts. Am. J. Roentgenol. 181, 177–182 (2003)
34. Buchberger, W., DeKoekkoik-Doll, P., Springer, P., Obrist, P., Dunser, M.: Incidental findings on sonography of the breast: clinical significance and diagnostic workup. Am. J. Roentgenol. 173, 921–927 (1999)
35. Kopans, D.B.: Breast cancer screening with ultrasonography. Lancet 354, 2096–2097 (1999)
36. Berg, W.A., Blume, J.D., Cormack, J.B., et al.: Combined screening with ultrasound and mammography vs. mammography alone in women at elevated risk of breast cancer. JAMA 299, 2151–2163 (2008)
37. Destounis, S., Young, W., Hanson, S., Somerville, P., Murphy, P., Zuley, M.: Automated Breast Ultrasound: A Pilot Study. Radiological Society of North America scientific assembly and annual meeting program. Radiological Society of North America, Oak Brook (2005)
38. Wenkel, E., Heckmann, M., Heinrich, M.: Automated breast ultra-sound: lesion detection and BI-RADSclassification–a pilot study. Rofo 9, 804–808 (2008)
39. Kaplan, S.S.: Clinical utility of bilateral whole-breast US in the evaluation of women with dense breast tissue. Radiology 221, 641–649 (2001)
40. Crystal, P., Strano, S.D., Shcharynski, S., Koretz, M.J.: Using sonography to screen women with mammographically dense breasts. Am. J. Roentgenol. 181, 177–182 (2003)

41. Fear, E.C., Li, X., Hagness, S.C., Stuchly, M.A.: Confocal microwave imaging for breast cancer detection: Localization of tumors in three dimensions. IEEE Transactions on Biomedical Engineering 47, 812–812 (2002)
42. Davis, S.K., Bond, E.J., Hagness, S.C., Van Veen, B.D.: Microwave imaging via space-time beamforming for early detection of breast cancer: beamformer design in the frequency domain. Journal of Electromagnetic Waves and Application 17, 357–381 (2003)
43. Kosmas, P., Rappaport, C.M.: FDTD-based time reversal for microwave breast cancer detection-localization in three dimensions. IEEE Trans. Microwave Theory Tech. 54, 1921–1927 (2006)
44. Winters, D.W., Shea, J.D., Kosmas, P., Van Veen, B.D., Hagness, S.C.: Three-dimensional microwave breast imaging: dispersive dielectric properties estimation using patient-specific basis functions. IEEE Trans. Med. Imag. 28, 969–981 (2009)
45. Joines, W.T., Jirtle, R.L., Rafal, M.D., Schaefer, D.J.: Microwave power absorption differences in normal and malignant tissue. Int. J. Radiat. Oncol. Biol. Phys. 6, 681–687 (1980)
46. Meaney, P.M., Paulsen, K.D., Chang, J.T., Fanning, M.W., Hartov, A.: Non active antenna compensation for fixed-array microwave imaging: art II - Imaging results. IEEE Trans. Medical Imaging 18, 508–518 (1999)
47. Fear, E.C., Meaney, P.M., Stuchly, M.A.: Microwaves for breast cancer detection? IEEE Potentials 22, 12–18 (2003)
48. Chen, Y., Gunawan, E., Kim, Y., Low, K., Soh, C.: UWB Microwave Imaging for Breast Cancer Detection: Tumor/Clutter Identification Using a Time of Arrival Data Fusion Method. In: IEEE Antennas and Propagation Society International Symposium (2006)
49. Bates, R.H.T., McDonnell, M.J.: Image Restoration and Reconstruction Oxford Eng. Science Series. Clarendon Press, Oxford (1986)
50. Hagness, S.C., Taflove, A., Bridges, J.E.: Two-dimensional fdtd analysis of a pulsed microwave confocal system for breast cancer detection: Fixed focus and antenna array sensors. IEEE Transactions on Biomedical Engineering 45, 1470–1479 (1998)
51. Klemm, M., Craddock, I., Leendertz, J., Preece, A., Benjamin, R.: Improved delay-and-sum beam forming algorithm for breast cancer detection. International Journal of Antennas and Propagation 2008, 9 (2008)
52. Li, X., Hagness, S.C.: A confocal microwave imaging algorithm for breast cancer detection. IEEE Microw. Wireless Components Lett. 11, 130–132 (2001)
53. Lim, H.B., Nhung, N.T.T., Li, E.P., Thang, N.D.: Confocal microwave imaging for breast cancer detection: Delay-multiply and sum image reconstruction algorithm. IEEE Transactions on Biomedical Engineering 55, 1697–1704 (2008)
54. Li, X., Davis, S.K., Hagness, S.C., van der Weide, D.W., van Veen, B.D.: Microwave imaging via space-time beamforming: Experimental investigation of tumor detection in multi-layer breast Phantoms. IEEE Transactions on Microwave Theory and Techniques 52, 1856–1865 (2004)
55. Sill, J.M., Fear, E.C.: Tissue sensing adaptive radar for breast cancer detection I Experimental investigation of simple tumor models. IEEE Transactions on Microwave Theory and Techniques 53, 3312–3319 (2005)
56. Lai, J.C.Y., Soh, C.B., Gunawan, E., Low, K.S.: UWB Microwave Imaging For Breast Cancer Detection I Experiments With Heterogeneous Breast Phantoms. Progres. Electro magnetics Research M 16, 19–29 (2011)
57. Sill, J.M., Williams, T.C., Fear, E.C.: Tissue sensing adaptive radar for breast tumor detection: investigation of issues for system implementation. In: Int. Zurich Electromagnetic Compatibility Symp., Zurich, Switzerland, vol. 53, pp. 71–74 (2005)

58. Kubota, S., Xiao, X., Sasaki, N., Kimoto, K., Moriyama, W., Kikkawa, T.: Experimental Confocal Imaging for Breast Cancer Detection Using Silicon on-Chip UWB Micro antenna Array. In: Antennas and Propagation Society International Symposium, pp. 1–4 (2008)
59. Salvador, S.M., Vecchi, G.: Experimental tests of microwave breast cancer detection on phantoms. IEEE Transactions on Antennas and Propagation 57, 1705–1712 (2009)
60. XiaoI, X., Liu, X., Liu, B.: Study on Microwave Imaging for the Early Breast Cancer Detection by FDTD with PML Boundary Condition. In: International Conference on Future Biomedical Information Engineering (2009)
61. Bialkowski, M.E.: Ultra Wideband Microwave System with Novel Image Reconstruction Strategies for Breast Cancer Detection. In: Proceedings of the 40th European Microwave Conference (2011)
62. Cutrupi, M., Crepaldi, M., Casu Mario, R., Graziano, M.: A Flexible UWB Transmitter for Breast Cancer Detection Imaging Systems. In: Proceedings of the Conference on Design, Automation and Test in Europe (2010)
63. AlShehri, S.A., Khatun, S.: UWB imaging for breast cancer detection using neural network. Progress In Electromagnetic Research C 7, 79–93 (2009)
64. AlShehri, S.A., Khatun, S., Jantan, A.B., Raja Abdullah, R.S.A., Mahmood, R., Awang, Z.: Experimental Breast Tumor Detection Using NN-Based UWB Imaging. Progress In Electromagnetics Research 111, 447–465 (2011)
65. Yusoff, N.I.M., Khatun, S., AlShehri, S.A.: Characterization of Absorption Loss for UWB Body Tissue Propagation Model. In: Proceedings of the 2009 IEEE 9th Malaysia International Conference, Malaysia (2009)
66. Zhuge, X., Hajian, M., Yarovoy, A.G., Ligthart, L.P.: Ultra-Wideband Imaging for Detection of Early Stage Breast Cancer. In: Proceedings of the 4th European Radar Conference, Munich, Germany (2007)
67. Bond, E.J., Van Veen, B.D., Hagness, S.C.: Multiple Window Based Ultra-wide band Microwave Imaging for Early-Stage Breast Cancer Detection. Sensor Array and Multichannel Processing (2006)
68. Khor, W.C., Bakar, A.A., Bialkowski, M.E.: Investigations into Breast Cancer Detection using Ultra Wide Band Microwave Radar Technique. In: Microwave Conference, APMC (2009)

Learning Automata-Based Reservation Scheme for Channel Allocation in Wireless Networks

Sudip Misra[1], P. Venkata Krishna[2], and V. Saritha[2]

[1] School of Information Technology,
Indian Institute of Technology, Kharagpur, India
sudip_misra@yahoo.com
[2] VIT University, Vellore, India
parimalavk@gmail.com

Abstract: In this paper, we propose a learning automata (LA) based channel reservation scheme, which determines the optimal number of reserved channels in a wireless network. The proposed scheme is tested on two different models named as Single Traffic No Queues (STNQ) with LA and Single Traffic With Queues (STWQ) using LA. STNQ deals with two types of calls as originating calls and handoff calls but maintain any queue for any type of call. STWQ deals with single traffic like real time or non-real time and maintains queue for both originating and handoff calls. These proposed algorithms are based on distributed dynamic channel allocation policies. Channel allocation based on the type of the cell and the user mobility increases the performance of the systems further. The results show that the proposed systems performance is better when compared to the bequest systems.

Keywords: dynamic channel allocation, cellular networks, bandwidth reservation.

1 Introduction

The available wireless network bandwidth needs to be used efficiently, as it scarce. In this regard, "reusability" concept, which is explained later in the paper, is applied to reuse the available channels. The channels can be reused when the cells are maintained a reuse distance, where the signal interference will not occur.

The basic channel allocation modes are fixed channel allocation procedure [3, 4], dynamic channel allocation procedure [5, 6], and hybrid channel allocation procedure [1, 2]. In fixed channel allocation scheme, the fixed number of channels is distributed to each base station. When a request for a channel arrives for a particular base station, the request is serviced, if the free channel is available; otherwise, it is blocked / dropped. The performance of this scheme is improved with the channel borrowing scheme [3]. There are two different schemes in dynamic channel allocation – distributed and centralized. Hybrid channel allocation is the combination of fixed and dynamic channel allocation.

An algorithm is proposed by Zeng et al. [12] to efficiently handle the handoffs. Priority is given by reserving some channels for handoff calls to reduce the dropping

J.J. Yonazi et al. (Eds.): ICeND 2011, CCIS 171, pp. 116–126, 2011.

probability. The author discussed about the single, multi-traffic systems, maintaining queues and modeled the system using Markov model.

Dynamic channel assignment scheme with reusability concept was proposed by Chen et al. [8]. There are huge research initiatives in effect to increase the capacity of the cellular systems. As a part of it, reuse partitioning is one of the techniques to achieve the increment in the cellular network capacity. The complete network region is partitioned and a fraction of channels are assigned permanently to each partition based on the reuse distance in dynamic channel assignment. The irregular and time-varying traffic may lead to channels assignment not to be optimum [15]. Any channel can be used by any user from different regions with co-channel interference constraints satisfied as channels are open to all incoming calls. Blocking probability can be reduced and the performance of the system can be improved by increasing the system capacity with flexible dynamic reuse partitioning provided with interference information under both uniform and non-uniform traffic distributions.

Boukerche [7] presented dynamic channel allocation protocol which is based on QoS for wireless and mobile networks. The network is divided into clusters and the base stations are assigned a group of channels based on the mutual exclusion paradigm. Reusability is done based on the three color theorem to increase the capacity of the system. The group is selected first to allocate the channel by the base station whenever required. If there is a free channel from the requested group, the call is serviced; otherwise, the call is blocked / dropped. This protocol improves the system performance by reducing the dropping probability by adjusting the number of reserved channels for handoff calls by periodically comparing the average dropping probability with the target probability.

Krishna et al. [9, 10] modified this system as each base station is assigned fixed number of channels based on the mutual exclusion paradigm to maintain reuse distance. A new parameter is introduced as reservation factor which is used to modify the number of reserved channels and is dependent on both the blocking and dropping probability. The number of reserved channels is increased when the average dropping probability increases more than the threshold value of dropping probability. Similarly, the reserved channels are decreased, when the average blocking probability increases more than the threshold value of the blocking probability. Whether the reserved channels are increased or decreased, the author selected the reservation factor such that both the average dropping probability and average blocking probability are less than their corresponding threshold values. In this scheme, the authors reserved some channels for originating calls also.

The author studied single traffic system and modeled the system using single dimensional Markov model in [9] and multi-traffic system which maintains queues for all types of calls and modeled the system using three-dimensional Markov model in [10].

In wireless networks, the continuous services need to be ensured to guarantee the quality of service [14]. Most of the channel allocation schemes do not consider the QoS as an important factor while providing services to the mobile users. Continuous QoS support is provided by distributed algorithm for dynamic channel allocation with an efficient adaptive channel reservation scheme by Boukerche et al. [13]. In congested cells, the dropping rate needs to be maintained less by reserving appropriate number of channels for handoff calls. Instead of reserving same number of channels in all the cells, it will be more appropriate if the channels are reserved based on the density of the traffic in a particular cell.

In this paper, we design a distributed dynamic channel allocation scheme with LA based Reservation (LAR) mechanism. In this scheme, LA determines the number of channels to be reserved for handoff calls. The use of LA for channel allocation is already introduced by Misra et al. [16] and we use the same approach in the LA-based channel reservation for handoff calls.

This scheme is tested on different systems – Single Traffic No Queues system (STNQ) [9] and Single Traffic With Queues system (STWQ). The comparison of the systems is given without LA implementation and with LA implementation and it is shown that the use of LA gives better performance

2 LA-Based Reservation Scheme for Channel Allocation

A comprehensive overview of LA can be found in the classic text by Narendra and Thathachar [11]. The number of reserved channels is determined by the Learning Automata based Reservation (LAR) mechanism. The automaton is stationed at every base station (BS) in the network. The input actions to the automaton are the number of reserved channels. Initially, the input action is selected randomly as all actions have equal probability. The action selected is rewarded / penalized based on the performance of the system which is dependent on the dropping probability and blocking probability. If the selected action is rewarded, the probability of the corresponding action is increased otherwise unchanged. In the next iteration, the action is selected based on the updated probabilities and the process is repeated until we obtain the optimum action whose action probability is ≈ 1, which can attain optimal blocking and dropping probabilities. This scenario is shown in Fig. 1 [16].

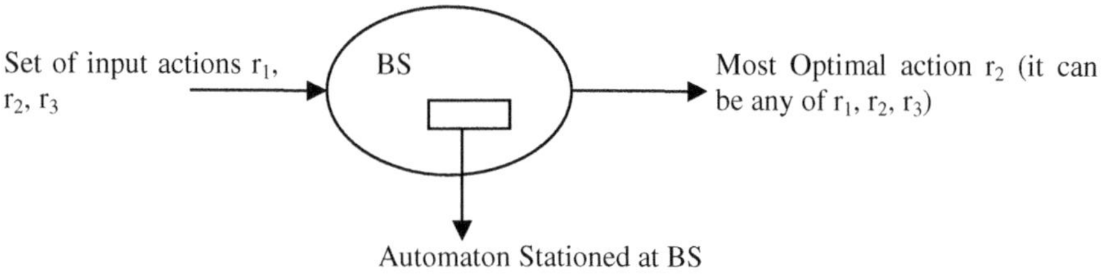

Fig. 1. BS with automaton stationed in it

Equations corresponding to the reward of the action:

$$\begin{aligned} P_{r_1}(n+1) &= P_{r_1}(n) + \frac{1}{\lambda}(1 - P_{r_1}(n)) \\ P_{r_{2,3}}(n+1) &= (1 - \frac{1}{\lambda})P_{r_{2,3}}(n) \end{aligned} \tag{1}$$

Equations corresponding to the penalty of the action:

$$P_{r_1}(n+1) = P_{r_1}(n)$$
$$P_{r_{2,3}}(n+1) = P_{r_{2,3}}(n) \tag{2}$$

The Algorithm

Inputs:
Number of Base stations
Set of actions for each BS
Number of reserved channels corresponding to each action

Output:
Optimal number of reserved channels corresponding to the action given as output of automaton

Steps:
1. Initialize the action probabilities
2. select any action randomly at every BS
3. goto 5
4. Select an action with highest probability at BS
5. if $Drop_{avg} > Drop_{th}$ then
6. penalize the selected action
7. else
8. reward the selected action
9. goto 4
10. if an action α_i probability ≈ 1 then
11. α_i is selected as optimal action

2.1 Extended Models of Traffic Systems

Two systems are discussed in this paper and are as stated below. The ideas are highly influenced by the works presented in [7], [8], [9], [10] and [17].

- Single traffic No queues system (STNQ)
- Single traffic and with queues system (STWQ)

The system with single traffic and no queues (STNQ) deals with single traffic like real time or non-real time originating and handoff calls. This system does not maintain any queue for any type of the call. This system is dealt in detail in [9]. The system with single traffic and with queues (STWQ) does not deal with real time and non-real time traffic but it maintains queues for both originating calls and handoff calls.

The complete network is divided into seven cells and all the available channels are divided into 3 groups. The number of groups is chosen to be three as this is the minimum number of groups to avoid co-channel interference. The number of groups can be divided into seven but when channels are divided into seven, reusability would be absent in this case as the number of cells is chosen to be seven. So, when the cells are more than seven, the groups of channels can be seven. In general, the number of groups is chosen based on the channel strength and co-channel interference. Three color theorem or mutual exclusion paradigm is used to distribute the groups among the base stations so that neighboring base stations will not have the same group of channels [10] as shown in the Fig 2.

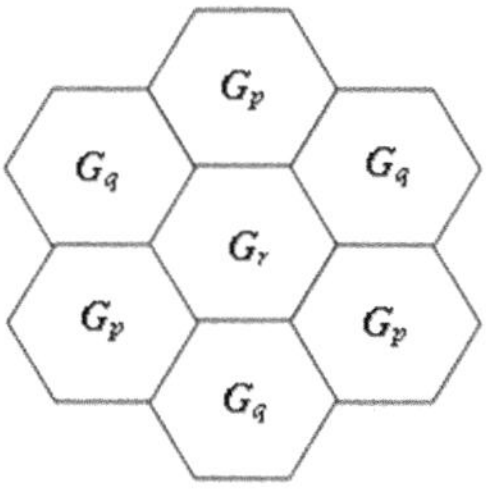

Fig. 2. Cellular network divided into seven cells and channels divided into three groups G_p, G_q, G_r

The capacity of systems is increased using reusability. Reusability makes the same channel to be used in different locations at the same time. So, the C channels in the cellular network may behave as S = (N*C)/g channels virtually, where N is the total number of cells in the cellular network, C is the total number of channels available in the network and g is the number of groups. The group allocation procedure is same for both the proposed algorithms and is based on mutual exclusion paradigm [9].

When three parameters – number of channels in the group, reserved channels and reservation factor are considered with uniform and non-uniform distribution, we obtain eight combinations [10].

These call rates influence the probability of call acceptance and it is difficult to model an exact scenario. So, some assumptions are made as follows:

- All users move at a random speed and to a random direction.
- Assume that mobile stations have GPS devices equipped in it.
- User mobility is in horizontal direction.
- All users are uniformly distributed in a cellular network.
- Let the probability of originating calls be λ_O
- Let the probability of handoff calls be λ_H
- Let the call service rate be μ

2.2 System with Single Traffic and with Queues (STWQ)

The total number of channels available are partitioned into three – CO, channels for originating calls, CC – common channels for both originating and handoff calls, CR – channels for handoff calls. STWQ system maintains individual queues for both originating calls and handoff calls. Originating calls queue Q_O length is represented as L_O and the handoff calls queue Q_H length is represented as L_H. STWQ system model is as shown in Fig. 3

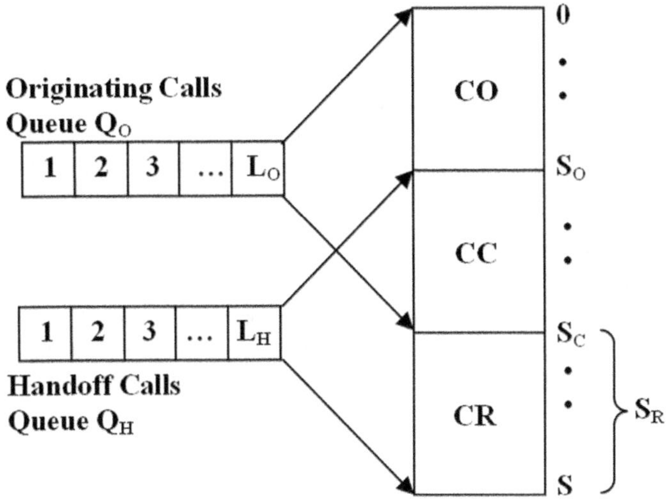

Fig. 3. System Model for STWQ System

2.2.1 Channel Allocation Procedure

1. When a call arrives at BS
2. if originating call then
    a. if free channel in CO then
        i. allocate channel in CO
    b. else
        i. if free channel in CC then
            1. allocate channel in CC
        ii. else
            1. if queue Q_o is not full
                a. call is queued
            2. else
                a. call is blocked
3. else
4. if handoff call arrives at BS
    a. if free channel in CR then
        i. allocate channel in CR
    b. else
        i. if free channel in CC then
            1. allocate channel in CC
        ii. else
            1. if queue Q_H is not full then
                a. call is queued
            2. else
                a. call is dropped
5. update group usage table
6. Exit

The type of call is verified to be originating call or handoff call arriving at a base station. When an originating call arrives at a base station, the call is served if the base station could obtain a free channel from CO or CC; otherwise, the call is queued if queue Q_O is not full. If Q_O is full, the call is blocked.

When a handoff call is arrived at a base station, the call is served if the base station could obtain a free channel from CR or CC; otherwise, the call is queued if queue Q_H is not full. If Q_H is full, the call is dropped.

2.2.2 Performance Analysis

Pair of two non-negative integers (i,j) is used to represent the state of a cell, where i is the sum of busy channels and j is the number of originating calls in queue Q_O. Two dimensional Markov chain is used to model the system. Fig. 4 shows the STWQ state diagram. Equilibrium probabilities P(i,j) are related to each other through the state balance equations. Since the sum of all state probabilities is equal to 1,

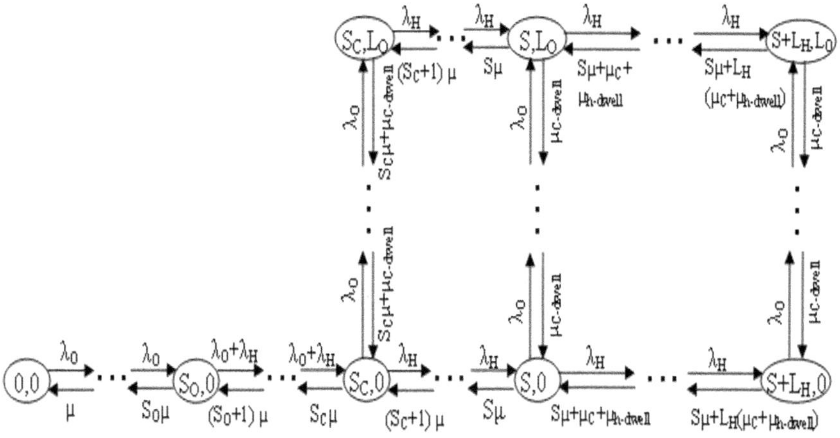

Fig. 4. State Transition Diagram for system model in Fig. 3

$$\sum_{i=0}^{S_C-1} P(i,0) + \sum_{i=S_C}^{S+L_H} \sum_{j=0}^{L_O} P(i,j) = 1 \tag{3}$$

Compute all the probabilities $P(i, j)$, where i = 0, 1, 2, …, $S + L_H$ and j = 0, 1, 2, …, L_O using SOR (successive over relation method). Based on the above $P(i, j)$'s

The Blocking Probability of Originating Calls can be given as

$$B_O = \sum_{i=S_C}^{S+L_H} P(i, L_O) \tag{4}$$

The dropping Probability of Handoff Calls can be given as

$$B_H = \sum_{j=0}^{L_O} P(S + L_H - S_O, j) \tag{5}$$

3 Results and Discussion

The results are taken from the simulation of the system by conducting various experiments and each experiment is carried out for 30 runs and the average is considered. The simulation parameters are presented in Table 1.

Table 1. Simulation parameters

Parameter	***Value***
Number of cells	7
Number of channels	30
Groups	3
Number of channels in each group – G_p, G_q, G_r (equal division)	10
Unequal channels among groups - G_p, G_q, G_r	13, 10, 7
Action values at BS (Reserved channels)	2, 3, 4
Target dropping probability	0.05
Target blocking probability	0.3

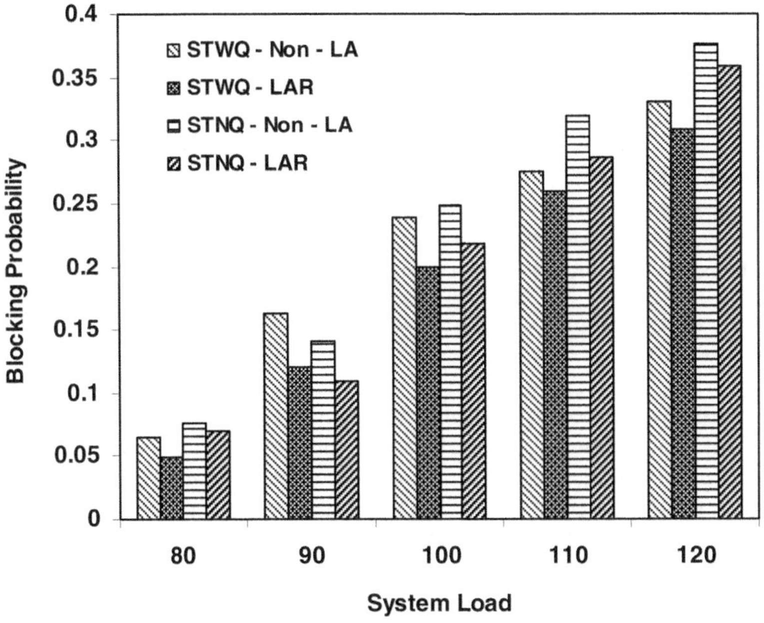

Fig. 5. Comparison of Blocking Probability for different systems (STWQ and STNQ) with and without LA

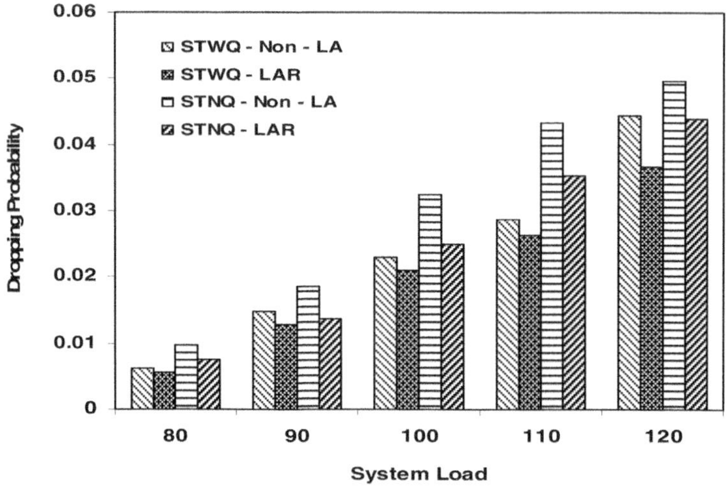

Fig. 6. Comparison of Dropping Probability for different systems (STWQ and STNQ) with and without LA

The performance of the 2 systems – STNQ and STWQ is tested using learning automata based reservation scheme and is shown in the Figs. 5 and 6. The performance of the systems in terms of blocking probability is shown in Fig. 5. The results are taken from the experiment carried out for all the combinations but the sample result is shown for the uniform distribution and non-uniform reservation factor. It can be observed that STWQ - LAR system performs well when compared with the other systems.

The performance of the systems in terms of dropping probability is shown in Fig 6. The experiment is carried out and the sample result is shown in the case of non-uniform distribution and non-uniform reservation factor.

4 Conclusions

In this paper, we proposed an LA-based channel reservation scheme which is tested on two different systems – STNQ (System with single traffic and no queues), STWQ (System with single traffic and with queues). Each system is analyzed individually using four different variations – uniform distribution and uniform reservation factor, uniform distribution and non-uniform reservation factor, non-uniform distribution and uniform reservation factor and, finally, non-uniform distribution and non-uniform reservation factor. The systems are chosen based on the requirement as they differ in cost efficiency and performance efficiency. It can be observed from the results that the behaviors of the systems are completely different from each other, i.e., when one system produces less blocking/dropping probability during non-uniform distribution and non-uniform reservation factor and the other system gives less blocking/dropping probability during uniform distribution and uniform reservation factor. Introduction of learning automata increases the performance of the system. The proposed systems are compared with and without using learning automata and are shown that the system with learning automata outperforms in case of both dropping probability and blocking probability.

References

1. Agrawal, D.P., Zeng, Q.-A.: Introduction to Wireless and Mobile Systems, 1st edn. Thomson Asia Pte Ltd., Singapore (2003)
2. Bedell, P.: Wireless Crash Course, 2nd edn. Tata McGraw-Hill, New York (2002)
3. Patra, S.S.M., Roy, K., Banerjee, S., Vidyarthi, D.P.: Improved Genetic Algortihm for Channel Allocation with Channel Borrowing in Mobile Computing. IEEE Transactions on Mobile Computing 5(7), 884–892 (2006)
4. Katzela, I., Naghshineh, M.: Channel Assignment Schemes for Cellular Mobile Telecommunication Systems: a Comprehensive Survey. IEEE Personal Communications 3(3), 10–31 (1996)
5. Kuck, S.S., Wong, W.C.: Ordered dynamic channel assignment scheme with reassignment in highway microcells. IEEE Transactions on Vehicular Technology 41, 271–277 (1992)
6. Boukerche, A., Huang, T., Abrougui, K., Williams, J.: A fault-tolerant dynamic channel allocation protocol for cellular networks. In: IEEE International Conference on Wireless Networks, Communications and Mobile Computing, pp. 342–347 (2005)
7. Boukerche, A., Huang, T., Abrougui, K.: Design and Performance Evaluation of a QoS-Based Dynamic Channel Allocation Protocol for Wireless and Mobile Networks. In: 13th IEEE International Symposium on Modeling, Analysis, and Simulation of Computer and Telecommunication Systems, pp. 445–452 (September 2005)
8. Chen, S.L., Chong, P.H.J.: Dynamic channel assignment with flexible reuse partitioning in cellular systems. In: IEEE International Conference on Communications, vol. 7, pp. 4275–4279 (2004)
9. Krishna, P.V., Iyengar, N.C.S.N.: Optimal Channel Allocation Algorithm with Efficient Channel Reservation for Cellular Networks. Int. J. Communication Networks and Distributed Systems 1(1), 33–51 (2008)
10. Krishna, P.V., Misra, S., Obaidat, M.S., Saritha, V.: An efficient approach for distributed dynamic channel allocation with queues for real time and non realtime traffic in cellular networks. Journal of Systems and Software (2009), doi:10.1016/j.jss.2009.01.043
11. Narendra, K.S., Thathachar, M.A.L.: Learning Automata. Prentice-Hall, Englewood Cliffs (1989)
12. Zeng, Q.A., Agrawal, D.P.: Modeling and Efficient Handling of Handoffs in Integrated Wireless Mobile Networks. IEEE Transactions On Vehicular Technology 51(6) (November 2002)
13. Boukerche, A., Huang, T., Abrougui, K., Williams, J.: A fault-tolerant dynamic channel allocation protocol for cellular networks. In: IEEE International Conference on Wireless Networks, Communications and Mobile Computing, pp. 342–347 (2005)
14. Krishna, P.V., Iyengar, N.C.S.N., Misra, S.: An Efficient Hash Table-Based Node Identification Method for Bandwidth Reservation in Hybrid Cellular and Ad-Hoc Networks. Computer Communications 31(4), 722–733 (2008)
15. Krishna, P.V., Misra, S., Obaidatand, M.S., Saritha, V.: Virtual Backoff Algorithm: An Enhancement to 802.11 Medium Access Control to Improve the Performance of Wireless Networks. IEEE Transactions on Vehicular Technology 59(3), 1068–1075 (2010)

16. Misra, S., Krishna, P.V., Saritha, V.: LACAV: an energy efficient channel assignment mechanism for vehicular ad hoc networks. Journal of Super Computing (2011), doi:10.1007/s11227-011-0552-1
17. Venkata Krishna, P., Misra, S., Obaidat, M.S., Saritha, V.: A New Scheme for Distributed Channel Allocation in Cellular Wireless Networks. In: Proc. of 12th ACM/SCS Communications and Networking Simulation Symposium (CNS), San Deigo, USA, March 22-27 (2009)

Modified IT-Project Management Interventions for an Increased Economic Impact

Christian Malus

University of Applied Sciences bfi Vienna, Department of Project Management, Wohlmutstrasse 22, 1020 Vienna, Austria
christian.malus@fh-vie.ac.at

Abstract. A combination of two selected qualitative research methods is a practical addition for project managers who need both: knowledge about reflections on project work and a bridge to reflective technical development in IT projects. By referring to the recently published enrichment of *refPM*, a reflective project management process model, and its application on the exemplary model Unified Process this paper shows that reflection in IT projects leads to more efficient project work. If project managers integrate these reflection activities into their projects more consciously, they will have the option to pay more attention to the economic impact of their projects because invested money is tied up in projects for a certain time and its paybacks are necessary for raising the companies' shareholder values in a long term. An empirical qualitative research study will report on this issue to show that reflection is a positive contribution especially for project oriented companies.

Keywords: IT Project Management, Process Models, Qualitative Research Methods, Knowledge Sharing, Shareholder Value.

1 Introduction

Action Research (AR) and Design Research (DR) often appear as two controversial disciplines because there are publications which see the term Design Research as the research about how to design artifacts [1], [2], [3], [4]. [1] refers to the situation that the design-science paradigm seeks to extend the boundaries of human and organizational capabilities by creating new and innovative artifacts. [3] reported on the development of a banking application where artifacts of a project have been developed, the Design Science Research Methodology has been applied for this. Furthermore [4] speaks about Design Science as the study of design. This is in contrary to researchers who see Design Research as the process of how to design research in general or how to design a new research method [5], [6]. Based on the early works of [7] in which he put forward arguments in favour of a pluralist approach to IS research, he suggested that research results will be richer and more reliable if different research methods, preferably from different (existing) paradigms, are routinely combined together. The intention of the underlying research paper is to show a deeper insight on the process on how to design artefacts as it is also described by [2] who maintains that Design Science and AR [8] share important assumptions regarding ontology and

J.J. Yonazi et al. (Eds.): ICeND 2011, CCIS 171, pp. 127–134, 2011.

epistemology. The motivation for the work in terms of a research problem is the lack of efficiency in current IS project management processes as well as the justification of this problem. The scenario in which this problem occurs will be explained when showing a deeper insight on the lacking of proper project controlling methods in the Unified Process, a (software) developing model on the one side and less *dynamic* on the other side. In this process *refPM* the author describes how it is possible to overcome the existing problem and making a more static model like the Unified Process more dynamically in terms of reacting quicker to project's environmental necessities for change. When working in projects it is always necessary to analyze (or: to reflect on) certain activities for getting sustainable success. Referring to [9] AR simultaneously assists in practical problem-solving and expands scientific knowledge, while collaboratively acting in a situation using data feedback in a cyclical process aiming at an increased understanding of change processes in social systems. In AR investigators try to fulfill the needs of their study subjects and, at the same time, generate new knowledge. One of the reasons for the emergence of AR and its subsequent use in the information systems (IS) field is the recognition that a research environment can be more deeply understood if the researcher becomes part of that environment.

In this research paper the author shows that the implementation of *refPM* [12] into an iterative software development model (UP) can be optimally used for regularly reconsidering actions (as artifacts) developed during the underlying project process and also its project environment. In a later section the economic impact of using the *refPM* model will be introduced to explain that this approach makes a positive contribution to the shareholder value of enterprises in a long term with special regard to project oriented companies. With respect to the above section and previous work of [10], [11] and [12] the combination of Action Research and Design Research has already been introduced to the scientific community to explain a solution to the above described problem.

2 The Unified Process and the Combined Interventions of Action Research and Design Research for Project Controlling Purposes

There is a need for a combination of Action Research and Design research which has been clearly defined by [13] but not exclusively by finding the similarities of both approaches but also on how the two methods can be best implemented together (or at least in addition to each other). Furthermore a project leader has the ability to choose between the described approaches in regard to each specific situation of the project process, the Unified Process project management discipline is defined as a support discipline, which is more an indication for an appendix than a well accepted methodology as proposed by the International Project Management Association (IPMA). On the other hand controlling is important in both frameworks and therefore a further missing link could be found, the project controlling. ARDR as a combination of AR and DR can be used throughout the whole development project; the four phases (inception, elaboration, construction and deployment) of the UP indicate this circumstance. In a nut shell, *ARDR* can be implemented in the project controlling sub discipline of the IPMA methology which is a better defined substitute from the original project management discipline of the UP. The implementation of *ARDR* in project controlling, integrated in the project management discipline the *refPM* model will support the project manager in a more formal way to reconsider project work than he or she has done it up to now. This *refPM* process model gives the UP approach a much more dynamic touch for future IT development projects and influences the economic result of a (project oriented) company.

3 Economic Impact on Companies: Problem Definition

The Free Cash Flow is one of the basic fundamentals to measure the increase of liquidity of a company. It is equal to the income that a firm has after subtracting costs and expenses from the total revenue: The Free Cash Flow [3] can be used for investments because it is of free disposal. It has its origin in a prior period where investments have been done and then the spending can happen in the current period. Due to the situation that project costs reduce the project's available budget, the liquidity of an enterprise will be reduced as soon as a project is officially launched. Projects are investments with a certain risk for a certain period of time: unless the project is finished successfully, there is a risk that the value of the enterprise is reduced. So regular reflections during a project also cause costs in regard to personnel, material, etc. Before or after the successful project closure there are normally paybacks from the project and inflows will raise the value of the company. In the figure below it is described how the reflections influence a project's budget and at long-sight the economic situation of a company:

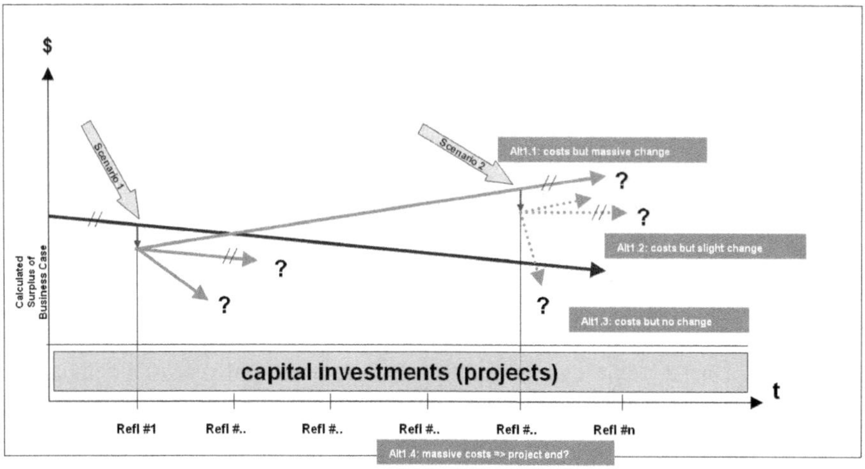

Fig. 1. Interventions & Business Issues / ARDR Interventions [14]

In figure 1 there are two scenarios described; the blue line shows the declining paybacks from the calculated Business Case which is used for reflections: at a certain point (Scenario 1) the *ARDR* reflections of the *refPM* model take place and after that the Business Case needs to be evaluated (cost could have been risen, so the Business

Case will have a curve with a more negative trend. The three grey lines show the uncertainty of this issue because after a reflection a Business Case can be calculated much more positively as it has been before the reflection. The worst situation happens when the Business Case looks like before the reflection, because in this case there were reflection costs but with no specific change. In Scenario 2 the reflections will happen for a second time and - again – there will be changes of the calculated Business Case. Finally, the more reflections take place the more will be changes of the Business Case which can have a positive effect on the future paybacks from the project or a negative impact, because when there are no or only a few reflections the project manager works with assumptions not suitable for the project. If there is no positive Business Case and the project owner did not end the project at a point earlier in the project the company may loose money which in return will reduce the company´s shareholder value.

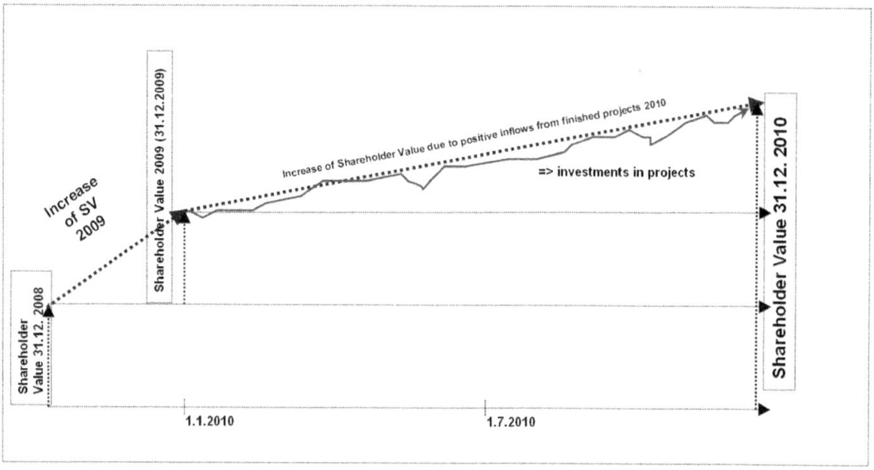

Fig. 2. Increase of Shareholder Value due to Positive Free Cash Flow from Project Activities [14]

In the above figure the shareholder value is explained in relation to the development of the paybacks from projects: the dotted blue lines describe the increase of the liquidity in 2009 and 2010; the red line below marks the Free Cash Flow. This is the sum of all financial back flows from all projects in one fiscal year of a company and describes the (financial) development of these projects throughout the year due to regular *refPM* reflections. On this figure the shareholder value is higher than in the beginning of the year so reflecting in projects has an (indirect) impact on the financial situation of a company.

4 Empirical Approach for Proving Theoretical Assumptions

4.1 Underlying Model of Empirical Research

For this research, the complete procedure model below has been developed. The author started with an overview of the complex model and sub divided it into 22 sub models:

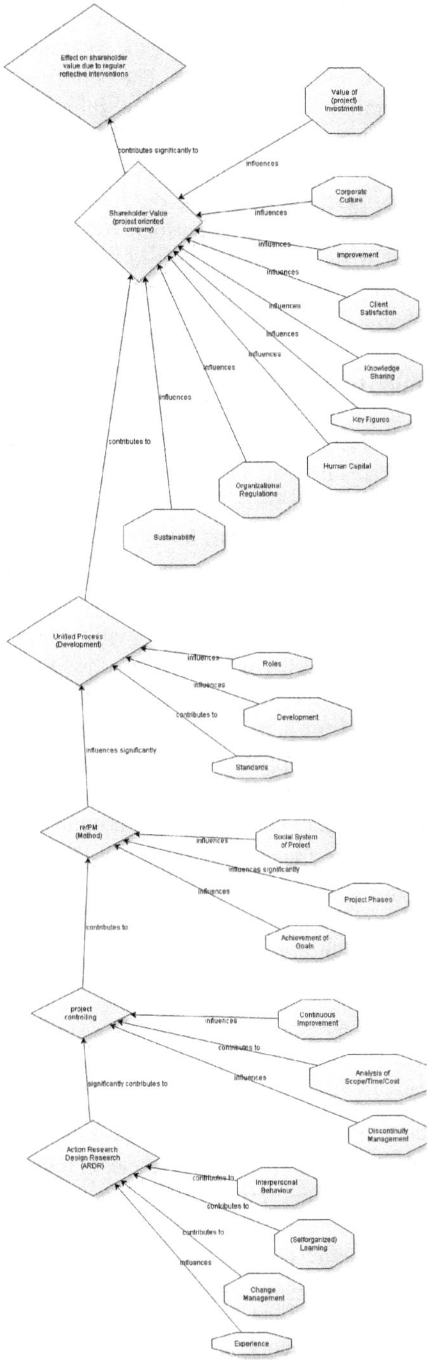

Fig. 3. *refPM*-Model (methodological approach, own design)

In the above model several sub models are combined and integrated into an overall goal: to answer the question about effects on the shareholder value due to regular reflection interventions in project (work). The interventions which have been described (ARDR) in detail in [11] and [12] are subject to the project controlling activities. These activities are embedded in the *refPM* method applied to the UP while developing software. The goal is to find out whether there are relations between reflective work on the one side and economic output on the other. The 22 sub models (which are not part of this paper) are described by clustering relevant nodes. The clusters are child nodes to the belonging parent nodes but some are parent nodes again. The parent nodes influence the top parent nodes which form the overall aim for the following empirical study.

4.2 Results from Qualitative Work

After definition of the above model and the 22 sub models, several expert interviews have been made with the result that the interviewees mentioned relevant aspects of reflections in project management.

After finishing the interviews there was a common consent that reflections in project work is necessary; neither the interviewees from academic nor the practitioner refused to accept reflections for improvement in their projects. In the study it was also subject to find out whether the conscious use of single- and double-loops for learning purposes is of relevance. Most of the interviewees agreed that learning is relevant for project work but it depends on the time project team members have during their projects. There was a clear signal for learning but the double loop approach can or should be done either in the pre-project phase or in the post-project phase. In the project phase itself there is to less time for reflecting on a formal basis with special focus on the governing values of a project. This refers to the double loop learning and the majority of the interviewees think that this should be easily done before or after a project. After the interviews there was a clear consent that (social) controlling leads to changes in business cases which will also change the financial impact on the company itself. This therefore means that the shareholder value of a company is subject to (reflective) changes in projects which can be especially observed in so-called "project oriented companies".

4.3 Further Steps

Only a few nodes of the above mentioned 22 sub models could not be loaded after the interviews and so the most relevant propositions and statements were taken for deeper research within the following quantitative research: a questionnaire will be developed for proving the opinions of the interviewees. By adding a quantitative method to the described research approach the author wants to find out whether more than 700 project leaders and other project team members agree on the interviewees´ opinions. After that the stated *refPM* approach will be subject for further research on the practical implementation in IT projects.

5 Conclusions and Further Research

Reflections during project management cause a higher cost oriented view on projects, for this reason a combination of Action Research and Design Research is needed for improving the work in specific environments, as it was introduced by [9], [2], [12] and [13]. IT Projects often last longer than they were originally planned which leads to a waste of resources and to an increase of costs and consequently to a reduction of the expected returns from this project investment. A proper controlling of projects, enriched to *refPM*, can reduce development time and costs. The consequent usage of reflections leads to the solution that developments in IT projects can be done much more effectively. A project manager developing an IT system needs to know when it is necessary to do further reflections in the projects. The lack of reflections causes uncertainty and a prolongation of projects and this further concludes in the increase of project costs and a decline of liquidity. In this paper the economic impact of modified interventions in IT project management has been explained to help project managers to contribute to the company's shareholder value. Higher paybacks from the Business Cases have a higher effect on the enterprise, e.g. expressed in higher productivity, liquidity, etc. A currently ongoing quantitative study accompanies this paper to gain further insight on the potentials of enriching project management for business reasons.

References

1. Hevner: Design Science in Information Systems Research. MIS Quarterly (2004)
2. Cole, R., Purao, S., Rossi, M., Sein, M.: Being Proactive: Where AR Meets DR. In: Avison, D., Galleetta, D., DeGross, J.I. (eds.) Proceeding of the Twenty-Sixth International Conference on Information Systems. Association for Information Systems (2005)
3. Becker, J., Weiss, B.: Developing a Business Modelling Language for the Banking Sector – A Design Science Approach. In: Proceedings of the Fifteenth Conference on Information Systems, San Francisco, California (2009)
4. Weedman, J.: Design Science in the Information Sciences. In: Encyclopedia of Library and Information Sciences, 3rd edn. (2010)
5. Gregor, S., Jones, D.: The Anatomy of a Design Theory. Journal of the Association for Information Systems 8(5), Article 2, 312–335 (2007)
6. Ivari: A Paradigmatic Analysis of Information Systems as a Design Science. Scandinavian Journal of Information Systems 19(2), 39–64 (2007)
7. Mingers: Combining IS research methods: Towards a pluralist methodology. Information Systems Research 12(3), 240–259 (2001)
8. Lück: Kurt Lewin. Beitz Taschenbuch (1996)
9. Rossi, M., Sein, M.: A proactive research approach. DR Workshop IRIS26 (2005)
10. Malus: AR and the Unified Process: Can they match? Emerging Trends and Challenges in Information Technology Management (2006a)
11. Malus: Using Process Models and Action Research for the Development of Competence Centres for Universities of Applied Sciences. In: Collaborative AR Network (Conference Paper) (2006b)

12. Malus: The Application of ARDR in IT project management as a basis for the Process Model 'REFPM'. In: 2011 ECIS European Conference of Information Systems (Conference Paper, 2011)
13. Sein, M., Henfridsson, O., Purao, S., Rossi, M., Lindgren, R.: Action Design Research. MIS Quarterly 35(2) (June 2011)
14. Malus: The Integration of Reflective Interventions in Projects as an Evaluation Model for Increased Liquidity. In: 2010 Collaborative AR Network (Conference Paper) (2010)

Management of Different Format Initial Data

Sylvia Encheva

Stord/Haugesund University College, Bjørnsonsg. 45, 5528 Haugesund, Norway
sbe@hsh.no

Abstract. Most available models and tools facilitating cooperative decision making are functional when initial data is presented in the same format. Real life situations however often require incorporation of initial data in f.ex. crisp values, interval values, and text at the same time.

In this work we apply many-valued formal concept analysis for answering queries when some of the initial data is available in text form and another part in with crisp values.

Keywords: Many-valued Galois connections, intelligent systems.

1 Introduction

A cooperative decision making usually focusses on providing sufficient information about the uncertain total payoff resulting from the final decision and at the same time improving on the individual welfare of each participant. Most available models and tools facilitating cooperative decision making are functional when initial data is presented in the same format. Real life situations however often require incorporation of initial data in crisp values, interval values, text, etc..

Parties interested to join a society for cooperative decision making are often following a Pareto optimal sharing rule, [7]. Utility functions related to that rule can be used only if the presented data, requirements, expectations, etc. are given in a form of numerical data. There is obvious need for developing effective methods for presenting different formats data in a 'unified' way that can be used as an input for f. ex. decision support systems.

One way to work out a solution to the above mentioned problem is to use the theory of the extended formal description, [10]. It is concerned with a mapping from the set of attributes to the power set of the values, assigning to each attribute the set of allowed values under some conditions. The extended formal descriptions are naturally ordered by preciseness, and then a concept lattice is obtained according to the theory of formal concept analysis [8], [21].

Many-valued Galois connections are defined with respect to similarity between attribute values in a many-valued context, [12]. In this paper we are further extending this method with respect to working with both numerical and linguistic initial data. The last due to real life occurrences where some human evaluators prefer text form for expressing their opinion and others are more comfortable with numerical values.

J.J. Yonazi et al. (Eds.): ICeND 2011, CCIS 171, pp. 135–144, 2011.

The rest of the paper is organised as follows. Section 2 contains definitions of terms used later on. Section 4 explains how to rank help functions according to personal responses. Section 5 contains the conclusion of this work.

2 Background

2.1 Approximate Reasoning Schemes

Rough Sets were originally introduced in [13]. The presented approach provides exact mathematical formulation of the concept of approximative (rough) equality of sets in a given approximation space. An *approximation space* is a pair $A = (U, R)$, where U is a set called universe, and $R \subset U \times U$ is an indiscernibility relation.

Equivalence classes of R are called *elementary sets* (atoms) in A. The equivalence class of R determined by an element $x \in U$ is denoted by $R(x)$. Equivalence classes of R are called *granules* generated by R. The following definitions are often used while describing a rough set $X, X \subset U$:

- the *R-upper approximation* of X, $R^{\star}(x) := \bigcup_{x \in U}\{R(x) : R(x) \cap X \neq \varnothing\}$
- the *R-lower approximation* of X, $R_{\star}(x) := \bigcup_{x \in U}\{R(x) : R(x) \subseteq X\}$
- the *R-boundary region* of X, $RN_R(X) := R^{\star}(X) - R_{\star}(X)$

In the rough set theory [14], objects are described by either physical observations or measurements. Consider an information system $\mathcal{A} = (U, A)$ where information about an object $x \in U$ is given by means of some attributes from A, i.e., an object x can be identified with the so-called signature of $x : Inf(x) = a(x) : a \in A$.

Approximate reasoning schemes (AR schemes) [15] are employed for approximation of specific properties of structured (complex) objects. The schemes are often presented in a tree structure where the root illustrates the satisfiability degree of a feature of a complex object and leaves show the satisfiability degrees of different features of the so called primitive objects. Every part of a structured object is connected to concepts describing its properties. A structured object is usually related to several ontologies of concepts [18] since concepts form a hierarchical structure.

Labelled approximate rules, called productions are used for constructing an AR scheme. They can be obtained from data using domain knowledge. Productions are also defined as parametrised implications with premises and conclusions built from patterns sufficiently included in the approximated concept. Concepts approximations are presented in [16] and [17]. It is assumed that it is possible to change some of the objects' properties by various actions. An action can be either defined by a set of attributes, or by training data describing objects before and after actions execution.

2.2 Concept Lattices

Let P be a non-empty ordered set. If $sup\{x, y\}$ and $inf\{x, y\}$ exist for all $x, y \in P$, then P is called a *lattice* [4]. In a lattice illustrating partial ordering of knowledge values, the logical conjunction is identified with the meet operation and the logical disjunction with the join operation.

A *context* is a triple (G, M, I) where G and M are sets and $I \subset G \times M$. The elements of G and M are called *objects* and *attributes* respectively [4], [21].

For $A \subseteq G$ and $B \subseteq M$, define

$$A' = \{m \in M \mid (\forall g \in A) \;\; gIm\},$$

$$B' = \{g \in G \mid (\forall m \in B) \;\; gIm\}$$

where A' is the set of attributes common to all the objects in A and B' is the set of objects possessing the attributes in B.

A *concept* of the context (G, M, I) is defined to be a pair (A, B) where $A \subseteq G$, $B \subseteq M$, $A' = B$ and $B' = A$. The *extent* of the concept (A, B) is A while its *intent* is B. A subset A of G is the extent of some concept if and only if $A'' = A$ in which case the unique concept of the which A is an extent is (A, A'). The corresponding statement applies to those subsets $B \in M$ which is the intent of some concepts.

The set of all concepts of the context (G, M, I) forms a complete lattice called the *concept lattice* of the context (G, M, I) and is denoted by $\mathfrak{B}(G, M, I)$.

Formal contexts are often represented by data tables where a $\times$ in the context row of o and in the context column of a means that object o has attribute a. A blanc entry however can have different meanings, f. ex. the object does not posses the attribute, information about possessing or not is irrelevant, or the relationship between o and a is unclear. Context where the last two cases occur are known as incomplete contexts.

3 Many-Valued Galois Connections

Many-valued Galois connections are discussed in [8] and [12]. Many-valued context has been recently applied in [11] for handling incomplete information. In [1] many-valued context has been applied for knowledge elicitation in case based reasoning processes. Various methods for data analysis can be found in [3] and [4] and [5].

Definition 1. *[12] Given a many-valued context (G, M, W, I) and a threshold $\theta \in [0, 1]$.*

1. *Two attribute values w_i and w_j of an attribute m are similar if and only if $|w_i - w_j| \leq \theta$.*
2. *Two objects g_i and g_j in G share an attribute m in M if and only if $m(g_i) = w_i$ and $m(g_j) = w_j$ are similar i.e. $|w_i - w_j| \leq \theta$. More precisely: g_i and g_j share $m_{[w_i, w_j]}$ (assuming that $w_i \leq w_j$). The interval $[w_i, w_j]$ is called similarity interval of m for g_i and g_j.*
3. *More generally a set of objects $S \subseteq G$ shares an attribute m whenever any two objects in A share m. The similarity interval of m for A is*

$$[\min_{g \in A}(m(g)), \max_{g \in A}(m(g))]$$

and the attribute m shared by objects in A is denoted by $m_{[\min_{g\in A}(m(g)),\max_{g\in A}(m(g))]}$.

Definition 2. *[12] A many-valued concept is a pair (A,B) where $A \subseteq G$ and $B \subseteq M \times J_\theta$ such that $A'_\theta = B$ and $B'_\theta = A$. A and B are respectively the extent and the intent of (A,B).*

Definition 3. *[12] Consider a many-valued context (G,M,W,I) and a threshold θ.*

1. *If (A_1,B_1) and (A_2,B_2) are many-valued concepts, (A_1,B_1) is a subconcept of (A_2,B_2) when $A_1 \subseteq_\theta A_2$ (which is equivalent to $B_2 \subseteq_\theta B_1$). In this case (A_2,B_2) is superconcept of (A_1,B_1) and we write $(A_1,B_1) \leq_\theta (A_2,B_2)$. The relation $\leq_\theta$ is the hierarchical order of MV concept.*
2. *The set of all MV concepts of (G,M,W,I) ordered in this way is denoted by $\mathcal{B}\theta(G,M,W,I)$ and called the many-valued concept lattice of (G,M,W,I).*

Definition 4. *[12]*

1. *A query is a set Y of weighted attributes where weights can be single values or intervals. In a many-valued concept lattice, a query is represented by a single concept (Y'_θ, Y) where Y'_θ is the set of attributes that share all attributes in Y.*
2. *An object g is relevant for a query Y whenever $g'_\theta \cap Y \neq \emptyset$ (i.e. g shares at least one of the attributes in Y).*

3.1 Pareto Optimality

Parties forming a group for cooperative decision making aim at applying a Pareto optimal sharing rule, [6] and [7], and [9]. This means using one sharing rule only where the utility of one party is increased without decreasing the utility of any other party. This however turns to be quite difficult in practice and leads to a number of Pareto non-optimal solutions, [22].

3.2 Incomplete Information

The Armstrong axioms can be applied to obtain new knowledge from incomplete information.

Armstrong axioms for arbitrary sets of attributes A, B, C and D to be applied:
If $\alpha \to \gamma$, then $\alpha \cup \beta \to \gamma$
If $\alpha \to \beta$ and $\beta \cup \gamma \to \delta$, then $\alpha \cup \gamma \to \delta$

The Armstrong axioms, [2] are sound in that they generate only functional dependencies in the closure of a set of functional dependencies (denoted as F^+) when applied to that set (denoted as F). They are also complete in that repeated application of these rules will generate all functional dependencies in the closure F^+, [2].

4 Combining Information in Text Format and Numerical Interval Data

One of the challenges in a shipbuilding process is related to issues of building of environmental friendly transport systems while improving on customers satisfaction. A holistic approach can be achieved by applying a decision support system incorporating different levels preliminary evaluations.

In this scenario six designer firms $F1, F2, F3, F4, F5, F6$ are evaluated by three experts where each expert is expressing his opinion related to a single criterion only. They submit their evaluations in different text formats. An additional criterion involving interval data is also included. The involved criteria are

- regular practice in the maritime business (RP),
- quality of design of modern vessels (DM),
- experience with platform supply vessels in years (EV), and
- focus on green ship technology (FG).

The goal is not only to rank the listed firms but to be able to provide answers to some queries as well.

Table 1 summarizes both numerical and linguistic form of evaluation. Empty cells indicate lack of data.

Table 1. Mixed evaluation of the six firms

	Regular practice RP	Quality of design DM	Years of experience EV	Green ship technology FG
F 1		moderate	EV $\geq$ 10	high
F 2	regular	very good	EV $<$ 5	medium
F 3	not that regular	very good	5 $\leq$EV $<$ 10	
F 4	regular		EV $\geq$ 10	medium
F 5	somewhat regular	good	5 $\leq$EV $<$ 10	high
F 6	regular	good	EV $\geq$ 10	

Table 2. Firms with the highest evaluation

	RP	DM	EV	FG
F 1			×	×
F 2	×	×		
F 3		×	×	
F 4	×		×	
F 5				×
F 6	×		×	

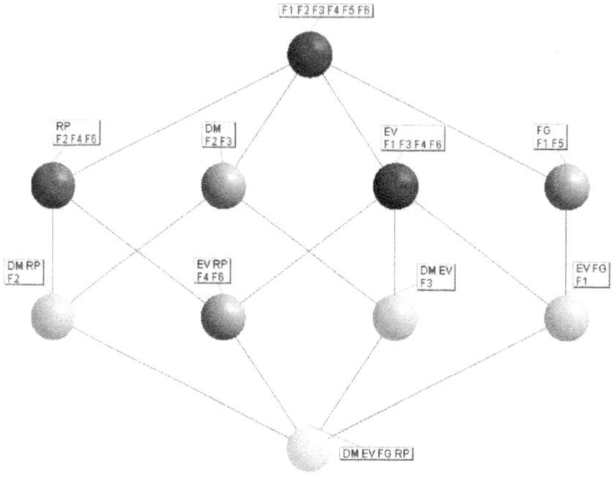

Fig. 1. Lattice of the context in Table 2

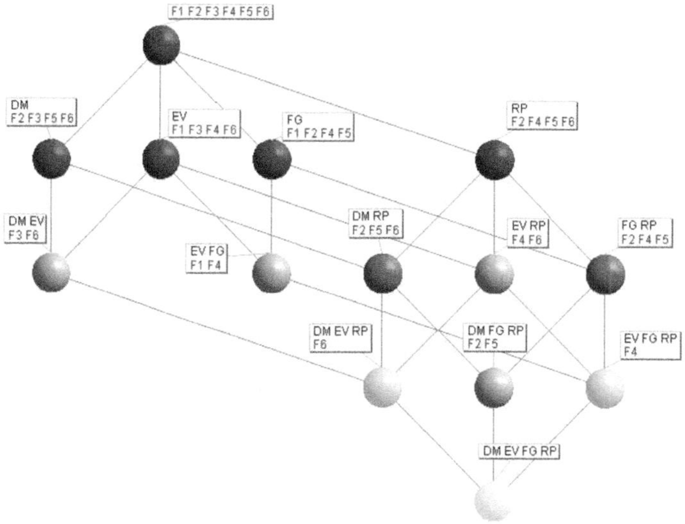

Fig. 2. Lattice of the context in Table 3

Table 2 shows which firms have received the highest evaluation with respect to the four criteria (RP), (DM), (EV), and (FG). Note that in case of removal or addition of new criteria the ranking could be considerably changed. The same effect can be expected in case of similar changes with respect to experts. The process appear to be even more complicated when changes in time have to be incorporated. A good solution to that type of problems is application of Yager's weights [20] and [19].

Table 3 shows which firms have received the highest and second highest evaluation with respect to the four criteria (RP), (DM), (EV), and (FG). Such evaluations are quite valuable to a decision maker since options receiving the highest evaluations are not always the easiest to implement.

The lattices in Fig. 1 and Fig. 2 show which firms possess certain attributes.

Information presented in Table 2 and Table 3 does not indicate to which degree an object satisfies a criterion. The initial information provided in Table 1 is normalized as in [5] as in Section 3 and presented in Table 4. In particular we first divide the available data in three levels. Each number in a cell is afterwards divided by the highest level in the respective column. The corresponding lattice can be seen in Fig 3.

The lattice in Fig. 3 can be used to find answers to queries like 'Which firms have obtained evaluation values on criteria RP and DM that are not more than $\theta = 0.4$ less than the best available?'. The answer is firms F2, F5 and F6, Fig. 4.

Such information is very useful when a ship owner has constrains on resources and time, i.e. the best services might not be available for a long period of time and or they can be far too costly.

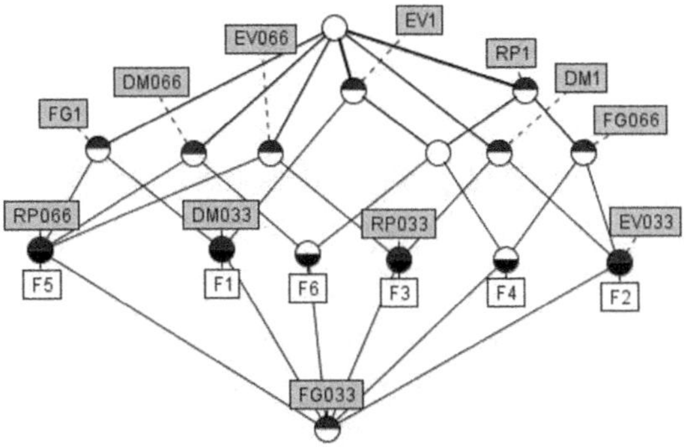

Fig. 3. Lattice of the context in Table 4

Table 3. Firms with the highest and second highest evaluation

	RP	DM	EV	FG
F 1			×	×
F 2	×	×		×
F 3		×	×	
F 4	×		×	×
F 5	×	×		×
F 6	×	×	×	

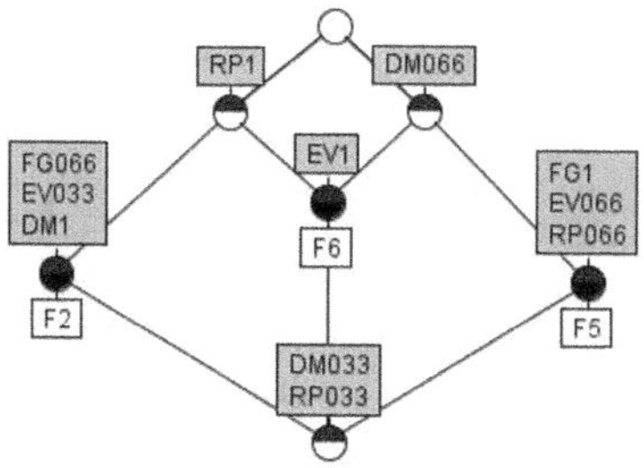

Fig. 4. Firms with good evaluations on criteria RP and DM

Table 4. Numerical results for the six firms

	RP	DM	EV	FG
F 1		0.33	1	1
F 2	1	1	0.33	0.66
F 3	0.33	1	0.66	
F 4	1		1	0.66
F 5	0.66	0.66	0.66	1
F 6	1	0.66	1	

4.1 Experts

Once the available information is presented in a consistent format we propose application of Approximate reasoning schemes (AR schemes) for achieving a final recommendation.

Suppose there are three experts taking part in a cooperative decision making process. They agree upon using linguistic form of grading - low, medium or high.

Production for concepts $C_i, i = 1, 2, 3$ is formed as a collection of simpler rules, called production rules, and is approximated by linearly ordered layers.

The presented case can be read as follows - if inclusion degree to a concept C_1 is at least low, to a concept C_2 at least low and to concept C_3 is at least medium then the inclusion degree to a concept C_4 is at least low; if inclusion degree to a concept C_1 is at least low, to a concept C_2 at least medium and to concept C_3 is at least high then the inclusion degree to a concept C_4 is at least medium; if inclusion degree to a concept C_1 is at least low, to a concept C_2 at least medium and to concept $C3$ is at least medium then the inclusion degree to a concept C_4 is at least medium. The concept from the highest level of production is called the target concept of production, whilst the concepts from the lowest level of production are called the source concepts of production. For example, in the case of production from evaluations made by Expert 1, as in Fig 5, C_4 is the target concept and C_1, C_2, and C_3 are the source concepts.

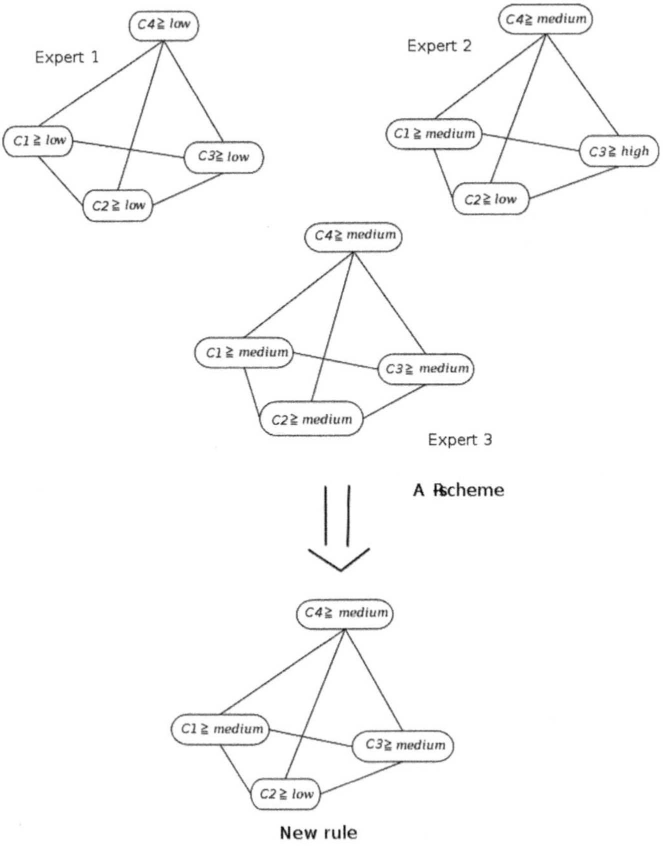

Fig. 5. Approximate reasoning scheme

The outcomes resulted from the evaluation of each expert are summarized in an AR-scheme. The final conclusion is presented as a new production rule. In this particular case it says that if $C_1 \geq$ 'medium', $C_2 \geq$ 'low' and $C_3 \geq$ 'medium', then $C_4 \geq$ 'medium'.

5 Conclusion

Application of many-valued Galois connections in contrast to formal concept analysis allows more flexible evaluations and provides inside information with respect to the degrees to which a particular object possess a particular attribute.

References

1. Daz-Agudo, B., Gonzlez-Calero, P.A.: Formal concept analysis as a support technique for CBR. Knowledge-Based Systems 14(3-4), 163–171 (2001)
2. Armstrong, W.W.: Dependency Structures of Data Base Relationships. In: IFIP Congress, pp. 580–583 (1974)

3. Carpineto, C., Romano, G.: Concept Data Analysis: Theory and Applications. John Wiley and Sons, Ltd., West Sussex (2004)
4. Davey, B.A., Priestley, H.A.: Introduction to lattices and order. Cambridge University Press, Cambridge (2005)
5. Djouadi, Y., Henri Prade, H.: Interval-Valued Fuzzy Galois Connections: Algebraic Requirements and Concept Lattice Construction. Fundamenta Informaticae 99(2), 169–186 (2010)
6. Doyle, J.: Reasoned Assumptions and Pareto Optimality. In: Proc. of the 9th IJCAI, pp. 87–90 (1985)
7. Feldman, A.M.: Welfare Economics and Social Choice Theory. Kluwer, Boston (1980)
8. Ganter, B., Wille, R.: Formal Concept Analysis. Springer, Heidelberg (1999)
9. Jia, Z., Ierapetritou, M.G.: Generate Pareto optimal solutions of scheduling problems using normal boundary intersection technique. Computers and Chemical Engineering 31, 268–280 (2007)
10. Lei, Y., Wang, Y., Cao, B., Yu, J.: Concept interconnection based on many-valued context analysis. In: Zhou, Z.-H., Li, H., Yang, Q. (eds.) PAKDD 2007. LNCS (LNAI), vol. 4426, pp. 623–630. Springer, Heidelberg (2007)
11. Liu, J., Yao, X.: Formal concept analysis of incomplete information system. In: Seventh International Conference on Fuzzy Systems and Knowledge Discovery (FSKD), pp. 2016–2020 (2010)
12. Messai, N., Devignes, M., Napoli, A., Smail-Tabbone, M.: Many-Valued Concept Lattices for Conceptual Clustering and Information Retrieval. In: Proceeding of the 2008 Conference on ECAI 2008: 18th European Conference on Artificial Intelligence. IOS Press, Amsterdam (2008)
13. Pawlak, Z.: Rough Sets. International Journal of Computer and Information Sciences 11, 341–356 (1982)
14. Pawlak, Z.: Rough Sets: Theoretical Aspects of Reasoning about Data, vol. 9. Kluwer Academic Publishers, Dordrecht (1991)
15. Polkowski, L., Skowron, A.: Rough mereological approach to knowledge-based distributed AI, Soeul, Korea, February 5-9, pp. 774–781 (1996)
16. Polkowski, L., Skowron, A.: Rough mereology: A new paradigm for approximate reasoning. International Journal of Approximate Reasoning 15(4), 333–365 (1996)
17. Polkowski, L., Skowron, A.: Rough mereology in information systems. A Case Study: Qualitative Spatial Reasoning 56, 89–135 (2000)
18. Staab, S., Studer, R. (eds.): Handbook on Ontologies. International Handbooks on Information Systems. Springer, Heidelberg (2004)
19. Yager, R.R.: OWA aggregation over a continuous interval argument with applications to decision making. IEEE Transactions on Systems, Man, and Cybernetics, Part B 34(5), 1952–1963 (2004)
20. Yager, R.R., Rybalov, A.: Noncommutative self-identity aggregation. Fuzzy Sets and Systems 85, 73–82 (1997)
21. Wille, R.: Concept lattices and conceptual knowledge systems. Computers Math. Applications 23(6-9), 493–515 (1992)
22. Woroniecka-Leciejewicz, I.: Decision interactions of the monetary and fiscal authorities in the choice of policy mix. Organisational Transformation and Social Change 7(2), 189–210 (2010)

Message Signal Encryption Based on Qi Hyper-Chaos System

Dennis Luke Owuor and Guoyuan Qi

Department of Electrical Engineering, Tshwane University of Technology,
0001 Pretoria, South Africa
dennisluke11@yahoo.com, guoyuanqi@gmail.com

Abstract. Chaotic secure communication is recently attracting large interest due to the simplicity in design and implementation over other encryption methods such as conventional methods. In this paper, Qi hyper-chaotic system is modeled and used in providing message signal encryption using Hyper Chaotic Shift Keying (HCSK) method. Simulation is carried out using MATLAB/SIMULINK. Simulink model is used because it reflects as close as possible a real scenario of practical implementation.

Keywords: Chaos, Encryption, Secure Communication, Hyper-Chaos.

1 Introduction

Mobile communication and internet networks have tremendously grown in the field of telecommunication. Associated with this swift growth, there is mounting requirement for security implementation [1].

Lately, chaos based secure communication has been proved in the literature [1-6] to be more advantageous over the conventional methods. It is unique because of its simplicity and high unpredictability which enhances its level of security [3-5].

In the literature, many chaotic secure communication methods have been presented. However, a few of them have been implemented [7-10]. This paper presents the implementation of Qi hyper-chaotic system [11-12] which is modeled and used in providing message signal encryption using HCSK method.

1.1 Qi Hyper-Chaos

Many proposed chaos-based encryption schemes have been totally or partially broken by different attacks. One reason is that the degree of randomness of simple chaotic system like lorenz and other hyperchaotic signals used therein are not high enough as compared to Qi-hyperchaos system.

Qi Hyper-chaos exits in to four-dimensional (4D) autonomous systems.

$$\begin{aligned} \dot{x}_1 &= a(x2 - x1) + x2x3 \\ \dot{x}2 &= b(x1 + x2) - x1x3 \\ \dot{x}3 &= -cx2 + ex4 + x1x2 \\ \dot{x}4 &= -dx4 + fx3 + x1x2 \end{aligned} \tag{1}$$

J.J. Yonazi et al. (Eds.): ICeND 2011, CCIS 171, pp. 145–155, 2011.

where

$xi\ (i = 1, 2, 3, 4)$: are the state variables and a, b, c, d, e, f are positive constant parameters.

Simulations of the dynamic equations using MATLAB/Simulink are given in Figs. 1 and 2.

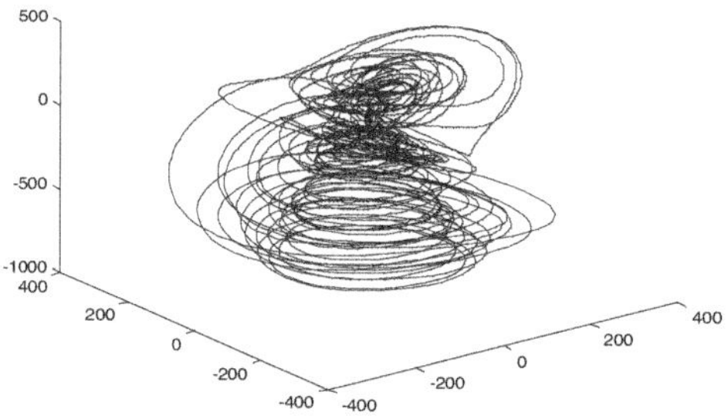

Fig. 1. 3-D view in the x_1-x_2-x_3 space of Qi hyper-chaos

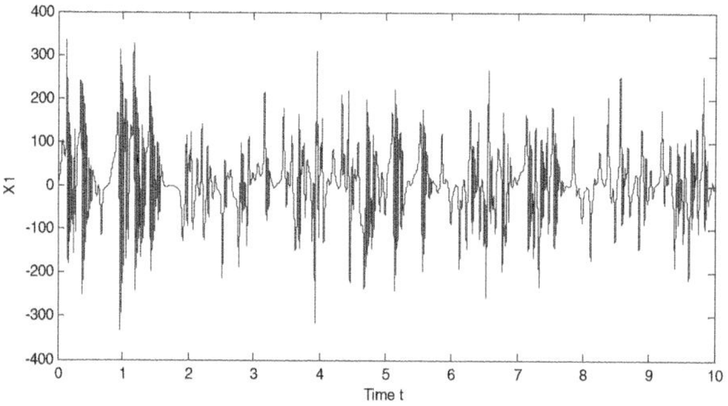

Fig. 2. The time against state $x1$ of the Qi hyper-chaotic system with $a = 50$, $b = 24$, $c = 13$, $d = 8$, $e = 33$, $f = 30$

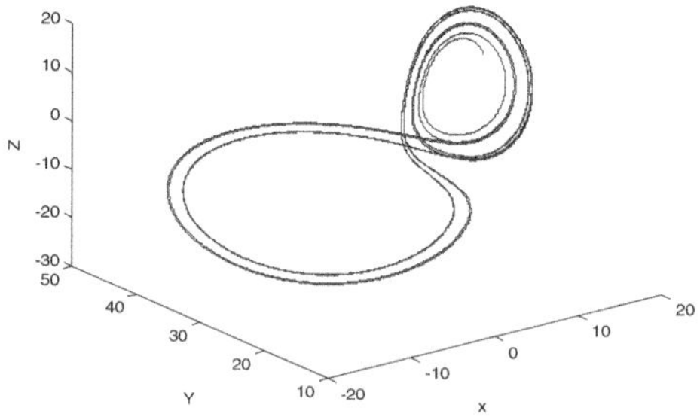

Fig. 3. 3-D view in the x_1-x_2-x_3 space of Lorenz chaotic system

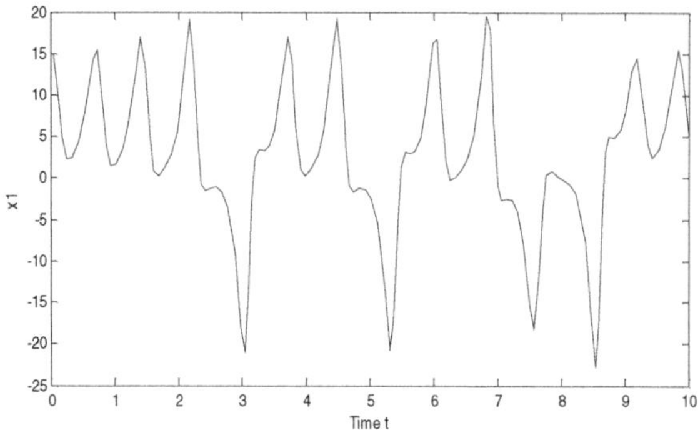

Fig. 4. Time series of x1 of Lorenz chaotic system

The basic Comparison of Qi Hyper Chaos and Lorenz Chaotic System is listed below:

- The attractor of Qi Hyper-chaotic system as shown in Fig. 1 has very irregular form, neither butterfly as the Lorenz's (see Fig. 3) that makes it more complex.
- The orbits of Qi-Hyper-chaotic systems as shown in Figs. 1 and 2 are more complicated and disordered than the Lorenz's (see Figs. 3 and 4).
- The orbits of the Qi-hyper chaos are extremely abundant and dense as compared to that of Lorenz.

Table 1. Similarity between Cryptography Properties and Chaotic properties

Cryptographic property	Chaotic Property
Pseudo-chaotic system -nonlinear transformation -finite number of state -finite number of iteration	Chaotic system -nonlinear transformation -infinite number of state - infinite number of iterations
Plaintext	Initial state
Cipher-text	Final state
Key	System parameters
Confusion	Ergodicity
Diffusion with a small change in the plaintext/secret key	Sensitivity to initial conditions/control parameter
Diffusion with a small change in one plain-block of the whole plaintext	Mixing property (topological transitivity
Algorithm complexity	Structure complexity

Based on the similarities in table 1, chaotic systems can be used to implement security during message signal communication [9].

2 Qi-Hyper-Chaos-Shift-Keying Encryption and Decryption

This is the encryption scheme where two hyper-chaotic signals are used to encrypt message signal at the sending end and at the receiving end decryption is done based on correlation technique [10].

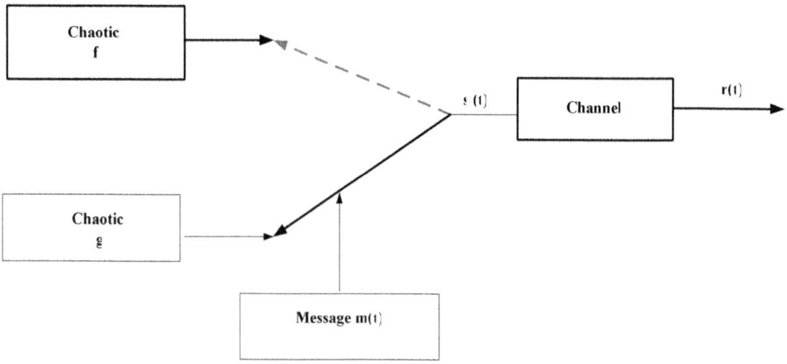

Fig. 5. Method of message m(t) encryption

Figure 5 depicts the chaos shift keying encryption where the transmitter consists of two chaos generators f and g, producing signal c (t) and c1 (t), respectively. During the l bit duration, i.e. [(l-1), lTb], if a binary “+1” is to be sent, c (t) is transmitted, and if “-1” is sent, c1(t) is transmitted.

$$s(t) = \begin{cases} c(t) & \text{when symbol "+1" is sent} \\ c1(t) & \text{when symbol "-1" is sent} \end{cases}$$

The encrypted signal $r(t)$ is sent through a channel of communication.

$$r(t)=s(t)+\xi(t). \tag{2}$$

Where $\xi(t)$ is the noise signal added to sent signal during communication.

The Decryption method is illustrated in Fig. 6.

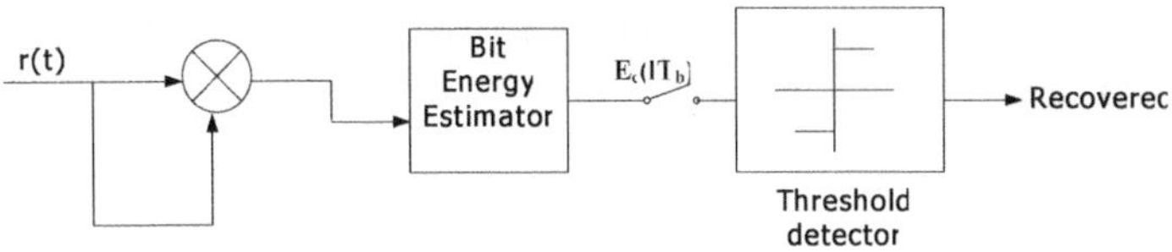

Fig. 6. CSK Decryption Based on Bit Energy Estimator

The decryption method used is called non coherent demodulation based on energy bit estimator. Decryption is done based on some distinguishable characteristics of the signal transmitted. The property used in this paper is the bit energy, which was deliberately made different for different symbols in the encryption process.

Qi Hyper-chaos generator is used to produce two chaotic signals of different bit energies with the use of two amplifiers of different gains.

At the receiving end, the bit energy can be estimated by a square-and integrate process.

Since additive noise corrupts the transmitted signal and the noise power is limited, therefore we have

$$r(t) = s(t) + \xi(t) \quad (3)$$

Then we squire the received signal $r(t)$ followed by integrating the $r(t)^2$ signal in-order to calculate the energy bit

$$\begin{aligned} r(t)^2 &= (s(t)+\xi(t))^2 = (s(t)+\xi(t))(s(t)+\xi(t)) \\ &= s^2(t)+s(t)\xi(t)+\xi(t)s(t)+\xi^2(t) \\ &= s^2(t)+2s(t)\xi(t)+\xi^2(t) \end{aligned} \quad (4)$$

Therefore:

$$r^2(t) = s^2(t) + 2s(t)\xi(t) + \xi^2(t) \quad (5)$$

So we integrate $r^2(t)$

Let energy per bit is= $y(lTb)$

$$\begin{aligned} y(lTb) &= \int_{(l-1)Tb}^{lTb} [s^2(t) + 2s(t)\xi(t) + \xi^2(t)]dt \\ &= \int_{(l-1)Tb}^{lTb} s^2(t) + 2\int_{(l-1)Tb}^{lTb} s(t)\xi(t) + \int_{(l-1)Tb}^{lTb} \xi^2(t)dt \end{aligned} \quad (6)$$

When the energy bit $y(lTb) > 0$ then binary "+1" was sent and when it is less than "-1" was sent.

3 Simulation of Qi-Hyper-Chaos-Shift-Keying Encryption and Decryption

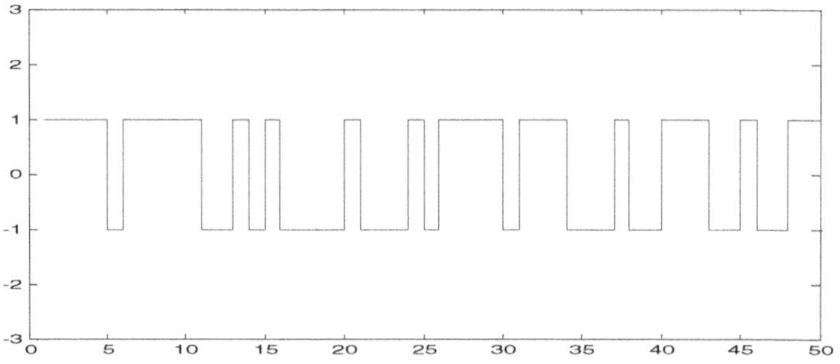

Fig. 7. Message signal *m* (*t*)

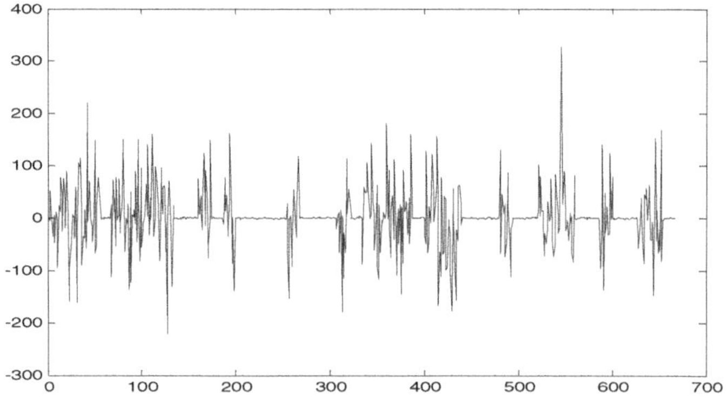

Fig. 8. Encrypted message signal

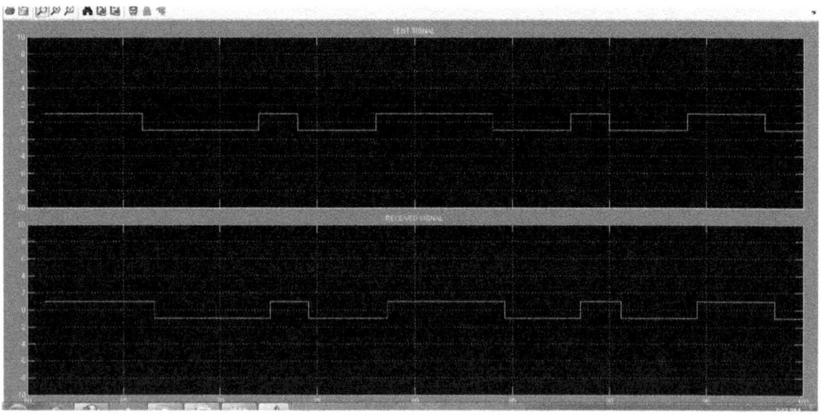

Fig. 9. Comparison between the sent signal and received signal as viewed in a scope

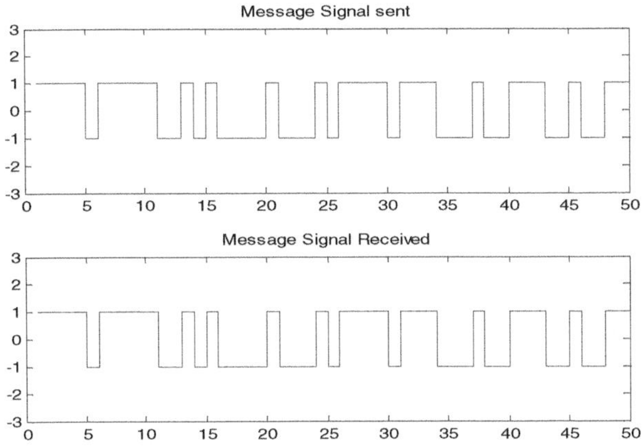

Fig. 10. Comparison between sent and received signal

The scope in fig 9 shows that there are some delays between the sent and the received signal but in fig.10 the delay is taken care of by introducing a delay to the sent signal while comparing with the received signal.

Fig 7 shows the encrypted message signal using Qi-hyper chaos. With the aid of a switch which acts as the controller between the first hyper chaotic signal and the second hyper chaotic signal based on the digital message signal sent. When message signal sent is greater than zero then the first hyper chaotic signal $c(t)$ is sent, when the message signal sent less than zero then the second hyper chaotic signal $c_1(t)$ is sent.

4 Message Signal Extraction Using Power Spectrum Analysis

Several methods have been proposed in literature [12 15] that attack chaotic encryption schemes. These methods are:

I. Autocorrelation.
II. Power spectrum analysis and filtering technique.
III. Return map analysis.

In this paper message signal encryption based on Qi hyper-chaos and message signal encryption based on Lorenz chaotic system are subjected to power spectrum analysis and filtering technique and the results is as show below.

Simulation results of power spectrum analysis employed on CSK based on Lorenz chaotic system.

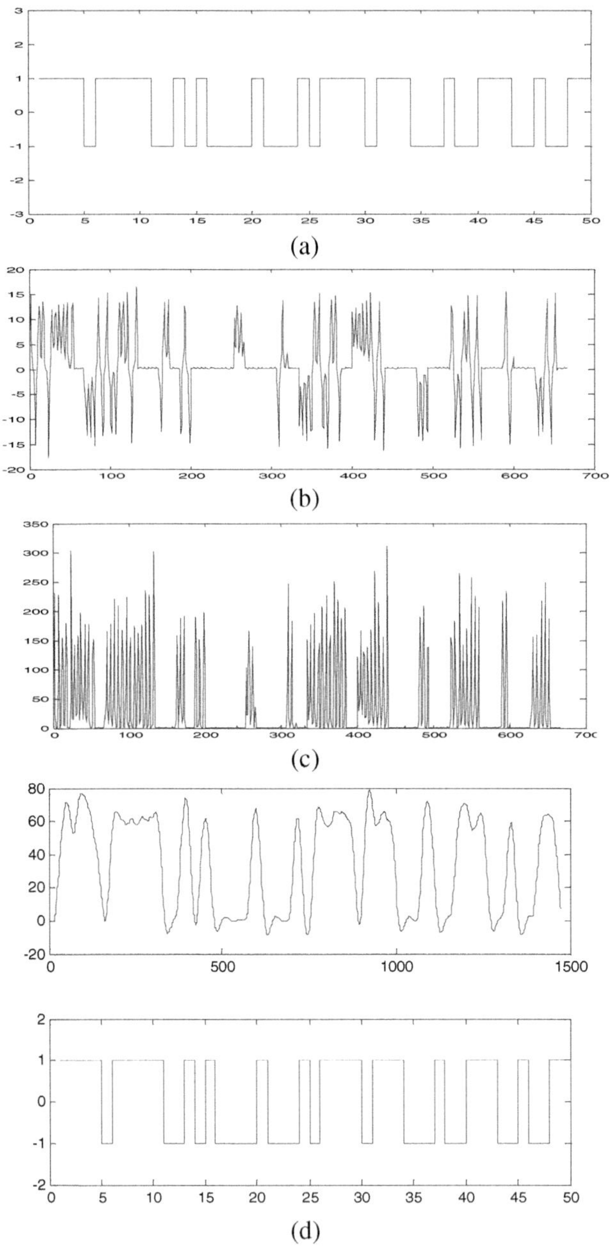

Fig. 11. Cryptanalysis attack on Lorenz based chaos shift keying method using Power analysis method. From up to down: plain text *m(t)*; cipher text *r(t)*.

Squared cipher text $r^2(t)$; low pass filtered squared cipher text signal and the reconstructed plain text $m'(t)$.

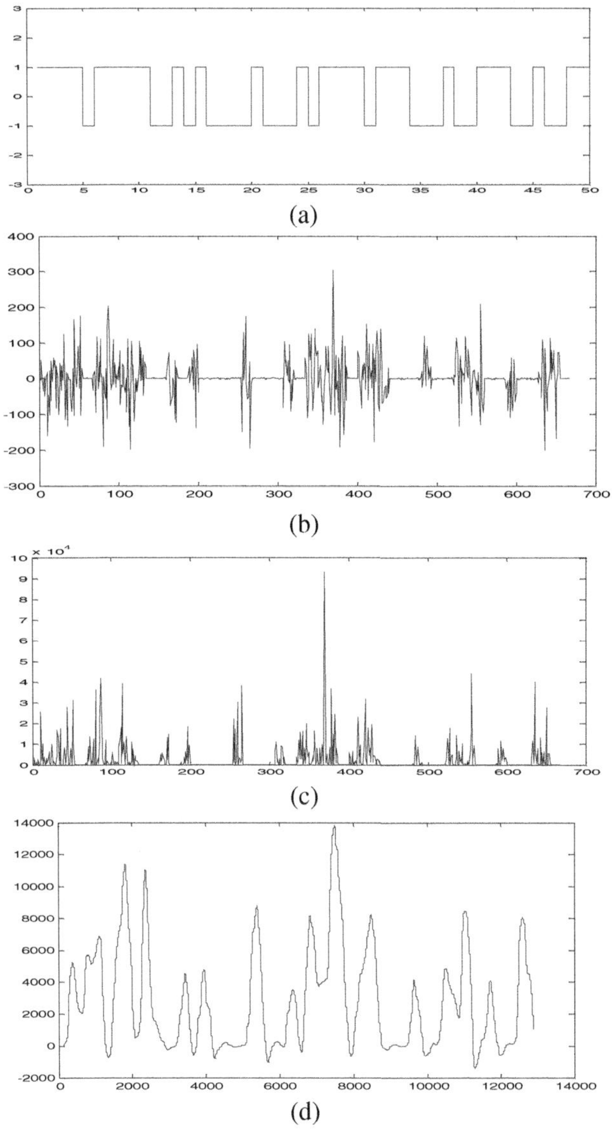

Fig. 12. Shows encrypted message signal $r(t)$, the square of cipher text which is $r^2(t)$ and the $r^2(t)$ after being passed through a low pass filter as that of Lorenz shift keying

NOTE: Even after passing $r^2(t)$ to a low pass filter it was very difficult to retrieve back the message signal sent, this is because The orbits of the Qi-hyper chaos are extremely abundant and dense as compared to that of Lorenz and once used to encrypt message signal it will require a very strong algorithm to retrieve the information.

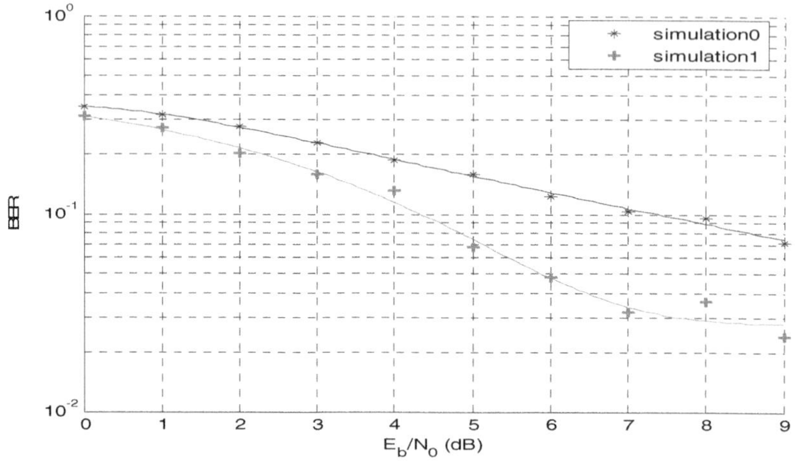

Fig. 13. Bit Error Rate (BER) performance between chaos shift keying based on Qi hyper chaos and chaos shift keying based on Lorenz chaotic system

Simulation 0 in fig 10 is BER of chaos shift keying based on Qi hyper chaos while **simulation 1** in fig 10 above shows chaos shift keying based on Lorenz chaotic system. The higher the signal-to-noise ratio the higher the quality of signal received. Many other times signal to noise ratio (SNR) is not used for digital communication but there is relationship between the system's SNR and BER. The higher the SNR, the lower would be the corresponding BER.

In the simulation of BER as shown in fig. 13 shows that Lorenz based CSK is more efficient since it has low BER than Qi based CSK. One interesting paradox between encryption and BER performance in communication scheme is how to Improving the security while maintaining a good BER performance.

5 Conclusion

In this paper hyper chaos messages signal encryption and decryption based on Qi hyper chaos has been implemented with the help of MATLAB\SIMULINK. Comparison between Qi hyper chaos and Lorenz chaotic was discussed. The simulation results show successfully encryption and decryption.

References

[1] Alverez, S.L.G.: Some Basic Cryptographic Requirements For Chaos-Based Cryptosystems. International Journal of Bifurcation and Chaos 16, 2129–2152 (2006)
[2] Baptista, M.S.: Cryptography with Chaos. Physics Letter A 240 (1998)
[3] Itoh, M.: Spread Spectrum communication Via Chaos. Internal Journal of Bifurcation and Chaos 9, 155–213 (1999)
[4] Stinson, D.: Cryptography: Theory and Practice. CRC Press, Boca Raton (1995)

[5] Abel, A., Schwaez, W.: Chaos Communication-Principles, schemes and systems. In: Proc. ASEE Gulf-Southwest Annual Conf.,Session (2002)
[6] Kennedy, M.P., Rovatti, R., Setti, G.: Chaotic Electronics in Telecommunications. CRC Press LLC, Boca Raton (2000)
[7] Chua, L.O., Lin, G.: Canonical Realization of Chua's Circuit Family. IEEE Trans. Circuits and Systems, 885–902 (1990)
[8] Rössler, O.E.: Phys. Lett. A, 71–155 (1979)
[9] Lorenz, E.N.: J. Atmos. Sci. 20, 130 (1963)
[10] Dedieu, H.: Chaos Shift Keying: Modulation and Demodulation of A Chaotic Carrier using Self-Synchronizing Chua's Circuits
[11] van Wyk, M.A., Qi, G., van Wyk, B.J.: On A New Hyper Chaotic System. Phys. Lett. A 372, 124–136 (2008)
[12] Feki, M.: Adaptive chaos synchronization scheme applied to secure communication. Chaos, Solution and Fractals (2003)
[13] Perez, G., Cerdeira, H.: Extracting messages masked by chaos. Phys. Lett. 74, 1970–1973 (1995)
[14] Alvarez, F.M.G., Romera, M., Pastor, G.: Breaking parameter modulated chaotic secure communication. Chaos Soliton Fract. 21, 783–787 (2004)
[15] Yang, T., Yang, L.B., Yang, C.M.: Breaking chaotic communications using a spectrogram. Phys. Let. A 247, 105–111 (1998)

A Multi-Agent Recommendation System for Energy Efficiency Improvement

Ovidiu Aritoni and Viorel Negru

West University of Timişoara,
4 Blv. Vasile Pârvan, Timişoara, Romania

Abstract. Our system is an ambient intelligent system that provides incremental recommendations in terms of behaviour, appliance usage and user-feedback. The purpose of this paper is to present the architecture of a recommendation system that has as objective to improve the behaviour of households or living spaces residents in order to increase the energy efficiency.

1 Introduction

In order to improve the life quality and to reduce the environmental pollution, the reduction of CO_2 emissions is an important challenge for all the researchers, academic and governmental institutions. The European Commission want to reduce the CO_2 emissions by 2020 with 20% [10]. More than 30% CO_2 emissions are due to the households and this proportion will grow up [9]. The purpose of our multi-agent recommendation system for energy efficiency improvement (**MARSEEI**) is to reduce the household's power consumption without to reduce the quality of live. The optimisation of the relation between the household residents behavior and the energy consumption is the problem that our system wants to solve.

The energy efficiency is defined in terms of power consumption, life quality and resources management. Energy efficiency means to use less energy to provide the same level of energy service to the user and to maintain the life quality. Information and communication technology (ICT) provide the technological support to improve the energy efficiency, and it can be used in a direct way in order to reduce the energy consumption [19].

The development of ambient intelligence (AmI)[1] is a solution to reduce the electricity consumption, natural gas, etc. An AmI system uses a sensor network to perceive the context, understands what is happen around him and it provides intelligent decisions that will be executed using actuators. There are two categories of AmI systems used to increase the energy efficiency.

The first category defines the "automatic house": it uses a sensor network and a lot of actuators that can close the windows, stopping HVAC, etc. The systems

[1] AmI refers to electronic environments that are sensitive and responsive to the presence of people.

J.J. Yonazi et al. (Eds.): ICeND 2011, CCIS 171, pp. 156–170, 2011.

from this category are proactive "building" that take some decisions in order to increase the energy efficiency. These smart houses use an elementary rule - based systems.

On the second category we find the AmI recommendations systems that understand the environment using sensor networks, but they don't have a direct impact in the house using actuators, they only make some recommendations. The AmI recommendation system use the humans as actuators, because they provide a set of recommendations and the human users try to apply these recommendations. The papers [22,16,15] prove that the recommendations systems can change the user behaviours, and in this way we can obtain more efficiency than using simple smart houses.

The MARSEEI context-awareness will be essential to reach the energy efficiency, the adoption of a multi-agent architecture has a major influence on the flexibility, scalability, proactivity and iterative systems features. As an example the user energy-awareness must to improve using an iterative collaboration between the system and the household residents and this implies that the system need to adapt.

The paper presents the recommendation system use-cases and functionality, from the users point of view. At the same time we define all the systems agents and the interactions between them. We concentrate on next section on positioning this paper in the young landscape of AmI recommendation systems for energy efficiency improvement. Thereafter, we will discuss the key concepts - especially the *profile* term and *iterative training* of household residents - and the system functionality. After, we outline the multi-agent architecture: how to integrate all the agents, the agent's capability and their interactions. We conclude the paper with the important fields of the future work and a discussion about the integration of this systems in the the real-life.

2 Related Work

In the energy efficiency context, ICT provides hardware devices and a framework for the system development. Several current-cost sensors such as CurrentCost, Kill-a-Watt, PlugWise are available. The first approaches for the energy consumption reduction was based on current-cost sensor. The simple fact of displaying the energy-consumption has a great impact on many household residents that take the initiative to reduce the power-consumption.

These solutions can broadly classified in two categories: the single sensor approach and the multiple sensor approaches.

The first solution consists in *a single current-cost sensor* which provides the aggregated consumption over the entire household or living space. This solution is easy to use due to it's low cost but it suffer from the fact that in some situations it is not very accessible to wiring around the household electricity meter. The Hydro One Smart Network project [20] uses only a single CurrentCost sensor, and provides to users (inhabitants from Barrie, Brampton, Lincoln, Peterborough and Timmins - Canada) real-time feedback about their energy consumption. The reduction in electricity consumption across the project was 6.5% at a high level of accuracy. Another project such as GooglePowerMeter [5], ETH Zurich initiative [19], Intel Home Energy Management [7] use a single sensor in order to provide real-time feedback about electricity consumption, without giving some advices of special recommendation to change the user behaviour. All the above project use only current-cost sensor data and does not take in to consideration the gas and the hot water consumption. The DEHEMS project [3] follows the same approach.

The second approach that uses *multiple sensors* can be divided in direct and indirect systems [19]. The direct systems use only current-cost sensors, and the indirect systems use also other context sensor such as light, movement, gas, RFID sensor. Project like AIM [6] use a wireless network of current-cost sensor and provides useful advices and recommendations. The project BeAware [4] uses also a wireless current-cost sensor network and the phone, the home lighting and lamps to communicate real-time alerts. The Energy Conservation and Homecare Network (ECHONET) project [18] develops a residential gateway for a home energy management systems. The ViriDiscope project [17] uses multiple current-cost and context sensors (light, movement, acoustic and electromagnetic sensor) to predict the future usage of household's appliance. The AIM, BeAware and ECHONET project develop a direct system, and the ViriDiscope project an indirect system.

3 Functional Requirements

In this section we present the MARSEEI functional requirements and some key concepts of the entire system.

3.1 The Iterative Recommendation Process

A recommendation is an action that is likely to be in the interest of the user. By providing recommendations, the MARSEEI system uses the household's resident feedback as well as the sensor data. The recommendations are used to change the household's residents behaviour, in order to improve the living space energy efficiency. The world wide web provides dedicated web-sites with many recommendations to reduce the electricity / gas bill such as [2]. MARSEEI is a training system for the users to adopt new behaviours and to be more aware about the problem of energy consumption. The residents training consist in a lot of recommendations. These recommendations are build using specific agents. Our system is a "step-by-step" training environment. MARSEEI uses an iterative process, as we can see on the figure 1.

The figure 1 explains the relations between our recommendation system and the house: the system provides to the user recommendations, the house residents try to "implements" these recommendations, and the house send as an output the resident's new behaviors and the context, and after that the recommendation system analyses and develops new recommendations. Each iteration of our system consist in:

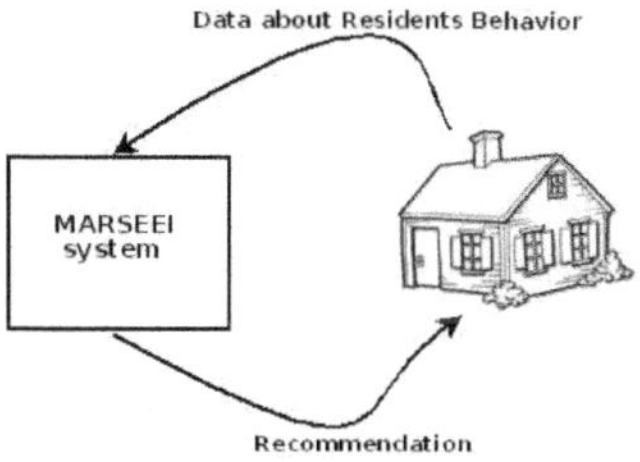

Fig. 1. Incremental Recommendation Process

- understanding the residents behaviours and the context in which they occur.
- making recommendations using the analysis of the rsidents behaviours and the context.
- the residents will change their behaviour using these recommendations.

On each iteration the system will build new recommendations, using as "input" the new context. The iterative process stop when the household have the lowest energy-consumption from a specific category. About household categories we will speak in next paragraph. The iterative process restart when the energy-consumption grows or we do some changes in the household structure: add new residents, build new rooms, add new appliances, etc. On each iteration we "increment" the recommendations: we can change the recommendations, we can add new recommendations, we can improve the old recommendations or we can delete recommendations.

We define seven main categories of recommendations, and for each category we build one agent that produce sugestions to increase the energy efficiency. The main recommendation categories are about:

- devices with malfunctions.
- the human actions or users habits that provide inefficiency in the energy usage.
- a realistic goal for the next month or next time period about the power consumption.
- automatic actions in the smart-house.
- tips and tricks from other families, but intelligently chosen.
- time intervals when the user can do some specific actions.
- how we can replace a device with a similar appliance from the same category and with the same functionality, in order to increase the energy efficiency.
- real-time and suggestive visualisation of power consumption (electricity / gas /etc).

3.2 Household Profiling

The household is the basic residential unit where the energy consumption is organized and carried out, similar as concept with a family residence or living space. Each household will be described in terms of profiles. The household owner specifies through web-pages data about:

- The Household Residential Profile: how many rooms are in the household, how many buildings are, wall width, wall height, etc. The residential profile includes a description of all the appliances and how they are located in that residence.
- The Household Behavioural Profile: how many inhabitants are in the household, their profession, their age, life style, inhabitants habits, etc.
- The Household Energy-Efficiency Awareness Profile: number of "ecological" appliances, user habits about interactions with devices, etc.

For each household we associate a residential profile, a behavioural profile and an energy-efficiency awareness profile. When the user introduces all the above data, we start an agent that has as main task to associate a unique profile. to the household.

The combination between specific residential profiles, behavioural profiles and energy-awareness profiles defines a households category:

$$Category = \langle \{ResidentialProfile\}, \{BehaviouralProfile\}, \{EnergyAwarenessProfile\} \rangle$$

A category is a triplet of three sets: a set of residential profiles, a set of behavioural profiles, and a set of energy-awareness profiles. Each set contains equivalents profiles. The household clusterisation process is based on profiles. A household category contains a set of equivalent residential profiles, a set of behavioural profiles and a set of energy-efficiency awareness profiles.

Through different processes, we establish for each household a *unique* residential/behavioural/energy-efficiency awareness profile, and finally a *unique* category. Firstly we associate with the household the residential profile. To establish the residential profile we need to define the energy efficiency class for the studied household. To calculate the energy efficiency class we follow the energetic audit workflow. After that we continue with associate the behavioural profile, based on the category that contains the finding residential profile. Finally we establish the energy-efficiency awareness profile.

Our system is able to define new profiles and new categories. The system defines new profiles when the user introduces particular data without any similarity with our profiles data. MARSEEI introduces new categories when we discover a profile which is not similar with any profile. The similarity between profiles is calculated using special metrics. We have defined complex metrics to compare household residential profiles and behavior profiles. For the energy-efficiency awareness we calculate a grade between 1 to 10 and the metric for the profiles similarity is based on the difference beween these grades. To define these profiles and categories we have developed a large statistical study of more than 850 household. This study was based on a questionnaire that follows a decision tree schema. We find 110 profiles and 35 categories. All the profiles and categories are stored in a database.

Also another important task is to validate the profiles and the category for a specific house. The behaviour profile is validated using the received sensor data, using a time interval of minimum one week. In this time period the household residents must have a similar behaviour with the description from the profile.

The validation of the residential and energy-efficiency awareness profiles uses database trigger technique.

The residential profile does not change in general, because it defines the general structure of the household. The behavioural profile and energy-efficiency profiles must change. The recommendations develop the transitions between the profiles. So, our system is dynamic due to the profile changes. All the recommendations are developed starting with these profiles. For each households category we have a lot of recommendations. So, the recommendations are clustered based on the household categories. We use the case-based reasoning in the recommendation process [14].

In order to obtain a good forecasting we can use a sensor data simulation process. The profiles are intensively used in the simulation process as input. As example, in these profiles we have details about the household appliances and how they are used, and we can produce time-series data. Also, using these profiles we can simulate the future residents behaviour. We can generate specific scenarious for a household using the behavioural profile. The simulation process allows the prediction of the inhabitants behaviour and establishes a new target for energy consumption with a good accuracy.

3.3 Sensor Data

Our system uses the sensors data, in the recommendation process. The data acquisition is delegated to a multi-agent middleware [11]. We use not only the current-cost consumption, but also the gas, hot water consumption and the thermique energy, in comparation with other approaches that use only power-consumption sensors. In the first stage, when the system learns the household's residents behaviour we use a complex sensor network: light level, movement, user-identification sensor, interior / exterior temperature, gas/ hot-water/ thermique-energy consumption, etc and current-cost sensors for each household socket and total electricity power consumption sensor. We use curent-cost sensor for each appliance because we want to learn the behaviour for each of them. When the system has learned the residents behaviour we use a small sensors network and we simulate data for the other sensors. On this stage we use only a user-identification sensor and the ussualy sensor for the total electricity power consumption, hot-water and thermique energy consumption.

The use-case diagram from Figure 2, illustrates the main functional requirements of our recommendation system.

4 Architecture

The Model-View-Controller architectural model has been chosen in order to respond all the requirements. The model contains the household profiles and categories repository, metamodels for recommendations, etc. The model is shared between the server and local systems. The multi-agent system that develop recommendation is the controller from the MVC architecture. We use an intuitive

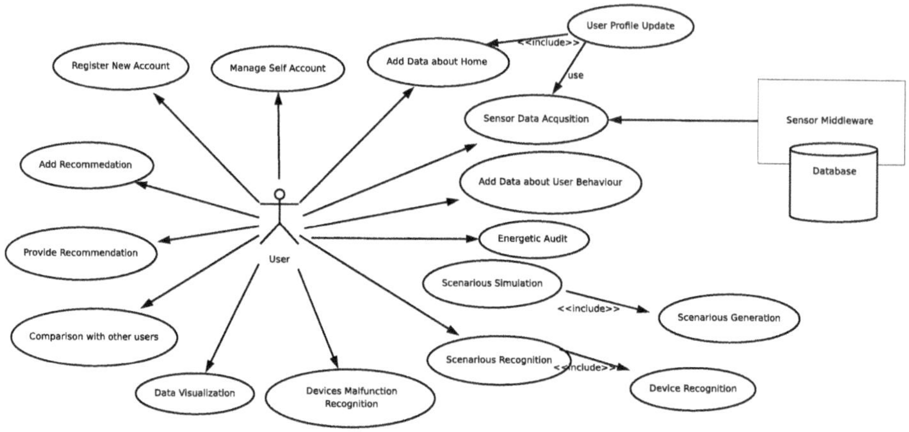

Fig. 2. Requirements

user interface, the communication between the system and the residence inhabitants it is developed in direct (recommendation system → users) and indirect way (especially when we receive the user feedback). We provide support to use in the communication process on the user-side: PDA devices, PocketPC, mobile phones, iPhone, etc. The architecture which we will describe here shows in general how the system works and the interactions between the agents in order to provide user services.

4.1 The Distributed Architecture

Our recommendation system uses a distributed architecture. The system consists in a central-server and several local subsystems for each household. On the server-side we develop web-services for:

- data-storage. The central-server store data about: household profiles, collected recommendations, the recommendation historic for each household, sensor-data readings, etc. To serve a large number of household is a big challenge, and for this we must to use a special solution for collecting data as is described in [21].
- user-profiling. We develop a repository that contains the descriptions of all the profiles used by our system. Also the central server provides services for working with the household residential / behavioural or energy-efficiency awareness profile.
- comparation between users habits, behaviours and power consumption.

The local subsystems are used for the data-acquisition and to develop recommendations. The sensor data acquisition is shared between the smart-house wireless sensors network and the central server: on each house we develop a wireless sensor network, and a gateway that collect all the data and send them to the central server [11]. All the recommendations are develop locally on each smart house subsystem. The agents have a local-view about the household context and can develop, on this way, good recommendations. When we build new agents in order to solve some problem, a knowledge transfer betwen the central-server and the agent take place. The figure 3 describes the distributed architecture of the MARSEEI system.

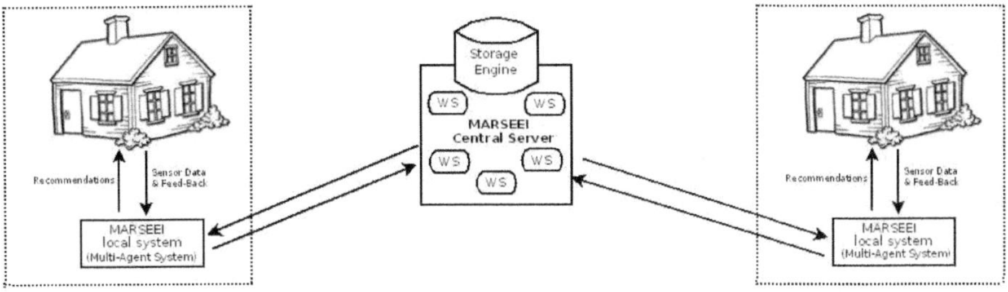

Fig. 3. The MARSEEI Distributed Architecture

4.2 Multi-Agent Approach

The incremental and iterative aspects are translated in the agent proactive feature, because the system will take the initiative to provide the next iteration. We use agents, because doing a recommendation needs to have a knowledge base about the problem. The agent solves the problem using the collected data about the user household and the lessons learned from other situations. Each recommendation agent has as capability to give a special kind of recommendation. The proactive feature of our system, the necessity to learn continuosly, the use of a knowledge base in the recommendation process motivate the multi-agent architecture of our system.

We use agents to solve all the tasks of our recommendation system such as: user "profiling", energetic audit, data simulation and off-course recommendations. Our architecture uses agents also for the direct communication between the system and users, in order to provide services for the user interface. A software agent is a software entity which works toward goals in a dynamic environment on behalf on another entity, without continuous direct supervision or control, and exhibits a significant degree of flexibility and even creativity in how it seeks to transform goals into action tasks [23].

In many situations agents use software modules that pursue sub-goals - on this situation are Scenarios Generation Agent, Scenarios Simulation Agent, Prediction Agent, etc. We use some conversational agents in the communication process between the user and the recommendation system through the user-interface. The sensor middleware agents are system agents that continuosly run in background with the purpose to receive and process the sensor data [11]. The Behavioural Profile Agent(BPA) is also a system agents that process the data that describes the human behaviour in the smart-house in order to update or to validate the behavioural profile.

The goal of our system is to develop context-aware recommendations that request a permanent update of each agent goal. This could mean, for example, that the Prediction Agent will use a new prediction model after the user profile was change. If in the past the main reason of inefficiency was the heating system and now the user change its habits and this problem was solved, actually we can have the problem of cooking in the peak gas, when the gas price is more expensive than in the rest of the day. In this situation the Prediction Agent does not use the gas model for heating, it use the gas model for cooking. Also the Recommendation Agent goal is not to reduce the gas consumption for heating, is to reduce the gas consumption for cooking.

The communication and the interactions between agents use a common language - Agent Communication Language (ACL). For each task we instantiate one or more software agents. We have choose Jade [13] as a framework to develop MARSEEI. All the task-agents registers their services using the Directory Facilitator(DF) agent. The system creates at start-up a DF agent and a controller agent. A controller agent is responsible to supervise activities in the local container, to interact with the daemon agents and to control the application life-cycle. In many situations the requirements are very complex, due to the solving problem complexity. This means that we need to define workflows to solve the complex task. We define,in this way, agents workflow. This is the reason why, in our case we use WADE [1]. Our agents communicate with the central-server via web-services using WSIG [13].

4.3 Agents Description

Next paragraphs describe the MARSEEI main classes. The interactions between the agents are described in the figure 4. To develop recommendations for one user the system instantiate all the agents from second and third level from the figure 4. The agents from the first level are daemon agents that are active all the time.

The **Energetic Audit Agent (EAA)** calculates the energy efficiency class of the user household. The user fills a web page questionnaire, with details about the house surface, walls width, electric appliances, etc. The energetic audit agent has its own knowledge about the geographical conditions and weather with significance in the process of estimating the user household energy efficiency. The energetic audit workflow and other important details are defined by the national government where is the house located, so this agent must to take into consideration this aspect[2].

The **Residential Profile Agent(RPA)**, **Behavioural Profile Agent (BPA)** and **Energy Efficiency Sensitivity Profile Agent(SPA)** associate to a household a residential profile, a behavioural profile and a profile for energy efficiency

[2] At the level of European Community and European Economic Space is the same policy to calculate the energy efficiency with insignificants modifications.

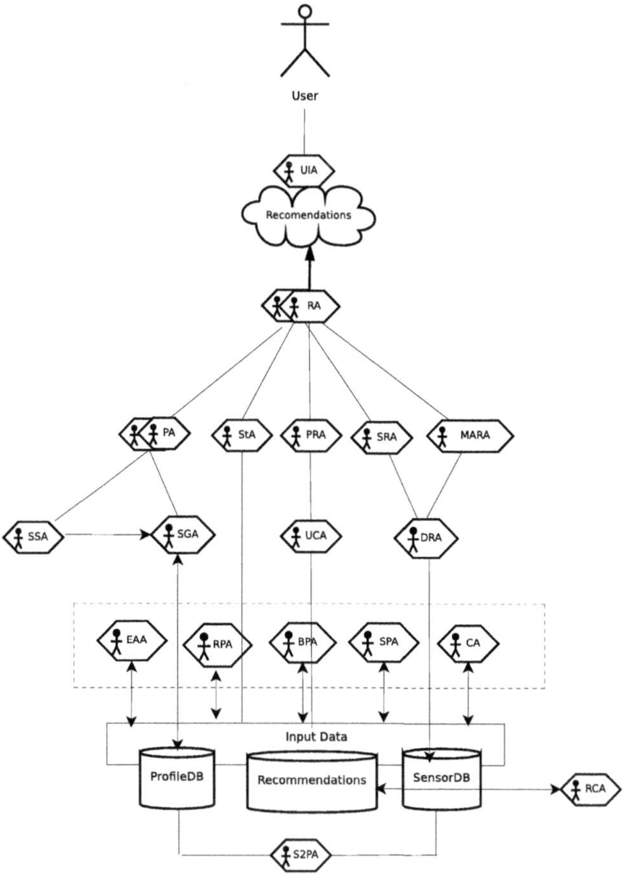

Fig. 4. Collaboration between agents

sensitivity. These agents use web form to receive data from users. These agents use some conversational agents which intermediate the user communication. The BPA and SPA are *daemon agents* that continuously are active, and update the user profile. These two agents also exchange data with other agents like the SA (Statistics Agent), UserComparatives Agent (UCA), PredictionAgent (UCA),etc. A daemon agent **SensorToProfileAgent (S2PA)** is used to update the user profile with knowledge from the sensor middleware.

Scenarios Simulation Agent (SSA) is an agent that simulates scenarios in order to build sensor data-streams [8]. A scenario describes the household inhabitants behaviour and the interactions between them. This agent uses as input a scenario written in **Scenarios Description Simulation Language (SDSL)**, approximately likely the natural language, received from the **Scenarios Generator Agent (SGA)** such as:

7:10 Paul wake up.
7:11 Paul turns on the light.
7:12 Paul goes to the bathroom.
....

The output is a data-stream of sensor-data records such as <sensorid, timestamp, value>. The SSA build sensor data-stream for many sensor categories such as: current-cost, gas/ water/ thermique-energy consumption, light level, temperature, movement level and user-identification sensors. Our simulator is based on real-life data acquisition. We used, for example, instant-consumption sensors which show the energy-consumption rate of a given object, bound to that, at any given time (6 second intervals). The output produced by the sensors was recorded in the form of time series for analysis. We used this data to fine-tune our simulator and get as close as possible to real-world results. The similarity coefficient between the simulated current-cost time-series an the real measurements time-series was in all the situation greater than 0.874/1 (1 means that the time-series are identicall). The project at hand is still a work in progress, however, results we obtained so far look very promissing. The energy-consumption data simulation output for electricity and water is very promissing and very close to real world consumption rates. Gas consumption still needs fine-tuning due to the lack of complete real-life measurments to base our simulations on. Manually inputed scenarios offer better results due to their higher accuracy, however, automatically generated scenarios are offering better results by the day.

Scenarios Generator Agent (SGA) generates scenarios using the behavioural and residential profiles. The SGA is a JADE agent that embed JESS code. The automatic scenary generator was develop using the JESS programming language. The algorithm is based on the using of decision trees and constraint programming principles. The using of constraints makes some actions to be not generated unless they have to: one man cannot use the gas cooker unless he is in the kitchen. When the user has a long historic in the MARSEEI system we will use the user-profiles updated with the results of statistics received from the Statistic Agent. At the moment we have defined the SDSL language, we have build our simulator for SDSL scenarious, and we have in progress the development of SGA.

The **DeviceRecognitionAgent (DRA)** [12] recognizes when the house's residents use an electric appliance, the exact time when a device is used and total power consumption when it is used. DRA can extract a data-stream segment for a specified electric appliance. The DRA agent is *an intelligent agent* that uses heuristic and pattern recognition techniques to achieve his goal.

The DRA services are used by the **Scenarious Recognition Agent (SRA)** and the Malfunctions Appliances Recognition Agent. The SRA agent has the capability to recognize the scenarios using the received sensors data-streams. It is an *intelligent agent* that use heuristic techniques and statistic calculus to obtain scenarios which describe what happens in the user house. The SRA goal is to translate the sensor time-series in to SDSL language instructions. We use this agent because we must to analyze the behaviour of household inhabitants. of The SRA agent is still under development.

The **Malfunctions Appliances Recognition Agent (MARA)** uses as input the power readings stream of a users device and produce as output: determination if the device is malfunctioning (health status) and other statistics. Our first goal was to define a set of rules, so that, given a set of energy readings, would evaluate the health of a device and pinpoint regions of faulty power usage. A set of reading has at its core two most evident states: ON and OFF. This information developed our first rule in evaluating device consumption. Thus, before going any further, we must extract the actual usage that characterizes the ON state of the device. Further information has to be provided about each specific type of device in order to effectively determine health status, and such information has to be accessible. Given that, as a general rule, the correct function of a device, as observed only by consulting the values representing the power consumption, has to fit between some boundaries: the maximum power consumption and minimum power consumption, the former, as observer earlier, having to reflect the ON state of the device. The device specifications sometimes include the maximum and minimum power consumptions. However, for the purpose of this project, these were taken from energy usage patterns. Using the developed agent, we analyzed the power consumptions of our laptops and successfully created charts that show that the deviations are negative, which means the devices operate under the minimum power consumption specification, making it optimal.

The **Communication Agent (CA)** intermediates the communication between the MARSEEI system and the local power / water/ thermique energy providers software systems. It can initiate the communication with all these providers system in order to obtain for example a historic about the user consumption along an entire year, or to update the prices for their services. The CA is an *interface agent* that has as capabilities to request information, to process them or to do conversation with another system, with the main goal to collect data about the MARSEEI users. All the gathered data are stored in the MARSEEI storage server.

The **StatisticAgent (SA)** provides statistics services about the user behaviour: how many electric appliances are in the house, which is the device the most used, average power consume, etc. Also, a noteworthy capability for this agent is to do calculus about the energy cost for the entire house / one specific appliance, etc. The **PatternRecognitionAgent (PRA)** uses the SA services and detect some behavioural patterns that describe the user habits. This agent update the MARSEEI database and add new habits that can be useful or not for other household.

PredictionAgent (PA) is an agent which provides forecasting services about: the user's behaviour in the near future, how and when will use the electric appliances, the total electric power or gas consumption, the future costs of energy for the entire house, etc. It can split itself into sub-agents which can perform sub-tasks and operate in parallel.

The **RecommendationsCollectorAgent** is a web crawler that periodically scans the web or selected portions of the web looking for recommendations about how to improve the energy efficiency. It is responsible to update the MARSEEI recommendations repository.

UCA (User Comparations Agent) is a noteworthy agent of our system. It is used to do a comparation between one user and others in term of: behaviour, total / maximum / minimum / average power consumption, total / maximum / minimum / average gas consumption or to compare the user profiles between them. In the comparativ process this agent uses metrics that can describe in a quantitative way a profile or a behaviour. Also this agent provides clustering services. Using UCA we can obtain user classes, where one or more user from the same class have approximately the same behaviour/power consumption/residential profile/etc. Also we need to compare the households from the same category. Our recommendation system use the case-based reasoning and this means that firstly we must to discover the most similar household with the studied household. This agent will provides services for the recommendation agent.

The **RecommendationAgent (RA)** is the most important agent in the entire architecture. It is an intelligent agent that uses others agents services to provide recommendations: UCA, MARA, etc. It uses the recommendation server storage. It sends the recommendations to **User-InterfaceAgents (UIA)**. The UIA agents communicate the recommendations via web-pages, mobile phones and other mobile devices. We have defined for each type of recommendations a special RA agent. Due to its behaviour, it splits itself into sub-agents or to clone itself. Because we have to analyse a complex living space, the RA agent splits itself, in order to give response at each aspect of the context. In many situations the RA agent clones itself: each of both will do recommendations for the user. The both recommendations will be exposed to user.

5 Conclusions and Future Work

On these article we have proposed a recommender system for the energy-efficiency improvement based on a large study of the household and it's inhabitants. This study about builds the household profiles. The recommendation process is based on these profiles, and the system evaluates the user behaviour after each set of recommendation in order to update the household profiles. The recommendation process is iterative.

Our system is still under development, due to the complexity of the problem. As future work we propose to develop an abstract model for the context-aware recommendations system for the efficient ressource management. We want to refactor this software prototype using the proposed abstract model. An important problem for our prototype is to develop metamodels and interfaces, in order to increase the interoperability of the system with another AmI systems. For a household we can have at the same time several AmI systems and the communication between them is very important. For example we can have an assistive recommendation system, another system for the house safety, etc and we must to interconnect all these system between them and with the municipality system. The future metamodels that we want to develop will provide support for the future extension of our prototype. We can extend our system with new recommendation categories. The validation of the entire system will be develop using our statictic study about the households across the Banat region of Romania. The system validation was started with our sensor data and scenarious simulator, which is ready at the moment.

Our proposed system, uses a heterogenous sensor network that contains multiple current-cost and context sensors. We use a multi-agent architecture that provides support for adaptivity and proactivity. Our software prototype is not a system which only informs the user about the total power consumption, it expose real and adaptable recommendations. Our approach is different from the others because we take into consideration: the household profile, the household resident behaviour, we collect tips and tricks from other users, we compare the users and we provide specific recommendations for each user. The profile concept used in our architecture and the iterative recommendation process provide a novelty in our architecture. The proposed system is and indirect system like the Viridiscope project [17], but we use an exhaustive sensor network only on the training stage, and after the simulation. Comparing with other indirect initiatives we provide services for household profiling and iterative recommendations.

Acknowledgement

The research leading to these results has received funding from the European Community's Seventh Framework Programme FP7 2007-2013 under grant agreement No224609 DEHEMS, and by the Romanian projects: DEHEMS-RO RO-PNII-20-EU/11.06.09 and PNII-ASISTSYS. The views expressed in this paper do not necessarily reflect those of the DEHEMS consortium members. Further information on DEHEMS can be obtained from http://www.dehems.eu.

References

1. http://jade.telecomitalialab.com/wade/html/home-getting.htm (retrieved: May 10, 2011)
2. http://www.auroraenergy.com.au/save_energy/green_scheme_house.asp (retrieved: May 10, 2011)
3. http://www.dehems.eu (retrieved: May 10, 2011)
4. http://www.energyawareness.eu (retrieved: May 10, 2011)
5. http://www.google.com/powermeter/about/ (retrieved: May 10, 2011)
6. http://www.ict-aim.eu/home.html (retrieved: May 10, 2011)
7. http://www.intel.com/embedded/energy/homeenergy/index.htm (retrieved: May 10, 2011)
8. http://web.info.uvt.ro/~oaritoni/smarthousesimulator (retrieved: May 10, 2011)
9. Climate change programme review (2005)

10. European commision press. Mars (2007)
11. Aritoni, O., Negru, V.: Sensors data-stream processing middleware based on multi-agent model vol. 11(1), pp. 19–32 (March 2010)
12. Aritoni, O., Negru, V.: A methodology for household appliances behaviour recognition in ambient intelligent systems. In: Proceedings of The First International Conference on Smart Grids, Green Communications and IT Energy-Aware Technologies (will appear, 2011)
13. Bellifemine, F.L., Caire, G., Greenwood, D.: Developing Multi-Agent Systems with JADE. Wiley, Chichester (2007)
14. Bridge, D., Mehmet, G., McGinty, L., Smyth, B.: Case-based recommender systems. The Knowledge Engineering Review 20(03), 315–320 (2005)
15. Fischer, C.: Feedback on household electricity consumption: a tool for saving energy? Energy Efficiency 1, 79–104 (2008), doi:10.1007/s12053-008-9009-7
16. Vekemans, G., Desmedt, J., Bael, J.V.: Influencing households energy behaviour, an in-situ measuring campaign
17. Kim, Y., Schmid, T., Charbiwala, Z., Srivastava, M.B.: Viridiscope: design and implementation of a fine grained power monitoring system for homes. In: UbiComp, pp. 245–254 (2009)
18. Kushiro, N., Suzuki, S., Nakata, M., Takahara, H., Inoue, M.: Integrated residential gateway controller for home energy management system. IEEE Transactions on Consumer Electronics 49(3), 629–636 (2003)
19. Mattern, F., Staake, F., Weiss, M.: Ict for green: how computers can help us to conserve energy. In: E-Energy 2010: Proceedings of the 1st International Conference on Energy-Efficient Computing and Networking, pp. 1–10. ACM, New York (2010)
20. Mountain, D.: The impact of real-time feedback on residential electricity consumption: The hydro one pilot. Technical report (2006)
21. Pungilă, C., Fortiş, T.F., Aritoni, O.: Benchmarking database systems for the requirements of sensor readings. IETE Technical Review 26(5), 342–349 (2009)
22. Wood, G., Newborough, M.: Dynamic energy-consumption indicators for domestic appliances: environment, behaviour and design. Energy and Buildings 35(8), 821–841 (2003)
23. Wooldridge, M., Jennings, N.R.: Intelligent agents: Theory and practice. Knowledge Engineering Review 10, 115–152 (1995)

Cyber Crime Detection and Protection: Third World Still to Cope-Up

Virginiah Sekgwathe[1] and Mohammad Talib[2]

[1] Directorate on Corruption and Economic Crime, Gaborone, Botswana
veesek@gmail.com
[2] Department of Computer Science, University of Botswana, Botswana
talib@mopipi.ub.bw

Abstract. Cyber-crime is typically understood to consist of accessing a computer without the owner's permission, exceeding the scope of one's approval to access a computer system, modifying or destroying computer data or using computer time and resources without proper authorization. Cyber-terrorism consists essentially of undertaking these same activities to advance one's political or ideological ends. Terrorist actions in the cyberspace could be done not only by isolated persons or terrorist groups, but one state against another. By that, cyber terrorism does not differ from other kind of terrorism in any way. The specific nature of the threat can range from denial of service to eavesdropping, fraud, sabotage, and theft of intellectual property and proprietary information. This paper aims to provide a broad overview of the challenges faced by the world in cyber crime and problems faced by law enforcement agencies and Information and Communication Technology security specialists in cyber investigations and the benefits that may be gained by the international community and of course the public-private partnerships (PPP) to the prevention, detection and prosecution of cyber crimes and how third world countries need to keep pace with the ever changing technologies and the manipulation of this technology by what we may term cyber criminals in order to make profit.

Keywords: Cyber Crime, Digital Evidence, Security, Hacking, Risk Analysis, Intellectual Property (IP), Cyber Terrorism, ICT.

1 Introduction

Internet has brought a host of problems haunting all those concerned with national security, privacy, IP rights, social decency, child protection, fighting, detecting and prosecuting crime. Innocent populace are falling prey to cheats, threats, money and identity losses, sexual abuses etc., and most of the victims around the World especially developing countries, are still ignorant of their rights on the Web and the methodology to bring a culprit to book. Computer crimes affect our daily lives and national security deeply, especially in this information epoch; we almost can't live without computers, the expanding wave of Internet connectivity and digital technologies bring us a lot of convenience, at the same time they also offer criminals more chance to commit crime. Traditional law enforcement tools, methodologies and disciplines do not successfully address the detection, investigation and prosecution of

J.J. Yonazi et al. (Eds.): ICeND 2011, CCIS 171, pp. 171–181, 2011.

cyber crime. This type of crime calls for a pro-active approach, for timely international cooperation, and for effective public private partnerships to ensure the upper-hand over criminals.

Cyber Crime may be defined as any criminal activity that uses a computer either as an instrument, target or a means for perpetuating further crimes comes within the ambit of cyber crime or unlawful acts wherein the computer is either a tool or target or both. Illegal computer-mediated activities that can be conducted through global electronic networks. Cyber Crime for the purpose of this paper may be categorized as follows:

a) A criminal act in which a computer is essential to the perpetration of the crime.
b) A criminal act where a computer, non-essential to perpetration of the crime, acts as a store of information, concerning the crime. This is to say that not only the crimes committed directly with a computer belongs to this field of no sense but also crimes where evidence could be found on computers or networks without necessarily using those devices to actually commit the crime.

Bank accounts can be hacked and credit card details can be stolen. When such cyber crimes are committed, we need digital evidence for investigators to catch the culprits. Though cyber forensics is doing a great deal to combat this crime, it faces many issues that have to be handled with care.

2 History

Cyber crime is not actually a new crime as the first recorded cyber crime took place in the year 1820, Joseph-Marie Jacquard, a textile manufacturer in France, produced the loom. This device allowed the repetition of a series of steps in the weaving of special fabrics. This resulted in a fear amongst Jacquard's employees that their traditional employment and livelihood were being threatened. They committed acts of sabotage to discourage Jacquard from further use of the new technology.

Cyber crime, is the latest and perhaps the most complicated problem in the cyber world, and may be said to be those species of which genus is the conventional crime and where either the computer is an object or subject of the conduct constituting crime. Cyber crime is characterized by:

i. Silent in Nature: Computer crime could be committed in privacy without reaching to scene of crime physically i.e. no eye witnesses. There is no signs of physical violence or struggle.
ii. Global in character: No national borders. By sitting comfortably far away from the country the entire economy of the country could be destroyed. As digital evidences are fragile in nature one has to respond quickly.
iii. Non existence of Physical Evidence: No physical evidence to indicate that crime has been committed. Only on a closer look the trained person could find out the evidences which are not in the traditional format but are in digital format.
iv. Creates high Impact: Impact is severe and may be long term. It can damage the victim system permanently. Loss of good will.
v. High Potential and Easy to Perpetrate: A software developer who did not get enough money or good job would turn to criminal world for their survival. Therefore, the computer crimes have a potential to increase. Hence organized mafia groups have entered into this sector.

2.1 The People on the Scene

The anonymity of cyberspace makes identity tracing a significant problem which hinders investigations. The ubiquity of computer technology throughout the civilian population will require full societal engagement if the national objective is a secure cyberspace. As the digital environment grows in scale and scope, so too will the need for a cyber civic culture to emerge to manage it.

Almost every computer criminal is knowledgeable with computers; some of them are even professional in computer science. They know how to commit computer crimes without leaving a trace, hence computer forensic professionals need higher level of computer science knowledge including hardware and software. They need to understand and be familiar with all kinds of computer forensic software.

Internet Corporation for Assigned Names and Numbers (ICANN's), Uniform Dispute Resolution Policy (UDRP) introduced a unified legal framework bringing all concerned subject to the same substantial law for dispute resolution. But if a parallel body revolts and sets up its own system, who will restrain? For instance the case of cyberstalking, the new weapon with criminals to threat or harass the addressee by use of e-communications on internet. Jurisdictional issue will come into contact in most of the situations. Lack of extradition treaties amongst most of the nations, make it a real game for the criminals to launch their operations from so called safe havens on the globe.

Law enforcement agencies are getting more organized and cooperating better, particularly in international investigations. At least 45 countries participate in the G8 24/7 High Tech Crime Network, which requires nations to have a contact available 24 hours a day to aid in quickly securing electronic evidence for trans-border cyber crime investigations. The private sector has a criminal case in Europe, the Middle East and the United States against alleged phishers throughout 2006 and 2007.

The solution looks simple, may be available but highly difficult to implement. Even all the component United States of America are not having consensus on many ethical and social issues and run different sets of laws and regulations for their respective citizens. Then, how other independent countries would allow universal rules to be adopted in their domains? Religious restrictions in many countries would also come in the way to accept one thing considered legitimate in the other. So far, even the institution of awarding domain names could not be globalized and many independent groups are granting domain names without any universal authorization or without any treaty authorizing them to collect subscriptions on such grants of domain names. Conflicts of award of domain names, while dealing with the different countries also cannot be resolved at present. However, there is a need to reach a consensus internationally.

2.2 Facing the Problem Head on

Traditionally, crime has been defined as an intentional violation of the legal code that is punishable by the state. Central to this definition is the premise that crime occurs within the boundaries of some physical reference point, such as a location that constitutes a specific jurisdiction. For example, when a conventional case of fraud occurs, one of the important considerations is where the actual offense took place so that questions of the appropriate jurisdiction for prosecution can be addressed. Law Enforcement officials need to know where the victim and offender came into contact with one another in the perpetration of the offense so that investigative and prosecutorial authority can be determined.

A global dependency on technology combined with the expanding presence of the Internet as a key and strategic resource requires that corporate assets are well protected and safeguarded. Cyber crime has become one of the major security issues for the law enforcement community, industry, e-business, judiciary and the academia. As already pointed out there is no difference between cyber crime and traditional crime in nature, with the advantages of convenience, anonymity and mobility of telecom and Internet, criminals are able to disguise their command center and disrupt the direction of investigation. Lawful enforcement officers need to make more effort in studying crime model and finding the way out to combat criminals. Cyber investigations used to be done on an ad hoc basis in many different divisions and programs.

The most distinct nature of cyber crime from traditional one is borderless and anonymous. By the help of pervasive network technology cyber crime is ramping over areas, regions, and countries. For investigators, it is really hard to get the true picture of the whole crime process because of dispersed elements in different places. Since new cyber crimes arise by the leap development of telecommunication and information technologies, investigators must face such challenges with a totally different thought and technical skills. The figure below depicts the nature of cyber crime simply as traditional crimes going high tech (fig 1). Traditional criminals are turning away from crime such as cash-in-transit robberies to an easy and well-paying life of cyber crime, which offers far greater rewards but less risk. Law enforcement agencies in developing countries are mostly far outpaced by these criminals.

Fig. 1. Evolution of conventional crime to digital crime delicate

Many law enforcement agencies that have to investigate cyber crimes usually are faced with jurisdictional, expertise, equipment, time issues. The jurisdiction issue related to the fact that online crimes are international by nature. It may sometimes be uncertain as to whether such an investigation should be handled by the country that initially received the complaint, which eventually led to an investigation or the country that is the destination.

The international community realized fully the cost from the cyber criminal thread hence signed the International Convention of cyber criminal by the representatives of EC countries and also US, Canada and Japan in November 2001. Governments must provide strong leadership in protecting critical cyber-assets, most of the efforts in this struggle must come from the private sector.

2.3 The Limits of the Private Sector in Response to Cyber Crime

The primary responsibility for cyber crime in commercial fields such as cyber banking or e-commerce belongs to individual businesses. However, the reality is that it is not possible to place all of the responsibility of cyber crime and security on them. The government must step in and devise a proper measure in response to cyber crime. However, a bigger problem is that cyber crime is not limited to just the private sector. There are no boundaries, no divisions between the government and the people. Good citizens and heinous criminals coexist in the same cyber space.

3 Cyber Crime Prevention to Be Adopted by Third World Countries

Organizations may employ prevention methods to prevent hacking by implementing policies since the largest threat is often from within an organization and ensure probe configured firewall protection to computer network as well as intrusion detection and other filtering software. Nonetheless, deterrence should be pursued as a mitigation strategy, because even limited accomplishments can prevent some crime incidents and provide some protection from an increasingly serious problem. Companies in branches that typically employ hackers can certainly be particularly helpful in deterring computer crimes, but the results of this study also indicate that all companies and organizations need to do more to actively prevent victimization, regardless of their branch. The education of employers, while definitely an important protective measure, is not the only contribution that will be required from organizations. They also need to start reporting all their victimization incidents to the authorities. The current situation, in which many organizations refrain from reporting incidents to protect their own interests and thereby harm the interest of all businesses, needs to be changed because, unless more incidents are reported, computer crimes are unlikely to become controllable. The benefits and detriments of a mandatory reporting system are debatable, but a reporting requirement would certainly benefit efforts to manage cybercrimes. It would put law enforcement agents in the position to decide which cases to devote their attention to rather than be dependent on the willingness of organizations to submit their cases in order to press charges.

3.1 Detecting and Protecting against Cybercrime

The International communities need to be dedicated to fighting cybercrime and helping to protect your online experience. We believe you have digital rights, similar to your rights in offline society. Not only do software vendors develop the world's leading security software to be used by 120 million customers worldwide but some even conduct extensive research into the nature and construct of the underground cybercriminal world. This knowledge allows is mostly shared internationally to provide global protection against an ever-changing battle ground. Internet Security and other utilities give business and individuals the power to deny cybercriminal attacks and keep them from wreaking havoc on business, family, finances, reputation, and even our life. We defend your digital rights to help you have complete control of your online experience. The best protections are careful system design, the use of products to detect known viruses and system intrusions, and user education, says the report. It adds that it is also essential to have proper contingency plans for system recovery. Each organization's implementation of cyber security requirements should evolve as technology advances and new threats to security arise. The nation's cyber security is being threatened because an important element in establishing it is not being emphasized enough citizen awareness and participation. Working against connected but weakly protected computer systems, hackers can steal information, make the systems malfunction by sending them false commands and corrupt the systems with bogus information.

4 Implementing Cybercrime Detection Techniques

For cyber crime to be detected a team of professionals need to work together and these include but not limited to law enforcement agencies, forensic scientist, Lawyers, and Computer security professionals. Detection helps organizations to determine whether or not someone attempted to break into the organization most critical asset that is system, if they were successful, and what they may have done. Almost daily, new techniques and procedures, are designed to provide information security professionals a better means of finding electronic evidence, collecting it, preserving it, and presenting it to client management for potential use in the prosecution of cyber criminals. The cyber crime detection techniques include but are not limited to;

- Auditing/log files
- Firewall logs and reports
- Email headers
- Tracing domain name/IP addresses
- IP spoofing/anti-detection techniques

Legislation alone cannot adequately combat the prevalence of cyber crime we face today. Private industry want to protect their businesses and customers provide the first line of defense. The private sector is usually ahead of Government on the latest technology, and must be willing to cooperate with law enforcement agencies. Technology holds the key to the future, and private businesses are leading the way in innovation and products, but if left unchecked, cyber crime will stifle that progress.

5 Collecting and Preserving Digital Evidence

While collecting electronic evidence it is best for law enforcement officers or security professionals to consider the rules of evidence to support an action against a cyber criminal, admissibility of evidence and complying with any existing standards for the admissibility of evidence and quality of evidence for which a strong evidence trail is necessary. The law enforcement officers also need to respond quickly and designate one person to secure evidence or maintain logs, immediately do a full file system backup and preserve that as evidence. The security professionals have to ensure they change root password and give to no more than two individuals with no remote root log-ins, Keep a hand written log of all root and sys administrator activities and preserve as evidence.

- Implement Excellent Logging; Install TCP Wrappers on victim system and log as much TCP activity as possible. Use Remote Hosts for Offline, Secure Logging. If to voluminous limit to untrusted networks and/or move users and data to another network leaving no authorized activity (sandbox). One can use a commercial product such as Etherpeek to monitor via dumb hub, try without giving IP address (w/o tcp stack).
- Request trap and trace with phone company if a dial up; Request trap and trace of connection by requesting complete logging by upstream system administrator (ISP or another victim network). Give upstream provider, date/time and IP#. Request he/she make the same request.
- Advise all legitimate users manually, telephone or directly. Have them verify last login was them.
- If no banner, attempt to manually get written consent to monitor from legitimate users that will continue to access machine.

5.1 Building the Cyber Case

The increase in computer-related crime has caused law-enforcement agencies to seize digital evidence in the form of network logs, text documents, videos and images. In specific cases like those involving terrorism, the need to extract and analyze every possible bit of evidence becomes crucial. The author also comments on how aggressive countries should be in its proactive cyber-spying activities.

When investigating the crime scene, what you can see is just one computer, several telephone lines, etc. The computer is the only item that you can detect evidence, digital evidence begin to play a significant role at that time. Knowledge of how to retrieve digital evidence is a prerequisite, how to recover deleted or damaged information, how to preserve digital evidence, etc. Also, Digital evidence, by its very nature, is very fragile and can be altered, damaged, or destroyed because of improper handling or examination. So it is important that digital evidence should be conducted by experienced computer forensic investigators. The expert then examines the digital evidence and gives a final report about the act complained of as a crime. This report is a determination of whether an act on a computer was a breach of any penal law or not. Therefore it should be made very carefully. It must be objective, based on indisputable facts, because law enforcers will connect the suspect to the act of the computer performed by a human. This connection therefore has to be beyond reasonable doubt. It is advisable to obtain and rely on professional legal advice at this stage. But above all, the existence of a regulatory framework and laws catering for cyber crimes in the country are quite different, what may constitute a crime may not necessarily be a crime in the country that the cyber criminal reside.

6 Challenges Faced by Cyber Crime Investigators in Third World

The changing world of technology presents a challenge for the courts to keep pace with new laws in addressing evidence and other legal issues involved. Computer forensic experts not only need to investigate and collect the criminal evidence, but also need to communicate the results clearly in the court. Actually, the judge and jury may not understand computers very much. When they enter computer crime scene, they must know where to look for useful information, where operations history is maintained, how files are deleted and how to use forensic tools to gather or recover deleted files or damaged files. Moreover, computer forensic professionals must know how to protect and preserve digital evidence; they also need to know how to present the digital evidence in court. Now computer forensics field is in great need of this kind of professionals.

The most important factor in understanding the limitations of generalizations when it comes to cyber crime is that malware and hack attacks can be launched from anywhere and by anybody. Likewise we have to be aware that criminals will go to great lengths to obscure their tracks. So drawing a definitive map of cyber crime is therefore far from an exact science and assuming any one country has sole rights to any one crime would be a mistake. Cyber crime is truly a global problem. Yet despite all this there are still some clear regional trends, though this is a far from comprehensive list. The question is how far the digital evidence collected by a computer expert fulfills the criteria set by the general law of evidence to prove guilt of a criminal. The lack of continuity and completeness of evidence can compromise the legal position. It is also required that the court be satisfied that the evidence has not been modified and is absolutely reliable. For this, hi-tech technical facilities, production of access control measures, or other supporting evidence should be used to justify integrity of digital evidence.

If a country's law enforcing agencies have no system in place or procedures to collect or store the electronic evidence, cyber crimes will go unpunished and expert's work of investigation will also go wasted and inadmissible. Scientifically, the results of the computer analysis should be able to withstand legal scrutiny. Details of imaging will play a crucial role in establishing the credibility of digital evidence in a cyber crime case. Cyber legislation in the developed countries has triggered a fierce debate, equipping the Police to monitor citizens' mail on the pretext of detecting cyber terrorists or child porn traders, is considered by citizen groups as permitting the Police to enter any one's house without permission. Courts have taken cognizance and began giving verdicts. Encryption softwares are under attack by the governmental agencies. Restrictions on export of encryption softwares were introduced to restrict spread of encrypted communications, restricting potential of law enforcing agencies to check the text in transit.

6.1 Recommendations

There is a review of current government action, an examination of how governments interact with the private sector and a consideration of the prospects for international cooperation and treaties. Although the world enjoys tremendous economic benefits from Internet development, the respective governments have to try to maintain tight control over the telecommunications industry and the public Internet use, and fight increasing cyber crimes. In order for the world to win the war against cyber crime, there is a dire need to establish a dedicated cell in each country and region which will not primarily detect but also prevent various cyber crimes that take place every day. It is also essential for countries around the globe, academia, business/industry and the international community to:

- Setting up an International Cyber Crime Investigation Cell
- Need for a Cyber Forensic Cell
- Join hands in the cyber war
- Educate individuals in cyber security
- It is quite natural for criminals to use advanced ICT technologies. There may not be faulty in practice with technology, but humans may make mistakes by using it. Investigators are able to find the breakthrough and combat these criminals.
- Enhance technical on-job training for law enforcement agencies to promote capability of investigation and criminal law
- From viewpoint of investigation, enhance horizontal coordination among all units in order not to waste resources. From strategy, increase international, cross-strait cooperation to combat cross-border swindler group.

Law enforcement needs to quantify the amount of cyber crime occurring within their jurisdictions to better grasp the magnitude of the problem. Corporations need better support on how to meet information security requirements as dictated by regulatory agencies, both need a better understanding that virtually no investigation, either civil or criminal, comes without digital evidence in some form. Clear reporting of crimes, and subsequent investigations, provides a basis for understanding the cyber crime problem. The development of a strategic approach to dealing with the issue will allow investigators to collaborate better on investigations over the long term. Additionally, the development of policy will help to guide investigators through the complicated process of cyber crime investigations. From the technical perspective, the focus lies on the tools and technologies available to cyber criminals, potential victims and law enforcement for the execution, protection against and prosecution of cyber crime, and digital forensics. From the organizational perspective, the focus lies on the cooperation between and responsibilities of all stakeholders in the field of cyber crime. From the legal perspective, the focus lies on criminalization of punishable activities targeted at computers largely related the field of substantive law and on establishing investigation and prosecution powers largely related to the field of procedural law.

Deterrence undoubtedly is an indispensable component in the control of all criminal behaviors, but it seems to be particularly suited to prevent cybercrimes. Most countries introduced Biometrics though it is not yet a mature technology, but it is rapidly developing, expanding with the proliferation of digital media. Some banks already offer print verification for cash instrument cashing, and biometric identification is being encoded into U.S. passports and Botswana recently implemented this. The technology underlies the Automatic Fingerprint Identification System (AFIS) now in use throughout most countries, Botswana inclusive. In controlled spaces, biometrics already serve to verify the identity of persons seeking entrance into secured and restricted areas in addition to a network of closed-circuit televisions (CCTV) in both public and private spaces, biometrics represent a capacity for locating wanted persons, even within the seeming anonymity of a crowd. As costly as bandwidth these days hence organizations require to detect users with abnormal bandwidth consumption in their organizations and automatically or manually restrict their activities.

7 Conclusions

Cyber crime is an international phenomenon that compels cooperation between multiple countries. The best protections are careful system design, the use of products to detect known viruses and system intrusions, and user education. It is also essential to have proper contingency plans for system recovery and engagement with the public as they are the weakest link in both the national and international cyber security about the role they play in cyber security. Internet is being used as a medium by many people to make fast money or to indulge in criminal acts. There is no limit to the way a human mind can think but it is in our hands to take precautions to prevent falling prey to such insidious acts. There is a need for a balanced international strategy to combat cybercrime also for round-the-clock cyber patrol and to equip the law enforcement officials with expertise in, and responsibility for, investigating and prosecuting cybercrime. A need has arisen for third world countries to work in partnership with industry to address cybercrime and security, where challenges can be discussed and develop effective solutions that do not pose a threat to individual privacy.

References

1. Boudreau, M.C., Gefen, D., Straub, D.W.: Validation in information systems research: A state-of-the-art assessment. MIS Quarterly 11(1), 1–16 (2001)
2. Brenner, S.: Defining cybercrime: A review of state and federal Law. In: Clifford, R.D. (ed.) Cybercrime: The Investigation, Prosecution, and Defense of a Computer-Related Crime, pp. 13–94. Carolina Academic Press, Durham (2006)
3. Broadhurst, R.: Developments in the global law enforcement of cyber-crime. Policing: An International Journal of Police Strategies and Management 29, 408–433 (2006)
4. Chawki, M.: Cybercrime in France: an overview. ComputerCrime Research Center (December 2005), http://www.crime-research.org/articles/cybercrime-in-france-overview/ (accessed November 23, 2009)
5. Chirillo, J.: Hack attacks revealed: A complete reference with custom security hacking toolkit. John Wiley, New York (2001)
6. Clough, B., Mungo, P.: Approaching zero: Data crime and the computer underworld. Faber and Faber, London (1992)

7. Curran, K., Morrissey, C., Fagan, C., Murphy, C., O'Donnell, B., Firzpatrick, G., et al.: Monitoring hacker activity with a honeynet. International Journal of Network Management 15(2), 123–134 (2005)
8. DARPA's role in developing the internet, go to the Internet Society, http://www.isoc.org/internet/history/brief.shtml
9. Wall, D.S.: Policing Cybercrime: Situating the public police in networks of security in cyberspace. Police Practice and Research: An International Journal 8(2) (2007) (forthcoming)
10. Davis, E., Wright, H., Tremaine, C.: Beyondphishing: pharmingand crimeware attacks (January 23, 2006), http://www.privsecblog.com/archives/phishingpharming-53-beyond-phishing-pharming-and-crimeware-attacks-.html
11. DOJ: H.R. 3402 Department of Justice Appropriations Authorization Act, fiscal years 2006 through 2009 (accessed June 23, 2009), http://www.gop.gov/Committee-central/bills/hr3402.asp (2005)
12. Erickson, J.: Hacking: The art of exploitation, 2nd edn. No Starch Press, San Francisco (2008)
13. Finny, T., et al.: Future challenge of cyber crime (September 2010), http://www.futuresworkinggroup.cos.ucf.edu/ (last accessed March 31, 2011)
14. Gordon, S., Ford, R.: On the definition and classification of cybercrime. Journal of Computer Virology 2, 13–20 (2006)
15. Internet Crime Complaint Center, Internet Crime Report and Kaspersky Labs' estimates (2007), http://www.ic3.gov/media/annualreport/2007_IC3Report.pdf
16. Kurzweil and his work can be found at, http://www.kurzweilai.net, http://www.kurzweilai.net
17. Taylor, R.W., Caeti, T.J., Kall Loper, D., Fritsch, E.J., Liederbach, J.: Digital Crime and Digital Terrorism. Pearson, Prentice Hall (2006)
18. Steffensmeier, D.J.: The fence: In the shadow of two worlds. Rowman & Littlefield, Totaw (1986)
19. Vacca, J.R.: Biometric technologies and verification systems. Elsevier, Amsterdam (2007)
20. Vielhauser, C.: Biometric user authentication for IT security: From fundamentals to handwriting. Springer, New York (2006)
21. Woodward Jr., J.D., Orlans, N.M., Higgins, P.T.: Biometrics: Identity assurance in the information age. McGraw-Hill/Osborne, New York (2003)

Sensor Network for Measurement and Analysis on Medical Devices Quality Control

Marek Penhaker, Monika Darebnikova, and Martin Cerny

VSB - Technical University of Ostrava, Faculty of Electrical Engineering and Computer Science, Ostrava, Czech Republic
{marek.penhaker,monika.derabnikova,martin.cerny}@vsb.cz

Abstract. The theme is the long-term measurement and verification of technical correctness shaker function of blood derivatives with subsequent signal analysis. We are scanning and processing signals containing information about the vibration shakers grids. To capture these signals is used accelerometers and measured data is then transmitted wirelessly via ZigBee technology from the mixer to the computer where the data is transmitted using TCP/IP communication to remote sites in the measurements. The data from the server, then shared the results to clients for processing. As a measurement, visualization and communication software has been used LabVIEW, which allows you to connect and communicate with the database created.

Keywords: Sensor Network, Data Transfer, Measurement, Quality Control.

1 Introduction

Blood is indispensable fluid necessary to recover the health and preservation of endangered human lives. Collection of blood and its subsequent processing is an integral part of every hospital. The processing of blood derivatives, there is several intermediate steps, which needs the support of preparation for reasons of Electrical and preserves the required properties of this precious liquid.

Platelets are involved in the process of blood clotting and stop bleeding. Platelet concentrates are stored in thromboembolism - an agitator or shaker in a temperature range of +20 to +24 ° C, with continuous shaking bag. Shakers are such devices, which can be placed in bags of platelets in a horizontal position. These bags are then shaken with a continuous speed in the horizontal axis amplitude of ca. 3 cm. Shakers also functions as a thermostat, because maintaining a constant temperature. Tromboconcenrate shaker kept at the time of manufacture for dispensing to the patient, ie. from 5 hours to 5 days. Shakers also tend to have an adjustable rate, to avoid foaming. Shaking frequency of 1 Hz is chosen.

Biomedical engineering is a challenge not only to monitor the basic life functions of individuals, but also focuses on various verification processes and feedbacks in the measurement of vital human functions or directly control the devices that these and other measurements are made. Monitoring and feedback are now required for each device, since it identifies errors, and then facility is able to remove or at least warn them.

J.J. Yonazi et al. (Eds.): ICeND 2011, CCIS 171, pp. 182–196, 2011.

One such problem is a technical demonstration of increased numbers trombo concentrate, which must be removed from the register and environment protection, probably due to poor work of agitators. These subjective impressions of blood center workers, together with an analysis of the entire process of preparing tromboconcentrate led to the analysis of technical operations and activities agitators. The clues leading to the long enough time devoted to monitoring the proper functioning agitators were also the possibility of the destruction of the samples due to sudden shocks or imperfect mixing, bouncing event bags wear of bearings and other options under consideration. In this article we will mainly focus on further data collection system for long-distance monitoring of blood agitators with off-line analysis.

The motivation for further work was the hospital request for verifying the functionality of agitators. More often the blood derivates in bags were smitten immediately after the shaking procedure finishing in one agitator then in others in the same time. We will try to acknowledge if the utility of agitator is proper or not. We will compare the utility of three agitators and we also made a several tests that were searching the effect of the events in near neighborhood. [1]

2 Measurement

Measuring string used for verifying the technical accuracy and functionality was implemented on the shaker the separation of blood components Hospital in Ostrava. Here, measurements were taken on the unit horizontal Agitator RL 45-B from Tool Company. Furthermore, in room the laptop for wireless measurement of vibrations from the accelerometer placed on the shaker. The room is also a UE device 650 from the Scientific business at which the measurement was carried out also.

The agitator blood derivatives were therefore scanned using accelerometry vibration sensors. Scanning was carried out at various locations within agitator or their surroundings. The figure 2 shows the local vibration measurements agitators marked points are sensing points. Measured data from the accelerometers were transmitted wirelessly to a computer at 2.4 GHz through the ZigBee technology. This technology eliminates the problems associated with cables and movement restrictions, reaching up to 20 meters over two walls and floors.

The shooting was to verify the technical requirements applied to these environmental influences for 10 seconds:

- strikes on the side of the shaker (of about 7 J)
- blow on the table underneath the apparatus (of about 10 J)
- jumps weighing 120 kg at 1m from the device
  a moderate impact to the hand shaker
- Walking from the door at the entrance to the room shaking and back
- status of 400 ml bottles, the shaker

2.1 An Accelerometers

For vibration sensing grids were used agitators two possible options. The first option was set XBee - MaxStream. The second option was to use to measure the accelerometer MMA7260Q from Freescale and XBee modules from MaxStream Company. The measured data is then two of these sensors were compared and the results are identical.

2.2 Measuring Board Accelerometer MMA7260Q and XBee Module

The device communicates wirelessly with the basic develop-exchange environment to several tens of meters. For the cordless PC networked ZigBee modules are used. Motherboard IDE is connected to a PC via a serial line (RS-232). Users are given basic information about the device using light emitting diodes.

Sensor Board containing the 3-axis accelerometer (X,Y,Z). There are three samples, IT = 3. The sampling frequency must be chosen as the greatest. XBee can sample up to 1 kHz, resulting in 100 Hz for the three inputs. In translation it is 10ms, set the IR = 10. [2]

Features of accelerometer MMA7260Q is in sensing acceleration in 3 axes (X, Y, Z); The possibility of external adjustment and the extent of changes in fixed increments ± 1.5g/2g/4g/6g bringing logic voltage levels 0 or 1 on two inputs g-Select; evaluation logic of the transfer acceleration acting on the output voltage signal, power supply: 3.3V, approximately 500μA , Sleep mode = 3μA; ± 2000 g maximum acceleration, frequency bandwidth acceleration measurements: X and Y = 350Hz, Z axis = 150Hz, max nonlinearity of ± 1% full scale; Output signal voltage 1.65 V at 0 g (temperature drift of ± 2 mg / ° C), sensitivity of 200 to 800mV / g (temperature drift of ± 2% / ° C).

Features of ZigBee XBee – MaxStream is in wireless communication with sensors through the 2.4 GHz band; to reach 100 on a line of sight; broadcast of 1mW (0dBm) RF data rate 250kbps, transmission methods DSSS / QPSK, sensitivity-92dBm, the supply voltage 2.8 - 3.4V, operating modes: standby, transmitting, receiving, and Configuration; supported topology: Point-to-point, point-to-multipoint, peer-to-peer mesh, the number of selectable channels is 16. [3]

3 Implementation

In the implementation of the measuring sensor system was needed to proceed in two steps. The first step was to address a local chain for the measuring of the Shaker Blood derivates in hospital. Another part of the remote data communications terminal to a local server for remote data storage and real - time visualization of measured data.

3.1 Measuring the String in the Blood Center

There were done more than forty independent measurements of the horizontal agitator's utility verification. In the Figure 4 shown complete measuring chain from the sensors placed in agitators to database in distance server with clients for processing the data. We used the accelerometer MMA7260Q for measuring the acceleration curves and we did several events that should affect the quality of agitation. For measuring the accelerometric data the acceleration sensors were put: sensor S1 - on the grate of the agitator, S2 - on the top of the agitator, S3 - on the blood bag in the agitator, S4 - on the floor. The events in near neighborhood that were simulated: knock on the side wall of agitator, plain plunge to the table, jumps by the person (120kg) in 1meter distant from the table, walking in the room, putting the bottle with 400ml of water on the agitator. All of the tests were made on the two agitators. [3]

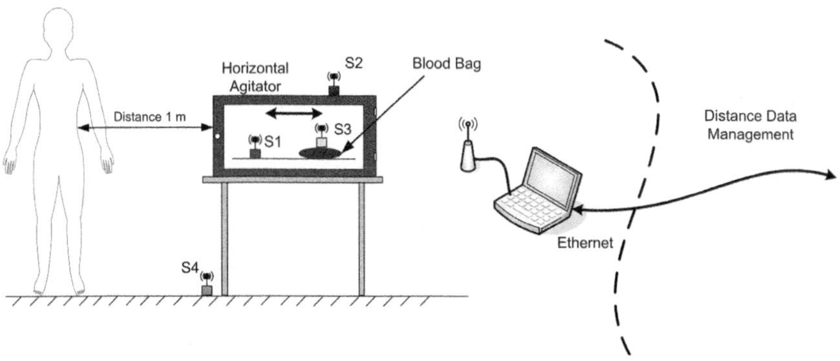

Fig. 1. The local chain for horizontal agitator vibration measuring with S1 and S3 sensors. The measurement surrounding vibration to pre-set influence of the environment on blood bags were also measured by S4 and S2 sensors.

Measured data from the accelerometers were transmitted wirelessly to a computer at 2.4 GHz through the ZigBee technology. This technology eliminates the problems associated with cables and movement restrictions.

Telemetry string more precisely consists of two modules, XBee (Zigbee MaxStream from the company). The first module is placed on the manufactured measuring board, which includes an accelerometer (MMA7260Q from Freescale), which measures acceleration. When moving a plate located on the gratings agitators the measured data from the accelerometer using the XBee transmit telemetry to the next block chain. In the last part of the telemetry chain block is LabVIEW, which allows communication with a serial interface with MySQL database created.

Data transfer within the Blood Center of agitator's blood derivatives was mediated via wireless communication, where the measured data from the accelerometers are stored on your computer's USB port. More data are already concerns of remote communication, which was carried out for continuous online monitoring.

3.2 Transfer of Measured Data - Remote Communication

The computer located at the Blood Center has been programmed application, which allows storage of measured data to the server database shaker. From this database, clients can re-created through the application of relevant data to retrieve and possibly further processed. To create the simulation application was used LabVIEW program.

Today is a big part of the database accessed remotely. The database, called "shaker" is centrally located on campus VSB. To access this site is should be an intranet or the Internet with a VPN client program, through which they can gain access to the internal network of TU. Type of data falls below the MySQL and php MyAdmin tool is created, which allows for easy Internet access and manipulate databases. Database "shaker" provides not least measured accelerometer data users who wish to continue with these raw data to work.

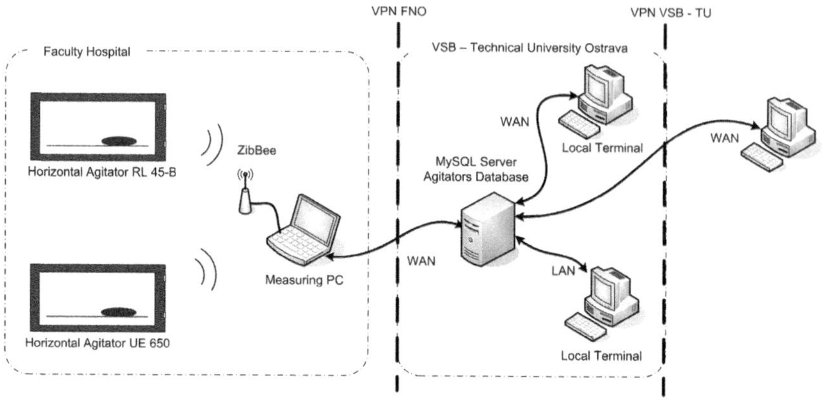

Fig. 2. Distance data measurement diagram for sensor network quality control

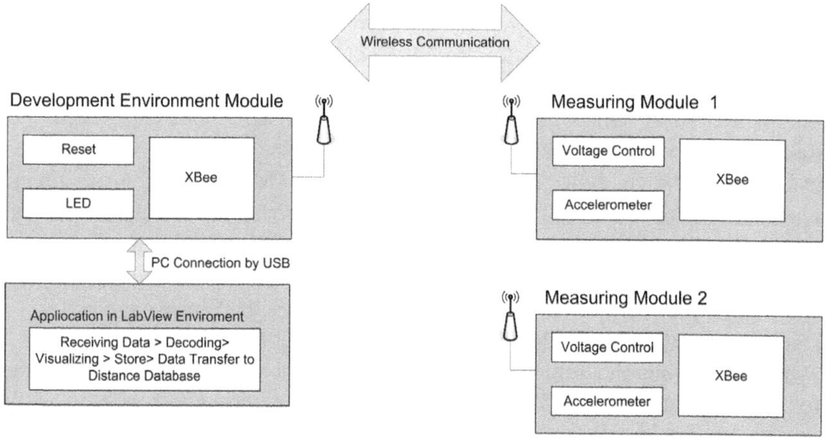

Fig. 3. Local measurement telemetry system at sensor part of measurement

4 Signal Evaluation

For the evaluation and processing of data was used MATLAB, a programming environment for scientific computing, algorithm design, simulation, modeling, analysis and data presentation, measurement and signal processing. MATLAB is an important part of the library known as Signal Processing Toolbox. The toolkit can help to simplify calculations and allow frequency analysis signals or sequences, filtering, modulation and demodulation. Also, it focuses on the design of filters display of amplitude and phase characteristics, etc. All signals in the MATLAB digital signals, as it always is a set of numbers. Processing of received signals proceeds from the mathematical treatment of curves.

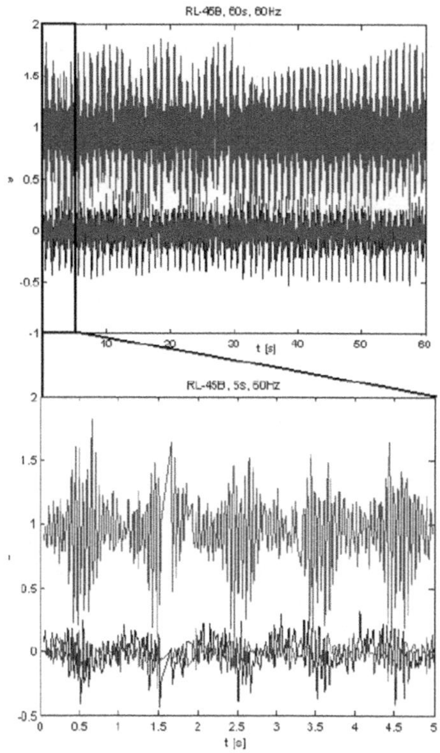

Fig. 4. The time course from 0 to 60 seconds added to zoomed section from 0 to 5 s from sensor placed on trombo concentrate

4.1 Signal Analysis in Time Domain

The result of acceleration sensors are measured values that are shown at three time axes (X, Y, Z). Since the accelerometer is expected to be susceptible to acceleration in the desired direction. For example, an accelerometer measuring the X-axis, measured in the plane of the parasitic Y and Z. The sensitivity ratio is expressed in ways not required, and against the wishes of the often causes a measurement error. In the case of motion grows shaker is likely dominance of the acceleration in the X and the other two axes are dependent on the vibration of grids in the working mode.

Due to the large volume of data obtained usually does not analyze the entire record, but only suitably chosen part or several parts of the record. The analyzed section is determined either randomly or in moments when they were shooting accelerometer data applied because of environmental influences verification of technical assumptions device. The length of selected segments depends on the purpose of analysis, were generally analyzed 30 or 60-second 5-second record with illustrative examples.

Legend to the following graphic display:

- Blue curve - the X-axis - measured in horizontal direction
- Green curve - the Y axis - measured in vertical direction
- Red curve - Z axis - measured in the axial direction
- The unit of measurement is grams, if the user requested output in units of m/s2, just the resulting value multiplied by the value of g, which has in our latitude, the size of 9.81.

4.2 Spectral Analysis

The aim of signal analysis is to calculate the required parameters or characteristics of the signals. When signal analysis, however, in many cases can not do with the parameters and characteristics calculated in the original (time) regions. To obtain more information about signals, Helping the spectral analysis. Spectral analysis is intended to find a description of the signal using its spectral components in the area, which is then supplementing the analysis in time domain. Knowledge of the spectral description is important because it allows explaining a number of practical things that would otherwise be difficult clarified. The signal can be characterized as a function of frequency. Such a statement is called spectrum, which allows analysis in the frequency domain. Correlation signals its spectrum is mathematically or algorithmically based on the use of various transformations. The most common use of Fourier transform, whose application can obtain the frequency spectrum given signal.

In the frequency domain to obtain the signal frequency spectrum (Fourier transform) analyzed the proportions of the various components and their changes. The sampling is of course subject sampling theorem. The data processing using frequency analysis, the resulting parameters frequency and amplitude.

For the real signal is a spectrum of one-sided. For sampling the analog signal with his full recovery to be followed Shannon - Kotelnik theorem: FVZ> 2fmax (sampling frequency must be at least twice the maximum frequency of the reconstructed signal). The results of the analysis of power spectra shakers UE 650 are illustrated in the following Fig. 38, which was considered the dominant axis X (horizontal direction of the record 60s removing the DC component of the signal) is selected FFT for N = 2m = 512th.

4.3 Time-Frequency Analysis

Classical spectral analysis of signals in the Fourier sense implies that the signal is analyzed during the analysis of change in terms of frequency content. This means that whenever the calculations of spectra are considered the signal. In the case of data measured in blood derivatives agitator's length is too long and the signal is a signal with parameters varying over time. Recording equipment output is continuously connected with a local computer, which is a very long record of data for calculating the FFT of the registration. Therefore, the calculation uses a different spectrum than the Fourier sense, or to apply Fourier analysis, but the original signal is divided into sections of finite length. Above each section is carried out by Fourier analysis.

Compressed spectral method is used props to show the frequency domain in three-dimensional projection. Gradually, the frequency curves calculated from the length of sections 2-4 seconds. Thus, the calculated frequency curve, then gradually rendered one after another in pseudo- three dimensional projections - (f, t, PSD (f)). The method of TFA is possible to monitor progress and changes in the frequency components over time - a description of the dynamic behavior of the signal in the frequency domain.

The advantage of data processing is arranged to record a longer stretch. In Fig. 40 is outlined the difference between the PSD and the CSA, which is illustrated in the case of the CSA to see how different spectral components vary in time. As seen, this is a short-range signal of each section ordered for him. Fig. 41 shows this case for one second and two-second segments.

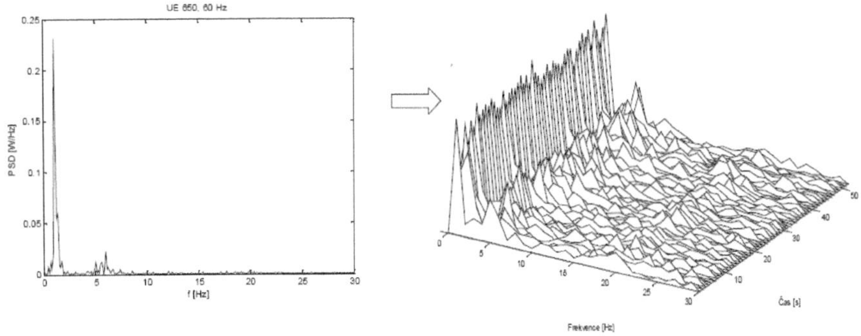

Fig. 5. Samples of one second TSA (left) and two-second segments (right)

4.4 Ties between the Shaker - Correlation Coefficient

When analyzing the signal can also use correlation analysis, which examines the relationship between the two different signals that were recorded simultaneously. To the degree of linear dependence between two signals from shakers comparison is not necessary to calculate the correlation function directly, but correlation coefficient:

$$\rho_{xy}(i,j) = \frac{C_{xy}(i,j)}{\sqrt{\sigma_x(i)\sigma_y(j)}}, \tag{1}$$

MATLAB array returned a value of 2 x 2 The matrix R is at positions R11 and R22 values equal to 1, which is the autocorrelation sequence accelerometer signals, the mutual correlation coefficients sequence alone with myself. The positions of R12 and R21 are sought correlation coefficients agitator UE 650 - RL 45-B.

As previously mentioned, the correlation coefficient becomes in the linear positive, respectively negative) dependence of the two variables limits ± 1 has zero correlation with the independence of the two sensed signals, where both polarities are equally probable. The values close to zero correlation, however, clearly does not imply independence, but it can be assumed that the link between these signals is very weak. When comparing the signals from both agitator, which was worked upon the files of 1000 measured values (samples), which corresponds to a record of about 20 s, was found a correlation coefficient value of 0.1507.

5 Tests and Results

To be able to compare both agitators have chosen the same input ranges of the measured signals and the sampling frequency that was selected 30 or 60 Hz. Measurements took place under the same environmental conditions and were trying to bring the two measurements - like the physical arrangement of sensors sensing the same settings, same route of transmission signals. Measurements were carried out with full service equipment, so the data capture is often well placed agitators trombo-concentrate.

Comparison of platelet agitators

The signal is removed from both types of blood derivatives agitators has a different character. From time to record Fig.7 and Fig.8 show that UE 650 has Shaker in the X (blue curve) the apparent sinusoidal. Same axis in the image on the right (RL shaker 45-B) has also outlined the nature of the sinusoidal signals with modulated as much higher frequency. The timing can not make any conclusions.

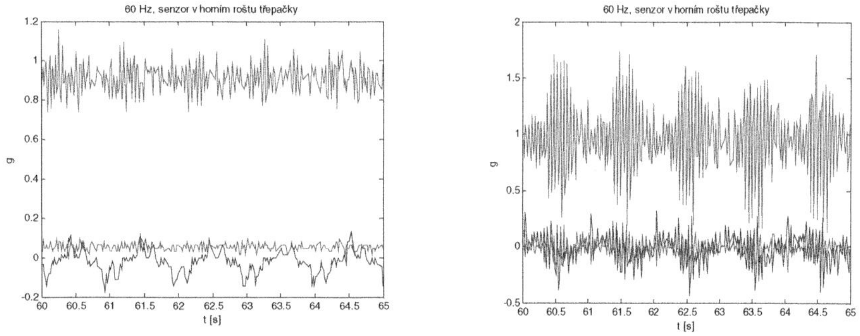

Fig. 6. UE650 shaker in the time domain in 60 Hz – left and Shaker RL45-B in the time domain in 60 Hz right

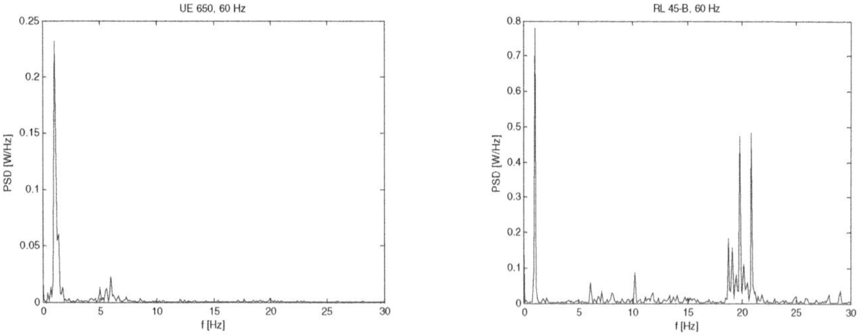

Fig. 7. Shaker UE650 - PSD major axis X – left and RL45-B shaker - PSD major axis X -right

Proceed to compare the measured signals in the frequency domain. In Fig.9-10 shows the power spectral density calculated by direct application of Fourier transform. The chart shakers RL45-B are shown outstanding frequencies - 1Hz, 21Hz, and 21Hz is present in the signal to a large extent. As demonstrated by comparing these graphs, the process of significant frequency components is substantially different.

Display using the CSA in the following chart gives a better localization of significant frequency components in time.

After the measurement and signal processing is possible to offset the effects of the events surrounding the processing of blood products with horizontal agitators. The influences are reflected in the records are processed due to the very activities of agitators. Differences in the processed records are measurable and can cause long-term problem with the appearance of samples processed incorrectly. In another part of the analysis we focus on the source of the artifacts caused either by failure, age, or agitator design fault. This finding may have significant impact on the quality and preparation trombo-concentrate.

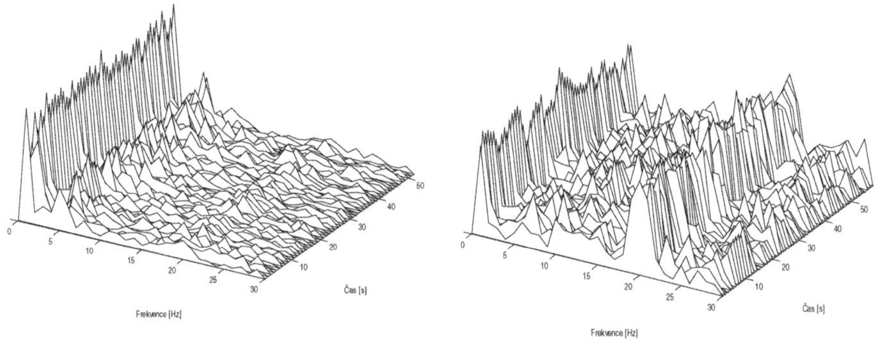

Fig. 8. CSA 60-second recording shaker UE 650 – left and CSA 60-second recording shaker RL 45-B – right

The result of this work is technical language code in MATLAB, enabling wider mathematical analysis of measured data. The data that was retrieved from the database was analyzed in next section. They were evaluated vibration signals going from shakers. When analyzing the FFT method was used, since this method gives information about the signal spectrum.

Graphs are compared in the spectrum of PSD plots the measurement results, but the result of frequency analysis. Based on the comparison of spectra were analyzed both shakers.

Both devices for storing blood products should at the very end to show the same activity. It should be borne in mind that both devices were manufactured by different manufacturers.

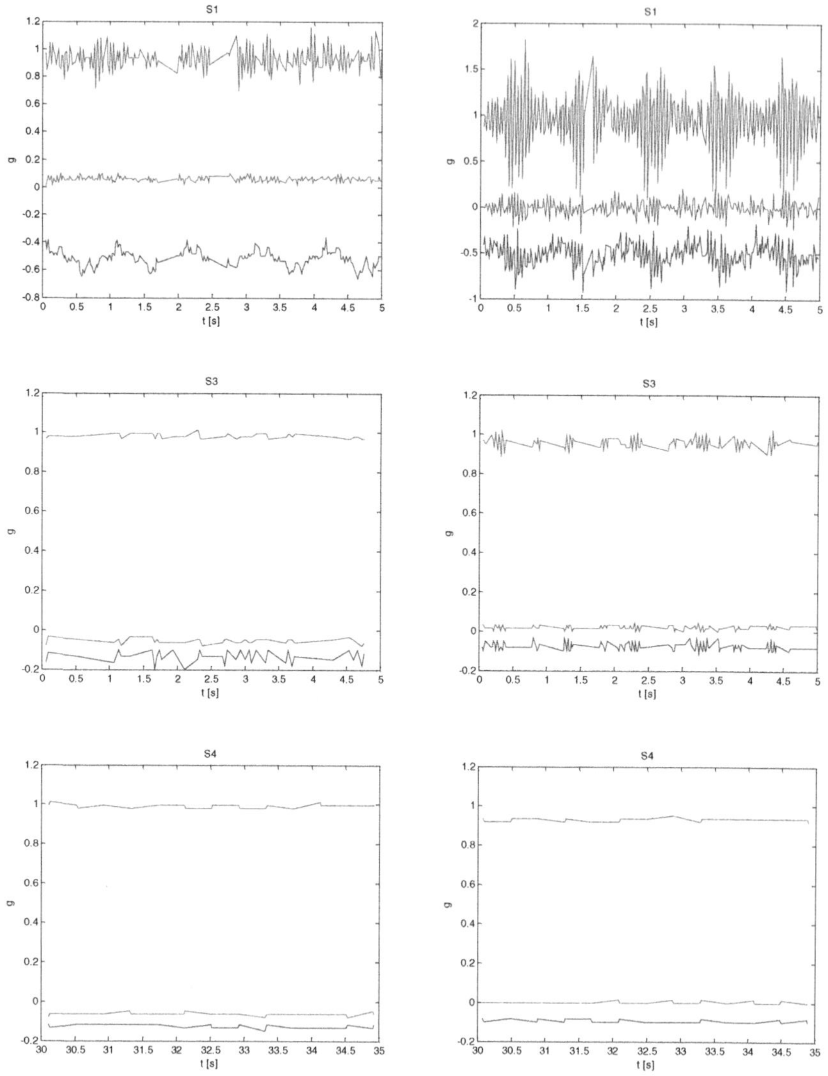

Fig. 9. Comparison of time course record in the individual measurement points in both agitators UE 650 and RL 45-B. Location of the sensors according the measured signal: S1-sensor grid shaker-S2 sensor on top of the shaker, S2 - the blood bag, S4-sensor on the floor in the room agitator.

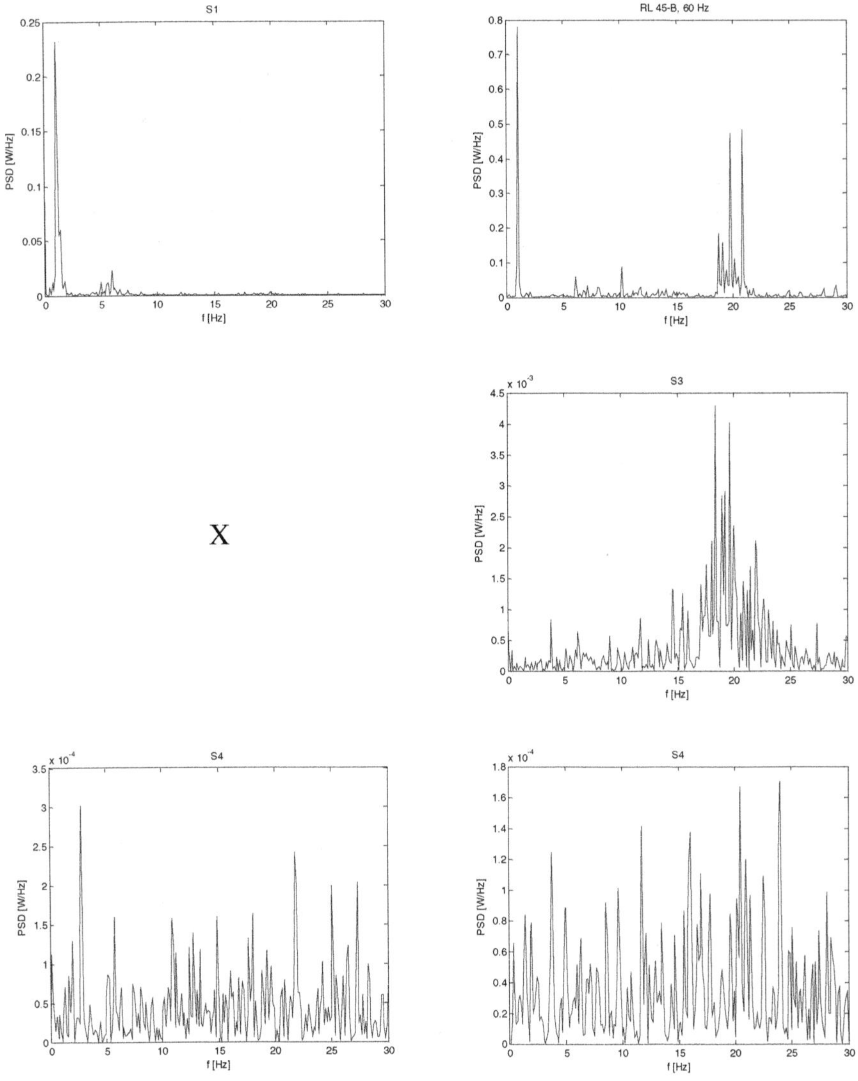

Fig. 10. PSD - power spectral density measurements at various points in both shakers UE 650 RL 45-B of the upper shaker-S4 sensor in the room on the ground

On the basis of the measurements and analysis it is clear that the similarity - the sameness of the functionality of both shakers vary. This conclusion is supported by the resulting graph analysis, that the shaker, RL 45-B shaker UE 650 over an increase in the frequency of 20 Hz, which may affect the shaking and the storage bags with tromboconcentrates.

6 Conclusion

The result of this study was to compare and verify the functionality of two agitators Blood Center University Hospital on the basis of vibration analysis. The work was the requirement for University Hospital, because of previous decay tromboconcentrate after shaking. This error occurred more frequently in one of agitators (Horizontal agitator RL 45-B from company Tool). The task of the thesis was therefore to verify functionality and accuracy of this shaker is similar to shaking UE 650 from the Scientific business, or has the effect of decay proportion tromboconcentrate other variable. It was therefore a comparison of the agitator and done a few tests that have been tasked to explore the environment.

Verification of long-term technical accuracy agitators blood products prior to scanning, processing and subsequent analysis of signals containing information about the vibration agitator grids. He developed and implemented to capture the measuring chain and long-term online monitoring equipment blood derivatives. To measure the acceleration sensors were used accelerometer Freescale.

Acknowledgment. The work and the contribution were supported by the project: Ministry of Education of the Czech Republic under Project 1M0567 "Centre of Applied Cybernetics", Student grant agency SV 4501141 "Biomedical engineering systems VII" and TACR TA01010632 "SCADA system for control and measurement of process in real time". Also supported by project MSM6198910027 Consuming Computer Simulation and Optimization.

References

1. Vasickova, Z., Penhaker, M., Darenikova, M.: Thee Functionality Control of Horizontal Agitators for Blood Bags. In: Bamidis, P.D., Pallikarakis, N. (eds.) XII Mediterranean Conference on Medical and Biological Engineering and Computing 2010, MEDICON 2010, Chalkidiki, Greece, May 27-30. IFMBE Proceedings, vol. 29, Part 2, pp. 859–862. Springer, Heidelberg (2010), doi:10.1007/978-3-642-13039-7_217, ISBN 978-3-642-13038-0 (Print) 978-3-642-13039-7 (Online), ISSN: 16800737
2. Datasheet for ZSTAR3 – DRM103 Designer Reference Manual. Arizona (USA). Freescale, 88s (2008)
3. Datasheet for MMA7361L - Three Axis Low-g Micromachined Accelerometer. Arizona (USA). Freescale, 11s (2008)
4. Kasik, V., Stankus, M.: Graphical development system design for creating the FPGA-based applications in biomedicine. In: XII Mediterranean Conference on Medical and Biological Engineering and Computing 2010. IFMBE Proceedings, vol. 29, Part 5, pp. 879–882, doi:10.1007/978-3-642-13039-7_222
5. Aidu, E.A.I., Trunov, V.G., Titomir, L.I., Tysler, M., Turzova, M., Szathmary, V.: Electrocardiographic ST segment changes as an indicator for localization of injury potentials. A Computer Simulation Study Kardiologia 15(1), 21–24, ISSN: 12100048
6. Kasik, V.: Acceleration of Backtracking Algorithm with FPGA. In: 2010 International Conference on Applied Electronics, Pilsen, Czech Republic, pp. 149–152 (2010) ISBN 978-80-7043-865-7, ISSN 1803-7232

7. Skapa, J., Siska, P., Vasinek, V., Vanda, J.: Identification of external quantities using redistribution of optical power - art. no. 70031R. In: Book Optical Sensors 2008, vol. 7003, pp. R31–R31 (2008) ISSN: 0277-786X, ISBN: 978-0-8194-7201-4
8. ŠimšíK, D., GaLajdová, A., Majerník, J., Hrabinská, I., Želinský, P.: The video analysis utilization in rehabilitation for moblity development. Lékař a technika. Česká republika, 4-5, Ročník 35, 87–92 (2004) ISSN 0301-5491,
9. Živčák, J., Petrík, M., Hudák, R., Tóth, T., Knežo, D., Kovalova, E.: Embedded tensile strenght test machine FM1000 - An upgrade of measurement and control. Diffusion and Defect Data Pt.B: Solid State Phenomena 147-149, 657–662, ISSN: 10120394, ISBN: 3908451655; 978-390845165
10. Krištof, M., Hudák, R., Takáčová, A., Živčák, J., Fialka, L., Takáč, R.: Contact pressure measurement in trunk orthoses. In: Proceedings of ICCC-CONTI 2010 - IEEE International Joint Conferences on Computational Cybernetics and Technical Informatics, art. no. 5491304, p. 175 (2010), doi: 10.1109/ICCCYB.2010.5491304, ISBN: 978-142447433-2
11. Klima, M., Pazderak, J., Bernas, M., Pata, P., Hozman, J., Roubik, K.: Objective and subjective image quality evaluation for security technology. In: Proceedings of IEEE Annual International Carnahan Conference on Security Technology, pp. 108–114
12. Garani, G.: Nest and unnest operators in nested relations. Data Science Journal 7, 57–64, doi: 10.2481/dsj.7.57, ISSN: 16831470
13. Havlik, J., Uhlir, J., Horcik, Z.: Thumb motion classification using discrimination functions. In: International Conference on Applied Electronics, AE, art. no. 4382963, pp. 55–57 (2006), doi: 10.1109/AE.2006.4382963, ISBN: 8070434422;978-807043442-0
14. Hozman, J., Zanchi, V., Cerny, R., Marsalek, P., Szabo, Z.: Precise Advanced Head Posture Measurement. In: Book Challenges in Remote Sensing - Proceedings of the 3rd Wseas International Conference on Remote Sensing (REMOTE 2007), pp. 18–26 (2007) ISSN: 1790-5117, ISBN: 978-960-6766-17-6
15. Cerny, M.: Movement Activity Monitoringof Elederly People – Application in Remote Home Care Systems. In: Proceedings of 2010 Second International Conference on Computer Engineering and Applications ICCEA 2010, Bali Island, Indonesia, March 19-21, vol. 2. IEEE Conference Publishing Services, NJ (2010) ISBN 978-0-7695-3982-9
16. Krejcar, O.: Large Multimedia Artifacts Prebuffering in Mobile Information Systems as Location Context Awareness. In: 4th International Symposium on Wireless Pervasive Computing, ISWPC 2009, Melbourne, Australia, February 11-13, pp. 216–220 (2009), doi:10.1109/ISWPC.2009.4800591, ISBN 978-1-4244-4299-7
17. Vasickova, Z., Augustynek, M.: New method for detection of epileptic seizure. Journal of Vibroengineering 11(2), 279–282 (2009) ISSN 1392 - 8716
18. Bernabucci, I., Conforto, S., Schmid, M., D'Alessio, T.: A bio-inspired controller of an upper arm model in a perturbed environment. In: Proceedings the 2007 International Conference on Intelligent Sensors, Sensor Networks and Information Processing, pp. 549–553 (2007) ISBN: 978-1-4244-1501-4
19. Krejcar, O., Cernohorsky, J., Fojcik, P., Janckulik, D., Martinovic, J.: Smartphone, PDA and mobile Embedded device clients of Biotelemetric System for monitoring of life functions. In: 5th International Conference on Innovations in Information Technology, Innovations 2008, Al Ain, United Arab Emirates, December 16-18, pp. 145–149 (2008), doi:10.1109/INNOVATIONS.2008.4781761, ISBN 978-1-4244-3396-4
20. Cerny, M.: Movement Monitoring in the HomeCare System. In: Dossel-Schleger (ed.) IFMBE Proceddings, vol. (25). Springer, Berlin (2009) ISBN 978-3-642-03897-6; ISSN 1680-07

21. Machacek, Z., Hajovsky, R., Ozana, S., Krnavek, J.: Experiments of Thermal Fields of Sensors Supported by Digital Image Processing. In: Mediterranean Conference on Control Automation, Ajjacio, France, p. 6 (2008) IEEE CFP08MED-CDR, ISBN 978-1-4244-2504-4
22. Ozana, S., Machacek, Z.: Implementation of the Mathematical Model of a Generating Block in Matlab&Simulink Using S-functions. In: Kamaruzaman, J., Mahmoud, S., Sivakumar, R. (eds.) The Second International Conference on Computer and Electrical Engineering, ICCEE 2009, vol. I. IEEE Computer Society, Los Alamitos (2009); Session 8. S. 431-435. ISBN 978-0-7695-3925-6
23. Korpas, D., Halek, J.: Pulse wave variability within two short-term measurements (2006); Biomedical papers of the Medical Faculty of the University Palacký, Olomouc, Czechoslovakia, vol. 150(2), pp. 339–344, ISSN: 12138118

Multi-Level Latent Class Analysis of Internet Use Pattern in Taiwan

Tsui-Chuan Hsieh and Chyan Yang

Institute of Information Management, National Chiao Tung University, 1001 University Road, Hsinchu, Taiwan 300
{terrynctu,professor.yang}@gmail.com

Abstract. This study reports the Taiwan Government survey results of the Internet use pattern by Multi-level Latent Class Analysis (MLCA). Based on the stratified random sampling with total sample size of 16,133, this study discovers the use pattern of Internet consists of seven segments: knowledgeable segment, traditional use segment, amusement segment, entertainment & online shopping segment, leisure & aloof segment, business segment, Interactive segment. At a higher level, the entire Taiwan is divided into three segments: Southern Taiwan, Northern Taiwan, and metropolitan. Besides, the Internet use behaviors of instant messenger, email, or IP-phone are uncorrelated. This study enriches findings of this research to provide researchers and practitioners a good guideline for its economic development policy setting.

Keywords: Internet Use, Digital Divide, Latent Class Analysis, Multi-level Latent Class Analysis.

1 Introduction

The rise of Internet extends the service hours into 24 hours a day; also, it attracts customers from all around the whole world. That is, for sellers, Internet alters the type of mass-production and service-providing in only a few assigned places, which buyers gradually start to have more bargain powers, including shopping around more conveniently through search, referring to others' experiences, and even, making a credit to the sellers to influence their sales volumes, etc [1]. Changes like these make service-providers or product- developers value users' needs and consumption behaviors in the Internet more than before [9, 15]. If a marketer on the Internet is able to identify potential early adopters and can understand their personality correlates, a positive image of the product or service, along with appropriate incentives, may be presented to the consumer to facilitate the adoption process and encourage subsequent positive word of mouth communication to later adopters [7, 8].

With the popularity of digital environment, Internet has influenced our daily life more than ours in the past. Plentiful, multi-dimensional, and convenient services here stimulate peoples' change in their lifestyle [6, 27]. Peoples' daily activities are gradually shifted from the physical circumstance into the virtual one. For example, hand-written letters are replaced by e-mails, or even by instant messengers. The

J.J. Yonazi et al. (Eds.): ICeND 2011, CCIS 171, pp. 197–208, 2011.

bulletin boards are evolved into web sites. Diaries change into blogs or micro-blogs. Also, the shopping environment is migrated from physical stores into online ones. It could be agreed that people are not doing anything particularly new – they are doing old things in new way and finding that some of those new ways suit their lifestyle better [2, 25]. Besides, more and more Internet users contribute to the generation of e-services, like online-shopping, e-banks, online movies, online games, IP-phone, e-news, and online booking. The place of Internet applications and services enrich peoples' life [2, 13, 14]. Internet also affects on others more and more, for instance, family life, learning, and work. The internet is popularly celebrated to be transforming all sectors of everyday life – from the economy to civic society, seems to be context-dependent and highly variable with and between households, patterns of participation in the information society [2, 19, 26].

2 Multi-Level Latent Class Analysis

In the social sciences research, many research questions investigate the relationship when both the categorical outcome and the predictor variables are latent. Categorical data analysis that has been and will continue to be useful in the analysis of sociological data and examples of which include survey data, and in empirical studies of latent types, latent variables, and latent structures [10]. In an attitude survey, researchers generally concerned more about the sample's potential group and the latent class model provides better fit to categories data, when attitude survey more appropriate use of Latent Class Analysis [16].

2.1 Latent Class Analysis (LCA)

A latent class model assumes that population of subject is divided into a few exclusive latent classes. LCA is a statistical method used to identify sub-types of related cases using a set of categorical and/or continuous observed variables. These sub-types are referred to as latent classes. The classes are inferred from the multiple observed indicators. They are not directly observed [11]. Suppose that dependent variable Yi is a binary variable, and only one independent variable. The LCA model [3, 17] can be expressed as follows:

$$P(Y_i = 1 \mid X_i, \beta) = \frac{e^{v_i}}{1 + e^{v_i}} \tag{1}$$

Where $v_i = \beta_0 + \beta_1 X_i$ is latent variables, predict by X_i. If depend variable Y_i are binary data, let X_i is a latent variables, categorical $s = 1, 2, \cdots, S$, then when the non-conditional probability can be expressed as equation (2).

$$P(Y_i = 1) = \sum_{s=1}^{S} P(X_i = s) P(Y_i = 1 \mid X_i = s) \tag{2}$$

Where $P(Y_i = 1 \mid X_i = s)$ is conditional probability, meaning if i is one member of class s, the probability when dependent variables are one. The classes are latent classes, it can't be directly observed, and it's estimated from data. Let X_i is a latent Class variables. When $P(Y_i = 1 \mid X_i = s)$ can be expressed as follows:

$$P(Y_i = 1 \mid X_i = s) = \frac{e^{\beta_s}}{1 + e^{\beta_s}} \tag{3}$$

Where β_s is the parameter that needs to estimated. $P(X_i = s)$ is a probability when individual i belongs to any latent classes, The equation can be presented like a multi-category logistic regression form, namely:

$$P(X_i = s) = \frac{e^{\gamma_s}}{\sum_{s'=1}^{S} e^{\gamma_{s'}}} \tag{4}$$

If depend variable Y_i are binary variable vectors, vector variable is assembled by Y_{ij}, if j is categorical $k = 1,2,\cdots,K$, i is an individual variable, k is one of a multivariate variable, if the other conditions unchanged, then we observed the non-conditional probability (when all the variables Y_{ik} are equal to 1) can be expressed as equation (5).

$$P(Y_i = 1) = \sum_{s=1}^{S} P(X_i = s) \Pi_{k=1}^{K} P(Y_{ik} = 1 \mid X_i = s) \tag{5}$$

Conditional probability $P(Y_{ik} = 1 \mid X_i = s)$, namely:

$$P(Y_{ik} = 1 \mid X_i = s) = \frac{e^{\beta_{ks}}}{1 + e^{\beta_{ks}}} \tag{6}$$

Such effect can be included by means of one or more concomitant variables, denoted Z_i, let it be assembled by Z_{it}, if $t = 1,2,\cdots,T$, then conditional probability $P(Y_{ik} = 1 \mid X_i = s)$ can be expressed as follow:

$$P\left(Y_{ik} = 1 \mid Z_i, X_i = s\right) = \frac{e^{\beta_{ks} + \sum_{t=1}^{T} \beta_{kt} Z_{it}}}{1 + e^{\beta_{ks} + \sum_{t=1}^{T} \beta_{kt} Z_{it}}} \tag{7}$$

Traditional LCA assumes that observations are independent of one another. However, multi-level data structures are common in social and behavioral researches are needed. For example, observations are not independent when the data structure includes citizen nested in city, employees nested in companies, or students nested in schools. Consideration and assessment of contextual level predictors in the framework of a latent class analysis has implications for many salient research questions in the social and behavioral sciences. These nested data structures require multi-level techniques. In response to these needs, Vermunt presented a framework for assessing latent class models with nested data [22].

2.2 Multi-Level Latent Class Analysis (MLCA)

Multi-level Latent class analysis (MLCA) has been suggested as a model-based tool for regular both individual (level 1) segmentation and group segmentation (level 2). [4, 11, 20, 22]. We apply MLCA to attain simultaneously city segmentation and cross-regional customer segmentation. Let Y_{ijk} denote the response of individual or level-1 unit i whin group or level-2 unit j on indicator or item k. Suppose data is available on an nationwide (Cross-regional) sample of customers, denoted $i = 1,.., I$, originating from a set of counties, denoted $j = 1,..., J$. For each individual i, it is recorded whether this person uses each function from a set of Internet use behaviors, denoted $k = 1,..., K$, where $Y_{ijk} = 1$, if customer i from City/County j use function k, and $Yijk = 0$ otherwise. The data of behaviors for an individual i is collected in vector Yij, and Yj denotes the observed data of behaviors for all consumers of country j. The in Cross-regional sample of customers is assumed to represent a limited number of *customer segments*, denoted $s = 1 ,..., S$. Furthermore, the counties under study are assumed to belong to a limited number of *City/County segments*, denoted $t = 1 ,..., T$. Discrete latent variables Xij and Zj represent the customer segment and City/County segment membership, respectively. A multi-level latent class model [22] consists of a mixture model equation for the customer level and one for the City/County level. For the customer level, we specify the probability of Internet use behaviors for a customer i from City/County j, conditional on membership of City/County j to City/County segment t, as follows:

$$P\left(Y_{ij} \mid Z_j = t\right) = \sum_{s=1}^{S} P\left(X_{ij} = s \mid Z_j = t\right) \Pi_{k=1}^{K} P\left(Y_{ijk} \mid X_{ij} = s\right) \tag{8}$$

Basically, equation (1) is a regular mixture model, with the novelty that the relative sizes of the latent classes (customer segments) depend on the city segment. At the city-level, a similar mixture model equation is specified, namely:

$$P\left(Y_{j}\right)=\sum_{t=1}^{T} P\left(Z_{j}=t\right) \Pi_{i=1}^{N_{j}} P\left(Y_{ij} \mid Z_{j}=t\right) \tag{9}$$

where *Nj* denotes the sample size in city *j*. Combining equations (8) and (9) yields:

$$P(Y_j)=\sum_{t=1}^{T}P(Z_j=t)\Pi_{i=1}^{N_j}\left(\sum_{s=1}^{S}P(X_{ij}=s\mid Z_j=t)\Pi_{k=1}^{K}P(Y_{ijk}\mid X_{ij}=s)\right) \tag{10}$$

The right-hand side of equation (10) consists of three components, respectively: a) the probability that City/County j belongs to a particular City/County segment, b) the probability that customer j belongs to a particular customer segment, given the City/County segment membership, and c) the probability of a customer's use behaviors in the Internet k, given the customer segment membership. Hence, the probability of observing the behaviors data is a weighted average probability, where the weights are the City/County segment and customer segment probabilities. Component c) of equation (10) captures the key differences between customer segments, namely the conditional probability that customers use a particular Internet function k. This is modeled in the form of a logic equation:

$$P\left(Y_{ijk}=1 \mid X_{ij}=s\right)=\frac{e^{\beta_{ks}}}{1+e^{\beta_{ks}}} \tag{11}$$

Component b) of equation (10) captures the key differences between the City/County segments, namely the relative size of each of the customer segments. This is also modeled through a logic equation [22]:

$$P\left(X_{ij}=s \mid Z_{j}=t\right)=\frac{e^{\gamma_{st}}}{\sum_{s'=1}^{S} e^{\gamma_{s't}}} \tag{12}$$

The parameters of the MLCA model can be estimated by Maximum Likelihood. Maximization of the likelihood function can be achieved by an adapted version of the Expectation-Maximization [8] algorithm [22].

3 Method

3.1 Samples

Data for all analyses were collected using the Research, Development, and Evaluation Commission, Executive Yuan, Taiwan (RDEC) Digital Divide Survey, which was to evaluate the status of information infrastructure implementation and current situation in

Taiwan. The survey was conducted using computer assisted telephone interviews (CATI) from July to August in 2009. Random sampling interview was used to interview a population segment of the Taiwanese interviewee at the age of 12 or above in 25 counties and cities. The survey collected 16,133 valid random samples with a response rate of 66.4%, and the sampling errors below ±3%. In this paper, we use 10 items of categorical variables about Internet use behavior as a research data set. The data are used in the exclusion of missing values for the 10,909 valid samples. In this paper, latent classes of Internet use behaviors among 10,909 Taiwan residents who live in one of 25 different cities/counties Taiwan are considered.

Ten categorical indicators were used to inform latent class membership. For example, Send/receive email (1=yes, 0=no), Internet for entertainment purposes(1=yes, 0=no), instant message(1=yes, 0=no), use Online telephone(1=yes, 0=no), E-banking(1=yes, 0=no), sell or buy products on the Internet(1=yes, 0=no), general information acquisition(1=yes, 0=no), search for work Information(1=yes, 0=no), news browsing(1=yes, 0=no), Internet search for public notices(1=yes, 0=no). Descriptive statistics for the Internet use sample see Table 2. For example, sample size of Taipei City is 1,355. In Taipei City, more than 92% of them use Internet for email, 97% of them also use Internet for entertainment. Besides, the others use instant messenger (78.1%), IP-phone (49.3%), on-line banking (40.6%), general information and news research (91.2%), job information and government information research (57.7%), respectively.

Table 1. Descriptive statistics for the Internet use sample

City / County	Sample Size	Internet Use (Sample Proportion)									
		Email	Enter-tainment	Messen-ger	IP-phone	Banking	Online shopping	Gen. info.	Job info.	News	Gov. info.
1 Taipei City	1355	92.0	73.3	78.1	49.3	40.6	65.5	91.2	80.7	86.7	57.7
2 Taipei County	1943	90.3	74.1	78.3	37.3	30.2	60.6	90.5	76.9	81.5	52.6
3 Keelung City	189	91.7	76.2	80.4	39.9	33.2	63.8	89.1	79.2	80.5	54.4
4 Yilan County	198	94.4	78.3	77.4	35.6	23.1	63.5	90.4	78.9	80.1	48.0
5 Taoyuan County	967	89.7	77.6	76.4	40.3	27.6	61.2	88.5	78.1	80.9	49.4
6 Hsinchu County	233	91.1	74.9	75.4	40.7	32.5	57.6	84.2	80.0	81.1	50.1
7 Hsinchu City	208	92.8	74.4	75.0	42.9	38.6	61.4	89.6	80.3	82.2	52.3
8 Miaoli County	256	92.5	75.7	77.8	36.1	28.5	59.9	87.9	80.7	83.2	51.3
9 Taichung County	726	89.4	78.2	76.9	36.3	25.4	57.2	86.8	80.2	77.6	49.3
10 Taichung City	573	92.7	72.2	74.8	50.2	32.1	58.9	88.6	80.3	80.5	56.2
11Changhua County	579	89.2	74.1	76.8	39.1	23.8	55.2	87.9	77.6	76.6	44.3
12 Nantou County	220	92.7	75.6	77.6	35.3	24.7	59.0	89.2	78.9	77.8	46.0
13 Yunlin County	265	91.1	81.5	77.6	34.7	27.5	53.5	85.0	80.2	75.6	46.1
14 Chiayi County	211	86.5	74.1	71.0	30.1	20.6	49.4	87.8	75.0	74.9	44.4
15 Chiayi City	131	89.1	77.5	72.3	37.8	30.3	55.1	90.4	81.7	82.5	52.4
16 Tainan County	499	86.2	76.3	68.8	32.6	20.7	54.3	84.9	77.7	79.1	47.4
17 Tainan City	353	91.9	76.2	74.8	37.1	25.6	56.7	83.2	78.1	78.4	50.0
18 Kaohsiung City	760	89.6	72.8	72.3	40.5	25.2	56.6	84.8	78.2	81.4	48.5
19Kaohsiung County	532	88.9	72.4	74.9	37.7	23.8	55.9	84.4	74.0	78.4	45.1
20 Penghu County	364	85.3	78.6	69.9	28.3	22.2	54.3	81.9	75.2	75.9	44.6
21 Pingtung County	36	91.2	79.6	78.6	34.5	24.1	60.2	90.3	79.2	82.5	50.2
22 Hualien County	158	88.9	76.4	72.8	42.1	31.6	66.3	90.8	80.2	80.6	56.0
23 Taitung county	104	89.3	74.0	73.1	32.7	27.1	70.0	89.1	72.7	80.1	56.6
24 Kinmen County	40	92.1	78.9	80.2	45.6	32.4	64.6	88.3	78.3	88.9	59.6
25 Leinchiang County	11	92.6	80.3	77.0	34.5	37.7	67.2	90.3	80.1	87.7	56.0

This study uses SPSS v12.0 to collate data descriptive statistics and the contingent table. The multi-level latent class methodology is manipulated in the computer program LatentGOLD v4.0 [4, 22, 23]

3.2 Model Fit

To study the similarities and differences between the patterns of behaviors in the Internet in 25 cities/counties, we applied the multi-level latent class analysis model. Model estimates were obtained for alternative numbers of consumer segments (S=1...10) and country segments (T=1,...,4). To account for sub-optimal solutions, we estimated the model 10 times for each combination of S and T with different random starting values. We retained the best solution for each combination. Table 2 reports model fit (in particular, the BIC value) for each combination of S and T. The optimal number of customer segments, applying the minimum BIC [11, 20, 22], varies between 6 and 7, which is fairly independently from the number of city/county segments. From the opposite perspective: when the number of customer segments is larger than two, the optimal number of city/county segments varies between two and three. We also check optimal number of customer segments, applying the maximum log likelihood [11, 21, 22] varies change may neglect not greatly. The overall minimum BIC is attained at 7 customer segments and 3 city/county segments (BIC=106,065; LL= -52,614), which we identify as the most appropriate solution. These results are presented in Tables 3.

Table 2. Model fit (BIC and LL) for alternative numbers of city/county

Number of User Segments	Number of City/County Segments							
	1		2		3		4	
	BIC	LL	BIC	LL	BIC	LL	BIC	LL
1	119131	-59519	119140	-59519	119149	-59519	119158	-59519
2	109101	-54453	109065	-54425	109063	-54415	109081	-54415
3	107316	-53509	107242	-53458	107243	-53445	107266	-53442
4	106565	-53083	106502	-53032	106509	-53018	106541	-53015
5	106248	-52873	106166	-52809	106175	-52790	106214	-52786
6	106158	-52777	**106086**	-52713	106108	-52696	**106144**	-52686
7	**106117**	-52705	106105	-52666	**106065**	***-52614***	106188	-52643
8	106144	-52667	106093	-52605	106160	-52601	106163	-52566
9	106204	-52646	106145	-52575	106175	-52548	106233	-52535
10	106265	**-52626**	106193	**-52543**	106216	**-52508**	106293	**-52500**

Table 3. Model fit for of models for indicators and clusters

Models for Indicators (level 1)				Model for Clusters(level 2)		
	Wald	**p-value**	**R2**		**Wald**	**p-value**
Email	746.49	0.00	0.38	T1:Southern Taiwan	327.49	0.00
Entertainment	952.51	0.00	0.24	T2:Northern Taiwan	299.89	0.00
Messenger	828.59	0.00	0.64	T3:Metro Area	285.94	0.00
IP-phone	942.07	0.00	0.18		**Covariates**	
Banking	934.74	0.00	0.35	age	534.94	0.00
Online shopping	902.91	0.00	0.37	eduction	1061.23	0.00
Gen. info.	720.46	0.00	0.26	Career	74.37	0.00
Job info.	1089.05	0.00	0.27	income	118.80	0.00
News	699.17	0.00	0.22	gender	66.08	0.00
Gov. info.	1166.02	0.00	0.30			

Table 3 reports model fit applying Wald test [5, 12, 18, 24]. The model for clusters (T1=327.491, p-value<0.00; T2=299.893, p-value<0.00; T3=285.941, p-value<0.00), with the contextual level divided into 3 segments is significantly different. In addition, models for ten categorical indicators in level 1 are significantly different. Hence, this results show that level 1 is divided into 7 segments, and level 3 is divided into 3 segments as the most appropriate solution.

4 Discussion

Internet use behavior within each consumer segment is presented in this section. To aid interpretation, we ordered the consumer segments in ascending order of behavior-penetration levels aggregated across the Internet use behavior. Integrated to explain about that individual level of the seven customer segments (referred to as S1 to S7) as follows:

S1, Knowledgeable segment: this group of people is knowledgeable to various Internet applications, such as email, messenger, general information research (eg. weather, traffic schedule), news, and job or work related searcher all above 90%. Among this group, 70% of them use Internet for banking and online shopping, the highest of all segments; even their use of entertainment reaches to 85% through a little lower than the segment 3 and 4.

S2, Conventional segment: majority of this group, for about 80%, use most traditional applications, such as email, news, and messenger. Only 30% of them use on-line banking, and 50% of them use IP-phone and on-line shopping.

S3, Amusement segment: more than 97% of them use Internet for email and instant messenger, and even entertainment. They do not to care about government information (25%). They rarely used on-line banking (2%), but they do use Internet for on-line shopping (34%).

S4, Entertainment and shopping segment: they are good at using communication tools, such as e-mail and instant messenger. 97% of them also use Internet for entertainment. They are also good at using Internet for information research related to daily life and their work. Their on-line shopping frequencies is relatively high (91%) and their participation of on-line banking is also significantly prominent (26%).

S5, Leisure segment: this group only moderately uses leisure-related services, such as general information research (65%), news (55%), and entertainment (40%). Compared to other groups, they don't frequently use communication tools, such as e-mail, instant messenger, and IP-phone. They do not to care about job or government information. Their on-line shopping frequencies is relatively low (20%) and their participation of on-line banking is also lower (7%).

S6, Business segment: they are good at using Internet for information research related to their work and business communication, such as e-mail (96%), general information research (96%), job (84%) and government information (70%). They also care about news (86%). There are relatively lower frequencies to use Internet for entertainment (44%) and online-messenger (12%).

S7, Interactive segment: this group is characterized by only using Internet for communication, such as email (74%), entertainment (81%) and instant messenger (69%). They do not use on-line banking (0%), and they seldom use Internet for on-line shopping (13%). They prefer instant messenger (eg. msn, yahoo), but they relative does not like to use IP-phone (7%). In other words, they prefer interactive forms to communication tools.

Table 4. Model results: user segments

		User Segments						
		Segment 1	Segment 2	Segment 3	Segment 4	Segment 5	Segment 6	Segment 7
Cluster Size		**0.20**	**0.18**	**0.17**	**0.17**	**0.13**	**0.10**	**0.06**
Email		1.00	0.97	0.98	1.00	0.44	0.96	0.74
Entertainment		0.85	0.62	0.97	0.97	0.40	0.44	0.81
Messenger		0.97	0.88	0.97	1.00	0.13	0.12	0.69
IP-phone		0.71	0.46	0.27	0.47	0.12	0.22	0.07
Banking		0.77	0.23	0.02	0.26	0.07	0.33	0.00
Online shopping		0.97	0.55	0.34	0.91	0.20	0.56	0.13
Gen. info.		0.99	0.91	0.91	0.98	0.65	0.96	0.37
Job info.		0.95	0.71	0.88	0.97	0.32	0.84	0.48
News		0.98	0.82	0.75	0.97	0.55	0.86	0.33
Gov. info.		0.90	0.56	0.25	0.54	0.15	0.70	0.07
City/County Segments								
G-Segment	G-Segment Size	Relative sizes of user segments						
T1	41%	0.16	0.19	0.17	0.16	0.14	0.11	0.08
T2	41%	0.21	0.16	0.16	0.19	0.12	0.09	0.06
T3	18%	0.27	0.18	0.19	0.13	0.11	0.08	0.03

Model results linking city/county and user segments are presented in the lower part of Table 5. Preliminary inspection of Internet use levels shows large differences across the city/county, but also some similarities. The entire Taiwan is divided into three city/county segments (referred to as T1 to T3), the size of each group's rate was 41%, 41%, 18%, respectively. To facilitate interpretation, we present city/county segment membership probability per category of each user segment, averaged across all categories (user segment) of the other city/county segment.

Three city/county segments of the composition are different. The metro area segment comprises higher proportion of knowledgeable and amusement user segments. The metro area segment comprises higher proportion of knowledgeable and amusement customer segments. The northern Taiwan segment comprises higher proportion of entertainment & online shopping customer segment. The southern Taiwan segment comprises less proportion of knowledgeable customer segment, and higher proportion of traditional use customer segment.

The composition of three city/county segments is different. The metro area segment comprises higher proportion of knowledgeable and amusement user segments. The metro area segment comprises higher proportion of knowledgeable and amusement customer segments. The northern Taiwan segment comprises higher proportion of entertainment & online shopping customer segment. The southern Taiwan segment comprises less proportion of knowledgeable customer segment, and higher proportion of traditional use customer segment.

Table 5. Model results in city/county segments

City/County segment	City/County	user segment 1	2	3	4	5	6	7	Subtotal
T1:Southern Taiwan	Hsinchu County	58	54	33	32	26	15	14	232
	Changhua County	141	111	74	88	70	62	33	579
	Yunlin County	57	50	39	40	29	28	23	266
	Chiayi County	49	28	26	33	35	25	16	212
	Tainan County	131	59	67	68	78	64	31	498
	Tainan City	91	67	57	49	41	16	31	352
	Kaohsiung City	201	123	118	106	106	71	35	760
	Kaohsiung County	104	83	86	80	77	55	48	533
	Penghu County	77	49	45	67	61	39	26	364
	Subtotal	909	624	545	563	523	375	257	3796
T2:Northern Taiwan	Keelung City	38	46	40	20	21	15	9	189
	Yilan County	36	38	41	31	23	22	7	198
	Taoyuan County	188	220	155	143	122	95	43	966
	Hsinchu City	43	66	26	25	22	15	10	207
	Miaoli County	49	63	39	33	32	24	15	255
	Taichung County	124	148	136	110	93	71	44	726
	Nantou County	48	38	41	26	27	28	11	219
	Chiayi City	31	26	21	20	17	9	7	131
	Pingtung County	8	7	7	5	4	3	3	37
	Hualien County	37	38	27	20	15	13	9	159
	Taitung county	20	24	17	11	16	10	5	103
	Kinmen County	8	11	7	5	4	3	1	39
	Leinchiang County	3	3	2	1	1	1	0	11
	Subtotal	633	728	559	450	397	309	164	3240
T3:Metro Area	Taipei City	288	492	162	154	146	75	38	1355
	Taipei County	407	537	178	294	235	241	51	1943
	Taichung City	134	174	55	92	68	39	11	573
	Subtotal	829	1203	395	540	449	355	100	3871

5 Conclusions

This study uses ten lists of data from the survey of digital divide related to the behaviors in the Internet made by RDEC (Research, Development, and Evaluation Commission) in Taiwan in 2009 to make a further analysis, for survey of Taiwan users' behaviors in the Internet all belong to categorical data, which traditional Factor Analysis Approach could not be applied. Hence, we choose L.C.M. (Latent Class Modeling) to analyze data and to choose models. In addition to significance of methodology and application, in social science related research fields, L.C.M. (Latent Class Modeling) could also further induce to the characteristics of the data. Also, it's helpful to discover potential factors behind the data, making researchers more understand the characteristics. Moreover, it aids researchers to cluster the attributes, so that they could research more deeply. In this study, we choose M.L.C.M. (Multi-level Latent Class Modeling), to discover those potential variables behind the behaviors in the Internet.

The results show that chief group of user segments into seven segments: S1 (Knowledgeable Segment), S2 (Traditional-use Segment), S3 (Amusement Segment), S4 (Entertainment & Online Shopping Segment), S5 (Leisure & Aloof Segment), S6 (Business Segment), and S7 (Interactive Segment).

In the future, we will analyze the data via different categorical variables, such as gender, education, salary and others, to gather deeper understanding of Internet using behavior of Taiwan citizens.

References

1. Ahuja, M., Gupta, B., Raman, P.: An Empirical Investigation of Online Consumer Purchasing Behavior. CACM 46, 145–151 (2003)
2. Kim, D.J., Ferrin, D.L., Rao, H.R.: Trust and Satisfaction, Two Stepping Stones for Successful E-commerce Relationships: A Longitudinal Exploration. Inf. Syst. Res. 20, 237–257 (2009)
3. FuLler, J., MuHlbacher, H., Matzler, K., Jawecki, G.: Consumer Empowerment Through Internet-based Co-creation. JMIS 26, 71–102 (2009)
4. Citrin, A.V., Sprott, D.E., Silverman, S.N., Stem Jr., D.E.: Adoption of Internet Shopping: the Role of Consumer Innovativeness. Ind. Manage. Data Syst. 100, 294–300 (2000)
5. Chang, M.K., Cheung, W., Lai, V.S.: Literature Derived Reference Models for the Adoption of Online Shopping. Inf. Manage. 42, 543–559 (2005)
6. Zviran, M., Glezer, C., Avni, I.: User Satisfaction from Commercial Web Sites: the Effect of Design and Use. Inf. Manage. 43, 157–178 (2006)
7. Chang, H.H., Chen, S.W.: The Impact of Online Store Environment Cues on Purchase Intention: Trust and Perceived Risk as a Mediator. Online Information Review 32, 818–841 (2008)
8. Anderson, B., Tracey, K.: Digital Living: The Impact (or Otherwise) of the Internet on Everyday Life. Am. Behav. Sci. 45, 456–475 (2001)
9. Yang, C., Chen, L.C.: Can Organizational Knowledge Capabilities Affect Knowledge Sharing Behavior? J. Inf. Sci. 33, 95 (2007)
10. Huang, J.H., Yang, C., Jin, B.H., Chiu, H.: Measuring Satisfaction with Business-to-Employee Systems. Comput. Hum. Behav. 20, 17–35 (2004)
11. Hsieh, N.C., Chu, K.C.: Enhancing Consumer Behavior Analysis by Data Mining Techniques. Int. J. Inf. Manag. Sci. 20, 39–53 (2009)
12. Yang, C., Wu, C.C.: Gender and Internet Consumers' Decision-making. CyberPsychology & Behavior 10, 86–91 (2007)
13. Tsou, C.S., Fang, H., Lo, H.C., Huang, C.H.: A Study of Cooperative Advertising in a Manufacturer-Retailer Supply Chain. Int. J. Inf. Manag. Sci. 20, 15–26 (2009)
14. Goodman, L.: Statistical Magic and/or Statistical Serendipity: An Age of Progress in the Analysis of Categorical Data. Sociology 33, 1 (2007)
15. Masters, G.: A Comparison of Latent Trait and Latent Class Analyses of Likert-type Data. Psychometrika 50, 69–82 (1985)
16. Henry, K., Muthen, B.: Multilevel Latent Class Analysis: An Application of Adolescent Smoking Typologies with Individual and Contextual Predictors. Struct. Equ. Modeling 17(2), 193–215 (2010)
17. Bartholomew, D.: The Analysis and Interpretation of Multivariate Data for Social Scientists. CRC Press, Boca Raton (2002)
18. Moustaki, I., Knott, M.: Generalized Latent Trait Models. Psychometrika 65, 391–411 (2000)
19. Vermunt, J.: Multilevel latent class models. Sociological Methodology 33, 213–239 (2003)
20. Bijmolt, T., Paas, L., Vermunt, J.: Country and Consumer Segmentation: Multi-level Latent Class Analysis of Financial Product Ownership. IJRM 21, 323–340 (2004)

21. Van Horn, M., Fagan, A., Jaki, T., Brown, E., Hawkins, J., Arthur, M., Abbott, R., Catalano, R.: Using Multilevel Mixtures to Evaluate Intervention Effects in Group Randomized Trials. Multivariate Behav. Res. 43, 289–326 (2008)
22. Vermunt, J., Magidson, J.: Latent Gold 4.0. User's Guide (2005)
23. Van Horn, M.L., Fagan, A.A., Jaki, T., Brown, E.C., Hawkins, J.D., Arthur, M.W., Abbott, R.D., Catalano, R.F.: Using Multilevel Mixtures to Evaluate Intervention Effects in Group Randomized Trials. Multivariate Behav. Res. 43, 289–326 (2008)
24. Buse, A.: The Likelihood Ratio, Wald, and Lagrange Multiplier Tests: An Expository Note. Amer. Statistician 36, 153–157 (1982)
25. Hox, J.: Multilevel Modeling: When and Why. Classification, Data Analysis, and Data Highways 2000, 54–85 (1998)
26. Phillips, P., Park, J.: On the Formulation of Wald Tests of Nonlinear Restrictions. Econometrica 56, 1065–1083 (1988)
27. Wald, A.: Tests of Statistical Hypotheses Concerning Several Parameters When the Number of Observations is Large. Trans. Am. Math. Soc. 54, 426–482 (1943)

A Model for Easy Public Searching of Web Services

Vitezslav Nezval[1] and Francois Bartolo[2]

University of Malta, MALTA
[1] Computer Information Systems Dpt., ICT Faculty
vnez@cis.um.edu.mt
[2] Francois Bartolo, Mathematics Dpt., Faculty of Science
francois.bartolo@gmail.com

Abstract. Web Services (WS) became an important means of developing distributed applications composed of a native code with references to remote web services. The problem is finding the desired web service by revealing details of the service, i.e. description of functionality of object methods exposed for public use. Several models have been suggested. Some have been implemented such as UDDI, the most known model. However, UDDI was abandoned by its inventors. This paper suggests a model which would allow for an easy way of finding the desired Web Service directly (using a browser and public search engines such as Google) without having to access any dedicated servers. The model also enables software vendors to publish the WS in a flexible way.

Keywords: Web Service, WSDL, XML, HTTP, WSSR, Search by Category, Search by Operation.

1 Introduction

Web Services (WS)

Web Service is software implemented by any object oriented language (e.g. Java, .NET languages, etc) following prescribed standards. It is hosted by a Web server as a module containing one or more classes defining various operations. The objects of the classes can be instantiated by a remote application (WS Consumer) by invoking its constructor and then by invoking the object's methods. The object and operations executed by the object methods are running on a server host.

The communication between a WS consumer/requester entity and server is done by exchanging messages through two standard protocols: SOAP and REST; both operating on top of the HTTP protocol.

SOAP uses XML for encoding the messages according to the W3C specification [1]. REST is indifferent to the component architecture and inner workings. A requirement of REST is that any resource which is used must have a URL. In order to execute an operation on the resource, the HTTP defined operations must be used. The most frequently used ones include GET and POST.

GET operations are primarily used when the consumer needs a current representation of the resource.

POST operations are used when a representation of a resource needs to be updated or created.

J.J. Yonazi et al. (Eds.): ICeND 2011, CCIS 171, pp. 209–222, 2011.

WSDL

To be able to use the Web Service the Client application (a program running at the WS consumer host machine) is to use a proxy (a middleware which maps local calls to the remote ones and then marshals the requests to the Web Service).

By standard a Web page presenting the Web Service is to have a URL reference to the WSDL (Web Service Definition Language) file which is necessary for the creation of a proxy used by the WS consumer application to invoke the remote services. WSDL is defined by the W3C specification [2].

The popularity of Web Services lies in an easy way of creating a proxy by downloading the WSDL file which contains all the XML encoded information necessary to create the proxy. When the WSDL file is downloaded a utility parser (also called *wsdl* and available for various computer platforms) generates the proxy in a chosen source code of the Client application.

Web Service Example

An example of a simple Web Service created by Fons Sonnemans©, Reflection IT [6] used throughout this paper for simplicity reasons is a Calculator. The web service, apparently used for illustration (rather than business) purposes, can be found on: http://www.html2xml.nl/Services/Calculator/Version1/Calculator.asmx

The web page of this Web Service (Fig. 1) follows the standards required for web services publishing.

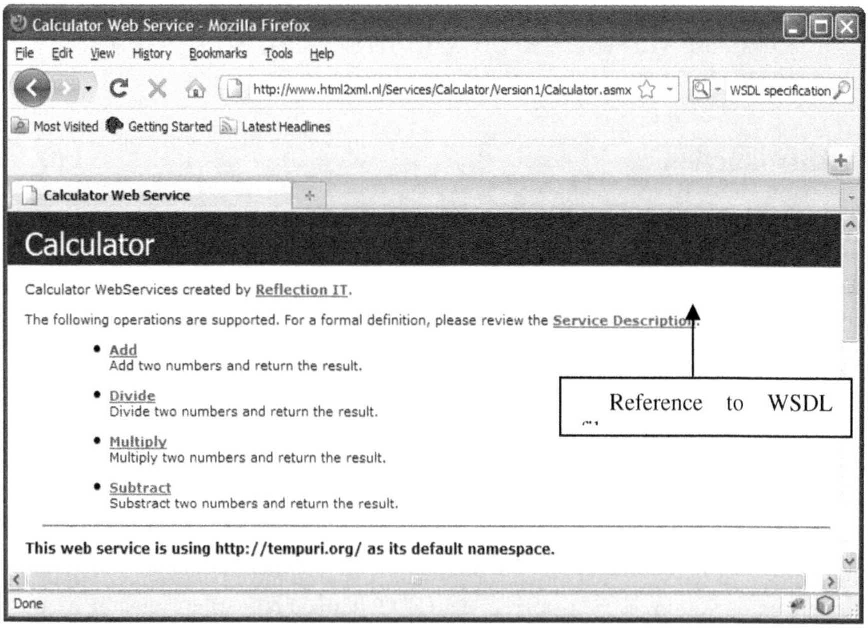

Fig. 1. Calculator Web Service

Note that the presentation page of this Web Service:

- includes brief information about the name of the service and its exposed operations
- provides the possibility to "try" the operations by example (by clicking on any operation presented)
- provides a reference to a WSDL file which can be downloaded by a prospective consumer in order to generate a proxy (by clicking on *Service Description* one can see contents of XML encoded WSDL file)

2 The State of Knowledge: Current Web Service Search Methodologies and Methods

Web Services available on the market are frequently of a complex nature representing software solutions of tasks used in business, education, banking, commerce, *etc*. And they are not free of charge. Irrespective of being free or licensed, all of them are published on the Web. However the problem is how to find a WS suitable for a particular Client application. [9][11]

UDDI (Universal Description, Discovery and Integration)
UDDI is a service that lets a Web Service provider register its services in a directory so that consumers have a central place to find their needed services. A UDDI directory is split into three major categories which are:

- White Pages – contain contact information about the service owner such as address and email as well as define the ownership of the service in question.
- Yellow Pages – contain information about the business classification according to recognized standards such as the North American Industry Classification System.
- Green Pages – these pages list the protocols and the technicalities of the service for instance the service, its binding details, and the parameters.[12]

However there arose a need to provide a common place where all the web services could be deposited and searched for. OASIS solved this problem by creating a central directory in which the services could be registered under a specific service category including the contact details of the individual responsible. This registry was then placed on the Internet so that it was easily accessible and searchable by consumers who were interested in using the service.

Another problem UDDI had to solve is how to present the service information in a standard way. OASIS has designed a model into their standard in which a service is presented. The specification document presented by OASIS specifies the model in which the information is stored in structures called tModels. [8]
tModels represent unique constructs used to describe compliance with a specification, a concept, a category or identifier system, or a shared design.
tModels types:

- *Specification tModels* are used to represent service type definitions
- *Category systems and identifier systems tModels*, together known as "value sets", enable the categorization and identification of entities registered in UDDI in accordance to these value sets.

Searching for Web Service description in a WSDL file
Another approach currently used attempts to search for web services by finding the associated WSDL files and retrieving as much information as possible from them. As specified in Appendix A, the WDSL provides some tags allowing to describe function of the web service. Refer to **Appendix A** specifying what information can be found in a WSDL file. However, this occurs in a rather unstructured manner without offering the possibility to reveal the category of the web service. [13]

Problems with searching for a suitable web service
a) UDDI Service
There is a criticism concerning the UDDI service.
Yu, J.J. & Zhou [3] state that due to the complex classifications and information stored in a UDDI system, a client can not perform search query efficiently to find the service needed.
Mintchev [4] argues that the information held by UDDI is mostly insufficient and is not needed by the WSDL consumers. He says that the only necessary information the tModels that store the web service definition provide is the name.
Rosanova [5] stressed that UDDI never caught up as a major public registry for the web services available but rather remained used by organizations to act as a register for their own services.
Due to the fact that UDDI is missing clear important features, WS providers implement their own non-standard functionality which results in loss of interoperability between systems due to these proprietary features [4].
As a result of the above stated problems the three major drivers in the project (Microsoft, SAP, and IBM) that provided a free public UDDI service have shut this public service down completely (Microsoft).
b) Search for WSDL description file
Fuzzy search for *.wsdl can result in finding intuitively a series of various web services with some indicative information about the service itself as well as its operations and further details.
However this information does not reflect the overall function of the Web Service so that the WS Consumer would not be in a position to decide whether it is convenient for him or not. There is a missing element of categorization.
c) Fuzzy search for web pages presenting Web Services can not be used (e.g. *. asmx is associated with web services created by ASP.NET technology, but other technologies, e.g. Java, use different file extensions)[10]

3 Proposed Model

Apparently there is no publicly available method of systematic search for Web Services.

The aim of this paper is to propose a model providing an easy but efficient way for the public to search for Web Services.

The model is based on a uniform, classified, description of a web service applicable to any brand of the service and a web searcher which is an easily implementable web crawling program runable on any browser used for the search of web services.

1 The Core of the Model - WSSR File

The core of the model is an XML encoded file providing all the details of the web service exposed by a Web Service provider in a defined way. A suffix suggested for this file is *.WSSR* (**W**eb **S**ervice **S**ea**R**ch). The file is to comply with the XML schema specification [7]

The WSSR file defines compulsory XML tags for the specification of:

a) web service name with a description of its function
b) web service operations (methods) with a brief description of their activity
c) web service category (e.g. science, banking, education, mathematics, ...) with multiple categories allowed
d) further description of any length and details
e) URL of the published presentation web page including the WSDL reference
f) name and e-mail address of the web service vendor

The WSSR files (with **.**WSSR suffix) can be easily found by any web crawler and parsed for retrieving information of web service by category as well by exposed operations/methods.

a) WSSR schema

The XML structure of the WSSR file consists of a root element whose name must be servicedescription. The root element must contain all the four top level child elements which are:

- documentation
- company
- categoryList
- operationList.

The *documentation* tag provides human readable information regarding the capabilities of the web service retrieved. Documentation of a service is essential by the person providing the service so that potential clients can check whether the service found meets their desired functional criteria. In the proposed schema the user must provide documentation on the service in general, on each operation provided by the service, and on the input-output parameters.

The *company* tag provides brief information about the entity providing the service. In the schema being proposed, the name of the company and its email address are set as compulsory information which must be specified. Other information can easily be included so as to provide useful information needed in order to start using the web service provided.

The *categoryList* and *operationList* tag enable the provider of the service to specify an unrestrained number of categories and information on operations offered by the service. The categoryList element may contain an unbounded number of child elements all with the tag <category>. Within each tag, the publisher can determine any category describing the function of the web service. This allows for the specification of the function of the web service by multiple categories. Similarly the operationList may contain an unbounded number of child elements with the tag <operation>. The operation tag has an attribute used to specify the name of the operation. A documentation element must also be designated within the operation element providing human readable information regarding the semantics of this single operation.

There are two types of operation tags. One type has a compulsory input tag followed by optional output and fault tags. The other type has compulsory output tag and optional input and fault tags. These operation tags were created to reflect all the possible message exchange patterns specified in WSDL:

- Request- response operation (input parameter followed by output parameter)
- Solicit-response operation (output parameter followed by input parameter)
- One-way operation (input parameter only)
- Notification operation (output parameter only)

For every parameter, or fault specified, the name of the element must be provided, and some documentation regarding the meaning of the parameter or the cause of the fault that was generated must be specified in order for the user to have a complete reference of the capabilities and functionality of the service being provided.

The schema defining the structure of the proposed WSSR file is spacified in **Appendix B.**

b) WSSR example - Calculator.WSSR file

The following is an example of a WSSR file for the Calculator web service mentioned previously as an example. The XML file shown complies with the WSSR XML schema proposed.

```
<servicedescription
serviceURI="http://www.html2xml.nl/Services/Calculator/Ver
sion1/Calculator.asmx" name="Calculator">
  <documentation>Calculator WebServices performing the 4
basic mathematical operations</documentation>
  <company name="Reflection IT">
    <email>example@example.com</email>
  </company>
  <categoryList>
    <category>Mathematics</category>
    <category>Calculation</category>
  </categoryList>
  <operationList>
    <operation name="Add">
```

```
    <operation name="Add">
      <documentation>Adds two numbers</documentation>
      <input name="AddIn">
        <documentation>The two numbers to be
added</documentation>
      </input>
      <output name="AddOut">
        <documentation>The result after
addition</documentation>
      </output>
    </operation>
    <operation name="Subtract">
      <documentation>Subtracts two numbers</documentation>
      <input name="SubtractIn">
        <documentation>The two numbers to be
subtracted</documentation>
      </input>
      <output name="SubtractOut">
        <documentation>The result after
subtraction</documentation>
      </output>
    </operation>
    <operation name="Multiply">
      <documentation>Multiplies two
numbers</documentation>
      <input name="MultiplyIn">
        <documentation>The two numbers to be
multiplied</documentation>
      </input>
      <output name="MultiplyOut">
        <documentation>The result after
multiplication</documentation>
      </output>
    </operation>
    <operation name="Divide">
      <documentation>Divides two numbers</documentation>
      <input name="DivideIn">
        <documentation>The two numbers to be
divided</documentation>
      </input>
      <output name="DivideOut">
        <documentation>The result after
division</documentation>
      </output>
    </operation>
  </operationList>
```

2 Search for Web Service Using WSSR File

WebSearcher

The *WebSearcher* is suggested web searching tool for a Web Service consumer to find out a narrow list of web services by analysing WSSR files found by the web crawler on the Web.

The *WebSearcher.HTML* file provides an interface for the consumer to enter data for fuzzy search by category as well as by operation. This results in the consumer receiving a list of applicable services to choose from.

Example of the *WebSearcher* page

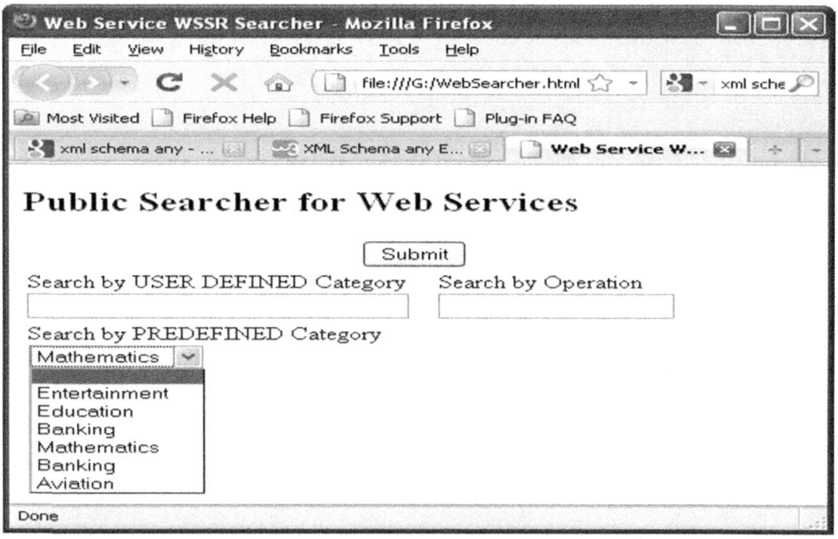

Fig. 2. Layout of Web Search GUI Interface web page with query by predefined category

Combined fuzzy search by user defined category and operation is possible as well. Ref. To Fig 3

Principle of *WebSearcher* operation

Referring to the query in Fig. 3, the web crawler is invoked in an attempt to find those *.WSSR* files with CATEGORY matching the substrings "maths" or "calcul" and OPERATION matching the string "subtract". The search results in the form of the following table specifying the list of possible applicable web services found.

By selecting the URL of a particular Web Service, the standard presentation page of that web service can be downloaded. This page is to have, apart from the prescribed reference to WSDL, also a reference to WSSR file as a standard. Here the consumer can use the example of the provided operation(s), and, by downloading and parsing the WSSR file, the complete information about the selected web service.

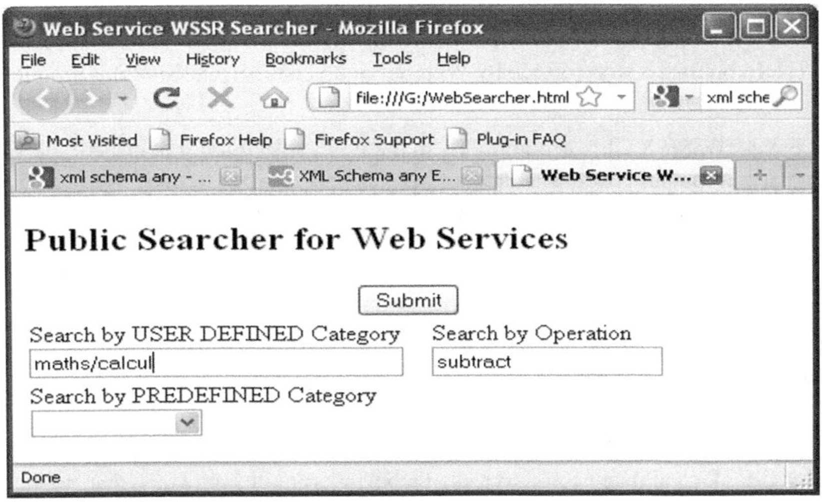

Fig. 3. Web Service fuzzy search query for user defined category combined with operation

Table of Web Services found

Name of Service	Description of Function	List of Operations with their descriptions	URL of Web Service presentation page	URL of WSSR file	Name and email of Web Service vendor

E.g. Should the Consumer opt for the Calculator then the web page with an incorporated reference to the WSSR will be downloaded:

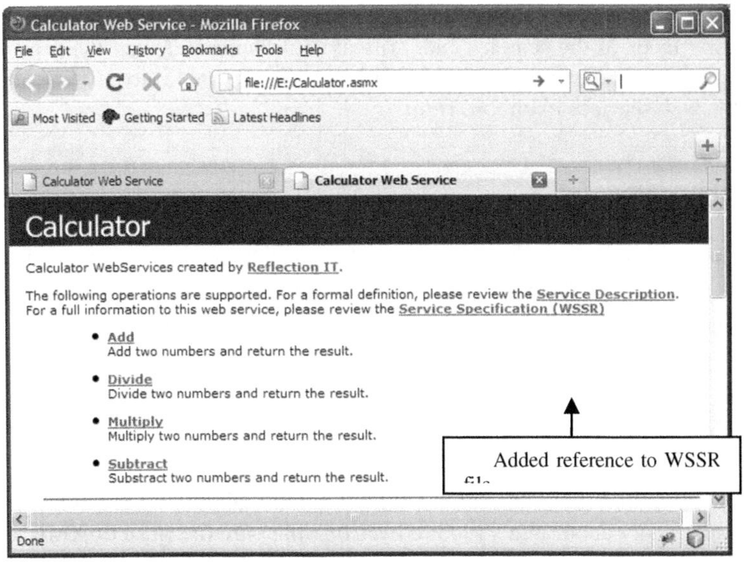

Fig. 4. Calculator Web Service with additional reference to WSSR file

3 Publishing Web Service Using the Proposed Model

The task to publish a web service by Web Service vendors (publishers) is simple. The steps are as follows:

a) create *.WSSR* XML file complying to the *wssr_schem.xsd* schema
b) place it on any web site and either leave it to be "found" by web search engines (e.g. Google) automatically or explicitly apply for the publishing
c) incorporate a reference to the WSSR description file to the Web Service presentation
page (refer to Fig. 4)

4 Performance

The ultimate goal of the proposed system is to enable a user to find a web service (or narrow list of candidate web services) to be incorporated into a client application program.

A part of the proposed model is the *WebSearcher* searching program consisting of a web crawler (any classical web crawling program) and an XML parser.

The crawler searches the web for *.WSSR* files (the proposed XML encoded files which must be associated with each web service complying with the proposed model).

After each *.WSSR* file is downloaded it is parsed in order to find out whether it contains matching string(s)/substring(s) corresponding to the user specification of the web service.It is the two XML child elements the *categoryList* and *operationList* with the corresponding <category> and <operation> tags (refer to the pargraph of the PROPOSED SYSTEM above) that contain web service area/operation description and guarantee a correct decision whether the currently analysed web service is to be accepted or ignored. The performance is enhanced by a fuzzy search within these tags to compensate for the user abbreviated, not exactly matching, specifications.

The time facor of the search is not critical as it happens during the process of the client application development, and also, it is desirable to download several applicable web services to choose from.

5 Conclusion

The suggested model has the advantage of providing a systematic search for Web Services available world-wide without the constraints of having to search on a particular server(s). The model provides two phases of operation:

Phase 1: The consumer searches for a web service by category/operation while getting a list of the possible services.

Phase 2: The choice is narrowed by selecting a particular Web Service having a reference to ALL details about the web service.

Its advantage is that the Web Service provider can make a FULL description of the web service to any depth in a structured yet flexible way (because of XML encoding) without affecting the standards adopted for presenting Web Services on Web.

References

1. http://www.w3.org/TR/soap/
2. http://www.w3.org/TR/wsdl
3. Yu, J.J., Zhou, G.: IEEE International Conference in Dynamic Web Service Invocation Based on UDDI at E-Commerce Technology for Dynamic E-Business (2004)
4. Mintchev, A.: Interoperability among Service Registry Implementations: Is UDDI Standard Enough? In: IEEE International Conference on Web Services (ICWS), Beijing, China (2008), http://ieeexplore.ieee.org/lpdocs/epic03/wrapper.htm?arnumber=4670242
5. Dan, R.: Why UDDI is Important, http://advice.cio.com/dan_rosanova/why_uddi_is_important?page=0%2C0
6. Sonnemans, F.: Trainer & Consultant, http://www.reflectionit.nl
7. http://www.w3.org/TR/xmlschema-1/
8. UDDI OASIS Standard, tModels, http://uddi.xml.org/tmodels
9. Eyhab, A.-M., Qusay Mahmoud, H.: Investigating Web Services on the World Wide Web. In: Proceeding of the 17th International Conference on World Wide Web, Beijing, pp. 795–804 (2008)
10. Janette, H., Madhusudhan, G., Weiyi, M.: Enhancing Discovery of Web Services through Optimized Algorithms. In: Proceedings of the 2007 IEEE International Conference on Granular Computing, Washington, DC, pp. 695–698 (2007)
11. Jianchun, F., Kambhampati, S.: A Snapshot of Public Web Services. SIGMOD Rec. 34(1), 24–32 (2005)
12. John, G., Yannis, P., Evangelos, S., Athanasios, T.: Web Service Discovery: Looking for a Needle in a Haystack? In: International Workshop on Web Engineering (2004)
13. Holger, L., Nathalie, S.: Survey of Current Means to Discover Web Services, Technical Report at Semantic Technology Institute, Innsbruck (August 2008)

Appendix A

WSDL Specification

WSDL specifications provide a model and an XML language used to describe a Web Service. The WSDL file indicates how potential clients of the service are to interact with the service including the protocol being used and the port where the service resides. The WSDL description separates the abstract functionality of the service from the concrete details of how and where the service operates. The abstract functionality of the service is described using the messages, types, and interface or portType tag in the WSDL document:

a) **Types:** Within the *type* tag the structure of the messages used by the Web Service isdefined. The information present in the *type* tag defines the content of the input and output messages when an operation is invoked. The information within the *type* tag is usually presented using an XML Schema containing information about all the messages which can be sent or received by the service.

b) **Message**: This tag was used in the WSDL 1.1 specifications but is not present in the WSDL 2.0 specifications. The data present within the message tag is an abstract, typed definition of the data being communicated. It can be divided into a certain number of parts making the description of the message more logical.

c) **Port Type/Interface:** The *PortType* tag in WSDL 1.1 has been replaced by the interface tag in WSDL 2.0. An interface consists of a set of operations where an operation can be defined as a sequence of input and output messages. Therefore, the interface tag outlines the operations that the service supports. Every operation must have some input or output parameters which are linked to either a message element in WSDL 1.1 or a type element in the case of WSDL 2.0.

The concrete details of the service are described using the binding and service tag. WSDL uses XML to describe the necessary properties for SOAP and REST services. Extensions for WSDL can easily be included in order to support other protocols such as Java RMI or RPC.

d) **Binding:** A concrete protocol and data format specification for a particular port type. The binding tag describes the implementation details necessary to access the service. The binding may specify the interface or portType which is linked to. In this case binding details must be specified for every operation and every parameter of the interface. A port is a single endpoint defined as a combination of a binding and a network address)

e) **Service:** A collection of related endpoints related by a common interface. For every endpoint, the name, the binding which the endpoint is linked to, and the address of the endpoint must be specified. This endpoint address will be a public URI where the service will be listening to the client requests.

Other tags which are important within the WSDL document are the *documentation* tag, *include* tag, and *import* tag. The documentation tag can be placed anywhere within the document and contains human readable information describing the functionality of the service. The include tag and import tag can be used to modularize the description of a WSDL document. The *include* tag is used to include components from WSDL documents which share a common namespace with the including description whilst the *import* tag is used to import a WSDL document from a namespace other than that of the importing description.

Appendix B

The XML schema of WSSR (wssr_schem.xsd file)

```
<?xml version="1.0" encoding="ISO-8859-1" ?>
<xs:schema xmlns:xs="http://www.w3.org/2001/XMLSchema"
           elementFormDefault="qualified">

 <xs:element name="servicedescription"
type="tservicedescription"/>

 <xs:complexType name="tservicedescription">
   <xs:all>
     <xs:element name="documentation" type="xs:string" />
     <xs:element name="company" type="tcompany"/>
     <xs:element name="categoryList" type="tlist"/>
     <xs:element name="operationList"
type="toperationlist"/>
   </xs:all>
   <xs:attribute name="serviceURI" type="xs:anyURI"
use="required"/>
   <xs:attribute name="name" type="xs:NCName"
use="required"/>
 </xs:complexType>

 <xs:complexType name="tlist">
   <xs:sequence>
     <xs:element name="category" type="xs:string"
minOccurs="0" maxOccurs="unbounded"/>
   </xs:sequence>
 </xs:complexType>

 <xs:complexType name="tcompany">
   <xs:sequence>
     <xs:element name="email" type="xs:string"/>
     <xs:any minOccurs="0" maxOccurs="unbounded"/>
   </xs:sequence>
   <xs:attribute name="name" type="xs:string"
use="required"/>
 </xs:complexType>

 <xs:complexType name="toperationlist">
   <xs:sequence>
     <xs:element name="operation" type="toperation"
minOccurs="0" maxOccurs="unbounded"/>
   </xs:sequence>
 </xs:complexType>

 <xs:complexType name="toperation" >
   <xs:sequence>
     <xs:element name="documentation" type="xs:string" />
```

```
      <xs:choice>
          <xs:group ref="request-response-or-one-way-
operation" />
        <xs:group ref="solicit-response-or-notification-
operation" />
      </xs:choice>
  </xs:sequence>
  <xs:attribute name="name" type="xs:NCName"
use="required" />
 </xs:complexType>

 <xs:group name="request-response-or-one-way-operation" >
  <xs:sequence>
    <xs:element name="input" type="param"/>
    <xs:sequence minOccurs="0">
      <xs:element name="output" type="param"/>
      <xs:element name="fault" type="param" minOccurs="0"
maxOccurs="unbounded"/>
    </xs:sequence>
  </xs:sequence>
 </xs:group>

 <xs:group name="solicit-response-or-notification-
operation" >
  <xs:sequence>
    <xs:element name="output" type="param"/>
    <xs:sequence minOccurs='0' >
      <xs:element name="input" type="param"/>
      <xs:element name="fault" type="param" minOccurs="0"
maxOccurs="unbounded"/>
    </xs:sequence>
  </xs:sequence>
 </xs:group>

 <xs:complexType name="param">
  <xs:sequence>
    <xs:element name="documentation" type="xs:string"/>
  </xs:sequence>
  <xs:attribute name="name" type="xs:NCName"
use="required" />
 </xs:complexType>
</xs:schema>
```

User Interactive Biomedical Data Web Services Application

Vladimir Kasik[1], Marek Penhaker[1], Vilém Novák[2], Radim Bridzik[2], and Jakub Krawiec[1]

[1] VSB - Technical University of Ostrava, Faculty of Electrical Engineering and Computer Science, Ostrava, Czech Republic
[2] Faculty Hospital Ostrava, Czech Republic
marek.penhaker@vsb.cz, caspenar@seznam.cz, petr.fojcik@vsb.cz, vilem.novak@fnspo.cz, radim.bridzik@fnspo.cz

Abstract. This paper deals with the usage possibilities of interactive web services for visualizing biomedical data measured with the possibility of complex mathematical algorithms for data processing. This possibility of data processing and evaluation is implemented using FPGA technology and link to existing databases and Web services. Interconnection of these technologies allows a large spectrum of users to quick access to evaluated biomedical data. This article discusses the possible topological solutions and implementation of that system.

Keywords: FPGA, Biomedical Data, SQL, Web Service, Database.

1 Introduction

Savings of biomedical data is not yet formed in any common standard. Many manufacturers of medical devices generally have their own data formats, which are mutually incompatible. The possibility of converting data between these formats is very limited. The trend today is to manage data through a Web interface that provides the user with many advantages. In that case, data storage using a standard XML format is often used and supported by many tools and programming languages.

For the purposes of medical practice, it is important that biomedical records are accessible from various web sites and networks without the need of specialized software. For this purpose, a system of storage and management of biomedical data has been designed, which is based on earlier work of the authors [1].

The system described in this article uses a web application that provides a view of stored biomedical data and also allows you to store records in one of three predefined formats – EDF, DAT and XML. As part of this web browser application is a viewer of stored records, which replaces the traditional programs and enables a view of recorded data directly on the website without need of additional programs. The system for storage and exchange biomedical data is based on ASP.NET 2.0 platform .NET Framework and Microsoft SQL Server.

For storage of biomedical data is used a data storage server. Every file uploaded to the server has its own unique name that is used as ID in the database. The basic

J.J. Yonazi et al. (Eds.): ICeND 2011, CCIS 171, pp. 223–237, 2011.

functions of Web applications provide: display a list of all records stored in a database, add a new record and manage users. The Web application has its own biomedical data browser that allows graphical display of such an EEG records from XML file.

Web site applications are for viewing records and allow for a direct interaction between the system and user. The layout was created in Photoshop CS4 Trial with CSS support in Visual Studio Web Developer. The web interface contains a home page, login page, catalog of saved records, and the administration page.

A significant part of the application is the browser of recorded biomedical data, which enables to display the 20-channels EEG records. It is also possible to modify the scale of the axis and to move the view in a direction of x axis. To display the data we used ZedGraph component, which is distributed under LGPL license.

Recently the system has been extended to evaluate the biomedical data with the detection of some time and quality parameters. These functions are implemented in specialized hardware with an FPGA chip. This hardware is exchanging data with a data server, but can also be connected to the analog inputs for on-line processing of biomedical signals.

2 Problem Definition

The current presentation of electrophysiological data is mostly going on local terminals with visualization of measured data using web applications. The processing of these data is done either by post-processing after measurement and in minor cases on-line. On-line processing puts high demands on hardware and so this process is destined only for specialized work. Enabling data processing on any number of remote terminals for users working with Web services currently represents significant progress in training of professionals - experts, cooperation and collaborations at the same time with rapid and inexpensive analysis of such data for educational and demonstration purposes.

The issue of distance evaluation of physiological data using web terminals is solved several ways. These methods of implementation will be discussed below, having a common feature in the installation of a powerful coprocessor with direct connection to server or database server, providing a web application platform and user cost-effective way of data evaluation.

To address such complex biological signal processing tasks can be advantageously used computational parallelism, high computational speed and very large scale integration with FPGA - Field Programmable Gate Array. Using FPGA technology with these features allows not only off-line processing of stored data, but also the possibility of on-line evaluation and data sharing to remote clients of Web applications.

3 New Solution

Connection of modern mathematical methods and powerful hardware are more requesting today. Today is usual to use very often wavelet transform which serve for before all to time frequency analysis of data and generalization of filtration and waveforms detection. It provides also some further possibilities such as compression of data with the little lost of the information value.

3.1 Joint Wavelet Transform

Today is usual to use very often wavelet transform (WT) which serve for before all to time frequency analysis of data and generalization of filtration and waveform detection.

The important characteristic of wavelet is intellectual simplicity familiar to the used Fourier accesses and also very important computer effective. Easy and quickly is possible to transform with the help of discrete wavelet transform (DWT) big files of data which is an opposite to the classical discrete Fourier transform (DFT).

A lot of wavelets bases exist which we can use for transform but for correct analysis is necessary bases to be orthonormal what these bases fulfilled. WT does a decomposition on signal components. The result of the transformation is a signal with the length one half of original signal and also cofactor is the same length.

The cofactor includes complementary information about a signal. Results of compression and decompression of particular signals are shown in table 1 and the compression was done on the one quarter of original length. In the table are these parameters: remained energy (r.e.), maximum error (m.e.) and standard deviation (σ).

From the table 1 we can find out that when we use the Daubechies (D) transformation base the partial deformation of the signal appears after the reverse decompression before all at the grade 2 what is caused by this that coefficients are tabulated as approximate values. At the compression and decompression was the transformation matrix W corrected in such way to suppress the periodicity of signal as it is shown in the first two lines in the table. In the third and fourth line was matrix W corrected not to be the periodicity of signal suppressed.

Results of decompression with the use Walsch-Paley and Haar's base are the same as at the base H1 - remained energy = 100 %, maximum error and standard deviation is in the rule e-33 ,this error is caused by around numbers during the calculation on the computer.

If we execute transformation of signal electroencephalography with the use of D base we obtain the signal it's course is nearly the same as the signal before the transformation, what we can verify by comparison of both signals.

WT transforms the signal with the use of windows or wavelet function. The main advantage of WT is its ability to analyze the signal with variable time frequency resolution.

WT enables analyze the signals with multiple resolutions that is done by application gradually expanded window´s function. For the analyze of high frequencies the narrow time window is used for analyze of low frequencies the time window broad. The signal is during this transform divided to the set of certain functions (wavelets).

The basic function of transformation is so called maternal wavelet. The next functions are derivated from the maternal wavelet with gradually widening and shifting in time. The original signal could be reconstructed by the inverse transformation. The joint WT is defined (1) a (2).

$$WT(\tau,l)=\int_{-\infty}^{+\infty} x(t).\Psi_{\tau,l}(t)dt \ . \qquad (1)$$

$$\Psi_{\tau,l}(t)=\frac{1}{\sqrt{l}}.\psi\left(\frac{t-\tau}{l}\right) . \qquad (2)$$

where :

τ	time shift of wavelet windows function (dilatation)
l	scale that could be recount to frequency
$\Psi\tau$,l(t)	wavelet function
ψ	transform function (basic – maternal wavelet)
x(t)	analyzed signal (signal)

The maternal wavelet ψ is the prototype for creation of the other windows function $\Psi\tau$,l(t). Wavele that are created from maternal wavelet have the different scale l and different position τ (shift), but the identical form. Constant $l^{-1/2}$ presents the normalization of energy.

If we install relation (2) into relation (1), we get the direct transcription for joint wavelet transform that represents the correlation between the input signal x(t) and function wavelet ψ.

$$WT\ (\tau,l)=\frac{1}{\sqrt{|l|}}.\int_{-\infty}^{\infty} x(t).\psi\left(\frac{t-\tau}{l}\right)dt \ \cdot \qquad (3)$$

3.2 Discrete Wavelet Transform

Analogous as discreet Fourier transform the algorithm was created that solves wavelet transform of discreet signals and it is called discreet wavelet transform (DWT). The discreet wavelet transform could be created by multidesintegration.

We could see the DWT as a matrix formula in which the calculation is base on the multiplication of vectors of data matrix coefficients of wavelet base. If we use the method of the multidesintegration then we can divide the signal in two parts (wavelet coefficients) namely on the compressed signal and orthogonal complement.

DWT enables to divide the signal into two parts namely on the part with the low frequency - approximate s_1 and on the apart with the high frequency – detailed (complementary) d_1. The proceeding is possible to repeat in this way that we transform the approximate part and we obtain the parts of the second stage s_2 a d_2. When we repeat the proceeding we obtain then parts of another levels. The result is one approximate supporting signal and a lot of detail components. By the reverse proceeding we can make the synthesis of the original signal.

This transform enables during the reverse syntheses some of data omit. For example if the signal contains the noise of the high frequency it is possible to filter it off during the reverse synthesis .WT enables to find out this part in which we want the noise to filtr off and it is the difference from another methods for noise filtration.

Then it is not need put the whole signal through filtration. It is very advantageous at these signals where noise is created only in the transient section.

For the selected area exists infinite many wavelet bases that must fulfilled of course some conditions to be possible to calculate the reverse transformation of the signal. Generally is possible to say that wavelet bases must fulfilled the condition of existence of inverse transformation with the possibility of reconstruction of the original signal.

For guarantee of reverse transform with the possibility of reconstruction of the original signal wavelet must fulfilled the condition of orthogonality and it is calculated from the dilatation formula $\phi(x)$.

$$\phi(x) = \sum_{k=0}^{M-1} c_k . \phi(2.x - k) \ . \tag{4}$$

$$\psi(x) = \sum_{k=0}^{M-1} (-1)^k h_{1-k} \phi(2x - k) \ . \tag{5}$$

where :

$\phi(x)$	dilatation function
$\psi(x)$	transform function (basic – maternal wavelet)
k	wavelet order
c_k	scale coefficients of filtration which warrants the orthonormality
M	Number of nonzero coefficients of wavelet base

Among the well-known wavelet bases belong Rademacher, Haar, Walsh, Walsh modified and Daubechies.

The example of dilatation formula for determination Daubechies base about four coefficients l_0, l_1, l_2, l_3 is following:

$$\phi(t) = l_0.\phi(2t) + l_1.\phi(2t-1) + l_2.\phi(2t-2) + l_3.\phi(2t-3) \ . \tag{6}$$

In the paper are described only the chosen bases which I work with and which I realize for further use on the computer in MATLAB environment.

3.3 Walsh (Walsh-Paley) Base

The advantage of Walsh base is that it is total in comparison with Rademacher base but it has this disadvantage that the index of lines does not respond to the number of zero points.

Walsh base is orthogonal in L_2, and it is formed by the product of Rademacher functions and functions $r_0(x) = 1$ according the relation (7).

$$W_0(x) = r_0(x) = 1 \ , \ \{W_n(x)\}_{n=1}^{\infty} \ , \ W_n(x) = \prod_{k=0}^{m} [r_k(x)]^{p_k} \ . \tag{7}$$

for $x \in \langle 0,1 \rangle$, number m, p_k are determined from the binary analysis of number n according the relation:

$$n = \sum_{k=0}^{m} p_k 2^k \,.. \qquad (8)$$

a) Walsh modified base

Another namely original base, which goes from Rademacher, and Walsh base is a modified Walsh base.

The advantage of this base is that the index of matrix lines responds to the number of zero points. This base we can construct recurrently from the Walsh base according the formula (8).

$$W_n^* = W_{2j+p}(x) = W_j(2x) + (-1)^{j+p} . W_j^*(2x-1) \, . \qquad (9)$$

b) Daubechies base

From a lot of various bases it is important to mention also Daubechies base. Daubechies base is determined by solution trigonometrical dilatation function and counted coefficients are tabulated.

For the calculation of wavelet transform with the use of Daubechies ortonormal base we use data vector of the length 2 – 10, by it is the transform wavelet Daubechies base formed.

Presented transform Daubechies base in formula (14) in the last rows transforms coefficients c_n on the beginning of matrix and by it is reached elimination of periodicity of the signal.

The Wavelet transform I have used in this study for the filtration of EEG record to eliminate possible failures and inaccuracy during the scanning. The compress quality of wavelet transform I then utilized for the saving of archive space for data storage on recording mediums.

Therefore I must the acquired EEG to compress with various types of transform bases into various depth (compression to 1/2, 1/4, 1/8 a 1/16 of the original signal length), without use of filtration (zeroing). Then it was also need to determine the suitable zero setting in the relation on the type (hard, soft, quintile, universal) and various sizes (60%, 80% a 100%).

It was a task to find out the best type of transform base for the compression of the signal, at the filtration the best type of zeroing (also the magnitude of zeroing) and in the end to integrate filtration and compression to save storage space on the disc. The graphical results of the transformation of the eeg record were consulted with physician. In Cupertino with the physician I had chosen as the maximum compression (at which is the signal for physician well readable – not distort) on 1/4 of its original length with the use of Daubechies base of the 2. Grade (D2). For filtration I had chosen the kvantil zeroing with the magnitude 90% - 100 % at base D8 namely at all compressions (1/2, 1/4, 1/8), from that the compression was set and the signal was decompressed. At 1/16 the distortion was manifested , and the physician could made the false diagnosis. It is why are rather better 1/2, 1/4 a 1/8. If we want to conclude, the best from physician point of view is:

- compression D2 to 1/4
- quartile zeroing with magnitude 90% - 100%at base D8

Diagram of evaluation of eeg by wavelet transform figure 2 contains the construction of representative pulse wave until the end because during the transformation rises distortion in some initial points of evaluated signal and it depends on the type of used base and it could affect the form of the resulting pulse wave. Therefore in contrast from the scheme of evaluation eeg record in time domain is better as a transformed signal to choose the whole eeg record. The entire processing

The choice of the suitable base

During the evaluation of signal compression it is not possible to check the quality only according the numeric values of particular parameters but it is also very important to evaluate it by eye of an expert. Such evaluation is also very important at all medical records. It is evident that results for Daubechies bases grade 4 give the best numeric results during the processing of the pulse wave. From it appears the applicability of its use for further processing. Even the expert verified this fact.

diagrams is also visible suppression or the use of periodicity of signal in the next period. At bases Walsh-Paley and Walsh-Paley modified suppression of periodicity is not used thanks to the difference of matrix coefficients structure.

For Daubechies base coefficients c_n of filtration are tabulated. In the chart are these parameters: retained energy (E_r), maximum error at comparing of original and decompressed signal (ε_{max}), standard deviation σ.

$$\varepsilon_{max} = \max\left(\left|X\right|\right) . \tag{10}$$

$$\sigma = \sqrt{\frac{1}{N}\sum_{i=1}^{N}\left(X_i - \overline{X}\right)^2} . \tag{11}$$

$$E_r = \left(1 - \frac{\sum_{i=1}^{N}\left(X_i\right)^2}{\sum_{i=1}^{N}\left(Y_i\right)^2}\right).100\ [\%] . \tag{12}$$

where:

X_i	difference between original and decompressed signal
Y	original signal
N	number of values of record

At Daubechies transform base is the original signal without use of periodicity after the reverse decompression very little distorted. It pays before all at Daubechies base of the 2nd level.

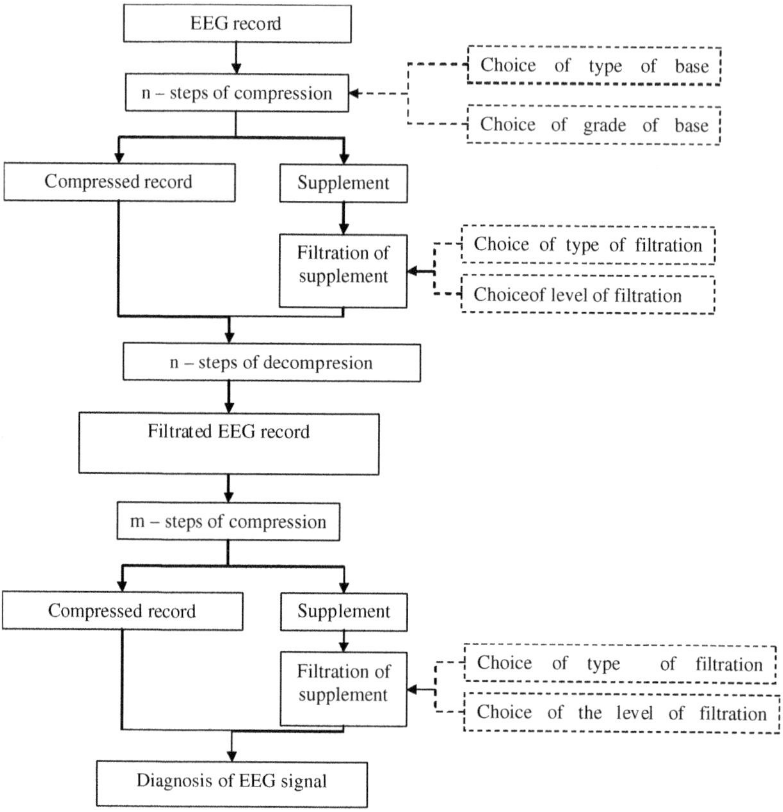

Fig. 1. Diagram of evaluation of eeg record by wavelet transformation

Table 1. Results of compression by Daubechies base

	D 2			D 4			D 8		
Pulse wave	E_r [%]	ε_{max} [mV]	σ [mV]	E_r [%]	ε_{max} [mV]	σ [mV]	E_r [%]	ε_{max} [mV]	σ [mV]
Original	99,86	0,17	0,0	99,99	0,03	0	99,99	0,005	0
Normed	99,82	0,31	0,0	99,92	0,13	0	99,99	0,024	0
Original with periodicity	99,72	0,29	0,0	98,76	0,53	1e-7	96,58	0,621	0,006
Normed with periodicity	98,77	0,86	0,0	95,09	1,06	1e-6	90,51	1,004	0,015

Number at base means the level of base (e.g.. D2 means that the base is 4 values).

At compression and decompression the transform matrix W was arranged into form in which the base inhibits the periodicity of the signal. Numeric results are shown in the first two lines of the chart. In the third and fourth lines matrix W was arranged in this way not to suppress the periodicity of signal.

Table 2. Results of compression by Walsch-Paley base (same as results of compression by Walsch-Paley modified base)

	W-P 2			**W-P 4**			**W-P 8**		
	W-Pm 2			**W-Pm 4**			**W-Pm 8**		
Pulse wave	E_r [%]	ε_{max} [mV]	σ [mV]	E_r [%]	ε_{max} [mV]	σ [mV]	E_r [%]	ε_{max} [mV]	σ [mV]
Original with periodicity	100	0,0	0,0	100	0,0	1e-7	100	0,0	e-7
Normed with periodicity	100	0,0	0,0	100	0,0	1e-6	100	0,0	e-6

Results from decompression with the use of Haar, Walsch-Paley and Walsch-Paley modified base are the same as at base H1, then retained energy = 100%, maximum error and standard deviation is place value of about 10^{-6} [mV], this error is caused by rounding of numbers during the calculations done by computer. These bases are not suitable for processing of compressed signal of pulse wave because they exhibits big distortion of its course.

From the text is visible that the results for Daubechies base of the level 2 do not have otherwise the best number results during the processing of pulse wave but after the consultation with the physician it was chosen as suitable. From it results that is possible to use it for further processing.

4 Implementation of New Methods

The processing of biomedical data often requires the detection of various events in recorded measurements. These events are evaluated in both qualitative parameters and the time parameters. Proper evaluation of caused events is usually not often easy, because the biomedical signals are strongly unsteady non-periodic and often stochastic in nature and may also be changed by parasitic physiological effects of interference. This is connected with the computing demands of data processing. The requirements for computing power increases mainly in the evaluation of biomedical signals in real time. Wavelet transformation currently provides a simple and efficient algorithm for detection and treatment of biosignals, which is used to implement various computations complexity, especially at the local workstations. Using the wavelet transform is not difficult due to the number of steps in one subscription - 2n, nevertheless for use on large real biomedical data it requires fully parallel computing with high performance. Implementation of this option can be currently done with only two possible architectural designs. One of them is a supercomputer and the second solution is a parallel computing with FPGA structures, which is comparable for these purposes with supercomputer performance. In this case, there seems to be three alternatives to fast signal processing as shown in Fig 3.

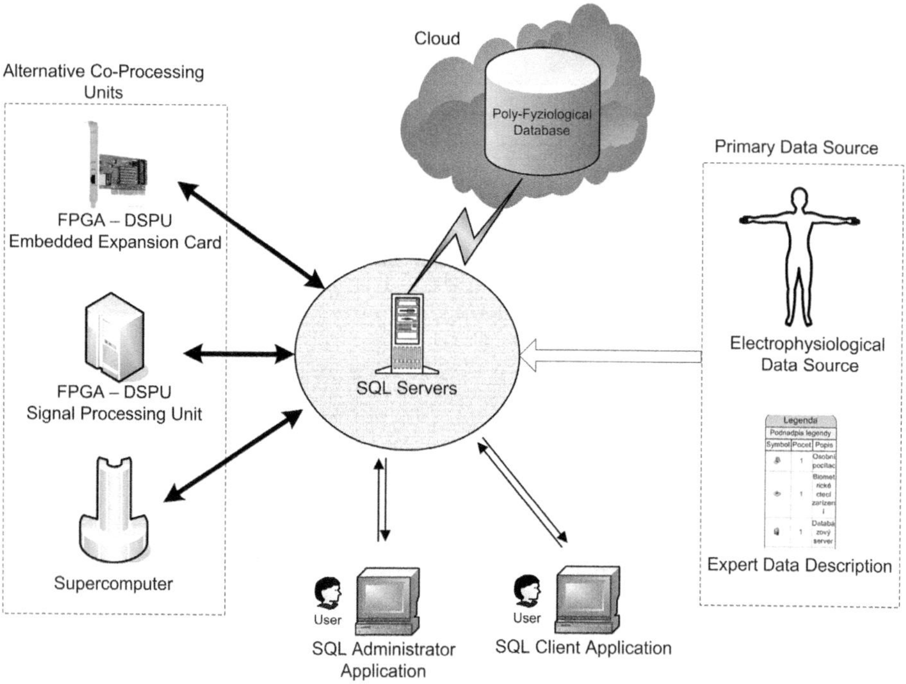

Fig. 2. Overall System Structure

That figure represents a system, which transmits stored biomedical data to the coprocessor unit for processing on user request. The data is returned after processing a data server, from which can be visualized in a web application.

Fig 3 shows the three possible alternatives of co-processing units: 1) FPGA – DSPU (Digital Signal Processing Unit) as Embedded Expansion Card, 2) FPGA – DSPU as stand-alone unit with an Ethernet connection and 3) Supercomputer as an alternative. The first two of these options are based on FPGA programmable logic, which uses both hardware and software approach for data processing. Hardware solution is based on the parallel implementation of some sub-algorithms in cooperation with the DSP units. Software solution allows you to process complex calculations and algorithms supporting MicroBlaze soft processor.

Conceptually, the co-processing unit with an FPGA is designed in two ways. The first solution is a PCI card for installation into a data server. This solution is elegant and allows a maximum data throughput between the server and the data processing unit. The main disadvantage is the need for a fixed location of the unit and modification of the data server configuration, which may not be desirable. Another solution of co-processing unit is a standalone module which can be connected via a communication network. In this case, a standard Ethernet network with TCP / IP protocol is used. The advantage of the solution is not only independence of data server location, but also a posibility of usage this unit with more servers and / or clients on the network. Network feature, however, poses claims on the network communication module, including requirements for adequate safety and security of data transmission on the network. These aspects and the issue of Ethernet's working load lead ultimately to a lower data throughput than in the first case. A significant feature of standalone unit is an expansion posibility of the analog inputs for on-line biomedical signals processing. For this function, the unit is equipped with A/D converter with an appropriate resolution. With the implementation of a Web interface extends the use of process units for additional functions when the web client can connect directly to the co-processing unit.

FPGA - DSPU Detailed Structure is based on Xilinx's Virtex 6 FPGA programmable logic. Its architecture allows to build logic for digital signal processing, wavelet transformation algorithms and implementation of a "System on the chip" with a MicroBlaze soft processor. The design includes a very fast block memories on the FPGA chip and larger but slower standalone memories. The FPGA is mounted on board, along with other supporting circuits including ADCs for On-Line measurement of signals. In the case of network featured unit the PCB contains Ethernet PHY chips. Operational status and basic diagnostic information of the system can be viewed on a VGA monitor connected to the FPGA interface.

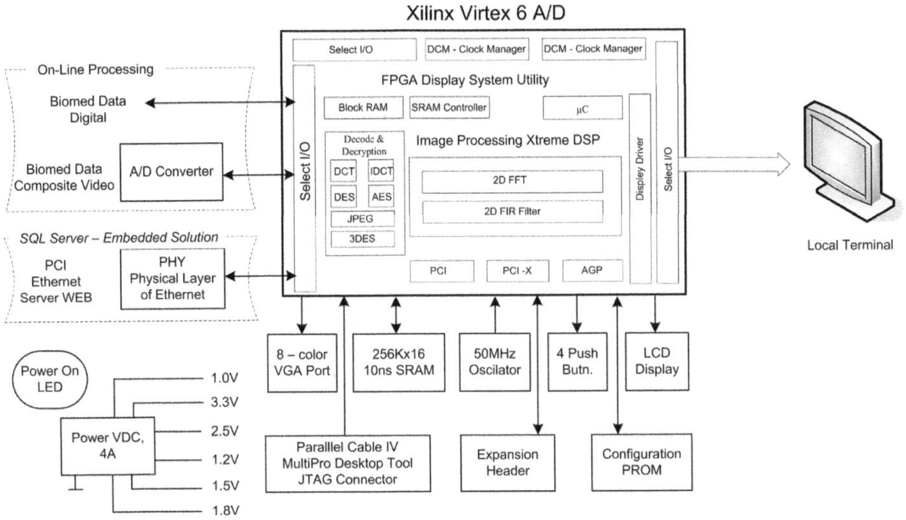

Fig. 3. FPGA – DSPU Detailed Structure

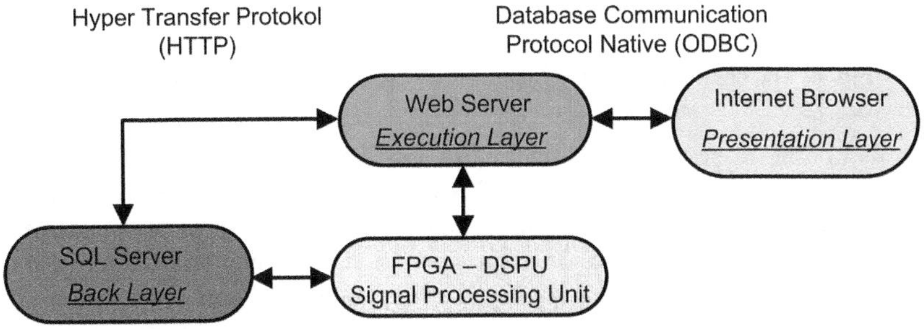

Fig. 4. Dataflow paths inside the system

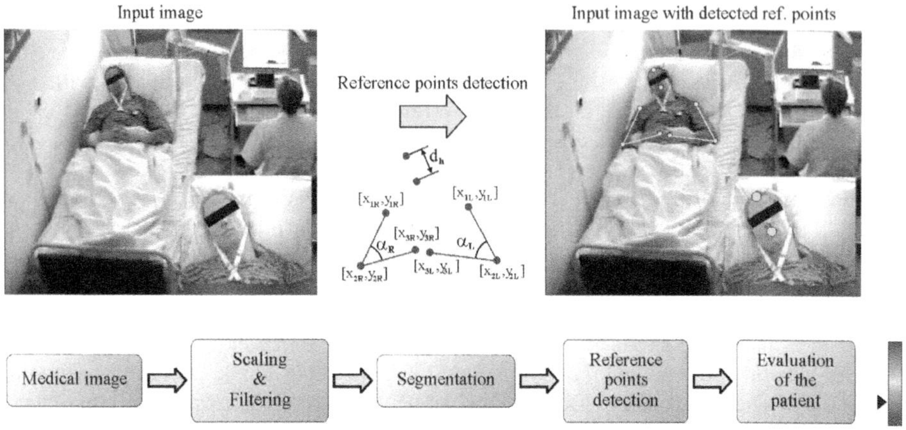

Fig. 5. Evaluation of Medical Image. Real-time processing of input image gives a result in terms of reference points, whose position is further evaluated.

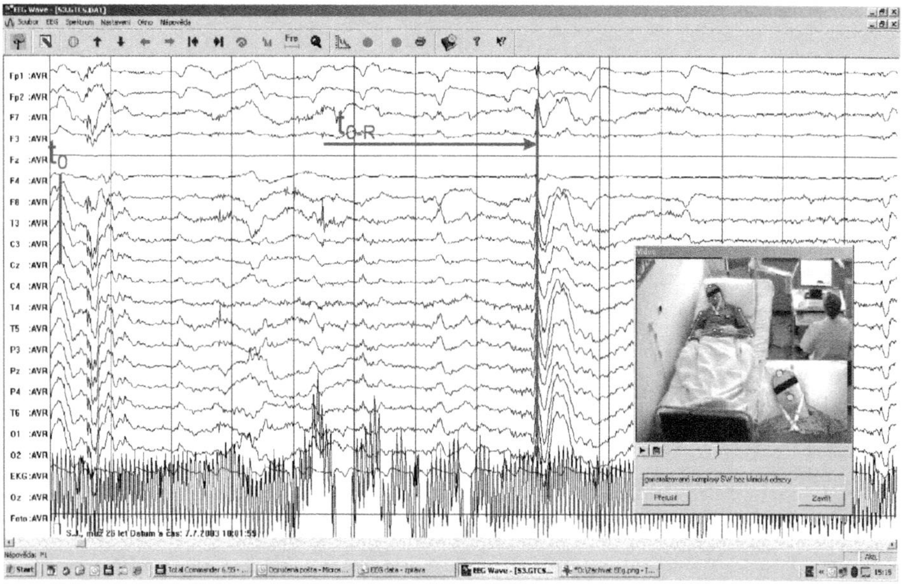

Fig. 6. The beginning of an epileptic attack far only detected on the EEG record

From a point of view of dataflow the FPGA – DSPU co-processing unit constitutes second link between web server and SQL server. The operation of FPGA is controlled by a web application that sends commands to the unit. Individual digital biosignal processing algorithms operate on data from SQL Server. The resulting data are processed by web applications and offered to the authorized user's web browser.

One of the projected features of the system was an EEG evaluation of patients and their association with epileptic attacks. To evaluate the EEG data was used wavelet transform methods. To evaluate individual patient images in clinical practice were used methods of digital image processing. Moments of epileptic attacks were evaluated by detection algorithm that was trained to locate some reference points in the image. Placement of these points and their movement is a basis for subsequent classification of the patient. Left image of Figure X is the input image and right image is updated with discovered reference points. In another analysis, the arm angles, hand position and movement, posture and movement of the head are observed. The result is an estimation of the overall condition of the patient, focusing on pathological states of the brain.

To detect epileptic attack from EEG record were used wavelet transform methods implemented on an FPGA platform. Among the fundamental parameters of signal derived from EEG data are mainly amplitude peaks and frequency spectrum. Furthermore, there was observed a delay between the first signs of attack in EEG and the corresponding motion signals (visible on Fig. 7).

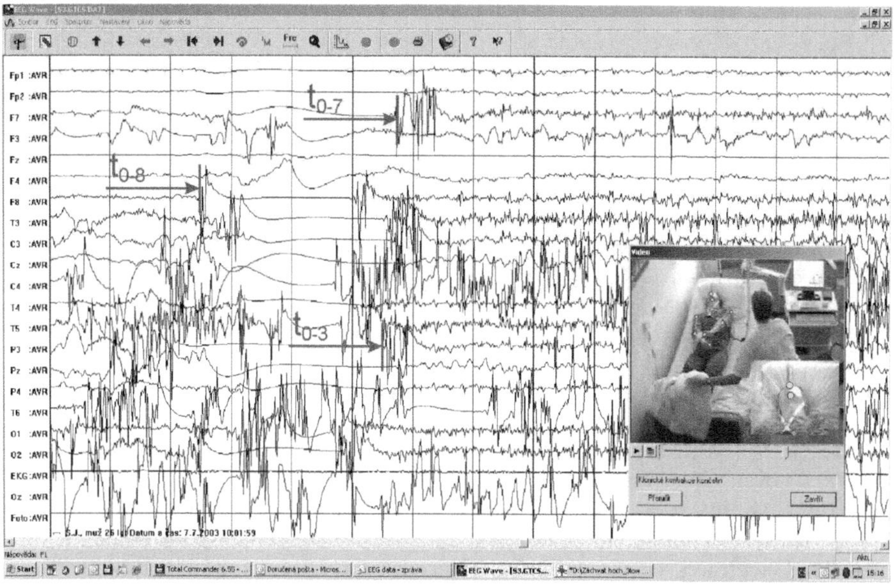

Fig. 7. Advanced epileptic attack and its symptoms in the EEG signal

5 Conclusion

Development of bio-signals currently comprises the majority of issues, which covers the field of biomedical engineering. Processing of these data in real time is very difficult to implement the task with high computational and financial demands of the workplace. The presented solution treatment and detection of signals in real time using FPGA brings new possibilities not only well equipped for a particular workplace, but also for users of web applications for visualization and processing the distance signals in real time. Using the appropriate topology for connecting the SQL and database servers, and digital signal processing unit can achieve comparable results as a supercomputer intended to be so complicated mathematical calculations.

The proposed system was tested on a specific polysomnographic recording video data and successfully detected using this system, an epileptic seizure and subsequent levels of nerve-muscle movements and to determine the strength of muscle contraction with respect to the degree of fit.

Acknowledgment. The work and the contribution were supported by the project: Ministry of Education of the Czech Republic under Project 1M0567 "Centre of Applied Cybernetics", Student grant agency SV 4501141 "Biomedical engineering systems VII" and TACR TA01010632 "SCADA system for control and measurement of process in real time". Also supported by project MSM6198910027 Consuming Computer Simulation and Optimization.

References

1. Krawiec, J., Penhaker, M., Krejcar, O., Novak, V., Bridzik, R.: System for Storage and Exchange of Electrophysiological Data. In: Proceedings of 5th International Conference on Systems, ICONS 2010, Menuires, France, April 11-16, pp. 88–91. IEEE Conference Publishing Services, NJ (2010), doi:10.1109/ICONS.2010.23, ISBN 978-0-7695-3980-5
2. Smith, T.F., Waterman, M.S.: Identification of Common Molecular Subsequences. J. Mol. Biol. 147, 195–197 (1981)
3. Simsik, D., Galajdova, A., Majernik, J., Hrabinska, I., Zelinsky, P.: The video analysis utilization in rehabilitation for moblity development. Lékař a technika. Česká republika, 4-5, Ročník 35, 87–92 (2004) ISSN 0301-5491
4. Dziakova, M., Zelinsky, L., Simsik, D., Majernik, J., Galajdova, A.: Objektivizácia účinku senzomotorickej stimulácie pomocou SMART-u. Rehabilitácia 44(4), 210-214 (2007) ISSN 0375-0922
5. Zivcak, J., Petrik, M., Hudak, R., Toth, T., Knezo, D., Kovalova, E.: Embedded tensile strenght test machine FM1000 - An upgrade of measurement and control. Diffusion and Defect Data Pt.B: Solid State Phenomena 147-149, 657–662, ISSN: 10120394, ISBN: 3908451655; 978-390845165
6. Kristof, M., Hudak, R., Takacova, A., Zivcak, J., Fialka, L., Takac, R.: Contact pressure measurement in trunk orthoses. In: Proceedings of ICCC-CONTI 2010 - IEEE International Joint Conferences on Computational Cybernetics and Technical Informatics, art. no. 5491304, p. 175 (2010), doi:10.1109/ICCCYB.2010.5491304, ISBN: 978-142447433-2
7. Sabol, F., Vasilenko, T., Novotny, M., Tomori, Z., Bobrov, N., Zivcak, J., Hudak, R., Gal, P.: Tradermal running suture versus 3M^{TM} Vetbond^{TM} tissue adhesive for wound closure in rodents: A biomechanical and histological study. European Surgical Research 45(3-4), 321–326, doi: 10.1159/000320837, ISSN: 0014312X
8. Klima, M., Pazderak, J., Bernas, M., Pata, P., Hozman, J., Roubik, K.: Objective and subjective image quality evaluation for security technology. In: Proceedings of IEEE Annual International Carnahan Conference on Security Technology, pp. 108–114
9. Garani, G.: Nest and unnest operators in nested relations. -Data Science Journal 7, 57–64, doi: 10.2481/dsj.7.57, ISSN: 16831470
10. Aidu, E.A.I., Trunov, V.G., Titomir, L.I., Tysler, M., Turzova, M., Szathmary, V.: Electrocardiographic ST segment changes as an indicator for localization of injury potentials. A Computer Simulation Study Kardiologia 15(1), 21–24, ISSN: 12100048

11. Havlík, J., Uhlir, J., Horcik, Z.: Thumb motion classification using discrimination functions. In: International Conference on Applied Electronics, AE, art. no. 4382963, pp. 55–57 (2006), doi:10.1109/AE.2006.4382963, ISBN: 8070434422;978-807043442-0
12. Hozman, J., Zanchi, V., Cerny, R., Marsalek, P., Szabo, Z.: Precise Advanced Head Posture Measurement. In: Book Challenges in Remote Sensing - Proceedings of the 3rd Wseas International Conference on Remote Sensing (REMOTE 2007), pp. 18–26 (2007) ISSN: 1790-5117, ISBN: 978-960-6766-17-6
13. Garani, G., Adam, G.K.: Qualitative modelling of manufacturing machiner. In: Book - 32nd Annual Conference on IEEE Industrial Electronics, IECON 2009, vol. (1-11), pp. 1059–1064 (2006) ISSN: 1553-572X, ISBN: 978-1-4244-0135-2
14. Cerny, M.: Movement Activity Monitoringof Elederly People – Application in Remote Home Care Systems. In: Proceedings of 2010 Second International Conference on Computer Engineering and Applications ICCEA 2010, Bali Island, Indonesia, March 19-21, vol. 2. IEEE Conference Publishing Services, NJ (2010) ISBN 978-0-7695-3982-9
15. Cerny, M.: Movement Monitoring in the HomeCare System. In: Dossel-Schleger (ed.) IFMBE Proceddings, vol. (25). Springer, Berlin (2009) ISBN 978-3-642-03897-6; ISSN 1680-07
16. Vasickova, Z., Augustynek, M.: New method for detection of epileptic seizure. Journal of Vibroengineering 11(2), 279–282 (2009) ISSN 1392 - 8716
17. Bernabucci, I., Conforto, S., Schmid, M., D'Alessio, T.: A bio-inspired controller of an upper arm model in a perturbed environment. In: Proceedings the 2007 International Conference on Intelligent Sensors, Sensor Networks and Information Processing, pp. 549–553 (2007) ISBN: 978-1-4244-1501-4
18. Krejcar, O., Cernohorsky, J., Fojcik, P., Janckulik, D., Martinovic, J.: Smartphone, PDA and mobile Embedded device clients of Biotelemetric System for monitoring of life functions. In: 5th International Conference on Innovations in Information Technology, Innovations 2008, Al Ain, United Arab Emirates, December 16-18, pp. 145–149 (2008), doi:10.1109/INNOVATIONS.2008.4781761, ISBN 978-1-4244-3396-4
19. Krejcar, O.: Large Multimedia Artifacts Prebuffering in Mobile Information Systems as Location Context Awareness. In: 4th International Symposium on Wireless Pervasive Computing, ISWPC 2009, Melbourne, Australia, February 11-13, pp. 216–220 (2009), doi:10.1109/ISWPC.2009.4800591, ISBN 978-1-4244-4299-7
20. Machacek, Z., Hajovsky, R., Ozana, S., Krnavek, J.: Experiments of Thermal Fields of Sensors Supported by Digital Image Processing. In: 2008 Mediterranean Conference on Control Automation, Ajjacio, France (2008); IEEE CFP08MED-CDR, ISBN 978-1-4244-2504-4, 6p
21. Korpas, D., Halek, J.: Pulse wave variability within two short-term measurements (2006); Biomedical papers of the Medical Faculty of the University Palacký, Olomouc, Czechoslovakia, vol. 150(2), pp. 339–344 (2006) ISSN: 12138118

Home Care Web Services Evaluation by Stress Testing

Ondrej Krejcar[1,2] and Leona Motalova[3]

[1] VSB Technical University of Ostrava, Center for Applied Cybernetics, Department of measurement and control, 17. Listopadu 15, 70833 Ostrava Poruba, Czech Republic
Ondrej.Krejcar@remoteworld.net
[2] University of Hradec Kralove, FIM, Department of Information Technologies, Rokitanskeho 62, Hradec Kralove, 500 03, Czech Republic
Ondrej.Krejcar@ASJournal.eu
[3] VSB Technical University of Ostrava, Department of measurement and control, 17. Listopadu 15, 70833 Ostrava Poruba, Czech Republic
Leona.Motalova@gmail.com

Abstract. Development of software applications result in complete application or solution. The last phase of developing process is the final testing of developed solution. The goal of our paper has focused on this problem in case of web services. The developed testing application can be used for any other software solutions with web service interface. The developed test environment, including application developed for the stress testing is based on Microsoft .NET Framework technology. Our stress testing application allows testing of selected problem areas to find any limitations before the tested developing solution will be set up at customer. By the help of our test application, the hardware solution for the server was selected on the base of selected home care agency needs.

Keywords: Stress testing, Response Time, Mobile Device, SQL Server.

1 Web Services Phenomena

The area of stress testing shows the tested system behavioral in case the data are accessed by several users simultaneously. For the testing of affection on the length of the time response by the number of the simultaneous accesses to the database, the special application was developed in C# language in the development environment of Microsoft Visual Studio 2008.

The developed application simulates simultaneous access of any number of users, on the methods implemented by the Web service and measure the response time of the web service for the requirement depended on the number of users who approach to service at the moment. The application measures and creates:

- The duration of one call of the given method
- The duration of the call of the method to the specified number of simultaneous user access
- The overall response time Web service by a given number of users including travel time requirement for Web services

J.J. Yonazi et al. (Eds.): ICeND 2011, CCIS 171, pp. 238–248, 2011.

- Build the required collection of data from the database
- The way of this collection back from Web service to the application
- The duration of the complete fulfillment of the requirement from the start button is pressed to the end of the test.

2 Implementation of Test Application

Our customization can be modified using the menu item "Settings" [Fig. 1, that allows the user to adjust the appearance of application windows, or better hidden (show) some items of the application window and a "Bar Chart", "Information about the test"," Summary information from the Web service", "Table of results of testing" and "data table from the database", This allows the user to customize the user interface to their specific needs. These items, the user can hide / show unchecking / checking the item in the menu "Settings". Furthermore, the window contains the Bar graph, for graphical display of test results, two text boxes, one displays information about just held testing and second displays information obtained from a Web service for the called method, is also entered into an indication of the direction the Web service on the duration of testing, which is the time needed to establish a connection with the Web service and its compilation, this statement is capable of distorting the results of testing. Apart from these two fields is the section with controls for setting the required test. At the bottom of application windows are then 2 tables, one contains data retrieved from the database server and the other information on the test is completed.

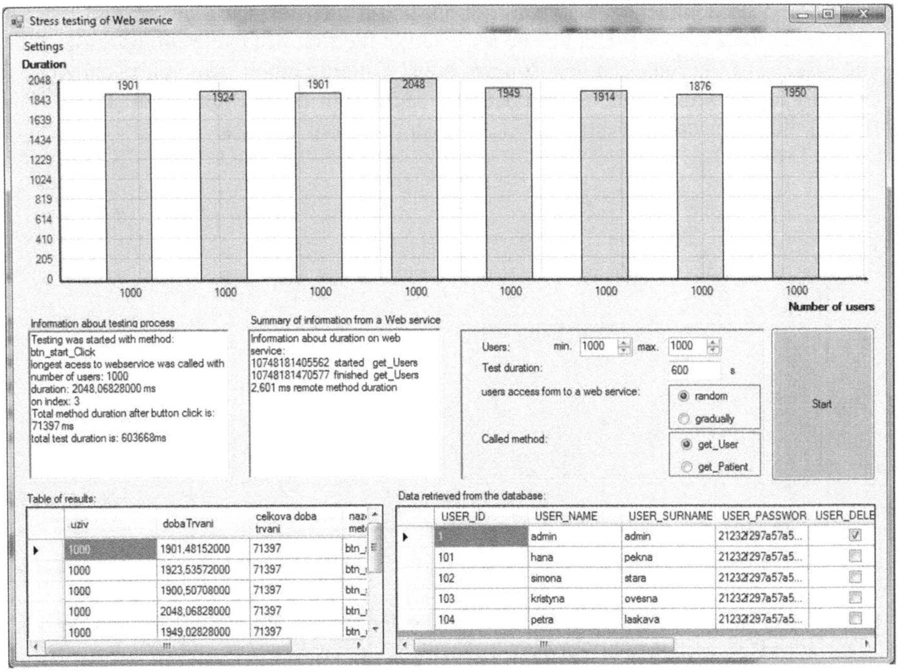

Fig. 1. Appearance of test application

Control section contains a selection method that is called (getUser or getPatient), the selector how the number will be generated by the user accessing the Web service (at random or sequentially), a text box for entering the period during which the test is to be conducted (in case of random access), an element for entering the step size in the progressive generation of users and components for entering the minimum and maximum number of users who have to simultaneously access a Web service.

The principles of UAS are used in proposed software application to allow user more comfortable work with application. We added an options to edit (add or remove) a remote PC location info, which is accessed during the testing of UAS. Thus, the user gets an opportunity to test responses to a rapidly increasing number of remote devices.

Furthermore, we are preparing the customized setting of categorized response. The user can set a maximal time value, beyond which the response is already not acceptable. The software application wills response on such problem by using of red color in the chart. The user can simply recognize values that exceeded the specified maximum time value limit.

2.1 Application Architecture and Ideas

If elected, progressive generation of the user, the method to simultaneously access the first minimum specified number of users in each cycle, the accession number of users increase the size of the specified step up to the maximum number of user specified person test.

This method of testing is shown in [Fig. 2] and [Fig. 3] Both images show exactly the same test results, with the difference being that [Fig. 2] shows the test result after switching on the program, in which case they must be before calling the method from a Web service connection between a client and a web service / server, and must be compiled into a Web service, this be reflected in the first test cycle (in this case call to one user), so he takes much longer than if the method was only called. For comparison, this test done even once. As seen from the difference in [Fig. 2] and [Fig.3], the connection is established and distortion took 287 ms.

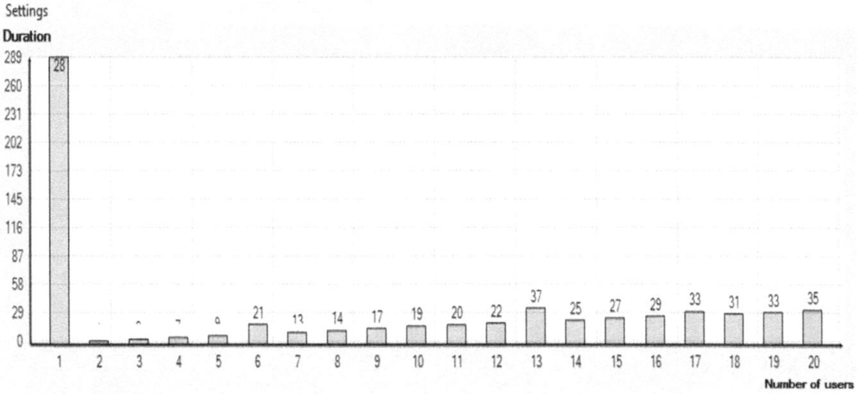

Fig. 2. Test conducted after the start - in the first column shows the bias of measurement when establishing a connection to the server and compile a Web service

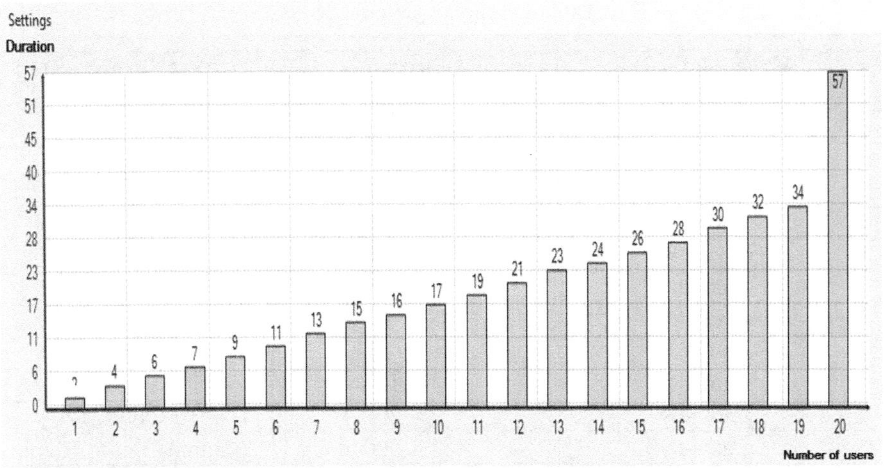

Fig. 3. Test without the overhead of Web service - it displays the test output obtained by measuring with active connection with the server and compiled the Web service

The first cycle of the first measurement was to use in the statistics and in averaging values of the measurements unusable, on the other hand, seeing time of activating connection of server with the Web service is interesting. To not state that during testing we forget to omit the test including initial directing of Web service that can the results of tests uncomfortable affected, the application was changed a bit, so that all Web service directing did not in the test data. This information is written to inform the user in the test results.

If elected, random generation of patients will be randomly selected number of users between the minimum and maximum number of users, given by a testing person and this number of users will be access to the chosen method. This procedure will be repeated until entered period of testing will expire. Once the term of testing is expire, calling method being completed, but another round of testing has not started.

The database was for an example deposited on two different machines and on both was measured duration. First, a powerful PC has processor 2x4GHz and 6 GB DDR2 RAM memory; the second PC contains a 850 MHz AMD processor and 512MB memory SD RAM.

3 Testing Methodology

Each type of tests listed in the table below are made in five iterations, all the values are then processed into arranged tables. For tests in which users are gradually generation, from these values are then calculated values "MODUS", "MEDIAN" and "arithmetic mean". Since it was measured only 5 iterations, not always experienced the same measurements values, therefore some items of calculated values contains value # N/A. Our measurements are not on the accuracy and repeatability values critical and diversity of individual measurements by a few milliseconds is not essential for us, it is only informative measurements, detecting how long time the server needs to respond to the request, which is also influenced by the current server utilization.

Table 1. Types of performed tests

Method of users generating	Users range	Test duration/step
2x4GHz, 6GB DDR2 RAM		
gradually	1 – 30	step = 1
gradually	1 – 1000	step = 50
gradually	100 – 200	step = 10
gradually	200 – 500	step = 20
gradually	500 – 800	step = 20
gradually	500 – 1000	step = 50
gradually	800 – 1000	step = 10
gradually	1 – 100	30 s, 60 s, 120 s
gradually	1 – 200	30 s, 60 s, 120 s
gradually	1 – 500	3 min, 5 min, 10 min
gradually	1 – 700	3 min, 5 min, 10 min
gradually	1 – 800	3 min, 5 min, 10 min
random	1 – 900	3 min, 5 min, 10 min
random	1 – 1000	3 min, 5 min, 10 min
random	1000	10 min
AMD 850MHz, 512MB SD RAM		
gradually	1 – 30	step = 1
gradually	1 – 1000	step = 50
gradually	100 – 200	step = 10
gradually	200 – 500	step = 20
gradually	500 – 800	step = 20
gradually	500 – 1000	step = 50
gradually	800 – 1000	step = 10
gradually	1 – 200	120 s
random	1 – 700	10 min
random	1 – 1000	10 min
random	1000	10 min

4 Tests Results

4.1 Gradually Generated 500 to 1000 Users

Graph shows how response of measurements gradually increase, by the increasing number of accession users. From individual columns can be seen that the values in each iteration of the same number of users slightly vary for both types of machines that are shown always for comparison for the number of users to each other. Variations of those values may be due to switching between processes on the server, that may not be able to handle our request exactly when it receives, it also may be network latency, etc.. The difference between each machine increases with the increasing number of simultaneous accesses. Looking at the graph it is seen that for 500 users is the difference between machines approximately 2.5 s, for 1000 users, this difference is even 5s.

Table 2. Calculated values for 500 - 1000 user-generated gradually

Calculated values:	2x4GHz + 6GB DDR2 RAM (Server)			AMD 850MHz + 512MB SD RAM (PC)		
Number of users	modus	medián	arithmetic mean	modus	medián	arithmetic mean
500	#N/A	895	985,8	3526	3526	3533,6
650	#N/A	1182	1258	4574	4574	4565,4
800	#N/A	1662	1616,6	#N/A	5645	5649,8
1000	#N/A	1797	1977	#N/A	7050	7046,8

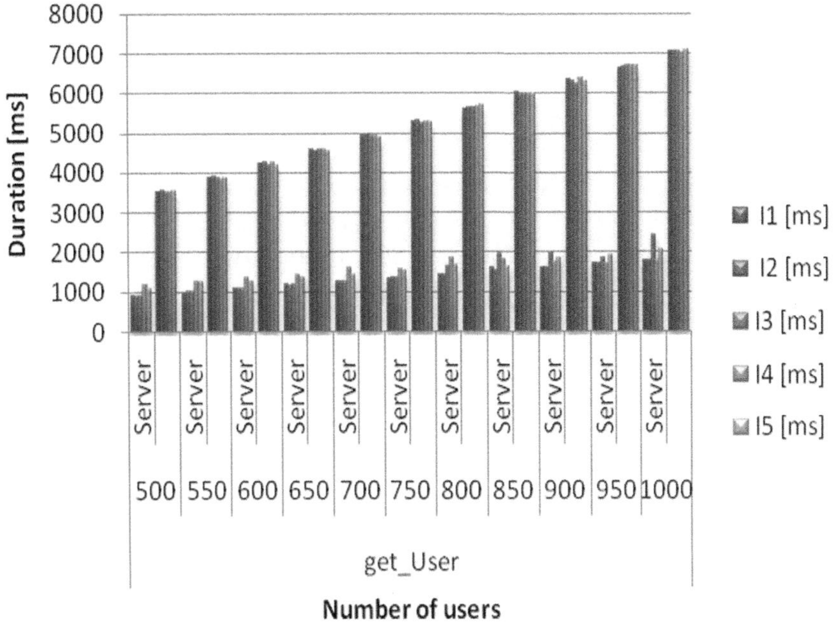

Fig. 4. Contingency graph for 500 - 1000 users - shows the results of all five iterations of measurement and both the PC machine type and the server machine type

Calculated values and graph of these values shows how these values with increasing number of users increase. Individual calculated values (median, mode and average) for one type of machine and the same number of users almost overlap, they are indeed almost identical, which you can see it on the table of values. This would change if it were used to calculate several iterations, for example, the arithmetic average would merely one very different value and this value could dramatically increase. In this case, however, the values in different iterations were very similar and therefore the calculated values are approximately equal.

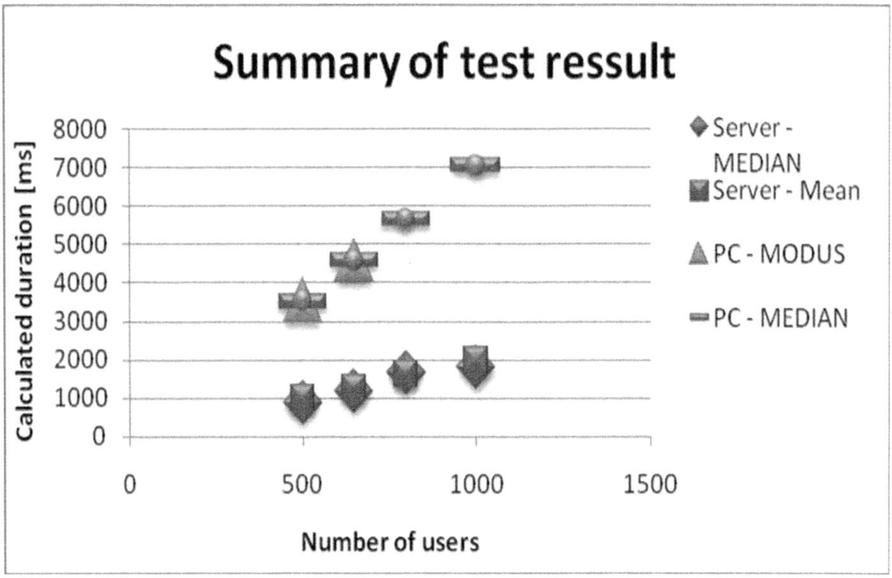

Fig. 5. Graph of calculated values for 500 - 1000 users generated gradually

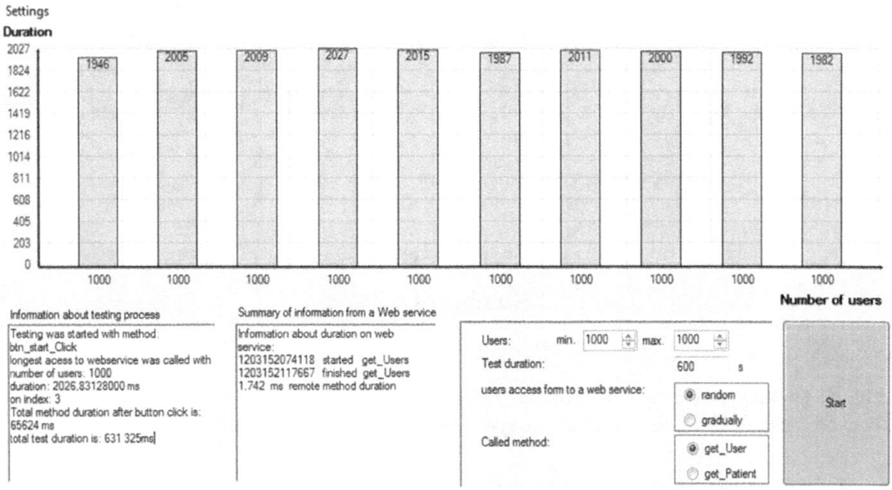

Fig. 6. Chart of results for the machine of server type - Iteration 5 - simulating 1000 simultaneous access to a web service at each step, the duration of the processing approaches are not very different from each other and reach a value of about 2 seconds

4.2 Randomly Generated 1000 to 1000 Users

In figure [Fig. 6] is output graph from the testing program. This graph was measured on a database stored on a PC with a processor 2x2 GHz with 6GB memory, shows how the response changes when we access by the thousands of users simultaneously over 10 minutes. As the chart shows, the values again differ only minimally, always moving around 2 seconds. Slight variations may be caused by the same causes, as it was in the progressive measurement [Fig. 4].

Figure [Fig. 7] shows the same measurement as [Fig. 6], but this measurement was made on the database stored on a PC with an AMD 850 MHz memory and 512 MB Response time for each call, same as above is slightly different. The only difference in these measurements is only that this slower machine has a response time long about seven seconds, compared with the previous measurements for 5 seconds more.

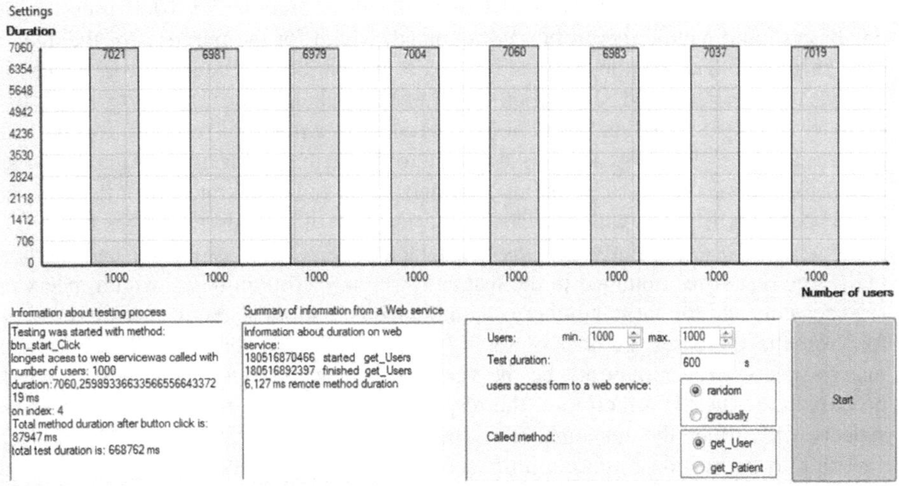

Fig. 7. Result of measurement for the machine of PC type - Iteration 5 - also simulates 1000 simultaneous access to a web service but on a weaker machine, access time of up to seven seconds

Results of the measurements indicate that the burden on Web service with growth in of the accession users increases in the hundreds of units of milliseconds. On the contingency chart [Fig. 4] can be seen that in the various iterations of measurement values fluctuate, but keeping approximately the same values for the same amount accession users differ in orders of milliseconds to tens of milliseconds, which is for the number of accession users allowed change. If occurs to the greater variation, such as in [Fig. 3], where response times for 19 users is 34 ms and 20 users have 57 ms which is for the number of simultaneous accesses a big difference, it may be because the server at the moment request came on the performance of another, more important process, so our demand is not executed immediately. Looking at Figure 2, for comparison of the difference in the responses is for 19 and 20 users, only 2 ms.

5 Discussion

Application allows measurement of response time of SQL Server to query based on the number of simultaneous access to data. The application was created within the development environment Microsoft Visual Studio 2008 and the database accessed by

Web services. The application allows you to measure the response time of database server, but also the time it takes delivery of the request to the server, packaging data collection and their subsequent transfer to the user. Period of the data processing in the developed application isn't at the time of the response included. The application also provides the user directing itself a Web service, which has delayed for the execution of user request a major impact. This delay includes the connection to database and subsequent compilation of web services. Data obtained by measurements are presented in a column chart and tables are summarized in text fields. The results indicate that the length of the response increases proportionally with increasing number of users and even the large number of 1000 users of the database should handle the problem of demand, which for the purposes of the agency over-sufficient. The response times but has a great influence machine on which the database server is stored. Test results shows that when using a desktop PC with a memory of only 512MB and tact 850MHz processor, amount of response for the 1000 user responses to long-7s, which is contrary to the requirement of the Agency, which called for the maximum response in 5 seconds. It is to be reckoned with the fact that the response will grow with increasing the number of records in the database. The machine, which is currently used as the database is 2x2GHz processor and memory 6GB. The responses obtained in the test achieved a maximum of 2s, which meets the requirements and the large number of simultaneous visitors also counts with a reserve to cover the increased number of records. Response times but also slightly affects many aspects. Server may not be the very moment when it is our request, ready to process the request. Furthermore, the response is affected by network latency. These aspects will affect the response time, but not substantially. This is only a slight variation in the response time in millisecond for a small number of users and tens of milliseconds for a larger number of users. For smaller agencies is not a problem to use the processing requirements through Web services. For larger agencies, however, processing of large amounts of data for simultaneous access to a large number of employees could take excessive time, therefore it is preferable to use the handle requests directly to the database.

6 Conclusion

Application has been tested by several stress tests for different numbers of simultaneous accessing users. The number of users has been gradually increased by the entered step or was generated randomness in the specified range. In the case the same number of users are accessing server, the time needed to process the query is almost unchanged. In this case the differences caused by network latency or the need to process the first request with higher priority results in the millisecond. The results showed that the time required to process the query is changed in proportion to the change of number of accessing users and depends on the performance of used machines. In the case the same number of users are accessing server, the time needed to process the query is almost unchanged. In this case the differences caused by network latency or the need to process the first request with higher priority results in the millisecond.

It is not a problem for agencies with smaller size to use the processing requirements through Web services. For larger agencies, however, processing of large amounts of data for simultaneous access to a large number of employees could take excessive time, therefore it is preferable to use the handle requests directly to the database.

Acknowledgment. This work was supported in part by (1) „Centre for Applied Cybernetics“, Ministry of Education of the Czech Republic under project 1M0567, (2) „SMEW – Smart Environments at Workplaces“, Grant Agency of the Czech Republic, GACR P403/10/1310 and (3) "User Adaptive Systems", VSB - Technical University of Ostrava under project SP/2011/22.

References

1. Abowd, G., Dey, A., Brown, P., Davies, N., Smith, M., Steggles, P.: Towards a better understanding of context and context-awareness. In: Gellersen, H.-W. (ed.) HUC 1999. LNCS, vol. 1707, p. 304. Springer, Heidelberg (1999)
2. Krejcar, O., Frischer, R.: Non Destructive Defects Detection by Performance Spectral Density Analysis. Journal Sensors, MDPI Basel 11(3), 2334–2346 (2011)
3. Nielsen, J.: Usability Engineering. Morgan Kaufmann, San Francisco (1994)
4. Haklay, M., Zafiri, A.: Usability engineering for GIS: learning from a screenshot. The Cartographic Journal 45(2), 87–97 (2008)
5. Evennou, F., Marx, F.: Advanced integration of WiFi and inertial navigation systems for indoor mobile positioning. In: Eurasip Journal on Applied Signal Processing. Hindawi publishing corp., New York (2006)
6. Arikan, E., Jenq, J.: Microsoft SQL Server interface for mobile devices. In: Proceedings of the 4th International Conference on Cybernetics and Information Technologies, Systems and Applications/5th Int. Conf. on Computing, Communications and Control Technologies, Orlando, FL, USA, July 12-15 (2007)
7. Jewett, M., Lasker, S., Swigart, S.: SQL server everywhere: Just another database? Developer focused from start to finish. DR DOBBS Journal 31(12) (2006)
8. Krejcar, O., Janckulik, D., Motalova, L., Kufel, J.: Mobile Monitoring Stations and Web Visualization of Biotelemetric System - Guardian II. In: EuropeComm 2009. LNICST. Springer, Heidelberg (2009)
9. Tucnik, P.: Optimization of Automated Trading System's Interaction with Market Environment. In: 9th International Conference on Business Informatics Research. LNBIP, vol. 64, pp. 55–61. Univ. Rostock, Rostock (2010)
10. Mikulecky, P.: Remarks on Ubiquitous Intelligent Supportive Spaces. In: 15th American Conference on Applied Mathematics/International Conference on Computational and Information Science, pp. 523–528. Univ. Houston, Houston (2009)
11. Krejcar, O., Janckulik, D., Motalova, L.: Complex Biomedical System with Biotelemetric Monitoring of Life Functions. In: Proceedings of the IEEE Eurocon 2009, St. Petersburg, Russia, May 18-23, pp. 138–141 (2009), doi:10.1109/EURCON.2009.5167618
12. Pindor, J., Penhaker, M., Augustynek, M., Korpas, D.: Detection of ECG Significant Waves for Biventricular Pacing Treatment. In: 2010 The 2nd International Conference on Telecom Technology and Applications, ICTTA 2010, Bali Island, Indonesia, March 19-21, vol. 2, pp. 164–167. IEEE Conference Publishing Services, NJ (2010), doi:10.1109/ICCEA.2010.186, ISBN 978-0-7695-3982-9

13. Augustynek, M., Penhaker, M., Korpas, D.: Controlling Peacemakers by Accelerometers. In: 2010 The 2nd International Conference on Telecom Technology and Applications, ICTTA 2010, Bali Island, Indonesia, March 19-21, vol. 2, pp. 161–163. IEEE Conference Publishing Services, NJ (2010), doi:10.1109/ICCEA.2010.288, ISBN 978-0-7695-3982-9
14. Labza, Z., Penhaker, M., Augustynek, M., Korpas, D.: Verification of Set Up Dual-Chamber Pacemaker Electrical Parameters. In: 2010 The 2nd International Conference on Telecom Technology and Applications, ICTTA 2010, Bali Island, Indonesia, vol. 2, pp. 168–172. IEEE Conference Publishing Services, NJ (2010), doi:10.1109/ICCEA.2010.187, ISBN 978-0-7695-3982-9
15. Brida, P., Machaj, J., Benikovsky, J., Duha, J.: An Experimental Evaluation of AGA Algorithm for RSS Positioning in GSM Networks. Elektronika Ir Elektrotechnika 8(104), 113–118 (2010) ISSN 1392-1215
16. Krejcar, O., Cernohorsky, J.: Database Prebuffering as a Way to Create a Mobile Control and Information System with Better Response Time. In: Bubak, M., van Albada, G.D., Dongarra, J., Sloot, P.M.A. (eds.) ICCS 2008, Part I. LNCS, vol. 5101, pp. 489–498. Springer, Heidelberg (2008)
17. Kotzian, J., Konecny, J., Prokop, H., Lippa, T., Kuruc, M.: Autonomous explorative mobile robot: Navigation and construction. In: Proceedings - 9th RoEduNet IEEE International Conference, RoEduNet 2010, art. no. 5541599, pp. 49–54 (2010) ISBN: 978-14244-7335-9

Weight Reduction of Players by Active Playing Using Accelerometers

Ondrej Krejcar[1,2]

[1] University of Hradec Kralove, FIM, Department of Information Technologies, Rokitanskeho 62, Hradec Kralove, 500 03, Czech Republic
Ondrej.Krejcar@ASJournal.eu
[2] VSB Technical University of Ostrava, Department of measurement and control, 17. Listopadu 15, 70833 Ostrava Poruba, Czech Republic
Ondrej.Krejcar@remoteworld.net

Abstract. The idea described in this paper deals with a connection of embedded sensors in current smart mobile devices and a game application for mobile devices which results in increased movement of player of these games. Active movement of players was found as one of possible solution how to reduce the weight of playes (users) because of well known global problem of the world is increasing obesity caused by the addiction on the PC games at the young people. This project connects pleasant with useful, respectively playing of the game with physical effort. By the help of the motion sensor (accelerometer) is possible to handle by simple games to whose operating is needed physical impulsion of the player. After it would be possible to take up on this project by the beat measurement of the player in order to check on effectivity of the suggested system. Software was developed in managed code using C# language and .NET Compact Framework platform. Some issues related to real development are also discussed in the rest of paper.

Keywords: accelerometer; weight reducing; mobile device, C#.

1 Introduction

This project is engaged in the interconnection of physical effort and playing of the games of mobile equipments in order to reduce the weight of the player. Is necessary to scan the movement of the whole body or its parts that in this project simulates hardware controlling elements. About that will care electronic component called accelerometer. Accelerometer is an appliance that measures vibrations or acceleration by the movement of the structures (constructions, parts of the machine etc.) The power causing vibrations or the change of the movement (acceleration), effects on the mass of the sensor, that than overpress piezoelectric element generating electric charge comparable to compression. Because the electric charge is comparable to energy and the mass of the sensor is constant, so also electric charge is comparable to acceleration [1]. By the accelerometer is possible to measure dynamic acceleration of the gravitation resulting from the movement of the player [2].

We can imagine accelerometer as a box that is in cosmic area – far- far from all of the cosmic orbs, or if is difficult to find such place, so at least as space ships orbiting

J.J. Yonazi et al. (Eds.): ICeND 2011, CCIS 171, pp. 249–260, 2011.

over the planet, where everything is in weightlessness. Imagine every wall is sensible on the pressure. If we will at once move by the field on the left (we will speed up acceleration 1g = 9,8 m/s 2), the ball will get at on the wall – X. We measure compressive energy and the output value on the axe X, that evolves the ball/ globule touching the wall [3]. For the practical realization was chosen linear 3-axes (x ,y ,z) accelerometer LIS3LV02DQ with digital exit and communication up to bus I2C/SPI.

The information obtained by the accelerometer can be transferred to the PC after the three communication interfaces. The first one parallel port, but that is rather outdated, and newer PCs are free. Another option is the serial port, after which it is not so difficult to communicate as after USB version for the third time. By using of the communication USB interface would be necessary to develop hardware that would be required to obtain information about location of the users hand from accelerometer, convert it to a data packed, and that send over USB. The development of that hardware is quite a complicated and too much time-consuming, when nowadays is ordinary converter between serial port and USB. From that follows that it is preferable to use serial communication interface. Standard RS-232, respectively the latest version of the RS-232C, from 1969, (also the serial port or serial line) is used as the communication interface of personal computers and other electronics. RS-232 allows connection and mutual serial communication between two devices, it means that the individual bits of transmitted data are transmitted in successively on after another (in series) over a single wire, similarly as by the network technology. Ethernet or USB interface [4]. In this paragraph have been described resources that would be used to build electronic equipment in order to reduce the weight of playing games on mobile devices.

For laboratory testing will be used mobile transmission equipment HTC Touch HD with just built-in accelerometer. By these devices motion sensor isn´t used just to recording the screen of display, but also to facilitate the control of various applications, without the use of buttons, both hardware and software. Method GetGvector returns the vector that describes the direction of gravitation and acceleration in relation to the device screen. When the unit face up on a flat surface methods are returned to quality 0, 0, -9.8. The value of -9.8 implies that the acceleration is in the opposite direction of the screen orientation. If the device is standing method returns to 0, -9.8, 0. The quality Y -9.8 means that the appliance accelerates in the direction of the bottom of the screen. Conversely, if the device is held upside down method returns 0, 9.8, 0 [5].

The values measured by an accelerometer, are than visualized by the application in this case the game that was written in Visual Studio 2008 C # for Windows Mobile platform. The application simulates acts as a jump, and the frequency of jumps over certain time. This game can play two or more players who compete with each other. The problem with the conversion of measured values from the accelerometer can occur with improper handling with mobile devices.

2 Problem Definition

The ubiquity of mobile phones in combination with an internet connection, built-in GPS chips, the location and other integrated sensors provide an excellent platform for collecting data about the individual and its surroundings [7].

The goal of the project is a using of C# language and .NET platform in the environment of Microsoft Visual Studio 2008 to implement a simple game for mobile applications that will use the motion sensor (accelerometer) with the result of increasing heart rate of players. The project will address the following issues:

1. Getting data from the accelerometer
2. The actual game programming

There are some examples of games which using motion sensors on the internet possible to download, but they don't provide a possibilities to use info from motion sensor to compute the amount of energy out by players body:

Caver

The task of the game is to safely fly ball, a series of cave complexes. Needless to say, touching the cave walls the game ends. Their scores are stored in tables and extra points can be obtained online by sending a proud result.

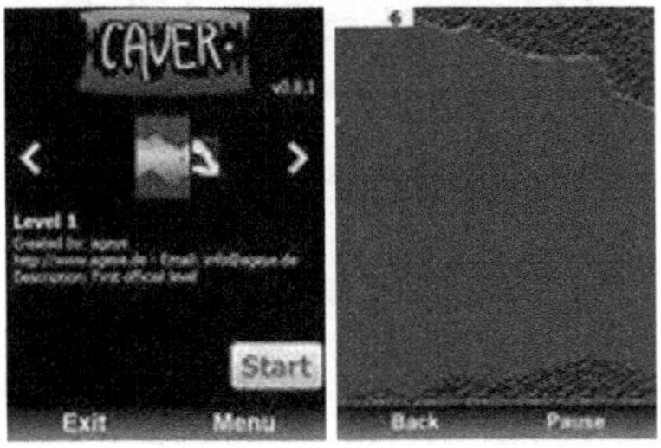

Fig. 1. Caver game

The application is also the possibility of calibrating the sensor. Initially you will appreciate the choice of difficulty.

G-Invaders

Using rackets and the firepower you need to find a way through ten levels of play. The number of enemies while in each of them increases geometrically, and the game becomes more difficult.

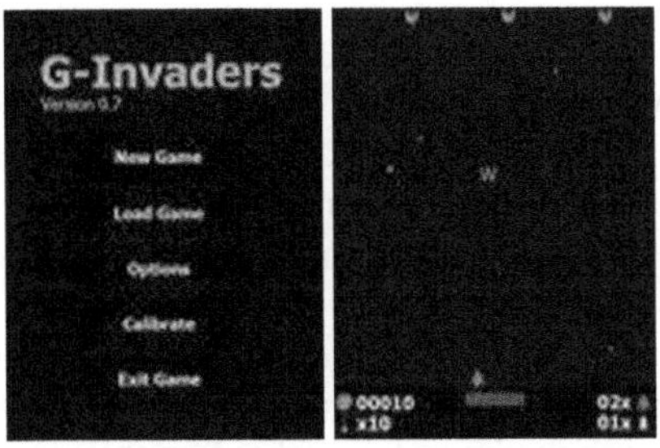

Fig. 2. G-Invanders

In addition to a pair of weapons can also use the shield when it is no longer the fire escape of unwanted guests.

SensorMaze

Another type of game in which the use of motion sensor offers literally, is a maze. SensorMaze just the mold of these games fall. The task of each maze is a way to show the mouse Emmental cheese delicacies. The graphics are very simple, to which indicates the size of the installation of less than 30 kilobytes.

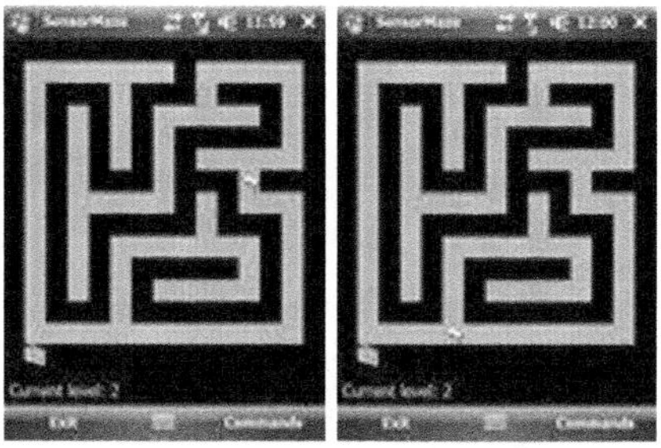

Fig. 3. Sensor Maze

Resco Bubbles

The first commercial game for Windows Mobile, which builds on the capabilities of gravitational chip. The player has the ball as quickly as possible to collect bubbles. It would not be so difficult were it not matter the order in which they will collect the bubbles.

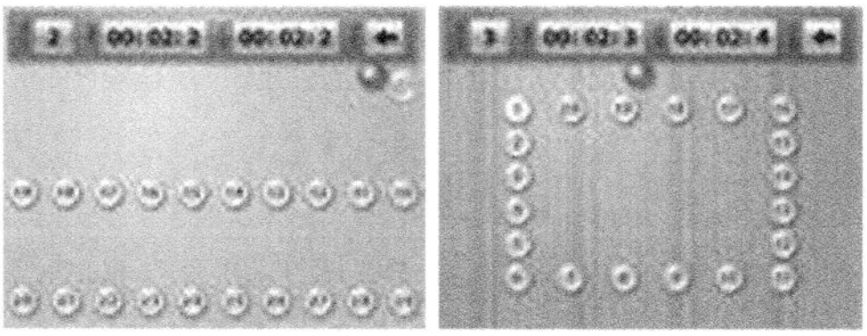

Fig. 4. Resco Bubles

Compared with freeware titles Resco Bubbles boasts very nice graphics. Producer price of the license provided for less than 10 USD (200 CZK). Newly promoted as the Samsung i900 Omnia.

All these games are (except the last) freeware and is involved in the development of amateur programmers. Also noteworthy is the application developed to iPhone4. This is a game Gun Range, which uses an accelerometer with a built-in gyroscope. This measure, unlike a rotary accelerometer. Averaging the data that come simultaneously from the accelerometer and gyroscope can get a relatively better estimate of the actual tilt equipment than what we obtained only by using data only from the accelerometer. This minimizes errors due eg braking on a train or boat leaning [8] Although this is a nice application, for our purposes are nedostaující because not enough players to move, so it is necessary to develop a game that the players will develop greater physical demands.

To work with G-sensor is used HTCSensorSDK.dll library. It should be noted that the algorithm using a library of conveying data from the motion sensor device works only on Windows Mobile 6.5. The code is a class HTCGSensor. This will enable us to capture and utilize state of the G-sensor in the device. The service will start using the algorithm for reading the information. Information, go to the pointer in memory where information is stored. After reading the requested data will terminate the service again. Upon termination of service is important to return everything to its original state, then reset all the variables. [9].

The movement effects on development-development effects on the move, thanks to the modern era full of technological innovations that lead to a reduction of movement and to decrease of physical exertion, is an irreplaceable factor for many companies to develop physical activity in gaming, which is directly linked to that to give physical proficiency. This combination of nice with useful leads to targeted result, respectively to weight loss of players during playing the games.

There are many games that needs physical exertion such as dancing simulators, virtual broad jump or mobile applications that by the help of accelerometer response on the tilt of mobile device as at the game „Cube Runner" , a simple game developed for iPhone mobile, iPhone 3G, iPod Touch. Controlled is the ship (arrow), which travels through a maze of cubes. To passing game is needed a ship without hitting the dice to the finish line. In this game control is very sensible, just very little to tilt the ship. Control is provided by a built-in accelerometer.

This game does not always bring such a great effect as the movement of player, it is de facto all about tilting of a mobile device [6].

Another way to move by playing games is using detection by help of 3D camera. The company Mgestyk presented the technology that allows you to control your computer just through simple gestures. It recognizes gestures by using 3D camera and can work with the most of programs under the Windows. It is about controlling your computer by using only hand gestures. You don´t need any peripherals like a mouse or keyboard. Just to connect special camera and buy special software by Mgestyk. There is no need to use sweeping gestures. It´s enough with saving moves by just one hand, in some cases you will use both. It is not known if some applications are so complicated that you would use also the legs, but if it happens, it will be especially the excesses. But the technology by itself in any case isn´t the excess. It should manage any application running under the Windows, and so in the full range of its possibilities. If you will learn to gesture and control computer by that, you will have no limits in its control [7].

iPhone 4 offers the games that are controlled by a gyroscope. You might ask why you should be interested in data from the gyroscope, while accelerometer provides directive angles in all of three axes. The answer is simple – we can´t always rely on the accelerometer. The results, even if the accelerometer is in a relatively stable position, are very sensitive to vibrations and to mechanical noise at all. This is the main reason why the most of the system for the measurement of inertial force uses a gyroscope to annihilation of errors of the accelerometer [8].

All of these methods how to achieve the movement of players by playing games have something good in itself and also some imperfections. In this project, when will be developed simple but effective game where the player will develop a physical activity and so that the mobile device THC Touch HD has just built-in accelerometer, which will be mounted on the body will do "sit-lye". The device will record the change in the tilt angles according to the number of changes within a given range. The result will be displayed on the display of the device. This game will play one or more players.

3 Software Platform Architecture

In this chapter we introduce with a specific solution. Developed applications for mobile device HTC Touch HD have the task of using G sensor, which is part of the device, scan the body position when performing the exercise (or movement in the simulation, simply by tilting the mobile device) called sit-lying. There are several types of sit-lying. One of them is that at the exercise, we lie on the ground. When sitting-lying, we lie on your back, bend the legs at the knees and feet push against the ground and hands can be in the rear. The movement begins slowly lift the upper torso from the ground through a rounded back. The scapulae should be lifted from the ground, while the lower back remains on the ground. In the second phase, the body return to its original position, but is not running the floor. During the exercise, it is necessary to maintain a neutral position of the cervical spine and regular breathing (stroke-touch return - exhale). Another type is to do sit-supine on an inclined bench. Lie on the bench upside down. The greater the slope, the greater burden. Slowly we lift the hull and hands crossed on his chest. The exercises on a inclined bench with his own body weight (you can add ballast in the form of wheel weights - it keeps on the chest) is graded load - the heaviest at the beginning of the exercise, when we were the lowest - surpass the greatest weight. This can be used during exercises tops - at the end of the exercise will remain in the down position and only a very short and slow movements up and down the muscles maximally heating up - here but watch out for injuries - strained or torn abdominal muscle and make it impossible for a few weeks of any workout! For better practice oblique muscle while moving up the appropriate body turns slightly left and right dial. The structure features is shown in (Fig.1).

Body of a program is a form on which the controls are initialized in the method FrmToCondition() and Initialization(). In the form is included TabControl, in which are two TabPages. In one are the elements of control and in the second are instructions. The main form (TabPage_1), are the following controls: The first is the ComboBox, which is used for the selection of activity (not implemented versions of choice for more activities). The second is the NumericUpDown-nudInterval-determined interval measurementactivity. One of the other Labek, one of the major is one that displays the number of repetition scores. Button-btnStart-used to start the exercise. Label-lblTime-The label displays the time practice starts and the time during which the exercise is conducted. PictureBox, PictureBox PictureBox3-in are two pictures that demonstrate the movement. Label - label6 this label displays the angle of rotation.

After initialization, the application will serve the main form load event FrmToConditional_Load. Here we set the head of file that is used for storing the measured values from the G sensor.

Event btnStart_Click used to initialize the element values before you start exercising. The method included features DataTime system time to recover. Next run timer, which is primetime for the calculation.

The event includes timer1_Tick as mentioned above calculation principle. If the time of exercise not equal to the system time + TimeInterval program continues the calculation otherwise, the info about the end of exercise. If the angle is greater than 50 and less than 150 in the BUP is changed from FALSE to TRUE. This applies to the situation when the angle increases. If the angle is greater than150 or less than 50 in bDown changes false to true. If both achieve both truei32Counetrer + +. Then BUP and bDown back to false. If-it will be when the angle of growth of less than50 and will fall again BUP'll always be in the condition is false, because the condition is not complete, which is such that for changing the status true, we need a angle greater than 50 and less than 150. This problem may occur for example when it is wrong to tutor training. In the eventbtnStart_click is contained in a file and saving. In the latest incident is resolved CloseMenu_Click quit. DialogResult, remembers what it was last pressed, then ask if dr == DialogResult if so, that application shall be terminated if not return.

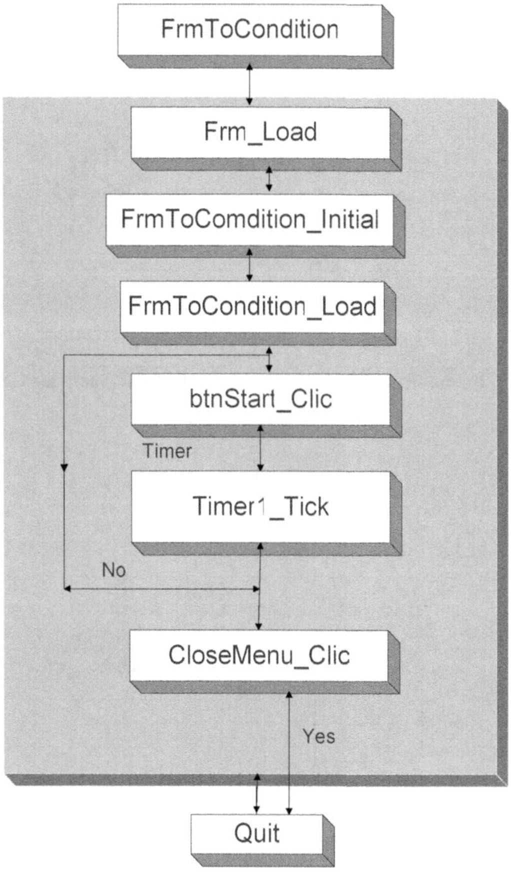

Fig. 5. Application Structure

The project is ready for further enlargement exercises. You need only get the code for the next exercise, therefore, is to write the formula for calculating algorithm danny issues such as handles and add the application graphically.

4 Implementation of Proposed Solution

This chapter will talk about how to implement new solutions. The application was developed using C # language compatible. NET in Visual Studio2010 from Microsoft. The application was created in the GUI, a graphical user interface library, in this case for mobile devices (mobile service). Were used as traditional components as Button, Label, PictureBox and components that run in the background like Timer and main menu. HCT_X7500 Mobile devices connected over USB to the PC and the connection and synchronize via ActiveSync program to play into the mobile device. You can then disconnect the mobile device from your PC and run the actual applicationHTC_X7500. Pressing the ToCondition application starts and loads the graphics window (Fig.2).

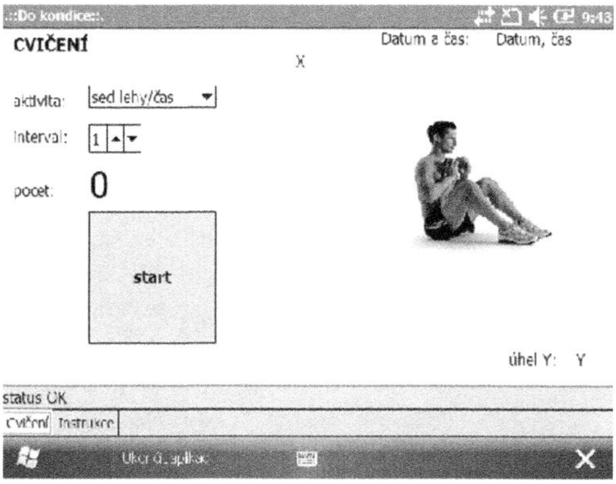

Fig. 6. Application GUI

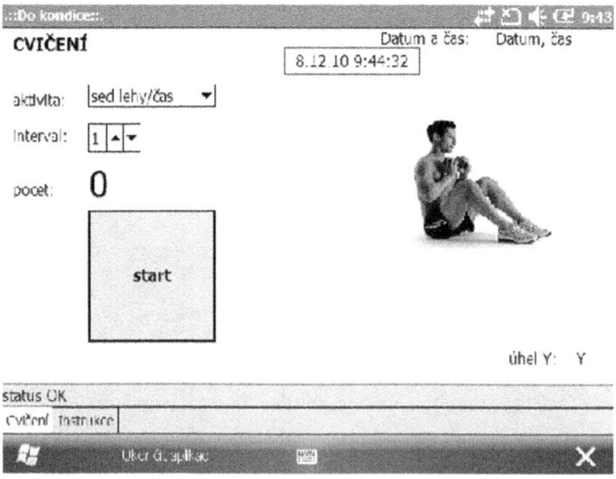

Fig. 7. Load startup time (ending time)

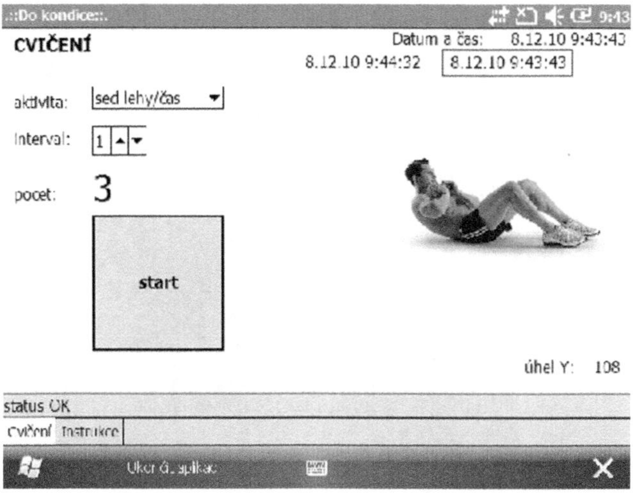

Fig. 8. Time Machine view (top)

After setting an interval workout that is every one minute, for example as shown in (Fig.2) user need to press Start. When pressed on the upper right shows the time when the end of the exercise (Fig.3).

After opening exercises the next time when the exercise will end the current time (Fig.4), a time that flows in real time and stops on a time basis, which is set to start after the Start button. After opening exercises the next time when the exercise will end the current time (Fig.4), a time that flows in real time and stops on a time basis, which is set to start after the Start button.

5 Testing of Developed Application

This chapter deals with the testing and applications created by comparing the results from other authors. Given that a similar application for mobile devices has been found will be tested only in testing applications developed. Task was to create an application for mobile devices, which already includes a built-in accelerometer (G sensor). In this project, namely HTC_X7500.

As a first test were tested, which took place after the first measurement interval setting exercise 1 minute and then another, without that application has been turned off. This means that after 1 min when it was done 34 sit-lying as the chart shows (Fig,5). Valid seven-Leh is one that is in the range of 50 - 150 The second measurement was performed five sit - the lying, as shown in the chart at the end (Fig, 5).

The second test was done to simulate the imperfect exercises or sit-angle, which would not be counted. The application is designed so that by making angle greater than 50 and less than 150 while the sit - lie valid, if so, the lack of angle of 50, which means that the instructor either writ on the ground or not come to the knee will sit-lie calculated as shown in (Fig. 6). Red dots represent unsuccessful attempts. The conclusion was one counted, because it met the set range.

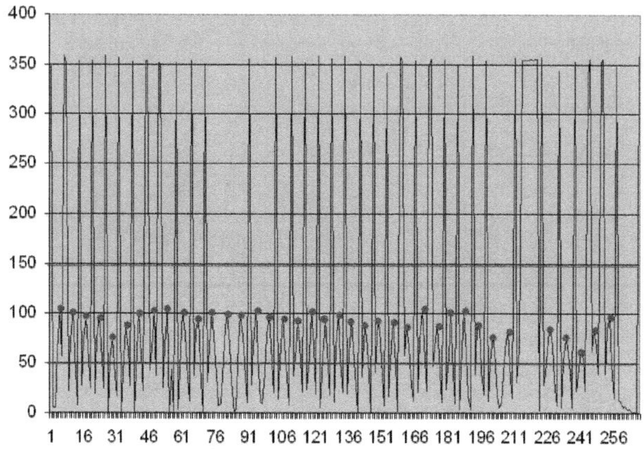

Fig. 9. Repeated exercises

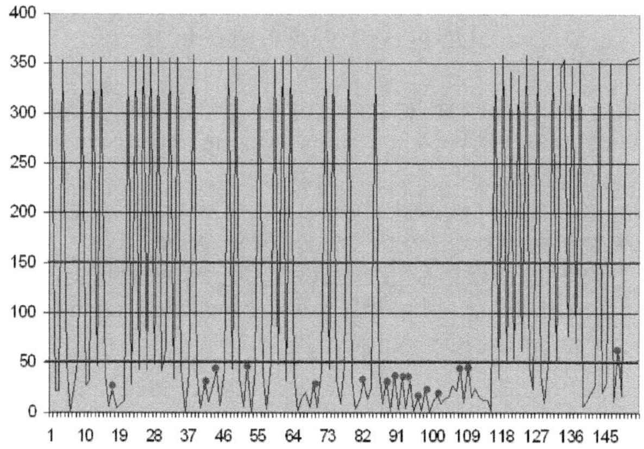

Fig. 10. Wrong exercises

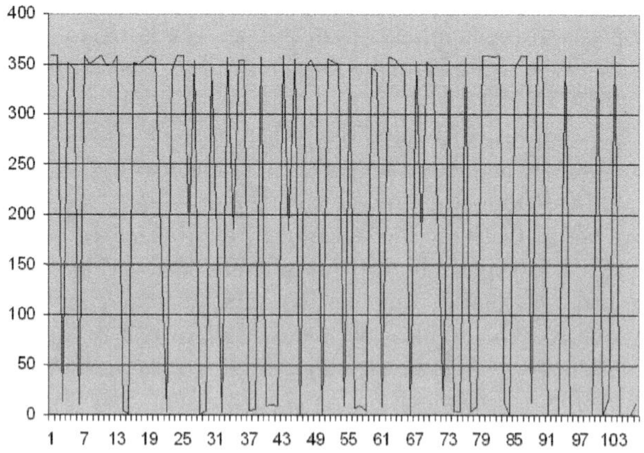

Fig. 11. Wrong handling of mobile devices

In the third test, was focused on improper handling, and that when the device is handled differently than the allowed (recommended for proper operation), i.e. in the Z axis or Y. In this case the application is broken and cannot see the number performed sit-lying position. Testing was done so that the mobile device is tilted in the Y and Z axis as shown in (Fig. 7) there was no valid test.

When testing an application has been tested in various speed training, namely three types of speed. From the slow movement across normal to move quickly, which represented the sit-lie exercise. In slow motion not occurrence slightest problem and applications flawlessly performed counting sit-ups. At higher speeds could be observed that the application is valid, although sit - lie counted, but it took a while before it appeared on the screen. Nothing less number of sit-lying position, which counted the application, was same as which was carried out in parallel by exercise. The testing of high speed, that even though the sit-lie done properly and was also entirety and not be counted because the number of measurements per second is somewhere between 3 to 5 It may therefore happen that the angle is not to be registered and therefore not counted valid attempt. A solution could be to use the timer or use a precise and distribution of the fibbers in this project which would result in speeding up processes, including multiple entry angles per second.

6 Conclusion

On this project we tried to work with the accelerometer control in the mobile deviceHTC_X7500. So everything related to getting from the accelerometer data from the device to communicate. We also tried working with graphics for mobile devices in mobile servicing and discovered some new features and commands.

Utilization of this project is such that at practice, we can concentrate fully on the exercises and you do not guard interval exercise or count the number of repetitions. The application was designed more as a game and therefore serves to entertain, such as two or more people who do much for the lying-sit any unit of time.

The application is ready, maybe in the future to extend to more activities such as push-ups and the like. It would be enough only to write up the algorithm and compute and modify graphics window.

Acknowledgment. This work was supported in part by (1) „Centre for Applied Cybernetics“, Ministry of Education of the Czech Republic under project 1M0567, (2) „SMEW – Smart Environments at Workplaces“, Grant Agency of the Czech Republic, GACR P403/10/1310 and (3) "User Adaptive Systems", VSB - Technical University of Ostrava under project SP/2011/22. We also acknowledge support from student Marek Smolon.

References

1. Krejcar, O., Frischer, R.: Non Destructive Defects Detection by Performance Spectral Density Analysis. Journal Sensors, MDPI Basel 11(3), 2334–2346 (2011)
2. Jung, D., Lee, D., Cho, H.: Implementation of Realistic Game Controllers using Three Axis Accelerometer and Wireless Communication modules. In: ICOIN: 2009 International Conference on Information Networking, pp. 152–155 (2009) ISBN: 978-1-4244-4526-4

3. Brida, P., Machaj, J., Duha, J.: A Novel Optimizing Algorithm for DV based Positioning Methods in ad hoc Networks. Elektronika Ir Elektrotechnika (Electronics and Electrical Engineering) 1(97), 33–38 (2010) ISSN 1392-1215
4. Tucnik, P.: Optimization of Automated Trading System's Interaction with Market Environment. In: 9th International Conference on Business Informatics Research. LNBIP, vol. 64, pp. 55–61. Univ. Rostock, Rostock (2010)
5. Mikulecky, P.: Remarks on Ubiquitous Intelligent Supportive Spaces. In: 15th American Conference on Applied Mathematics/International Conference on Computational and Information Science, pp. 523–528. Univ. Houston, Houston (2009)
6. Krejcar, O., Janckulik, D., Motalova, L.: Complex Biomedical System with Biotelemetric Monitoring of Life Functions. In: Proceedings of the IEEE Eurocon 2009, St. Petersburg, Russia, May 18-23, pp. 138–141 (2009), doi:10.1109/EURCON.2009.5167618.
7. Pindor, J., Penhaker, M., Augustynek, M., Korpas, D.: Detection of ECG Significant Waves for Biventricular Pacing Treatment. In: 2010 The 2nd International Conference on Telecom Technology and Applications, ICTTA 2010, Bali Island, Indonesia, March 19-21, vol. 2, pp. 164–167. IEEE Conference Publishing Services, NJ (2010), doi:10.1109/ICCEA.2010.186, ISBN 978-0-7695-3982-9
8. Labza, Z., Penhaker, M., Augustynek, M., Korpas, D.: Verification of Set Up Dual-Chamber Pacemaker Electrical Parameters. In: 2010 The 2nd International Conference on Telecom Technology and Applications, ICTTA 2010, Bali Island, Indonesia, March 19-21, vol. 2, pp. 168–172. IEEE Conference Publishing Services, NJ (2010), doi:10.1109/ICCEA.2010.187, ISBN 978-0-7695-3982-9
9. Brad, R.: Satellite Image Enhancement by Controlled Statistical Differentiation. In: Innovations and Advances Techniques in Systems, Computing Sciences and Software Engineering, International Conference on Systems, Computing Science and Software Engineering, ELECTR NETWORK, December 03-12, pp. 32–36 (2007)
10. Augustynek, M., Penhaker, M., Korpas, D.: Controlling Peacemakers by Accelerometers. In: 2010 The 2nd International Conference on Telecom Technology and Applications, ICTTA 2010, Bali Island, Indonesia, March 19-21, vol. 2, pp. 161–163. IEEE Conference Publishing Services, NJ (2010), doi:10.1109/ICCEA.2010.288, ISBN 978-0-7695-3982-9

SemanticXO: Connecting the XO with the World's Largest Information Network

Christophe Guéret and Stefan Schlobach

Vrije Universiteit Amsterdam, Amsterdam (Nederlands)
{c.d.m.gueret,k.s.schlobach}@vu.nl

Abstract. The XO, powered by a dedicated graphical environment Sugar, is a low cost, robust and connected laptop suitable for usage in developing countries. The Web of Linked Data is the largest decentralized information network ever crafted so far, containing factual information about millions of "things". The community project SemanticXO is about connecting the two, providing Sugar with dedicated tools to harness the power of the Web of Linked Data. In this paper, we introduce the project, its current status and the goals.

Keywords: Semantic Web, Linked Data, Sugar, SemanticXO, Serious Games.

1 Introduction

Over the last decades, the invention of network protocols enabled data sharing among groups of locally connected computers. The birth of the Internet connected all these local networks into one giant network upon which the World Wide Web (WWW) was built as a global, decentralized, publication system. As proven by its success, the publication of documents on the Web suits many information needs. However, the coarse level of document-level information aggregation does not fit the need of publishing atomic fact such as a date of birth, or a city of residence, so that it can be interpreted (or "understood") by some other computer program. On a typical biographical web page, such information will have to be manually harvested from the document. Although this is an easy task for human Web user, this becomes a daunting problem for a computer program. As a result, a Web browser can process a request phrased as "show me the personal Web page of Mr X" but can not give any definitive answer to "what is the date of birth of Mr X?". It can even less merge the content of several web pages to find information scattered among them, or combine such information.

It is based on this observation that the Word Wide Web Consortium (W3C) initiated the research on the Semantic Web in 2001 with the goal of establishing standards for the publication of structured information on the Web [1]. Using such standards, one can indicate that a particular date on a page is a birth-date, thereby providing any program parsing that page with the information it needs to give definitive answers. In the past few years more and more data-sources have been published and made public in what is now often called the *Web of Linked*

J.J. Yonazi et al. (Eds.): ICeND 2011, CCIS 171, pp. 261–275, 2011.

Data. The ultimate goal of this is a "Web 3.0": a Web combining a network of documents and data suitable for both human and machine processing. In this Web 3.0, programs are expected to give more precise answers to queries as they will be able to associate a meaning (the semantic) to the information they process. Sugar, the graphical environment found on the XO, is currently Web 2.0 enabled but has no dedicated tools to interact with the Web 3.0. The goal of the SemanticXO project is to make Sugar Web 3.0 proof.

Contribution of this paper. This paper reports on the first results of the SemanticXO project and highlights the current work and further directions of research. In order to give a better intuition on the potential of the proposed technology we will describe a prototypical use-case in knowledge acquisition of traditional amerindian world-views based on serious games built on top of our semantic infrastucture. The main research contributions are to:

- show that it possible to run a "triple store" on the XO, and
- to indicate how end users can benefit from having a triple store.

Outline. The rest of this paper is organized as follows: after a brief description of the SemanticXO project in Section 3 we give an introduction to the Web of Linked Data and the related key concepts, Section 4 describes the technical choices made and report on the initial performance results. Section 5 then shows a simple use-case activity exploiting the developed software stack. Finally, Section 6 concludes on the opened questions, upcoming challenges and opportunities for the project.

2 The Project SemanticXO

In this section, we describe the SemanticXO project. Its goal is to provide the infrastructure that is needed to integrate semantic information from the Web of Data into programs running in the Sugar environment on an XO computer which are provided through the OLPC initiative.

2.1 One Laptop Per Child (OLPC)

One Laptop Per Child is a non-profit organization whose goal is to empower the world's poorest children through education by providing them with a rugged, low-cost, low-power and connected laptop: the XO. This device connects them to each other and to the World via the Internet. They are five core principles observed whenever the XO are deployed in a school [2]:

1. Every child **owns the laptop** he receives. He takes it with him when he goes home or to the school. This way, everyone is free to use the machine whenever he wants;
2. The action is **focused on early education**, for children aged from 6 to 12;
3. Every child in classrooms and schools get a laptop at the same time so that **no one gets left out**;

4. Because there is plenty to learn from the Web and from others, the XO is a **connected device** which connects to other XOs and/or the Internet;
5. The XO must include free and open source software to be **free to grow and adapt** with the needs of the child.

The software available on the XO is designed for joyful and self-empowered learning getting children engaged in their own education. The core of the Human Interface for the XO is addressed by "Sugar", an easy to use environment that is built around activities rather than application windows. Most of the activities can be shared among different machines. For instance, several children can collaborate on a same drawing simultaneously in the Draw activity and one can share an e-book he is reading in the Read activity.

Although being aimed at children, Sugar is a fully functional environment that is suitable for usage by anyone. This, added to the physical robustness of the XO, makes it an interesting tool for usage within rural communities.

2.2 SemanticXO

SemanticXO is an OLPC contributor project started in October 2010 for an expected duration of one year and is granted with 3 refurbished XOs from the first generation (XO-1). The goal of the project is to investigate the technical possibilities and the advantages of setting up a "Semantic software stack" for Sugar, empowering it with the latest advances in knowledge representation on the Web. This is expected to be beneficial to Sugar itself, to the developers of activities and to the end users.

Benefits for Sugar. Sugar uses a data store that abstracts the file system details from the developers and the end users. It also grant them the possibility to store meta data for the elements saved on the machine. Knowledge representation techniques focused on structured data are designed to cope with meta data about diverse item and thus fit perfectly the functional needs of such a data store. The popular desktop indexers Tracker [3] and Strigi [4] have both already adopted these technologies to index the content of the file system, for the Gnome and KDE desktop environments, respectively.

Benefits for activities developers. As highlighted in the introduction, it difficult to integrate information within a given activity. The access to Linked Data on the Web gives allows the developers to combine information from different sources into their activities. For instance, combine a description of a city from Wikipedia with it's coordinates as found on Geonames. Semantic technologies also facilitate the storage of meta data in different languages.

Benefits for the users. In its vision statement, the Web Foundation see the Web as the medium that will enable a World where everyone "communicate and collaborate, create valued content, and access the information that they need to improve their lives and communities". Semantic Web technologies are the next evolution of the Web, improving information access by making it suitable from consumption by programs. Empowering Sugar with Semantic technologies will connect the users with the Web of Data, the largest structured information network ever created so far. It will also improve communication among individuals. The Network Institute [5] in Amsterdam is actively working with the Web Foundation on projects for improving the life of persons living in developing countries. Especially through the Web Alliance for Regreening in Africa [6], a project focused on improving information sharing among African farmers. SemanticXO as the potential to contribute to this effort, providing indirect benefits to its users.

3 The Web of Linked Data

The World Wide Web (WWW), launched around 20 years ago, is a decentralized system enabling the publication of documents and links between these documents on the Internet. This Web has proven to be very successful and currently links more than a trillion documents served by machines all over the world [7]. But documents are an aggregated representation of information that is only accessible through an interpretation of the content: individuals would not be able to make sense of page on Wikipedia wrote in English, unless they are able to understand that language. This makes impossible digging out any specific information out of the document. Applications are like individuals not speaking any of the languages the Web is made of.

Let's consider a simple knowledge acquisition problem: finding the number of inhabitants of Amsterdam. An easy solution for an individual is to go on Wikipedia and look for the information (in a language she understands). A software will have to be programmed to dig out that explicit information out of the Web document - a working but tricky technical solution, not robust again chances and targeted to a specific need. The Web of Linked Data (WoD) is a decentralized publication system for publishing **structured data**. It can also be seen as a distributed data base over the Web and, as a data base, it is possible to express a query asking for one information in particular. The following query asks the WoD for the population of Amsterdam (1211503 persons):

```
SELECT ?population WHERE {
     dbpedia:Amsterdam dbprop:populationTotal ?population.
}
```

Listing 1.1. Asking the WoD for the number of inhabitants in Amsterdam

Both programs and individuals are able to get the query to be executed and are able to interpret its result. It is also important to note that this query returns *only* the information sought, rather than a complex document full of different information.

This query is expressed in SPARQL, one of the many standards the Web of Linked Data relies on. We will hereafter spend some time going through the different key concepts and standards of the Web of Linked Data necessary to the understanding of the rest of the paper.

3.1 Key Concepts

The WoD is a network connecting resources with typed relations.

Definition 1 (Resource). *A resource is a named entity which represents a thing in the WoD. The things represented on the WoD can either be a physical entity of the real world or a document on the WWW. For instance, the resource* `http://dbpedia.org/resource/Amsterdam` *represents the city of Amsterdam on the Web of Data and the resource* `http://google.com/index.html` *is the document returned by Google as a welcome page.*

The example given in this definition uses the mechanism of Uniform Resource Identifier (URI) to assign a name to the things. This is one of the requirement of publishing linked data on the Web [8]:

1. Use URIs as names for things.
2. Use HTTP URIs so that people can look up those names.
3. When someone looks up a URI, provide useful information, using the standards [defined by the W3C].
4. Include links to other URIs. so that they can discover more things.

Because URIs are long, "namespaces" are used to compress their notation.

Definition 2 (Namespace). *Namespaces are syntactical shortcuts for resources. For instance, the namespace "dbpedia" is commonly used to refer to the address* `http://dbpedia.org/resource/`*, allowing to write* `dbpedia:Amsterdam` *instead of* `http://dbpedia.org/resource/Amsterdam`*. The web site* `http://prefix.cc` *maintains a list of the most commonly used namespaces.*

Unlike the WWW where the links between documents don't convey any specific meaning, the links between resources on the WoD are semantically rich and defined as predicates.

Definition 3 (Predicate). *Predicates are explicit relations used to bind resources. These predicates are defined in vocabularies (also called "ontologies"), they are used in conjunction with a subject and an object in statements referred to as "triple". The predicates are also resources having a URI and can thus be used on the Web of Data like any other resource. Because of this, the Web of Data is a network that contains both its content and the information about its interpretation*

The triples are expressed using a standard from the W3C, the organism in charge of the standardization of the Web(s). They are stored in specialized data bases called "triple store" and queried using the SPARQL protocol through a "SPARQL end point".

Definition 4 (SPARQL). *SPARQL is a query language for data expressed in RDF. It is similar to other data bases query language such as SQL and is meant to be used in conjunction with SPARQL end points.*

By making use of these publication concepts, a growing number of data publishers are taking part into the creation of this Web of Data. Each of them contributing a few more triples to this one global graph.

3.2 What Is Out There?

The current size of the Web of Data is estimated to be around 27 billion triples [9]. That is, 27 billion factual information about things as diverse as persons, movies, research papers or proteins. The Linked Open Data cloud [10] shown in Figure 1 is a well known representation that, although being non exhaustive, gives a fair appreciation on the current content of the WoD. One of the bubble in this picture is DBpedia, which we referred to in our introductory example. DBpedia is a Linked Data version of Wikipedia containing factual information extracted from the info boxes found on the pages of Wikipedia.

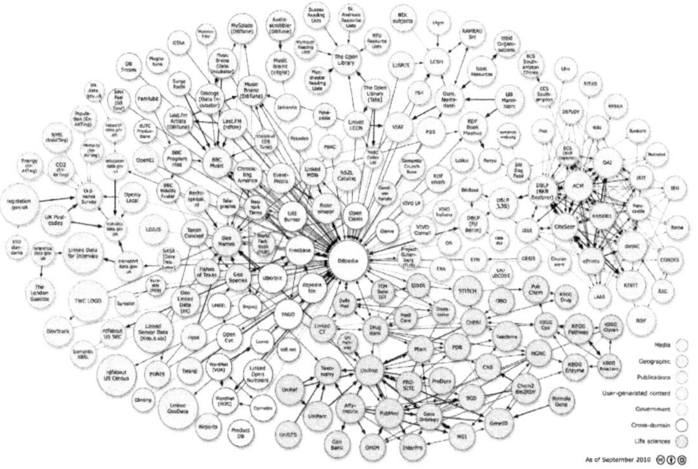

Fig. 1. A common representation of the Web of Linked Data, showing the data sets manually reported on the Comprehensive Knowledge Archive Network (CKAN) web site

Enhancing the XO with a proper software stack will enable every activity wrote for Sugar to both take advantage of the WoD by consuming the data out there but also to be part, by publishing data according to the Linked Data principles.

4 SemanticXO Software Stack

There are two tasks the software stack must address: the publication and the consumption of data. Publishing data means creating triples connecting different resources and making them available to the rest of the Web of Data. Consuming is the complementary process of using the data published by others.

Before going into the details of the software stack, we should not here that the idea of extending a desktop environment with such a semantic software stack is not new. The most remarkable work in this direction being the NEPOMUK project [11], which was funded by the European Community between 2006 and 2008, and resulted in the integration of Semantic functionalities into the KDE desktop for the benefit of the KDE users who can now annotate anything on their machine. As it was designed to be used on Desktop machine significantly more powerful, the software developed for this project can not be directly deployed on the XO. However, some other results of the project, such as the best practices learnt and the vocabularies developed [12], will be re-used in SemanticXO.

In order to facilitate the consumption and publication of Linked Data, the software stack must contain:

- **A triple store** in charge of storing the triples created by the activities running in Sugar. Because the triple store can only store triples and not, for instance, PDF files it has to be associated with **some file system based storage** for these documents.
- **An HTTP server** serving as a public interface to query the triple store, provide de-referencable URIs for the resources (*cf.* the third requirement of Linked data publishing) and serve the files.
- **A common interface** (Application Programming Interface - API) for accessing the triples stored either on the local Sugar environment, on an other Sugar or elsewhere on the WoD.

The security of the data stored within Sugar is an important issue that must be considered by every one of these components. Most of the activities are developed by third party contributors and are directly made available, without any vetting process. It must then be ensured that no malicious activity would be able to wipe out the entire content of the data stored by other activities. The data store in charge of storing the Journal information provides some sandbox-typed security mechanisms [13]. Because the publication and the consumption of Linked Data is made over HTTP, we directly benefit from all the security solutions made available for this protocol like the HTTP Authorization header [14].

The different components along with their interaction with external applications, Sugar activities and the WoD are depicted on Figure 2. Applications developed in Sugar can choose to either use the dedicated API or query the SPARQL end point over HTTP if the API does not address some specific needs.

4.1 Development of the Software Stack

There are several Triple stores available with Jena TDB [15], Virtuoso [16], 4Store [17] and OWLIM [18] being the most commonly cited names. These tools are all of very good quality but are aimed at storing millions of triples on modern and reasonably powerful hardware. With its 433Mhz Geode processor and

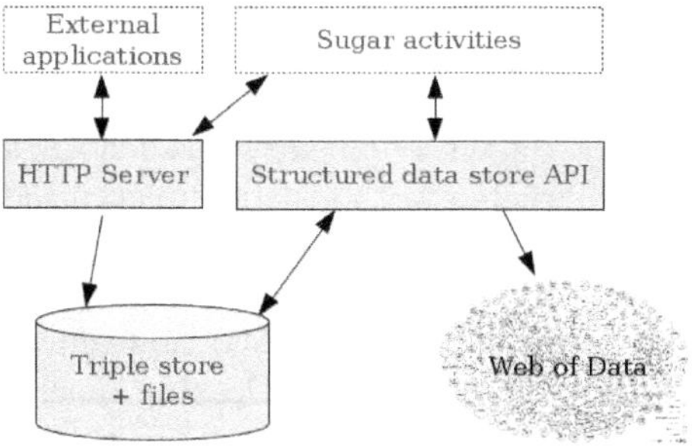

Fig. 2. The different components involved in SemanticXO and their interaction

256MiB of memory, the XO is not capable of supporting any of these well established pieces of software so we opted for a newcomer called Redstore [19]. Redstore is a lightweight, simple, yet featureful triple store that can be installed on the XO. It is also a free and open source project, which fits the guidelines for software use within the Sugar environment.

Unlike the rest of the software stack which is developed in Python, Redstore is a native application that has to be compiled to run on the XO. Because there is currently no pre-packaged version of Redstore for Fedora (the GNU/Linux distribution powering the XO), that compilation must be done by hand. The interested reader is invited to read [20] for the technical details of the compilation procedure. The full source code of the SemanticXO software stack is hosted on GitHub at `https://github.com/cgueret/SemanticXO`.

4.2 Performance of the Software Stack

They are two potential bottle necks that may affect the performances of the software stack in terms of response time. The first is Redstore ability to deal with limited hardware resources and the second the latency when querying data sources from the WoD, over Internet. In the following, we focus on assessing the performances of the former, the latter being essentially due to external factors upon which we have limited influence.

The performances of a triple store are commonly assessed using a benchmark with a triple generator and some pre-defined queries. Out of the two popular benchmark suites are LUBM [21] and SP^{2}Bench [22] we picked the latter which is focused on testing data access for different access pattern. LUBM is targetted towards testing the reasoning capabilities of the triple store, a feature we will not be using for the moment.

In the following, Redstore was configured to use the "SQLite" storage for its internal data.

Loading a set of triples. We used the SP^{2}Bench data generator to create 50k triples describing fictive research publications. This number of triples is considered as an upper bound for the amount of triples the XO will have to store. It is admittedly based on our personal experience and testing in real usage context will prove us true, or wrong.

Speed. It takes about 43 minutes to upload all these 50k triples into Redstore, this gives an average of 53 milliseconds per triple or 19 triples per second. That should be fast enough to have an API allowing to store a some triples with an acceptable response time. We can note here that the typical average "Ping time" on the Internet, that is the minimum time needed to send a query to a server and get a result, is also around 50 milliseconds (with peaks around 100-200 ms).

Size. The data takes 4MiB of disk space on the XO for an initial RDF file of about 9.8MiB. Triple store can efficiently compress the text used as literals in the triples or to write the URIs. This 4MiB are small enough to consider the impact of Redstore on XO's storage capacity (1024 MiB) as being minimal.

Issue the test queries. Once the data have been loaded into the triple store, the next step consist in running the queries contained in the benchmark suite. SP^2Bench comes with 17 queries of various levels of complexity. We executed them on a modern laptop, using the SPARQL end point on the XO (the technical details of the testing setup are available in [20]). Some of the queries did not provide any result after 1h running time and where thus considered to fail. Table 1 lists the queries that could be executed, the number of results returned and the time needed to process them , in second.

The queries that failed, q4 to q9 and q12(a,b), feature some nasty patterns like implicit joins, single and double negations that makes them difficult to solve even on bigger hardware [22]. It is thus expected that Redstore running on the XO can not answer them but we can also expect that no query alike these ones - designed to be challenging - will be used by the API or the external application accessing the store.

An interesting result from Table 1 is that the response time does not seem to be correlated with the number of results. q10 is the query which reflect the most what the API will have to do most of the time: fetch all the properties that apply to a particular resource.

Table 1. Execution time for some of the queries for the SP^2Bench benchmark suite

Query	Textual description of the query	Time	Results
q1	Return the year of publication of "Journal 1 (1940)"	14.23 s	1
q2	List all inproceedings (ordered by year) and nine of their `dc:creator`, `bench:booktitle`, `dc:title`, `swrc:pages`, `dcterms:partOf`, `rdfs:seeAlso`, `foaf:homepage`, `dcterms:issued`, and optionally `bench:abstract`, properties	44.19 s	965
q3a	Select all articles with property `swrc:pages`	21.51 s	3647
q3b	Select all articles with property `swrc:month`	19.50 s	25
q3c	Select all articles with property `swrc:isbn`	19.66 s	0
q10	Return all subjects that stand in any relation to Paul Erdoes	3.94 s	307
q11	Return (up to) 10 electronic edition URLs starting from the 51th publication, in lexicographical order	4.69 s	10
q12c	Check if the person John Q Public exists in the database	3.54 s	*boolean*

5 Use-Case: Knowledge Acquisition of Traditional Amerindian Worldviews Using Serious Games

In this section we describe an application that was recently built as a prototype for a project about knowledge acquisition of traditional Amerindian worldviews using serious games. This is a project we are planning to start up in cooperation with ethno-linguists from the University of Leiden and the the National Museum of Ethnology (NME) also in Leiden, NL. Although we describe the application for reference the focus is on the underlying technical contribution, ie. to show how SemanticXOs software stack can be used to implement such an application.

The NME manages an extensive collection of objects cataloged using western taxonomies. The museum world has now, in light of new 'best practices' policies, come to focus on sharing its objects with the communities from whom these objects were acquired, in an attempt to learn more about its collections, and to provide a more truthful access to them. The ways in which representatives of those communities speak of these objects are fundamentally different from the way the western heritage world perceives these objects. These discrepancies hamper museums' efforts to truthfully and respectfully deal with the objects in their care e.g. in exhibitions and even storage.

In a first set of experiments we are currently setting up a project for extracting the world-views of 4 indigenous communities in Suriname. The core idea for verifying and extending the original worldviews of these communities will be through *serious games*[1]. These games will provide an accessible and fun mechanism to acquire this invaluable cultural knowledge.

A first prototypical experiment will be a clustering activity, where players from the communities sort objects in clusters, and will be provided with scores when those clusters match. Technically this clustering activity stores triples describing items the user has to sort into boxes. This game is asynchronously collaborative: users can share items by making them publicly available. Every item made public appears in the left area on the activity once it's run on an XO in the same network.

5.1 Interface of the Clustering Activity

The interaction with the activity is centered around drag&drop manipulation. Using either an external mouse or the touchpad of the device, the user click on an item on the left part of the application and drag it to one of the boxes on the right. It is also possible to drag&drop items from a box to another box or back into the area on the left.

Items are currently provided externally with a dedicated script. A feature currently being developed will allow the user to select an image from his journal

[1] Such as "games with a purpose" `http://www.gwap.org`, "Freebase apps" `http://games.freebaseapps.com/`, Google Image Labeler `http://images.google.com/imagelabeler/`, word games from edict `http://www.edict.com.hk/studyguide/games.htm` or UC Dublin `http://afflatus.ucd.ie/`

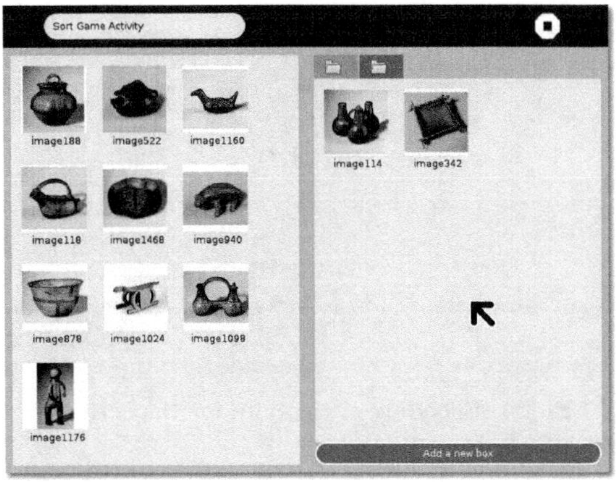

Fig. 3. Screenshot of the clustering activity

and import it into the application. In plus, the user will be able to decide whether the imported item should be made public for use on other XOs as well. The underlying, expected, usage scenario is a field trip where students of a class room would go out taking pictures of several things they see. Once back in school, they all start to classify their snapshots and share the best images with others. Using a global query over all the XOs, the teacher can then gather the content of all the boxes, compare and discuss them with the class.

5.2 Under the Hood

The data model of the activity is simple: a set boxes and a set of items, items may be assigned to one box at a time and item not assigned to any box as set on a reserve list. Among the many possible encoding possibilities for this data, we opted for a graph - the format that suits best RDF. The encoding shown on Figure 4 uses to specific resources named "Item" and "Box". Items and boxes are also resources, they get connected to either the Box or Item resource to indicate their type. Boxes are connected to the items they contain by a relation "hasItem". Every item has a name and a depiction file. Both properties are textual values rather than resources, this difference is made visually but using rectangles instead of ellipses. This is common practice for plotting RDF graphs.

Figure 4 is split in two parts, the upper part is the schema part and the lower part is that is usually referred to as the instance data. The schema part essentially indicates the different type of things the data set contains. The instance part contains the things themselves, and their connections. We reported on Table 3 part of the content of the later as the different triples it is made of. They are 40 triples in total: 3 per item, 2 per box and 2 to state that two of these items are set into one of the box. Table 3 shows a subset of them.

It is relevant to note here the flexibility of that data model: The assignment of one item to the only box is stated by a triple using the predicate "hasItem",

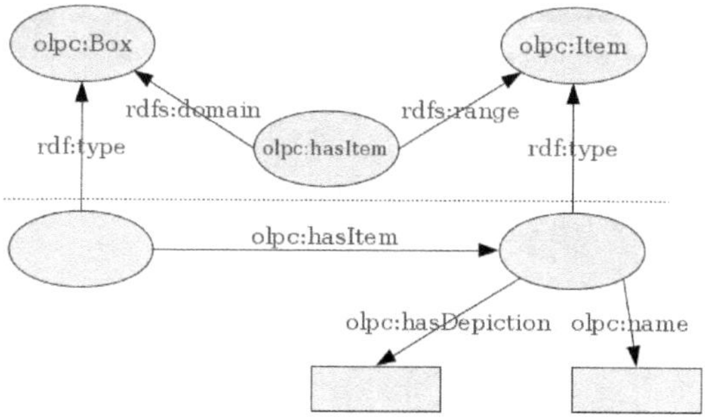

Fig. 4. Encoding of the data for the activity

Table 2. Part of the content of the triple store storing the data from the activity shown in Figure 3

subject	predicate	object
olpc:resource/a05864b4	rdf:type	olpc:Item
olpc:resource/a05864b4	olpc:name	"image114"
olpc:resource/a05864b4	olpc:hasDepiction	"image114.jpg"
olpc:resource/a82045c2	rdf:type	olpc:Box
olpc:resource/a82045c2	olpc:hasItem	olpc:resource/a05864b4
olpc:resource/78cbb1f0	rdf:type	olpc:Box
...	...	...

one of the box is empty because there is no such statement linking it to an item. A varied number of similar triples can be used, without any constraint and the same goes for actually all the triples in the system. There is no requirement for a set of predicates all the items must have.

Let us illustrate the usage that can be made of this data through three different SPARQL queries, introduced from the simple one to the most sophisticated.

List the URIs of all the boxes and the items they contain. This query is expressed as asking for all the resources that are of type `olpc:Box` and are connected to an item by a `olpc:hasItem` relation. There are two triple to query for, as shown in the resulting query in Listing 1.2.

```
SELECT ?box ?item WHERE {
  ?box rdf:type olpc:Box.
  ?box olpc:hasItem ?item.
}
```

Listing 1.2. List the URIs of all the boxes and the items they contain

The result of the query is a list of assignments of resources to the two variables queried (see Table 3). It returns two lines for two items in the first box. Because the second box has no items in it, it is not listed.

List of the items and their attributes. The previous query asked for a specific property of a particular type of resource. This next query is about asking

Table 3. Results from the query 1.2

?box	?item
olpc:resource/a82045c2	olpc:resource/a05864b4
olpc:resource/a82045c2	olpc:resource/843f4d66

for all the properties of a particular type of resource. Fortunately, it is not need to know all the possible properties an item can have. Rather, there is again only two triples needed, the second one allowing any predicate value (*cf.* Listing 1.3).

```
SELECT ?item ?property ?val WHERE {
  ?item rdf:type olpc:Item.
  ?item ?property ?val.
}
```

Listing 1.3. List of the items and their attributes

The results for this query are reported in Table 4

Table 4. Results for the query in Listing 1.3. For the sake of space saving, the list of statement is truncated to the same subset as in Table 2

?item	?property	?val
olpc:resource/a05864b4	rdf:type	olpc:Item
olpc:resource/a05864b4	olpc:name	"image114"
olpc:resource/a05864b4	olpc:hasDepiction	"image114.jpg"
...	...	...

List of the items that are not in a box. Because the presence of an item in a box is stated by the existence of a triple, our last query needs to search for non existing triples. This is done by first allowing optional result for the boxes: we ask for items and eventually the box they are in, if any. Then, we filter the results to keep only the ones where no box could be found. The query is in Listing 1.4.

```
SELECT ?item WHERE {
  ?item rdf:type olpc:Item.
  OPTIONAL {
    ?box rdf:type olpc:Box.
    ?box olpc:hasItem ?item.
  }
  FILTER (!bound(?box))
}
```

Listing 1.4. List of the items that are not in a box

The only result of this query is reported in Table 5. Because we do not ask for it in the "SELECT" statement, the value of the variable `?box` is not returned.

Table 5. Results for the query in Listing 1.4. For the sake of space saving, the list of statement is truncated to the same subset as in Table 2

?item
olpc:resource/a05d2814
...

6 Future and Ongoing Work

In the following, we go through the current list of "to-dos" for the SemanticXO project and explain the motivations and the work there is to do.

- **Implement an alternate data store using the triple store**
  The data store is the component in Sugar in charge of storing the content of the journal. It contains items and metadata about these items, every activity is also able to store entries in it.
- **Extend the clustering activity with collaboration features**
  As highlighted during the presentation of the activity, there is still some work to do to implement all the needed functionality. In particular, the data communication between the XOs and the possibility to import images from the Journal are pre-requisites to the field trip use-case we introduced.
- **Provide an interface to the WoD**
  There are plenty of Linked Data out there activities could benefit from, making them easily accessible to activities is a goal of SemanticXO. There is an interface in the works that aims at providing a transparent access to this big source of information. This interface will dialog with CKAN to get a list of SPARQL end point to query.
- **Package the software stack for Fedora**
  The operating system of the XOs is based on Fedora, a popular GNU/Linux distribution. The installation procedure described in Section 4 is manual because of a lack of pre-compiled package for Redstore on Fedora. In order to facilitate the installation of Redstore, it will be necessary to make a proper package for it.

7 Conclusion

Pushed by the development of standards for the next generation of the Web, there is a Web of Data that is becoming available and growing steadily in size. This Web provides structure information about several things, from movies to research publications to places in the World. In this paper, we presented the first results of the SemanticXO project aimed at enhancing the XO with the tools necessary to take part of this Web of Data, both in term of data publication and consumption.

We shown that despite its limited computing resources, the XO can accommodate a triple store (the *de facto* data storage for the Web of Data). We also introduced an activity showing how applications developed for the XO can benefit from using the triple store to store their data.

References

1. Berners-Lee, T., Hendler, J., Lassila, O.: The semantic web. Scientific American 284(5), 34–43 (2001)
2. OLPC Foundation: Olpc mission, part 1: Principles and child empowerment (2008), http://www.youtube.com/watch?v=c-M77C2ejTw

3. Tracker (2011), http://projects.gnome.org/tracker/
4. Strigi (2010), http://strigi.sourceforge.net/
5. The Network Institute (2011), http://www.networkinstitute.nl/
6. W4RA: Web Alliance for Regreening in Africa (2010), http://www.w4ra.org/
7. Alpert, J., Hajaj, N.: We knew the web was big... in Official Google Blog (2008)
8. Berners-Lee, T.: Linked data (2006), http://bit.ly/kYc4M3
9. Bizer, C., Jentzsch, A., Cyganiak, R.: State of the LOD Cloud (2011), http://www4.wiwiss.fu-berlin.de/lodcloud/state/
10. Cyganiak, R., Jentzsch, A.: Linking open data cloud diagram (2011)
11. Groza, T., Handschuh, S., Moeller, K., Grimnes, G., Reif, G., Minack, E., Mesnage, C., Jazayeri, M., Reif, G., Gudjonsdottir, R.: The NEPOMUK Project - On the Way to the Social Semantic Desktop. Management, 201–211 (2007)
12. Open Semantic Collaboration Architecture (OSCA) Foundation: Shared desktop ontologies (2006), https://sourceforge.net/projects/oscaf/files/
13. Krstić, I.: OLPC Bitfrost (2007), http://wiki.laptop.org/go/OLPC_Bitfrost
14. Network Working Group: RFC 2616. Hypertext Transfer Protocol – HTTP/1.1 (1999), http://www.w3.org/Protocols/rfc2616/rfc2616-sec14.html#sec14.8
15. Jena Development Team: TDB - A SPARQL database for Jena (2007), http://www.openjena.org/TDB/
16. OpenLink: Virtuoso Universal Server (2010), http://virtuoso.openlinksw.com/
17. Harris, S.: 4store - Scalable RDF storage (2009), http://4store.org/
18. OntoText: OWLIM Semantic repository (2000), http://www.ontotext.com/owlim/
19. Humfrey, N.: Redstore (2010), http://www.aelius.com/njh/redstore/
20. Guéret, C.: Redstore running on the XO (2010), http://wp.me/p1ffiZ-l
21. Guo, Y., Pan, Z., Heflin, J.: Lubm: A benchmark for owl knowledge base systems. Web Semantics Science Services and Agents on the World Wide Web 3, 158–182 (2005)
22. Schmidt, M., Hornung, T., Lausen, G., Pinkel, C.: SP2Bench: A SPARQL performance benchmark. In: 25th International Conference on Data Engineering (2009)

Digital Marketization of e-CRM in Effective Delivery of Financial Engineering in Global Organisations: Trends, Benefits and Critical Meta-Dynamic Issues

Ezendu Ariwa[1] and Daminni Grover[2]

[1] London Metropolitan University, UK
[2] IILM Institute for Higher Education, New Delhi, India
e.ariwa@londonmet.ac.uk, e.ariwa@ieee.org

Abstract. In recent years CRM has made significant strides world over as an effective aid to serve customers. There may be hardly any organisation which in some way or the other is not using CRM philosophy. CRM received fillip with the advent of internet and related web enabled technologies. As companies make the transition from a product-only focus to a customer focus, CRM emerges as a technology that brings customers closer to organizations to retrieve information online. In view of considerable research and developments in web enabled CRM area during last two decades it becomes necessary to take stock of emerging technologies and identify emerging opportunities and bottlenecks in implementation. In this paper it is attempted to review developments in e-CRM that facilitates online service to customers. Apart from review of technology related developments, the study focuses on identification of thrust areas resulting benefits and implementation strategies.

Keywords: Customer relationship management, e-CRM, customer relationship path, implementation strategies.

1 Introduction

Customer Relationship Management is a comprehensive strategy and process of acquiring, retaining and partnering with selective customers to create superior value for the company and the customer (Parvatiyar and Sheth, 2001). To support this capability, customer relationship management is evolving into electronic CRM. An increasing number of companies are considering implementing e-CRM systems to satisfy the growing expectation of customer service. e-CRM systems have unique characteristics that support customer-business interactions that are linked to internal business processes and systems across different areas for operational and analytical purposes.

Today companies are being confronted by an increasingly sophisticated customer universe, which expects and demands a higher level of immediate service across multiple access channels. Customers feel that customer service should occur via the channel of communication that they specify to be communicated, or at least the channel through which contact with a company was initiated. Customers not only

J.J. Yonazi et al. (Eds.): ICeND 2011, CCIS 171, pp. 276–284, 2011.

want to shop and get customer service through multiple communication channels, such as the telephone, web chat, electronic mail, and the web, they desire the ability to move seamlessly from one medium to another.

e-CRM enables to serves customers online and covers areas like content management, product and pricing models, customer service support, problem resolution and automated response agents and campaign management functions. In order for a company to provide unified customer communications at different customer interface points, it should be kept in mind that online customers can relate with a company through several channels. In view of multi-point contact with customers, e-CRM implementation requires organisations to have several devices and technologies in place such as e-mail inbound/outbound support, chat/browser control, voice-over internet protocol (VoIP), multi-language support; messaging, work-flow and web measurement devices.

e-CRM embraces the front-office business functions of sales, marketing and customer service, and supports the back-office business and analysis operations spanning these functions, all in a web-centric fashion (Talisma, 2001). Fig. 1 illustrates how e-CRM functionality supports each of the five business components of marketing, sales, customer service and support, e- commerce and the electronic processes in the back-office analysis.

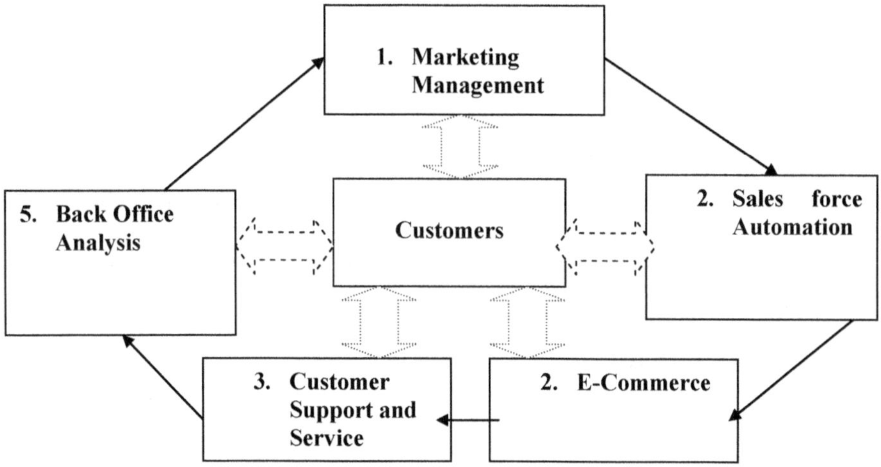

Fig. 1. e-CRM through the customer lifecycle

2 Customer Sales Path

A 'sales path' comprises of phases that take a consumer from a prospective to a buying customer (Fig. 2). This automatically brings various e-CRM components into pictures such as marketing, sales cycle, customer service, back-office support and e-commerce that engage to convert the prospective customer into a confirmed buyer. These components are described below.

Marketing Management. The first phase in any sales process is to create awareness, interest, and desire in a company, its brand or its offerings. This is the task of typical marketing management function as a substitute of traditional advertising (Dru, 2002, p. 180). Interactive technologies such as Internet has provided a real meaning to CRM. Federal Express transformed itself when it allowed customers to track their packages online. That interactive experience became an integral part of the FedEx brand (Dru, 2002, p. 181). Marketing automation covers a wide range of interactive capabilities such as e-mail response systems, campaign management and execution tools, and management and distribution of marketing materials to sales people and partners (Greenberg, 2002, p. 28).

Sales Cycle. The 'sales cycle' takes over in the process of converting the prospect within the sales path and the next phase in the path is the research phase. This evokes interest to possibly buy a product or service and the information made available through Internet facilitates him to make up his mind and buy the product. The Internet has simplified this phase with companies displaying their offerings on websites. Depending on the offering, consumers often demand a demonstration prior to purchase (Dru, 2002, p. 182). The sales cycle, specifically 'sales-force automation' takes over at this stage which covers activities such as lead qualification, generation and tracking, opportunity and contract management, and account management (Greenberg, 2002, p. 28).

E-Commerce. Mass customization became a reality with the Internet when companies like Dell created new business models enabling customers to customize individual products from online catalogues prior to purchase (Dru, 2002, p. 181). Digital technologies such as e-Commerce, that facilitates online order processing, billing and payment, also play an important role during 'purchase phase'. PlayStation took pre-orders for its PS2 product on its website prior to the product launching. Similar to global online book retailer *Amazon.com,* an Indian online retailer named *Kalahari.net* also uses a virtual shopping cart for customers to buy online during the 'purchase phase'. e-CRM ensures that vital customer behaviour and information is monitored and captured during the 'purchase phase'.

3 Customer Relationship Path

Internet and digital interactivity helps customers to get closer to brands. They can interact and experience brands directly and can gain immediate new benefits on a one-to-one, often customized basis (Dru, 2002, p. 179). A typical 'customer relationship path' integrates customers with the supplier and continues from where the 'customer sales path' ends (Fig. 2 and 3).

'Customer relationship path' begins with the 'sales path' and comprises of a number of phases that aid in taking the consumer from a prospective buyer to a loyal supporter; e-CRM supports the business components of marketing, sales, customer service and e-commerce throughout this path. e-CRM system architecture needs to permit easy round-the-clock access by both customers and company users from all supported access points. An open architecture is necessary to provide scalability, flexibility and easy maintenance. Digital technologies play a key role in cost-effective tailoring of one-to-one communications, mass customization and the sophisticated segmentation of customer databases (Fig. 3).

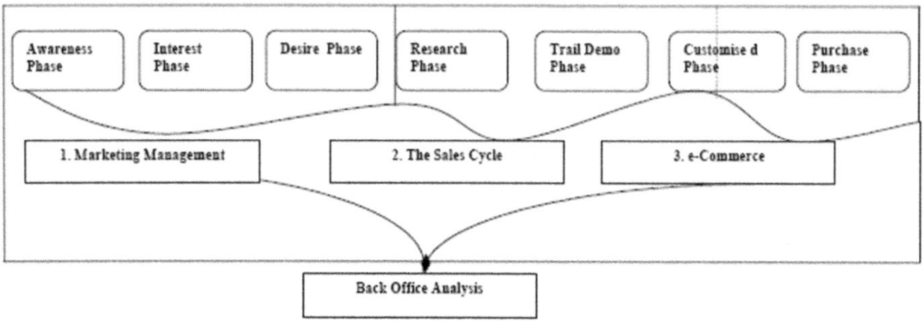

Fig. 2. Customer Sales Path

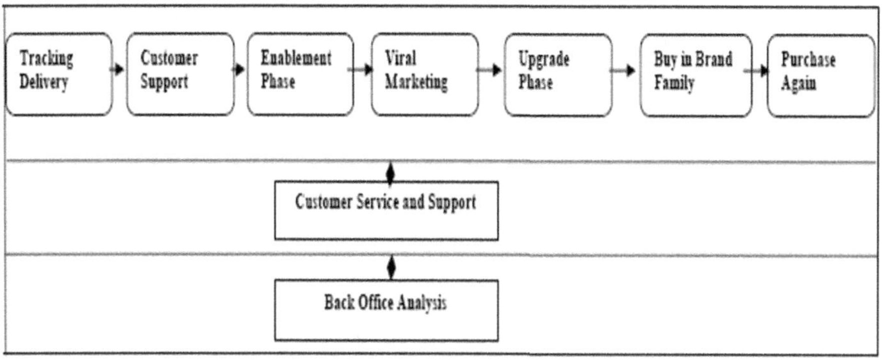

Fig. 3. Customer Relationship Path

4 e-CRM Technology

An e-CRM system is to be accessible to customers including company users and administrators from all access support points, round-the-clock on a 24/7 basis (Technosoft, 2003 p. 1). The e-CRM system should provide access to customers through a variety of touch points namely web self-help, e-mail, web forms, chat, VoIP, fax, phone, wireless and face-to-face contact. It should also provide access to system users through various client systems such as personal computers, mobile phones and personal digital assistants (PDAs).

The e-CRM system needs to support integration with customer interactions taking place in web based media, such as e-mail and web forms including those from traditional channels such as telephone. Given that interfacing with customers is fundamental to e-CRM, the system must also have facilities to maintain a complete organised history of a customer's contacts with a company, regardless of the communication channel used. Ideally, an e-CRM solution should feature three-tier architecture to provide scalability, offer flexibility and simplify maintenance (Technosoft, 2003 p. 1). An open architecture is necessary to allow e-CRM solutions to be extended and integrated with external systems on all three levels, or tiers. The three tiers are listed below:

Presentation tier. The 'presentation tier' includes interfaces for various types of access methods from both the customer and client user or administers point-of-view. Depending on available technology and its accessibility provision there is to be flexibility to access Local Area Network (LAN), Wide Area Network (WAN) , wireless, portal and remote access via the Internet and offline connectivity (Technosoft, 2003, p.1).

Business logic tier. This tier consists of the core application logic, the accompanying objects and services.

Data tier. This tier should comprise of a full-function database management system which could be software such as Microsoft SQL Server or Oracle.

Security. Although it was not originally included as a tier, the author of this study is of the opinion that Information Security Architecture (ISA) should feature as a separate tier within the e-CRM architecture.

5 Benefits of e-CRM

Most organisations invest huge sums in defining and automating their core business processes. No doubt, they have benefited by standardizing the processes, yet there are several areas which remain unresolved where e-CRM can play effective role. The following benefits can be realized with proper e-CRM implementation:

Increased customer loyalty. An effective e-CRM system enables a company to communicate with its customers using a single and consistent voice, regardless of the communication channel. This is because with e-CRM software, everyone in an organization has access to the same transaction history and information about the customer. Information captured by an e-CRM system helps a company to identify the actual costs of winning and retaining individual customers.

More effective marketing. Having detailed customer information from an e-CRM system allows a company to predict the kind of products that a customer is likely to buy as well as the timing of purchases. In the short to medium term, this information helps an organization create more effective and focused marketing/sales campaigns designed to attract the desired customer audience (www.epiphany.com). e-CRM allows for more targeted campaigns and tracking of campaign effectiveness. Customer data can be analyzed from multiple perspectives to discover which elements of a marketing campaign had the greatest impact on sales and profitability, for example (Greenberg 2001).

Improved customer service and support. An e-CRM system provides a single repository of customer information. This enables a company to serve customer needs quickly and efficiently at all potential contact points, eliminating the customer's frustrating and time-consuming "hunt" for help (www.epiphany.com). e-CRM-enabling technologies include search engines, live help, e-mail management, news feeds/content management and multi-language support.

Greater efficiency and cost reduction. Automating customer data mining saves valuable human resources. Integrating customer data into a single database allows marketing teams, sales forces, and other departments within a company to share information and work toward common corporate objectives using the same underlying statistics (www.epiphany.com). Examples of this are identifying unproductive/underutilized resources, closer tracking of costs, better forecasting for the pipeline and setting realistic project metrics and measurements to quantify return on investment.

6 Implementation Strategies for e-CRM

Once a company has identified the need for e-CRM, it has to plan for implementation for which following aspects need to be taken into account.

Developing customer-focused business strategies. The objective of this step is not to try to change the customer to the company's goals but to listen to the customer and try to create opportunities beneficial to both. It is important to offer customers what they are currently demanding and anticipate what they are likely to demand in the future. This can be achieved by providing a variety of existing access channels for customers, such as e-mail, telephone and fax, and by preparing to provide for future access channels such as wireless communication.

Retooling business functions. Starting to do business via e-CRM requires disruptive organizational change in order to determine which departments/functions are truly servicing the customer and which ones are only adding to overhead. After identifying and reducing surplus manpower, administrative time and cost should come down. A major factor here is that the changes needed during an e-CRM implementation will only be possible with buy-in from the top levels of management and with company-wide accountability of all stakeholders. Positive organizational change will not simply materialize on its own. It is the responsibility of senior management to ensure that all employees understand the need of the changes, how the new structure will benefit from them, and how it will enhance their ability to serve their customers better.

Work process re-engineering. Departmental role and responsibility changes from restructuring business functions will needs adopting new work processes. Choices here are to take the traditional step-wise approach or an integrated one towards improving work efficiency. Under the step-wise approach, departments are treated as separate efficiency entities. This rarely produces good results because the goals of each department can become too parochial, and departments tend to compete internally for their own benefit at the expense of what's best for the company.

Technology choices. The focus here is to consider the company's industry, the company's position within its industry, which e-CRM implementations are good candidates for the company in particular. Criteria for technology selections includes scalability of software, tool set flexibility for customization, stability of the existing e-CRM application code, compatibility of e-CRM application with legacy and Internet systems, level of technical support available during and after implementation, upgradable support, availability of additional modules and security.

Training and implementation. This thrust area is apparently the most important one in e-CRM implementation effort. Depending on the number of users, training times will vary from company to company. Training of employees should occur before the new e-CRM system has been implemented to ensure a seamless transition for customers. Examples of training include sending users to training facilities at considerable cost or bringing in an on-site consultant. Anyone who requires access to the system should receive full, appropriate and timely training. Training should be an ongoing, managed activity as systems must continuously change and evolve. All training and tools used should be thoroughly documented for existing, new and future employees. Without proper documentation, e-CRM system may not work. A firm should plan to spend about 5-7 per cent of its total e-CRM implementation on training (Patton, 2001b).

7 Difficulties Commonly Encountered during Implementation

In an attempt to quickly implement e-CRM, too many companies start spending huge sums before developing a comprehensive e-CRM strategy. The following list outlines potential pitfalls with e-CRM implementation process often encounters and needs to be overcome.

- Mismatch between a company and the vendor's CRM software. Every effort must be made to find a vendor whose product is flexible enough to emulate the company's best practices and does not force the company to adopt the vendor's best practices. Realistically, no single software solution will handle all e-CRM needs equally well. Therefore, each company should select the solution that best handles the critical customer-facing functions and maintains robust links to the existing ERP system.
- A poor understanding of the company's business processes. Each of the business processes should be reviewed, analyzed and documented before shopping for a vendor.
- e-CRM implementations that take more than 90 days have a high failure rate. A company should be skeptical about implementations that are considerably longer than the 90 days.
- Vendor stability should be a criteria used in selection. Financial stability of the vendor needs to be checked to assess whether or not it is likely to be able to survive a softening economy.
- Rejection by end users is always is a possibility when business functions are restructured. If the new processes required for a successful e-CRM implementation are not developed with the knowledge, help and acceptance of the employees who will be relied upon to use them, the project may fail.
- Size of project. Some e-CRM implementations have failed because their initial scope was too broad. The risk associated with a failed pilot is much lower than for a full rollout, and it gives your company the opportunity to evaluate the positives and negatives of the pilot as one plans for a larger-scale implementation.

Unfortunately, avoiding these 'pitfalls' is, in many cases, easier said then done. Often this is because sales and marketing teams are reluctant to adopt the new, automated CRM systems.

8 Recent Trends in e-CRM

Recent developments in the field of e-CRM include a CRM package evaluation/procurement service, hosting of CRM component applications and the use of Online Analytical Processing (OLAP) tools to develop *customer intelligence* in order to enhance the effectiveness of e-CRM.

CRM Package Evaluation/Procurement Service. ITenol is a California based company that offers a service called CRM Solution Acquisition Manager for automating the stages involved in choosing and implementing a CRM package (Bednarz, 2001). All phases are covered, from defining a company's requirements and evaluating vendors to negotiating contracts and generating purchase orders. Once the service is set up, users collaborate to specify business objectives and generate a request for proposal (RFP). ITenol contacts vendors when an RFP is available and vendor reps can collaborate online in response. The service is free of charge to CRM vendors. Once a company has purchased a CRM package, ITenol supplies web-accessible project management tools to help the company install the software.

Hosted CRM Component Applications. The market for hosting of fully-fledged e-CRM solutions is in decline, partly because of the current economic climate and partly because the levels of customization demanded by client businesses to meet their particular needs are too complicated to provide in a packaged solution. Nevertheless, the market for hosted CRM component applications, such as a hosted package from Satmetrix for gauging customer satisfaction, is faring better. The level of investment required is much lower, yet the hosted applications do provide added value to the client companies (Pepe, 2001).

Customer Intelligence (CI). As mentioned previously, integration of a company's legacy systems, especially it ERP system, with e-CRM functionality is critical to the success of any e-CRM implementation. Taking this one step further, customer intelligence focuses on applying the insights derived from customer analysis to e-CRM strategies, and then acting upon these strategies to build value into customer relationships. The customer intelligence enabling technologies must be tightly integrated with the ERP and e-CRM solutions in order to provide near-real-time data access and analysis. (Harvey, 2001). OLAP tools, available from companies like Cognos, are the core enabling technologies that make the advanced analytics required by customer intelligence possible. The OLAP software enables predictive modeling, data mining and data visualization that are needed to uncover hidden relationships in customer data that hold the keys to understanding customer behavior and determining customer value.

9 Concluding Remarks

e-CRM has evoked considerable interest about its effectiveness and risks amongst many organizations and researchers. e-CRM remains a priority for organizations, even as economic conditions cause IT budgets to be scrutinized. This paper has shown how e-CRM can add to traditional marketing concepts. e-CRM is not here to change the marketing but instead to enhance it. This paper examines problems that can accompany an e-CRM implementation and how to avoid them. In addition, critical issues have been identified that companies need to consider while starting e-CRM implementation. In addition, customer-centric and corporate benefits of implementing an e-CRM solution have been reviewed with the understanding that e-CRM efforts will only succeed when organizations make their customers win.

When companies understand customer buying behaviour they can avail cost savings and increased customer loyalty. Identifying products customers want is the first step of product mix expansion, new product launches and product differentiation. e-CRM can successfully implement new products, launch new marketing campaigns, and satisfy customer needs and wants. To be successful e-CRM requires that organizations allocate sufficient resources for building customer relationships and continuously evaluating e-CRM initiatives.

The evaluation and benefits realization mechanisms can expedite the organizational learning process and help make e-CRM work to the benefits of all customers and external partners, whether viewed from a narrow buyer/seller perspective or a broader supply chain perspective. e-CRM is an essential tool for any organization's high performance and depends on worker's effectiveness more than their efficiency. By doing so, companies can engage their customers in an ongoing knowledge exchange in which the company can learn more about market and customer needs and work to develop and deliver the products and services that can exceed the customers' expectations and leap ahead of market trends.

References

Bednarz, A.: CRM painkiller debuts. Network World (September 24, 2001)

Talisma: Critical Steps to e-CRM – Best Practice, White Paper (Internet) (2001), http://www.talisma.com (accessed on: March 15, 2003)

Dru, J.-M.: Beyond Disruption: Changing the Rules in the Marketplace. John Wiley & Sons, Inc., New York (2002)

Harvey, L.: Building Customer value Across the Enterprise. Patricia Seybold Group (2001)

Greenberg, P.: CRM at the Speed of Light: Capturing and Keeping Customers in Internet Real Time. McGraw-Hill, New York (2002)

Greenberg, P.: Capturing and Keeping Customers in Internet Real Time. McGraw-Hill, New York (2001)

Pepe, M.: Is there a market for hosted CRM solutions?, Computer Reseller News (2001)

Technosoft: What is e-CRM (Internet) (2003), http://www.technosoftusa.com (accessed on: May 28, 2003)

Reputation Based Trust Management System Supporting Collaboration in a Medical Application

Roman Špánek[1,2], Daniel Kouřil[3,4,5],
Martin Kuba[3,4,5], and Michal Procházka[3,4,5]

[1] Technical University of Liberec, Czech Republic
[2] Institute of Computer Science, Czech Academy of Sciences, Prague, Czech Republic
[3] Institute of Computer Science, Masaryk University, Brno, Czech Republic
[4] CESNET, Prague, Czech Republic
[5] Faculty of Informatics Masaryk University, Brno, Czech Republic
roman.spanek@tul.cz
http://www.cs.cas.cz/spanek/

Abstract. In a small group of people it is quite easy to start a collaboration based on shared trust, because people quickly recognize quality of each other. But this is not true when we move to the highly distributed environment with hundreds of users, not only from one institution or town, but even from different countries. It becomes very complicated task to distinguish experienced an trusted people from malicious users.

In the paper a reputation system proposed particularly for a medical environment supporting collaboration among physicians is presented. The system provides tools for sharing knowledge and expertize in form of modules which can be seamlessly connected to each other provided more advanced functionality. The reputation system is designed to help physicians selecting the right (the most reliable) module from set of all modules within the system. The selection is made on trust being managed by the proposed reputation system.

Keywords: Trust, Reputation System, Security.

1 Introduction

People can usually achieve particular goal easier and faster if they share knowledge and experience. From that point of view sharing information is crucial for every contemporary research discipline. However, the dark side of information sharing is a variable quality of results since results based on inaccurate or faulty inputs are not valuable. Each piece of information that comes as input should be properly assessed as to its quality.

A possible way of information evaluation is to assess its originator. When seeking a particular piece of knowledge, i.e., a suggested procedure to solve a problem, people tend to accept information coming from a trusted person/source, who is known to be familiar (an expert) with the problem.

J.J. Yonazi et al. (Eds.): ICeND 2011, CCIS 171, pp. 285–297, 2011.

Such approach can be quite easily applied in a closed environment consisting only of several people. However, it is much more difficult to mount the same mechanism in an open and distributed environment where people have even not met each other, but still want to collaborate on the same topic.

In this paper we present a reputation system designed for a MediGrid environment designed to support collaboration between experts in BioMedicine.

2 Knowledge Sharing in MediGrid

The goal of the MediGrid project [11,12] is to provide a platform supporting sharing knowledge in the biomedical domain. The knowledge that can be handled by the system must be expressed algorithmically and is inserted into the system as a *module*. Each user using the MediGrid system can use modules produced by others and they can also produce their own modules that can be used by other users, i.e. every user of the MediGrid can act both as the producer and the consumer of modules (in this way the MediGrid behaves in the same way as Peer-to-peer network).

Each module in the system has a detailed description of its functionality. Particularly the following data are required to be added to each module:

- list of scientific publications describing the functionality realized by the module,
- description of inputs and outputs (together with data types),
- several examples of input and output data to test the module implementation,
- modules can be assigned with tags, which help users searching for a module providing desired functionality.

Modules are grouped into so called *kits*, which are supposed to collect modules from various parts of medicine, e.g. neurology, urology, pediatrics etc. or modules used in one place, e.g. in an emergency room or in a genetic laboratory. A kit is a kind of working desktop on which user (users) may group modules and eventually connect more modules to provide more sophisticated functionality.

From a user point of view, a module providing desired functionality has to be somehow validated that provided outputs are correct and reliable. This is not an easy task, as MediGrid is aimed to be totally distributed environment. Solving this issue by traditional security systems (like PKI, passwords, etc.) is not sufficient in such environment.

Situation is getting even more complicated as every registered user can insert her own modules, can access modules of other registered users and create her own kits. In order to simplify the decision, a reputation system was designed with respect to all peculiarities of the MediGrid system. The main purpose of the designed reputation system is to assign a reputation to each module in the system. The score is then used for ordering modules from the most reputable users (note that all modules fulfilling filtering criteria are listed).

3 Calculation of a Module Reputation

Reputation system is designed to accept several variables as an input and to produce a real number output representing reputation of selected module, kit or author. In the following we describe basic points influencing the reputation systems design together with definition of a module, user and kit reputation.

3.1 Reputation System Design

The design requirements were directly influenced by the MediGrid environment peculiarities. As was already mentioned, the MediGrid is aimed to be a system based on Computing Grid ideas proving an extensive support to knowledge sharing within Biomedicine environment. The main target - knowledge sharing - should be supported by a very flexible, open and easy to use solution as users are experts in biomedicine,but may be af limited knowledge in computer science.

The following list summarizes set of requirements being observed when designing reputation of a module.

- Reputation of a module has to be based on:
  - reputation of the module author,
  - reputation of a kit the module is placed on,
  - popularity of the module (how many times the module has been used).
- The output of the reputation system should be simple and easily understandable by regular users.
- users should have a possibility how to evaluate quality of modules manually (by giving a positive or negative feedback).

The most of requirements are simply based on the proposed MediGrid structure (modules grouped on kits), but some are also motivated by a fact, that end users are highly educated in biomedicine, but have limited experience in computer science. The former observation is particularly important as most of known reputation systems are aimed for users being at least familiar with computers. In the MediGrid this is no longer valid.

3.2 Designing Reputation Calculation

The idea of the algorithm is that the reputation of a module depends on several components (mentioned in the previous subsection 3.1).

In order to give users rating of selected module as simple as possible, the five stars rating scale was used. Such rating are very often used and easily acceptable by most of common users.

The following list gives a basic informal definition of reputations:

- **Module**: The reputation of a module is calculated from
  1. its own rating given by users on the scale from one to five stars,
  2. on the number of times the module has been used, and
  3. on reputation of its author.

- **Author**: The reputation of the author depends on
  1. the reputation of all the modules the user has created,
  2. the reputation of the kits the user has created.
- **Kit** The reputation of kits depends on:
  1. the reputation of modules on a given kit,
  2. the number of times the kit has been used.

From the definition above it is clear that reputation of a module cannot be computed in one step as the module reputation depends on the reputation of its author; the author reputation uses reputation of kits and also the reputation of the modules used has created. Such situation is graphically depicted in figure 1 and it is well known for example in database systems as a *deadlock*.

Taken literally, such reputation definition would create a circular dependency, as the reputation of a module depends on reputation of its author which depends on reputation of his/her modules. On the other hand, omitting of any of the reputation components (the author reputation, kits reputation) would result in less reliable output. In order to remove the circular dependency, the reputation of a module is computed in three parts, marked a,b and c, where a expresses the average rating, b expresses the number of usages and c expresses the reputation of the author. When computing reputation of an author or a kit, only the parts a and b are used, as the c part cannot be determined in that time.

The algorithm for a given module produces a real number by calling the function `module_reputation(module)`.

The three parts are real numbers between 0 and 1. The final real number is produced by the following formula:

$$reputation_{module} = (a+1)^{(1/wa)} \times (b+1)^{(1/wb)} \times (c+1)^{(1/wc)} - 1 \quad (1)$$

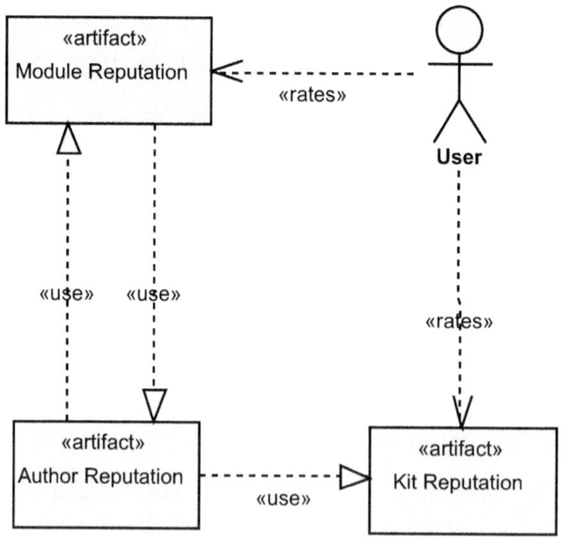

Fig. 1. Diagram depicting dependences between a module, kit and author reputation

The formula uses the following weights wa,wb,wc that have to satisfy the following criterion:

$$\frac{1}{wa} + \frac{1}{wb} + \frac{1}{wc} = 1 \tag{2}$$

Similarly, the reputation of a user (author) is computed in two steps marked d and e, where d expresses reputation of the user's kits and e expresses reputation of all of the user's modules. The parts are subsequently weighted by using the following formula:

$$reputation_{author} = c = (d+1)^{(1/wd)} \times (b+1)^{(1/we)} - 1 \tag{3}$$

where weights hold the following condition

$$\frac{1}{wd} + \frac{1}{we} = 1 \tag{4}$$

The reputation of a kit is computed in the same fashion. Particularly, by dividing the total reputation into two parts g and h, where g expresses the number of times the kit has been used and h expresses the reputation of all the modules on the kit. The parts are also weighted using the following formula

$$reputation_{kit} = (g+1)^{(1/wg)} \times (h+1)^{(1/wh)} - 1 \tag{5}$$

where proposed weights wg and wh satisfy the following condition:

$$\frac{1}{wg} + \frac{1}{wh} = 1 \tag{6}$$

Introduction of the weights was necessary for the fact that scales of the reputation components are different. The given formulas require parameters a, b, c, d, e, g, h to be on 0 and 1 scale and the formulas produce a number on the same 0 and 1 scale. Parameters c, d, e, h are products of weighting or averages of weightings being also of 0 to 1 interval. The other parameters are computed as simple ratios:

- a is the rating divided by the length of rating scale,
- b is the number of module usages divided by the number of all usages of modules being on the same kits as the given module (note that a module can be possibly used on many kits simultaneously),
- g is the number of kit usage divided by the number of all usages of all modules.

The weights used in the reputation components can be set as a constant. On the other hand, it is required to give more importance to a rating provided by more users (simply larger group of users has been determined to give a same/similar either positive or negative rating). Thus weight wa is computed with respect to the overall number of users providing the rating feedback.

Weights wc, wd, we, wg, wh are global constants, and each module is given by its own weights wa, wb.

Calculating components a, b of reputation of authors and kits cannot use the same weights wa, wb, so another pair wam, wbm is introduced fulfilling the following criteria:

$$\frac{1}{wam} + \frac{1}{wbm} = 1 \tag{7}$$

The algorithm uses the following functions for obtaining primary data from the MediGrid:

- `author(module)` returns user who is the author of the module given as the parameter
- `created_kits(user)` returns a set of kits that the user created
- `created_modules(user)` returns set of modules the user created
- `modules_in_kit(kit)` returns set of modules in a given kit
- `used_num(module)` returns int, the number how many times the module has been used by other users (omitting the module author)
- `used_num(kit)` returns int, number expressing how many times the kit has been used (omitting the kit author)
- `all_usages()` returns int, number expressing overall number of module usage, each usage of a module in a kit
- `usages_similar_modules(module)` returns int, total number expressing how many times modules in the same kits have been used (including the module the function is called for)
- `all_rating_users_num()` returns int, total number of all users who put any feed back on any module in the system
- `rating_users_num(module)` returns int, number of users who have given a feedback for a given module
- `last_user_ratings(module)` returns set of tuples [user,rating], set of ratings of the module from all users who has given a feedback (except for the module's author). the function returns only the latest rating for each user.

The following pseudo code describes the functionality and it fives several implementation details.

```
#the final module reputation
function module_reputation(module) returns real
   [a,b] = module_reputation_a_b(module)
   c = scalarize_user_rep(user_reputation(author(module)))
   return scalarize_module_rep(module,a,b,c)
end function

#the parts A and B of a module reputation
function module_reputation_a_b(module) returns [real,real]
   a = rating(module)/5
   if usages_similar_modules(module)==0 then
     b = 0
   else
     b = used_num(module)/usages_similar_modules(module)
   end if
```

```
   return [a,b]
end function

function compute_weights(module) returns [real,real,real,real]
   wa = all_rating_users_num() / rating_users_num(module)
   wb = 1 / (1 - 1/wa - 1/wc)
   wam = wa
   wbm = 1 / (1 - 1/wam)
   return [wa,wb,wam,wbm]
end function

# average evaluation of the module from all users
function rating(module) returns real
 sum = 0
 num = 0
 forall eval in last_user_ratings(module) do
     sum = sum + eval.rating
     num = num + 1
 end for
 if num==0 then return 3 else return (sum/num) end if
end function

#user reputation in three parts
function  user_reputation(user) returns [real,real]
   d_sum = 0
   d_num = 0
   forall kit in created_kits(user) do
      d_sum = d_sum + scalarize_kit_rep(kit_reputation(kit))
      d_num = d_num + 1
   end for
   if d_num == 0 then
      d = 0
   else
      d = d_sum / d_num
   end if
   e_sum = 0
   e_num = 0
   forall module in created_modules(user) do
      e_sum = e_sum + scalarize_module_a_b(module,module_reputation_a_b
      (module))
      e_num = e_num + 1
   end for
   e = e_sum / e_num
   return [d,e]
end function

function kit_reputation(kit) returns [real,real]
   g = used_num(kit)/all_usages()
   h_sum = 0
   h_num = 0
```

```
   forall module in modules_in_kit(kit) do
     h_sum = h_sum + scalarize_module_a_b(module_reputation_a_b(module))
     h_num = h_num + 1
   end for
   h = h_sum / h_num
   return [g,h]
end function

function scalarize_module_rep(module, [a,b,c] ) returns real
   [wa,wb,wam,wbm] = compute_weights(module)
   return (a+1)^(1/wa) * (b+1)^(1/wb) * (c+1)^(1/wc) - 1
end function

function scalarize_module_a_b( [a,b] ) returns real
   [wa,wb,wam,wbm] = compute_weights(module)
   return (a+1)^(1/wam) * (b+1)^(1/wbm) - 1
end function

function scalarize_user_rep( [d,e]) returns real
   return (d+1)^(1/wd) * (e+1)^(1/we) - 1
end function

function scalarize_kit_rep( [g,h] ) returns real
   return (g+1)^(1/wg) * (h+1)^(1/wh) - 1
end function
```

4 Experiments

MediGrid system is a real application being currently used by a group of biomedicine experts. The proposed reputation system has been implemented in Java accepting required data coming from a relational database (data about usage, ratings etc.) and storing/modifying reputation of modules, kits and authors into the same database. MediGrid web interface then accesses stored data and produces a set of screens giving user lists of modules, kits and also users with additional information about their reputation (see figure reffig:medigridexample).

The main aim of the experiments was to experimentally verified the weights and also parameters in the reputation formula are set properly and also to verify their influence on the reputation system functionality.

The experiments have to be run in background, as MediGrid is used by biomedicine experts so any unexpected behavior might be very unpleasant causing unwillingness to use MediGrid. Therefore the experiment was setup in the following manner:

- Four new accounts had been created and assigned to four different users (coauthors of this paper).
- Each user has been given by a role in the system:

- a proper user, producing modules of high quality,
- a standard user producing few modules of limited quality mostly consuming provided functionality,
- a fake user, trying get better reputation by copying modules, creating kits from highly rated modules etc.

For the fact that none of coauthors is an experts in the biomedicine area, the experiments have to be limited to just this group of users (new modules were created from existing modules in the system based on the global knowledge of expertize of users in the MediGrid).

The experiments have shown, that weight has strong impact on the reputation of modules (kits and users). As a result, tho following weights has been identified as the most reliable configuration $wc = 4$ $wd = 2$ $we = 2$ $wg = 1.5$ $wh = 3$.

In figure 2 is shown an example listing of modules with calculated reputation (depicted in a five start scale). The listing also shows values of each component (this is mainly for experimental purposes).

5 Related Work

5.1 Trust Management

Policy based approach has been proposed in the context of open and distributed services architectures [2],[3] as well as in the context of Grids [1] as the solution to the problem of authorization and access control in open systems. Its focus is on the trust management mechanisms employing different policy languages and engines for specifying and reasoning on rules for the trust establishment. Since the primary aim of such systems is to enable access control, trust management is limited to verification of credentials and restricting access to resources according to policies defined by required resources owner [6].

On the contrary, *Reputation based* trust management systems provide a way in which entities may evaluate and build a trust relationship between resource provider and requester. Reputation approach emerged in the context of electronic commerce systems, e.g. eBay. In distributed settings, reputation-based approaches have been proposed for managing trust in public key certificates, P2P systems XREP, mobile ad-hoc networks, and recently, also in the Semantic Web [4], NICE [13], DCRC/CORC [7], EigenTrust [9], EigenRep[10].

Social network based trust management systems utilize, in addition, social relationships between entities. In particular, the social network based system views the whole structure as a social network with relationships defined amongst entities. Examples of such trust management systems include Regret [17], NodeRanking [16].

5.2 Dynamic Trust Management

Trust is in some application a static phenomena, but in many other environments (e.g. Peer-To-Peer networks (P2P), mobile databases, the semantic web, the real human society) trust is highly dynamic.

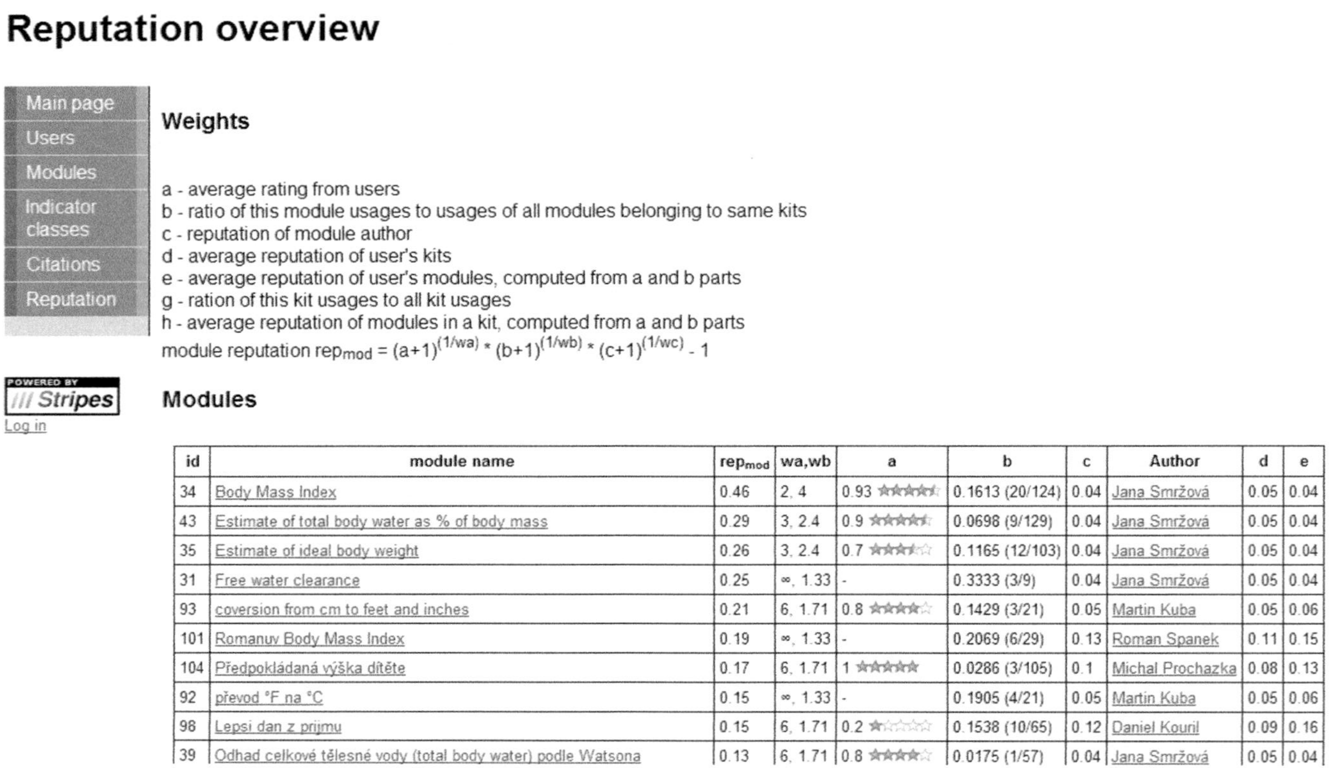

Fig. 2. Example listing of modules in the MediGrid system with calculated reputation

In most dynamic approaches trust is defined as a vector comprising few factors contributing to the overall trust value (e.g. [5]):

- the *short term trust factor*,
- the *long term trust factor*,
- the *penalty factor*.

These factors are then combined into one value of *dynamic trust metric* of a particular connection between entities. The purpose of the factors can be generalized as an effort to accommodate sudden deviation in normal behavior of an entity (so-called oscillation) together with long term behavior observation. The penalty factor is concerned to make reaction of the system (decrease or increase of trust level) satisfactory.

5.3 Trust Management System Standardization

Many systems have been designed without any standardization. In other words, trust management systems have been proposed and designed particularly for a target environment. Such situation was identified as a possible issue and several works have tried to identify some common parts [15], [14]. Such studies are very important as it is shown that despite differences in for example computational models, the same main building blocks can be found in each or at least majority of trust management systems. As trust management systems using reputation as the basis have been studied in the first place we present the common parts selected for such systems [8]:

- gathering behavioral information,
- scoring and ranking entities (peers, nodes, agents, and sensors),
- entity selection,
- transaction,
- and rewarding and punishing entities.

6 Conclusion

Paper describes a reputation system designed particularly for MediGrid environment that is aimed to be an open infrastructure based on computational grids supporting collaboration and knowledge sharing between experts in biomedicine. The reputation system design was driven by the fact that users in such open infrastructure lack of decision support which module/part is more reliable and will provide better service with higher probability.

The reputation system was shown to be proper solution providing users, who are not computer experts, with a simple and straightforward way how to find out which modules, kits and authors are the most reliable/trustable.

Reputation system was successfully implemented as a new module into the MediGrid environment. The experiments have shown that such solution is well accepted by the end users.

Acknowledgments

This work was realized under the state subsidy of the Czech Republic within the research and development project "Advanced Remediation Technologies and Processes Center" 1M0554 - Programme of Research Centers supported by Ministry of Education

References

1. Basney, J., Nejdl, W., Olmedilla, D., Welch, V., Winslett, M.: Negotiating trust on the grid. In: 2nd WWW Workshop on Semantics in P2P and Grid Computing, New York, USA (May 2004)
2. Becker, M.Y., Sewell, P.: Cassandra: distributed access control policies with tunable expressiveness. In: 5th IEEE International Workshop on Policies for Distributed Systems and Networks, Yorktown Heights (June 2004)
3. Bonatti, P.A., Olmedilla, D.: Driving and monitoring provisional trust negotiation with metapolicies. In: 6th IEEE International Workshop on Policies for Distributed Systems and Networks (POLICY 2005), pp. 14–23. IEEE Computer Society, Stockholm (2005)
4. Damiani, E., di Vimercati, S.D.C., Paraboschi, S., Samarati, P., Violante, F.: A reputation-based approach for choosing reliable resources in peer-to-peer networks. In: Proceedings of ACM Conference on Computer and Communications Security, pp. 202–216 (2002)
5. Duma, C., Shahmehri, N., Caronni, G.: Dynamic trust metrics for peer-topeer systems. In: Proceedings of 2nd IEEE Workshop on P2P Data Management, Security and Trust (in connection with DEXA) (August 2005)
6. Grandison, T., Sloman, M.: Survey of trust in internet applications. IEEE Communications Surveys 3(4) (2000)
7. Gupta, M., Judge, P., et al.: A reputation system for peer-to-peer networks. In: Thirteenth ACM International Workshop on Network and Operating Systems Support for Digital Audio and Video, Monterey, California (2003)
8. Hoffman, K., Zage, D., Rotaru, C.N.: A survey of attack and defense techniques for reputation systems. ACM Computing Surveys 42, 1–31 (2009)
9. Kamvar, S., Schlosser, M., et al.: The eigentrust algorithm for reputation management in p2p networks. In: WWW, Budapest, Hungary (2003)
10. Kamvar, S.D., Schlosser, M.T., Garcia-Molina, H.: Eigenrep: Reputation management in p2p networks. In: Proceedings of 12th International WWW Conference, pp. 640–651 (2003)
11. Kuba, M., Krajíček, O., Lesný, P., Vejvalka, J., Holeček, T.: Grid empowered sharing of medical expertise. In: Proceedings of HealthGrid 2006, pp. 273–282 (2006)
12. Kuba, M., Sebestianová, Z.: Web deployed interface for a medical knowledge grid. In: The Second International Conference on Internet and Web Applications and Services, ICIW 2007 (2007)
13. Lee, S., Sherwood, R., et al.: Cooperative peer groups in nice. In: IEEE Infocom, San Francisco, USA (2003)
14. Mekouar, L., Iraqi, Y., Boutaba, R.: Reputation-based trust management in peer-to-peer systems: Taxonomy and anatomy. In: Handbook of Peer-to-Peer Networking: Part 6, pp. 689–732. Springer Science + Business Media, Heidelberg (2010)

15. Mrmol, F.G., Pérez, G.M.: Towards pre-standardization of trust and reputation models for distributed and heterogeneous systems. Computer Standards Interfaces 32, 185–196 (2010)
16. Pujol, J., Sanguesa, R., et al.: Extracting reputation in multi agent systems by means of social network topology. In: First International Joint Conference on Autonomous Agents and Multi-Agent Systems, Bologna, Italy (2002)
17. Sabater, J., Sierra, C.: Regret: A reputation model for gregarious societies. In: 4th Workshop on Deception, Fraud and Trust in Agctn Societies, Montreal, Canada (2001)

Challenges Associated with ICT Asset Disposal in Tanzania

Daniel Koloseni and Faith Shimba

The Institute of Finance Management,
Faculty of Computing, Information Systems and Mathematics,
Shaaban Robert Street,
P. O. Box 3918, Dar es salaam, Tanzania
{koloseni,shimba}@ifm.ac.tz

Abstract. Government and non–Government institutions are heavily investing in Information and Communication Technologies (ICT) to enhance their businesses and operational activities. This trend has partially been inspired by the lift of computer ban in 1980s where millions of ICT assets had been imported. Subsequently, there is a rapid increase of Internet Service Providers (ISPs), Mobile Service Providers (MSP), and ICT asset vendors' country-wide. This implies a massive increase in imported ICT assets as well as the number of ICT assets that are going out of the ICT asset life cycle.

In order to study challenges facing Tanzania in disposing end of use ICT assets, two (2) dumping sites and two (2) recycling sites were visited with the aim of observing waste management practices on site, and the survey were conducted through web link sent to respondents over the email and Facebook (a social networking site).The survey was stopped after reaching 12 respondents out of 15 targeted respondents for Waste Management Organizations and 9 respondents for selected organizations which are major consumers of ICT.

Challenges that were found facing Tanzania in disposing end of use ICT assets include; lack of ICT asset disposal policies and procedures, lack of ICT management plan, storage challenges, lack of trained personnel and disposing infrastructures, challenges in legal aspects, recycling capacity, privacy, confidentiality and information security concerns.

Keywords: End of use ICT assets, disposal, e- waste, Tanzania.

1 Introduction

With the proliferation of ICT asset importation and usage at home, offices and the business environment, the task of managing ICT asset disposal is not an option anymore. In recent years the Government of Tanzania and non- government institutions have significantly increased the usage of ICT assets particularly computers to enhance business activities with the purpose of offering quick and efficient services to their customers.

In 1986, there were approximately 700 computers in Tanzania [1]and at least three computer vendors country-wide [2].Currently there are approximately 350,000 computers in use in the country and hundreds computer vendors [3].

J.J. Yonazi et al. (Eds.): ICeND 2011, CCIS 171, pp. 298–308, 2011.

As a consequence, the number of Internet Service Providers (ISPs), Data Service Providers (DSPs), and Mobile Service Providers (MSPs) has increased. Currently, there are about 23 ISPs, 16 DSPs and 6 major mobile operators, including Tigo, Vodacom, Zantel, TTCL and Airtel, 16 data services providers and 23 Internet service providers [4]. All of these are directly or indirectly contributing to the increase of importation and usage of ICT assets.

Accordingly, the increase in ICT asset importation contributes significantly to e-waste generation. For example, all MSPs are importing massive numbers of cellular phones and related accessories which in turn contribute to e-waste similar to the DSPs, ISPs, government and non-government institutions which imports data communication equipments of all sorts. This prolific increase of ICT asset importation and usage is driven by government's removal of all taxes and duties on computers and their peripherals.

In this paper we examine and discuss challenges facing the government, and non–government institutions in Tanzania and the public in general in management and handling end-of-use ICT assets considering that the majority of them are made up of harmful chemicals both to humans and environment.

Furthermore, we suggest workable solutions to the challenges concerning ICT asset disposal to alleviate these problems.

2 Literature Review

In this section, we provide definitions of key concepts and terminologies that are used in this paper. Moreover, an assessment of the current situation in e-waste management policies and regulations in Tanzania will be provided.

2.1 Definition of Key Terms

E-waste
E-waste is defined as end-of-use or end-life of electronic products, components and peripherals such as, computers, fax machines, phones, Personal Digital Assistant (PDA), radios and TVs [5].

Decommissioned ICT assets
An ICT equipment that has been removed from active state and no longer useful in business processes is referred to as decommissioned ICT asset.

E-Waste recycling sites
This refers to the space allocated specifically for recycling e-waste or end-of-use ICT assets.

2.2 Current Status of E-Waste Management in Tanzania

The review of existing literature shows that Tanzania has no specific policy or regulation related to e-waste management. However, there are a number of policies and regulations which aim at protecting the environment and human settlements. An example of these policies are Environmental Policy [6], the Sustainable Industrial Policy [7], National ICT Policy, [8] among others. An overview of the different e-waste related policies is given in table 1.

Table 1. An overview of Policies related to e-waste management in Tanzania

Policy	Aims and Objectives	Relevancy
National Environmental Policy [6, 9]	Guarantees sustainability, security and an equitable use of resources for now and the future with no compromise on safety and health.	Sets an overall framework for environmental management in Tanzania
The Sustainable Industrial Development Policy [7]	Achieving sustainable industrial development	Promotes pollution free industrialization and sustainable use of resources
National Science and Technology Policy [10]	Encourages the use of science and technology as means for economic development.	Capacity building on e-waste management. Research and development
Human Settlement Development Policy [11]	Guarantees sustainable human settlement development.	Pollution from solid and liquid waste should not endanger human settlements. e-waste is among solid waste.
National Water Policy [12]	Guarantees the participation of beneficiaries in planning and management of community-based water sources.	Prevents water pollution. Efficient e-waste management prevents water pollution
National ICT Policy [8]	Provides a national framework for ICT to contribute in economic development of the country.	Recycling of e-waste might result in collaboration between manufacturers and designers, and users of ICT equipments
National Energy Policy [13]	Guarantees the availability of reliable power supply.	Fosters the use of energy efficient equipment. Promotes the use of electrical and electronic equipment hence generation of e-waste.
The Small and Medium Enterprises Development Policy [14]	Promotes job creation and income generation.	E-waste recycling activities can lead to SMEs dealing with e-waste management.
National Trade Policy [15]	Increasing efficiency and linkage in domestic production.	Value creation from e-waste can contribute to the policy
National Health Policy [16]	Advancing the health of Tanzanians with particular attention to those at high risks.	Promotes safe disposal of hazardous waste including e-waste.

Table 2. A summary of regulations, aims and objectives and the impact on e-waste management of different acts and regulations in Tanzania

Regulation	Aim and Objective	Impact on e-waste management
Merchandise Marks Act [17]	Makes illegal supply of fake products, unsafe products and those which do not meet specified standards	High as it ensures safety of consumers and the environment.
Tanzania Bureau of Standards Act [18]	Establishes the Tanzania Bureau of Standards. Sets the standards for products and the environment quality	High as it sets the standards for products including electrical and electronic products.
Local Government (Urban Authorities) Act [19] and Local Government (District Authorities) Act [20]	The act makes available the management of waste from different human activities	Low as the act is not specific on other types of wastes, specifically, e-waste.
Atomic Energy Act [21]	Promotes safe use of nuclear and atomic energy.	Low as they does not have a direct relation to e-waste
Fair Competition Act [22]	Promotes effective and fair competition in trade.	High because it aimed at protecting consumers from unfair market practices and counterfeit product which may harm environment and health of consumers
Occupational Safety and Health Act [23]	Protect workers and non-workers from health hazards	High because it deals with the protection of workers' health and safety
Tanzania Food, Drugs and Cosmetics Act [24]	Provides a framework for control and regulation for manufacture, importation and distribution of foods, drugs, medical devices, cosmetics, etc. for human consumption	Low as it does not touch directly electrical and electronic products, and waste
National Environmental Management Act No. 20 [25]	Establishes principles for management, impact and risk assessment, prevention and control of environmental pollution.	High because it provides the framework for waste management.
Water Resources Management Act No.11 [26]	Controls management of water resources. Provides an institutional framework for management of water resources at national and local level.	Low it does not deal with e-waste pollution.
The Environmental (Solid Waste Management) Regulations [27]	Establishes principles for management of solid waste.	High provides the framework for solid waste management of which e-waste is one of them.
Environmental Management (Hazardous Waste Control) [28]	Establishes principles for the management of hazardous waste.	High provides principles for hazardous waste management; e-waste may be hazardous if not properly disposed.

The review of these different policies reveals that there is a need for e-waste-specific policies to address the different challenges and issues of e-waste management.

There are also a number of regulations and laws that provides an institutional framework for a sustainable management of the environment in general. Among others, the Environmental Management Act (EMA) No. 20 of 2004 is the cornerstone legislation in Tanzania. This legislation provides key principles for environment management, waste management, and impact and risk assessment among other things. A summary of the different regulations, their objectives and impact on waste management is given in table 2.

Table 2 provides a summary of the different regulations in Tanzania which are linked to e-waste management. A review of these regulations reveals that there is still a need for e-waste management specific legislation which will specifically address the different challenges in e-waste management.

2.3 E-Waste Management Specific Regulations

Tanzania lacks e-waste management specific legislation. Nonetheless, e-waste management is carried out through the Solid Waste and Hazardous Management Acts [27, 28] under the Environmental Management Act [25]. E- waste, and specifically electrical and electronic waste, is addressed in section 4 of the Environmental Management Act [25].

Different regulations in the act provide principles and guidelines on how e-waste should be handled. For example, regulation 35 (1), requires that any persons in possession or in control of electrical or electronic goods, to separate or segregate e-waste from other types of waste, and dump them separately as prescribed by different national or local authorities [19, 20]. The separation also applies to collection of waste, its transportation and the final dumping or disposal (refer schedule eight of the regulations). Schedule eight (8) of the regulation also classifies electrical and electronic equipments such as large households appliances, IT and Telecommunication equipment, among others. Section 37 (1) of the same regulation allows for manufacturers and/or vendors to set-up and operate recycling systems for electrical and electronic equipments from consumers. The role of local government (local authorities) is detailed in section 39.

The government through the Prime Minister's Office, environment division, has developed a strategy and an action plan [29]. This strategy, among other things, addresses the issue of e-waste management. The plan aims at, as its goal in e-waste management, minimizing of environmental and health risks resulting from improper handling of e-waste through stakeholders' participation. The specific objectives of the strategy and action plan are; to review different policies and regulations related to e-waste management, awareness creation on e-waste management, and promotion of recycling and material recovery. However, the strategy is yet to be implemented.

3 Research Approach

Two (2) different sets of survey were distributed. The first set survey targeted companies or organizations dealing with waste management, and the second organizations which are major consumer of ICT assets.

The aims of the survey were:

- To establish if Organizations have in place ICT management plan, asset disposal policy, and whether asset disposal policy include ICT assets.
- To understand how organizations store or treat end of use ICT assets.
- To establish if there exist a collaboration between organizations (consumer of ICT assets) and recycling industry to recycle ICT assets.
- To understand whether waste management practitioners are trained on waste management practices.
- To understand methods used by waste management companies or organizations to destroy wastes in damp sites.

In addition, two (2) dumping sites - Vingunguti and Mtoni-mtongani, and one (1) recycling site - located in Ada Estate Kinondoni, were visited. The aim was to observe waste management practices on site.

The surveys were conducted through web link sent to respondents over their email addresses and Facebook (a social networking site). The survey was stopped after reaching 12 out of 15 targeted respondents for the first set of survey and 9 respondents for the second set of survey. The results were analyzed in section 4.

4 Results Analysis and Discussion

The purpose of this study was to examine the challenges associated with disposal of ICT assets in Tanzania. The survey data used in this study come from twelve (12) organizations dealing with waste management and nine (9) which are major consumer of ICT assets.

In this survey, twelve (12) organizations responded out of fifteen (15), yielding an effective respond rate of 80% for waste management organizations and nine (9) which are major consumers of ICT out of nine (9) yielding an effective respond rate of 100%. The analysis of characteristics of respondents is shown in Table 3 bellow.

Table 3. A summary of respondents' characteristics

Nature of Organization	Academic	0%
	Ministry	8.3%
	Government Agencies	16.7%
	Other Organizations	75%
Geo-location	Ilala	33.3%
	Kinondoni	33.3%
	Temeke	33.3%
Experience in using ICT assets	More than 10 years	75%
	Between 5 - 10 years	8.3%
	Between 2 - 5 years	8.3%
	For 1 year	8.3%
Type of waste collected	General wastes	100%
	Medical wastes	0%
	Electrical wastes	0%
	Other	0%

Geographical location of respondents and the number of respondents are not a representative of a general population; we believe this will not bias the results, since selected organizations are located in Dar es Salaam which is the headquarter of many organizations surveyed. The study shows 75% of respondents have been using ICT assets in their organizations for more than ten (10) years. This aspect increases the reliability of study results as the majority of respondents are experienced users of ICT assets therefore are thought to be more familiar with ICT issues.

The study found the following challenges facing Tanzania in disposing safely end-of-use ICT assets.

Lack of ICT Asset Disposal Policy

The study found out that of nine (9) organizations which are major consumers of ICT assets, 37.5% of them do not have ICT asset disposal plan and policy that include ICT asset. This is a challenge as ICT asset disposal policies and procedures provide guidelines for disposing ICT assets in the organization [30]. The guidelines help determine assets to be disposed and procedures for disposing of ICT assets with value for money in mind. Without these policies and procedures, disposing of ICT asset will be handled improperly, or the decision to dispose may be delayed and therefore keeping the organization in stalemate of either to re-deploy or dispose the ICT. Similarly, there is a possibility of disposing of ICT assets which are still of value to the organization.

Lack of Storage Facility for end-of-use ICT Assets

Furthermore, this study found that storage of decommissioned ICT assets and e-waste in general needs special attention. 75% of surveyed organizations had no specialized rooms with enough space to store end of use ICT assets. This increases the chance of leakage. Standard operating procedures for e-waste for companies in India, for example, require organizations to allocate sufficient storage space with each type of e-waste placed differently to ensure safety [31]. Some components of ICT assets are made up of hazardous chemicals, i.e. batteries of phones and cartridges which contain carbon, lithium and other chemical elements [32]; Cathode Ray Tubes (CRTs) found in televisions and computer monitors contain mercury, phosphorous, cadmium, barium and lead; these may leak if stored carelessly. In this regard, sensing mechanisms to detect any leakage should be installed in storages of end-of-use ICT assets.

Lack of Trained Personnel in E-waste Management

Another challenge is lack of well trained personnel in waste management and allocation of dumping sites. It is shocking to find out that none of waste management organizations surveyed has trained personnel in waste management. Handling hazardous waste is different from other wastes; therefore it requires well-trained personnel and specialized equipment. Moreover, it requires strategic allocation of recycling, landfills or dumping sites to decrease the effect on the environment. Unfortunately this is not the case in Tanzania. The study found out that many recycling, landfills and dumping sites are near residential areas. This poses a very dangerous situation to health and environment as most of waste management organizations - 55.6%, prefer fire to destroy wastes (including e-wastes).

Lack of Proper Re-cycling Initiatives and Partnership

Tanzania has few institutions specialized in the recycling of waste products. Most of them target plastics (plastics containers), and metal related products, and none e-waste products. Therefore, to deal with categorized waste such as e-waste will be more difficult. This situation could have been improved if ICT assets consumers could forge partnerships with waste management organizations to recycle end-of-use ICT assets. In this study, it was found that 100% of organizations surveyed has no partnerships with recycling industry to recycle end of use ICT assets.

Additionally, due to rapid increase in users of mobile phones, televisions, internet [33], increase in importation of computers, photocopiers, printers and other computer peripherals to Tanzania, it is obvious that the existing recycling capacity is not sufficient to absorb the potential e-waste generated by these activities.

Privacy and Confidentiality

Finally, the study observed that privacy and confidentiality of information is in jeopardy as only 8.3% of respondents sanitize storage devices such as hard disk to wipe out the data permanently. If these devices, hard drives, are not wiped effectively or destroyed, privacy, confidentiality and security of information stored in may fall in the wrong hands and cause disaster.

5 Proposed Solutions

Suggested solutions to the challenges identified in Section 4 have been given as follows; there is a need of formulating ICT assets disposal policies and procedures, improving of end-of-use ICT assets storages, training and improving of disposing infrastructures and equipments, legal framework re-use, launching of awareness campaigns to the public and proper treatment of hard drives.

Formulation of ICT Asset Disposal Policies and Procedures

As the research results have shown, most organizations lack ICT asset disposal policies and procedures. As a result, formulation of ICT asset management policies and procedures will lay down principles, guidelines and procedures in disposing of ICT assets and clearly pave the way for the whole process in disposing of end-of-use ICT assets.

In addition, ICT asset disposal policies and procedures will build a sense of responsibility and accountability related to ICT asset management within organizations, in order to make sure that value for money concept is realized during ICT asset disposal exercise.

Storages Improvements

Storage of end-of-use ICT asset needs to be addressed seriously. To tackle this challenge, organizations and institutions need to make sure enough storage space is allocated for storing end-of-use ICT assets. Storages need to be equipped with sensing mechanisms to detect any leakage or emission of radioactive materials found within end-of-use ICT assets. Meanwhile, we recommend organizations to cut off time taken to keep in stores the end-of-use ICT assets before taking them out for disposal.

Reduction of delay-time will mean that organizations will not need large space for storing end-of-use ICT assets.

This will ultimately help to mitigate all risks associated with storage for long term end-of–use and decommissioned ICT assets including leakages and emissions of radioactive materials found in ICT assets.

Training and improvement of disposing infrastructures

Training of people working in waste management sector and improvement of infrastructure for disposing end-of-use ICT assets is a crucial step towards curbing ICT assets disposal challenges. Techniques related to personal protection, handling of hazardous products, first aid and combating fire and flames are essential for people working in this sector. The waste management sector is not getting the attention it deserves. Workers in this sector are not trained, equipped and are lowly-paid.

Considering the ICT growth trends in Tanzania, there is no doubt that within the next few years these challenges will be realized, and therefore building and improving infrastructure is not an option any more, it is a necessity. Kenya, Nigeria, South Africa, Egypt and many other West African countries have already started shaping their waste treatment infrastructure to accommodate e-waste [34], [35], and [36].

Deliberate Support for Recycling Initiatives

Due to rapid increase in importation of ICT assets and usage at homes and offices, it is clear that e-waste is becoming a "time ticking bomb". Recycling activities in Tanzania are mainly focusing on plastic and metal scrap only. Van de Brink and Szrimai's study of the Tanzania scrap recycling, showed that we have large surplus of scrap and the players in metal scrap industries are not capable of utilizing all available scrap [37]. Additionally, little has been done to support plastic recycling. This can be evidenced by the fact that few plastic products producers are engaging in recycling activities.

From [37] we can deduce that deliberate support for recycling initiatives and recycling activities is urgently needed to extend recycling initiatives and activities to accommodate e-waste products in order to curb this alarming problem before is too late.

Proper Hard drives Cleaning

Proper hard drives cleaning is essential for guaranteeing privacy and confidentiality of information stored in end-of-use ICT assets. Deleting a file or formatting a hard drive does not sterilize completely computer hard drives. When a hard drive is formatted, information stored in is still alive and can easily be recovered using data recovery software.

There are a lot of software available that are capable of deleting a file permanently, i.e. delete file permanently [38]. They clean hard drives without destroying the sectors and leave no trace of information. This makes it impossible for information stored to be recovered. Therefore, in order to safeguard privacy and confidentiality of information, it is recommended that organizations should apply secure data cleaner software that conforms to DoD 5220.22-M standard, which requires overwriting of all addressable locations with a character, its complement, then a random character and verify [39].

Conclusion

The findings illustrate that disposing of end-of-use ICT asset is an alarming situation and therefore needs special attention. Government and non-government organizations should set and enforce ICT asset disposal policy and work in collaboration with recycling industries to recycle end-of-use ICT assets safely. Furthermore, main importers of ICT assets should be involved in raising awareness to users of ICT assets regarding safe disposal of ICT assets and be involved in e-waste recycling initiatives.

Tanzania is one of the signatories of Basel Convention on the control of trans-boundary movements of hazardous wastes and their disposal which was ratified on 7 April, 1993. Unfortunately, Tanzania has not dealt seriously with the problem of importation of sub-standard ICT assets which are donated to majority of African countries as means of off-loading e-waste from developed countries. It is now high time for the Government of the United Republic of Tanzania to amend its Environment Law to accommodate the Basel Convention. This will prevent Tanzania from becoming a dump site for end-of-use ICT assets. Amendment of environmental law will make Tanzania part of worldwide team that prevents illegal e-waste trade and at the same time help hold responsible people importing sub-standard ICT assets and disposing of them irresponsibly. Additionally, the decision to slash all taxes and duties on computers and their peripherals needs to be revisited in order to save our environment for present and future generations.

References

1. Ndamagi, C.: National Informatics Policies in Tanzania: A Practitioner's Point of View. In: National Information and Informatics Policies in Africa, UN Economic Commission (1988)
2. Sheya, M.A.G.K.: The State of Informatics in Tanzania: Policy Issues and Strategies. In: Contribution of Informatics to Economic Development, UN Economic Commission (1987)
3. TCRA, Status of Telecom Market (2009)
4. URT, Tanzania National ICT Policy (2006)
5. e-WasteGuide. E- waste definition (2009), `http://india.ewasteguide.info/e_waste_definition` (cited on December 12, 2009)
6. URT, National Environmental policy, Government of Tanzania (1997)
7. URT, The Sustainable Industrial Development Policy (1996-2020), Government of Tanzania (1996)
8. URT, National ICT Policy. Government of Tanzania (2003)
9. URT, National Environmental Policy. Government of Tanzania, Tanzania (2003)
10. URT, National Science and Technology Policy. Government of Tanzania (1996)
11. URT, Human Settlement Development Policy. Government of Tanzania (2000)
12. URT, National Water Policy. Government of Tanzania (2002)
13. URT, National Energy Policy. Governmet of Tanzania (2003)
14. URT, The Small and Medium Enterprises (SMEs) Development Policy. Government of Tanzania (2003)
15. URT, National Trade Policy. Government of Tanzania (2003)
16. URT, National Health Policy. Government of Tanzania (2007)
17. URT, Merchandise Marks Act. Government of Tanzania (1963)
18. URT, Tanzania Bureau of Standards Act No. 3. Government of Tanzania (1975)

19. URT, Local Government (Urban Authorities) Act No. 8. Government of Tanzania (1982)
20. URT, Local Government (District Authorities) Act No. 8. Government of Tanzania (1982)
21. URT, Atomic Energy Act. Government of Tanzania (2003)
22. URT, Fair Competition Act. Government of Tanzania (2003)
23. URT, Occupational Safety and Health Act. Government of Tanzania (2003)
24. Tanzania Food, U.R.T.: Drugs and Cosmetics Act. Government of Tanzania (2003)
25. URT, National Environmental Management Act No. 20. Government of Tanzania (2004)
26. URT, Water Resources Management Act No. 11. Government of Tanzania (2009)
27. URT, The Environmental (Solid Waste Management) Regulations. Government of Tanzania (2009)
28. URT, Environmental Management (Hazardous Waste Control). Government of Tanzania (2009)
29. URT, National Waste Management Strategy and Action Plan. Government of Tanzania (2009)
30. LondonMetropolitanUniversity. Disposal of ICT Assets Policy (2009), `http://www.londonmet.ac.uk/londonmet/library/o49519_3.pdf` (cited on December 12, 2009)
31. e-WasteGuide. Standard Operating Procedures for E- waste (2009), `http://india.ewasteguide.info/standard_opreating_procedure_for_e_waste_management` (cited on December 12, 2009)
32. Brigden, K., Santillo, D.: Determining the presence of hazardous substances in five brands of laptop computers. Greenpeace Research Laboratories Technical Note 05/2006, p. 20 (2006)
33. CIA. The world fact book (2010), `https://www.cia.gov/library/publications/the-world-factbook/geos/tz.html` (cited on January 12, 2010)
34. Wanjiku, R.: Kenya opens first e-waste management plant. In: IDG News Service (2008)
35. Finlay, A.: E-waste Challenges in Developing Countries: South Africa Case Study. APC "Issue Papers" Series Association for Progressive Communication, pp. 1–22 (2005)
36. Moubasher, H.: BCRC-Egypt E-waste Activities (2006-2009)
37. Brink, J., Szirmai, A.A.: The Tanzanian scrap recycling cycle. Technovation 22(3), 187 (2002)
38. Deletefilepermanently. Protect your privacy!delete file permanently (2010), http://, `http://www.deletefilespermanently.com/` (cited on January 12, 2010)
39. DoD., National Industrial Security Program. Operating Manual. Defense Technical Information Center (1995)

Malay-English Cross-Language Information Retrieval: Compound Words and Proper Names Handling

Nurjannaton Hidayah Rais, Muhamad Taufik Abdullah, and Rabiah Abdul Kadir

Department of Multimedia,
Faculty of Computer Science and Information Technology,
Universiti Putra Malaysia,
43400 UPM Serdang, Selangor,
Malaysia
jannahhidayah@gmail.com, {taufik,rabiah}@fsktm.upm.edu.my

Abstract. Cross language information retrieval (CLIR) deals with the use of queries in one language to access documents in another. A popular CLIR approach is to translate the query into the language of the documents being retrieved. The simplest yet most effective method for query translation is bilingual dictionary approach. However, direct translation using bilingual dictionary prune two problems: proper names and compound words translations. In this study, a series of experiments were conducted to test and evaluate the effectiveness of the Malay-English CLIR using proper names and compound words translation. We believe by using concept-based indexing and translations, makes proper names and compound words translation possible. The best retrieval performance was obtained from the combination of query translation approach-select all translations listed in the dictionary, the alternative weighting scheme and proper names identification and translation.

Keywords: Concept-based IR, Cross-language information retrieval, Query translation, Bilingual dictionary, Proper names identification and translation.

1 Introduction

The increasing availability of information in different languages and the growing number of people speaking different mother tongues who want to find information have been motivating research on cross-language information retrieval (CLIR). CLIR is responsible for receiving search requests expressed in one language and retrieving documents written in another language. The key different between CLIR and monolingual IR is that the query and the documents cannot be matched directly.

The main approaches in CLIR are query translation, document translation and hybrid method where both query and documents are translated. Since it is more economical to translate queries rather than documents, query translation often preferred. Three main resources for query translation are machine translation (MT), bilingual dictionary and parallel or comparable corpora.

Dictionary-based and machine translation-based methods are incapable of finding equivalents for proper nouns not registered in dictionaries. The parallel corpus-based

J.J. Yonazi et al. (Eds.): ICeND 2011, CCIS 171, pp. 309–317, 2011.

method is unable to find equivalents of proper nouns appearing for the first time, since the term does not occur in the corpus. In this study, a series of experiments were setup to test and evaluate the effectiveness of Malay-English dictionary-based CLIR using compound words and proper names translation.

The paper is organized as follows. Section 2 discusses the previous works on concept-based IR and CLIR using bilingual dictionary. Section 3 reviews the query translation events involve in Malay-English CLIR using bilingual dictionary and relevance concept words. Section 4 represents the experimentation setup to test the effectiveness of dictionary-based CLIR system using relevance concept words. Section 5 is the results of our experiments. Summarization and future works is given in Section 6.

2 Related Work

Information retrieval (IR) deals with the representation, storage, organization of, and access to information items. An IR system prepares for retrieval by indexing documents and formulating queries, resulting in document representations and query representations, respectively; the system then matches the representations and displays the documents found and the user selects the relevant items.

In the cognitive view of the world, there exists the presumption that the meaning of a text (word) depends on conceptual relationships to objects in the world rather than to linguistic or contextual relations found in texts or dictionaries. A new generation information retrieval model is drawn from this view. We call it concept-based information retrieval model. Sets of words, names, noun-phrases, terms, etc. will be mapped to the concepts they encode [1].

Cross language information retrieval (CLIR) is a special case of information retrieval (IR). CLIR addresses this initial task of filtering, selecting and ranking documents that might be relevant to a query expressed in a different language. In [2], [3], the authors applied latent semantic indexing approach on Malay-English CLIR. In this study we used vector space model involve the computation of the degree of similarity between each document stored in the system and the user query [4]. The main translation approaches in CLIR are: query translation [5], [6], [7], document translation [8] and hybrid method [9], [10], [11], where both query and documents were translated. Since it is more economical to translate queries rather than documents, query translation often preferred.

The main problems reported in direct translation dictionary-based CLIR are: the problem of inflection, translation ambiguity, compounds and phrases and their handling, proper names and other untranslatable words and their handling, and lack of structuring [5]. However, we will focus on two problems in dictionary-based system: compounds translation and proper names translation.

Particularly, dictionaries do not contain proper names, such as the names of capital cities and countries. However, in document collection consists of news documents, proper names are considered important text elements. A common methods used to handle untranslatable keywords is to include them as such in the target language. Proper names should be identified and often need to be translated [12].

A compound word is defined as a word form from two or more root words. From the IR point of view, compounds may content bearing words in natural language sentences and therefore important for retrieval result. Compound words handling does not applied in direct translation. As result, compound words, such as *angkasa lepas*, *kapal terbang* and *kapal selam*, were wrongly translated and caused dropped in retrieval performance. These compound words should be translated as whole. Several approaches applied to CLIR system to translate compound words. English-Japanese CLIR system proposed by [13], focusing mainly in translation of technical compound words. The approach to acquiring compound word translation for English-Chinese CLIR system were applied by [14] based on self-learning mechanism, where automatically and dynamically expanding the translation dictionary of compound word.

Researchers in [15] analyzed the query translation in cross lingual IR based on feature vectors and usage of context information during the query translation. They pointed out that by using information external to the query, such as the ontologies and document collections, the effect of disambiguation and polysemi can be reduced. This study focused on bilingual dictionary approaches for Malay-English CLIR using relevance concept words. These approaches were query translation, the alternative weighting scheme and the proper names identification and translation approach.

3 Dictionary-Based CLIR Using Relevance Concept Words

3.1 Relevance Concept Words

For experiment purpose, list of concepts word were built manually, consists of proper names such as country names, capital city names, people, titles, places and events, and compound words. There were 282 entries in Malay and English concepts word based on 35 queries has been created for this experiment. These lists of concepts were applied in document and query indexing process and query translation process. The example of relevance concepts word in Malay and English were as follows.

Example 1: Relevance Concept Words
Malay Concepts word: cuti bersalin, Perdana Menteri, Wilayah Ekonomi Pantai Timur, Pusat Konvensyen Kuala Lumpur.

English Concepts word: maternity leave, Prime Minister, East Coast Economy Region, Kuala Lumpur Convention Centre.

3.2 Concept-Based Indexing

In concept-based IR, sets of words, names, noun phrases are mapped into the concepts they represent. In these approaches, a document is represented as a set of concepts. The indexing process involved four main tasks, Tokenization, Create Multiword Phrases, Concepts Identification, and Term Weighting.

As represented in Fig.1, the indexing process begin with getting documents/queries text. Then, the documents/queries texts were tokenized into single terms in Tokenization process. Next, we combined two to five terms to create multiword phrases and these phrases were identified as concepts words in Concepts Identification task. The phrases that were identified as concepts word will be added as index terms. The *tf.idf* weighting scheme were applied in Term Weighting task as we defined weights to each index terms.

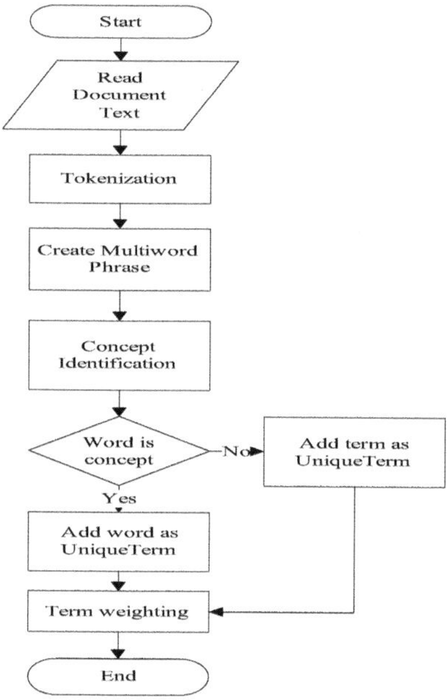

Fig. 1. Documents and queries indexing processes

3.3 Concept-Based Translation Using Bilingual Dictionary

Concept-based translation process consists of concept-based tokenization, general dictionary look-up, proper name identification, proper name dictionary look-up, query construction and query weighting. First, punctuation marks, digits and hyphens were removed from user query before concept-based tokenization take place. Concept-based tokenization will produces query keywords based on relevance concept words. All relevance concept words existed in the query will be treated as one keyword.

There were two types of dictionaries being used in this experiment, general dictionary that contains root words and compound words, and proper names dictionary consists of translation for proper names. After tokenization task was completed, general dictionary look-up was performed to translate root words and compounds words. Concept-based tokenization was the key process that makes compound words translation possible. Example 2 shows the Malay to English translation process performed for Query 28.

Example 2:- Compound word translation
Query 28: pelancaran kapal selam pertama negara
Concept-based Tokenization: (pelancaran)(kapal selam)(pertama)(negara)
General dictionary look-up: (launching) (submarine) (first) (country)

3.3.1 Proper Names Identification and Translation

Proper names such as country names, city names, titles, events and places were written in capital letter. The simplest method to detect proper names in the text is by detection on capital letter. In order to allow proper names detection, query terms will not be converted to lowercase during tokenization process. Proper names identification based on relevance concept words performed right after concept-based tokenization. Proper names translations were applied in proper names dictionary look-up. Example 3 below show an example of proper names identification and translation approach for Query 8.

Example 3:- Proper names identification and translation
Query 8: Anugerah seni bina Aga Khan di Pusat Konvensyen Kuala Lumpur (KLCC)
Concept-based Tokenization: (anugerah) (seni bina) (Aga Khan) (di) (Pusat Konvensyen Kuala Lumpur) (KLCC)
Proper names identification: (Aga Khan) (Pusat Konvensyen Kuala Lumpur) (KLCC)
Proper names dictionary look-up: (Aga Khan) (Kuala Lumpur Convention Centre) (KLCC)

4 Experimentations

In order to evaluate the effectiveness of query translation approaches in concept-based Malay-English CLIR system, a series of experiments were conducted using Malay-English alignment corpora. The English-Malay corpus contains 1, 446 news articles collected from Bernama News (www.bernama.com). For experiments purpose, we created 35 Malay queries covering a number of major events occurred in Malaysia during the period when the newspaper collection was built. For English monolingual IR, 35 Malay queries were manually translated to English language. The relevance judgments for Malay-English news collection were established manually. We then built term-document matrix for Malay and English documents.

For CLIR experiments, we were using unidirectional bilingual dictionaries for Malay-English queries translation. The Malay-English bilingual dictionary contains 21,176 entries and English-Malay dictionary consists of 22,228 entries. The dictionaries were collected from translation website. A program was built to translate 35 queries from Malay to English, and vice versa. The program involves tokenization, dictionary look-up, query construction and query weighting.

Two translation approaches for query translation were tested in this experiment: Method1: selecting the first translation listed in the dictionary, referred as CLIR1, and Method2: selecting all the translations for each query, referred as CLIR2. The combination of query translation approach, Method2 and alternative weighting scheme was tested in this experiment, we called CLIR3. CLIR1 and CLIR2 involve four processes: concept-based tokenization, general dictionary look-up, query construction and query weighting. For CLIR1, the first translation listed in the dictionary was selected in dictionary look-up process. While in CLIR2, all translations listed in the dictionary were selected. Alternative weighting scheme was applied to the query processes in experiment CLIR3. In CLIR4, proper name identification and translation process were combined with query translation approach-method1. In CLIR5, query translation approach-Method2 was applied with alternative weighting scheme and proper name identification and translation. In CLIR6, query translation approach-Method2 applied with proper name identification and translation.

The experiment results were evaluated using Mean Average Precision (MAP). We compared MAP results for CLIR with MAP result for monolingual IR, respectively.

5 Results and Discussions

As can be expected, the retrieval performance of the direct translation method is lower than that of the equivalent monolingual methods. Table 1 shows the MAP results for CLIR experiments. For Malay document collection, English queries were translated into Malay language automatically. The MAP results for CLIR1 and CLIR2 were lower than Baseline, 5.7% and 4.7%, respectively. Query translation approach, select all translations listed in the dictionary outperformed query translation approach select the first translation listed in the dictionary result by 1%.

For English document collection, Malay queries were translated into English language. The MAP results for CLIR1 and CLIR2 were 7.4% and 9.6% lower than Baseline result. For English document collection, query translation approach, selects the first translation listed in the dictionary outperformed CLIR using query translation approach, select all translation listed in the dictionary by 2.2%.

The alternative weighting scheme applied with query translation approach, select all translations listed in the dictionary seems to improve MAP results for Malay and English document collection. For Malay collection, MAP result for experiment CLIR3 improves 0.8 % compared to experiment CLIR2 result. For English collection, MAP result for experiment CLIR3 improves 6.4 % compared to experiment CLIR2 result.

The proper names identification and translation approach applied in experiments CLIR4, CLIR5 and CLIR6 can improve retrieval performance for Malay and English document collection. For Malay document collection, the combination of query translation approach, select the first translation listed in the dictionary, the proper names identification and translation approach and the alternative weighting scheme in experiment CLIR5 outperformed experiment CLIR3 by 0.2 %. Experiment CLIR6 which was the combination of query translation approach, select all translations listed in the dictionary and the proper names identification and translation approach improved MAP result by 0.5 % compared to MAP result of CLIR2. However, performance of experiment CLIR4 slightly dropped 0.2 % compared to CLIR1 result.

For English document collection, the combination of query translation approach, select the first translation listed in the dictionary and the proper names identification and translation approach in experiment CLIR4 improve 3.1 % compared to CLIR1 MAP result. Experiment CLIR5 outperformed CLIR3 MAP result by 2.6 % and experiment CLIR6 outperformed CLIR2 result by 6%.

For English and Malay document collections, as shown Table 1, the best retrieval performance was obtained from experiment CLIR5, the combination of query translation approach, select all translations listed in the dictionary, the alternative weighting scheme and the proper names identification and translation. These approaches solved three query translation problems discussed in [5]: translation ambiguity due to multiple translations obtained for one query term, compound words translation and proper names identification and translations.

Table 1. Comparison of MAP results of experiment CLIR1, CLIR2, CLIR3, CLIR4, CLIR5 and CLIR6 with monolingual IR (baseline) for Malay and English document collections

Experiments	MAP Results	
	Malay Document	**English Document**
Monolingual IR (Baseline)	0.811	0.746
CLIR1 (First translation)	0.754	0.672
CLIR2 (All translations)	0.764	0.650
CLIR3 (All translations + Alternative weighting)	0.772	0.714
CLIR4 (First translation + Proper name Handler)	0.752	0.703
CLIR5 (All translations + Alternative weighting + Proper name Handler)	0.774*	0.740*
CLIR6 (All translations + Proper name Handler)	0.769	0.710

(* indicate the best result obtained from cross-language information retrieval (CLIR) experiments)

The characteristics of compound words in Malay and English languages reported in [7]. In Malay language, compound words either written separately or link together when they are bound by circumfix or when they are considered as stable words. In English language, compound words in English language are written in three ways: hyphenated compound, an open compound and a solid compound. Included all compound words in bilingual dictionaries is the easiest yet effective way to translated compound words. Compound words such as *kapal terbang* and *kapal selam* were considered as solid compounds but written separately in text. By using concept-based indexing in documents and queries, these compounds were taken in as one index item and can be translated directly by dictionary. However, since the new compound words emerge every day, we need an approach to automatically acquire new compounds as suggested in [14].

In [12], proper names in texts often need to be translated. Country names, city names and events, often written with capital letter at the beginning of each character. The simplest way to identified proper names from document text was by detection of capital letter. However, these approach cannot detect proper names written at the beginning of the sentences since capital letter were applied at the beginning of each sentences. Proper names translation using dictionary was efficient depends on the coverage of the dictionary. It is possible to build proper names dictionary for Malay-English language pair, but it require more times and cost. We suggest generating proper names dictionary automatically based on documents in the internet or document collection analysis.

6 Conclusion

In this study we were evaluated the effectiveness of bilingual dictionary approaches for Malay-English CLIR using proper names and compound words translation. The relevance concepts words consists of compound words and proper names has been created based on 35 queries used in the experiment. Relevance concepts words were applied in document/query indexing and query translation tasks. Concept-based indexing makes compound word and proper names translation possible.

The best experiment result was obtained from experiment CLIR5 which was the combination of query translation approach, select all translations listed in the dictionary, the alternative weighting scheme and proper names identification and translation. For both, Malay and English document collection, compound words and proper names translation show improvement in CLIR system.

References

1. Haav, H.M., Lubi, T.-L.: A Survey of Concept-based Information Retrieval Tools on the Web. In: Proc. of 5th East-European Conference ADBIS, Vilnius, "Technika", vol. 2, pp. 29–41 (2001)
2. Abdullah, M.T., Ahmad, F., Mahmod, R., Sembok, T.M.T.: Application of Latent Semantic Indexing on Malay-English Cross Language Information Retrieval. In: Sembok, T.M.T., Zaman, H.B., Chen, H., Urs, S.R., Myaeng, S.-H. (eds.) ICADL 2003. LNCS, vol. 2911, pp. 663–665. Springer, Heidelberg (2003)
3. Abdullah, M.T.: Monolingual and Cross-Language Information Retrieval Approaches for Malay and English Documents. Ph.D thesis, Universiti Putra Malaysia (2006)
4. Baeza-Yates, R., Ribeiro-Neto, B.: Modern Information Retrieval. Addison Wesley, Reading (1999)
5. Pirkola, A., Hedlund, T., Keskustalo, H., Jarvelin, K.: Dictionary-Based Information Retrieval: Problems, Methods and Research Findings. Information Retrieval 4, 209–230 (2001)
6. Fujii, A., Ishikawa, T.: Japanese/English cross language information retrieval: Exploration of query translation and transliteration. Computers and the Humanities (2001)
7. Rais, N.H., Abdullah, M.T., Kadir, R.A.: Query Translation Architecture for Malay-English Cross-Language Information Retrieval System. In: International Symposium on Information Technology 2010 (2010)
8. Hayurani, H., Sari, S., Adriani, M.: Query and Document Translation for English-Indonesian Cross Language IR. In: Peters, C., Clough, P., Gey, F.C., Karlgren, J., Magnini, B., Oard, D.W., de Rijke, M., Stempfhuber, M. (eds.) CLEF 2006. LNCS, vol. 4730, pp. 57–61. Springer, Heidelberg (2007)
9. Bian, G.W., Chen, H.H.: Integrating Query Translation and Document Translation in a Cross-Language Information Retrieval System. Springer, Heidelberg (1998)
10. Kishida, K., Kando, N.: Hybrid Approach for Query and Document Translation with Pivot Language for Cross-Language Information Retrieval. Lecture Notes in Computer Science, vol. 4022, pp. 93–101 (2006)
11. Rahman, S.A., Ahmad, N., Hashim, H.A., Dahalan, A.W.: Real Time On-Line English-Malay Machine Translation (MT) System. In: Third Real-Time Technology and Application Symposium (2006)

12. Grefensette, G.: The Problem of Cross-Language Information Retrieval. In: Cross-Language Information Retrieval. Kluwer Academic Publishers, Dordrecht (2000)
13. Fujii, A., Ishikawa, T.: Cross-Language Information Retrieval using Compound Word Translation. In: Proceedings of the 18th International Conference on Computer Processing of Oriental Language (1999)
14. Zhang, Y., Isihara, H.: Acquiring Compound Word Translations Both Automatically and Dynamically. In: PACLIC. Waseda University,Tokyo (2004)
15. Lilleng, J., Tomassen, S.: Cross-lingual information retrieval by feature vectors. Lecture Notes in Computer Science (including subseries Lecture Notes in Artificial Intelligence and Lecture Notes in Bioinformatics), pp. 229–239 (2007)

From UML Sequence Diagrams to Labeled Generalized Stochastic Petri Net Models Using Graph Transformation

Mouna Bouarioua, Allaoua Chaoui, and Raida Elmansouri

MISC Laboratory, Department of Computer Science, University Mentouri Constantine, Algeria
{mouna.bouarioua,a_chaoui2001}@yahoo.com,
raidaelmansouri@yahoo.fr

Abstract. UML sequence diagrams are used to describe concepts related to behavioral view of systems. In other hand, Petri Nets models are tools for the performance analysis of distributed systems. Graph grammars aims to bridge the gap between semi-formal models and formal notations. In this paper we propose an approach for transforming UML sequence diagrams to labeled generalized stochastic Petri nets. Since the input and the output models are graphs, we use Java based graph transformation to perform this process automatically.

Keywords: UML, Sequence Diagrams, Generalized Petri Net, LGSPN, graph transformation.

1 Introduction

Nowadays, technology is looking for distributed applications to develop and increase its domains (network, telecommunication, …). This kind of applications is known by a high complexity. Formal verification methods [26] are the most used techniques to raise concurrent systems questions because of their ability to describe systems behaviors without ambiguity.

The unified modeling language UML [21] [9] is a standardized language compatible with object-oriented development methods for specifying and visualizing software systems. It includes a large set of graphical notations called diagrams which allow capturing different aspects of the systems such as structural view and behavior. UML sequence diagrams [4] are an interaction diagrams (subset of behavior diagrams) that show communication among processes taking in account some timing constraints. These diagrams describe how and in which order objects operate, and the relations between them in a visual and intuitive manner. Sequence diagrams, as their name indicates; order messages sequentially according to their occurrence in time. They are used to explore the logic of methods and services and also for model scenarios.

Our goal being performance analysis and validation, UML lacks a precise formal semantic which hinders the formal evaluation and verification [6] of system structure, and still needs more semantic bases for its notation.

J.J. Yonazi et al. (Eds.): ICeND 2011, CCIS 171, pp. 318–328, 2011.

Petri nets [2], Predicat/Transition nets [11] and in particular, labeled generalized stochastic Petri nets (LGSPN) [2] are formal and graphical methods [26] for modeling complex systems in distributed environments. LGSPN capture many aspects of systems, the most important are concurrency, synchronization and conflicts.

To reach our goal, UML sequence diagrams are projected into LGSPN models for managing systems performance, and the result of formal analysis can be back-annotated to the UML models.

To manage the complexity of the system, we need to raise the level of abstraction in the development process by building a tool that generates our needed formalisms. This step is very important since it allows modeling models themselves. So in this case meta-models [22] [25] are the definition of models. The mapping between two models also called models transformation [22] must be semantically well-defined in a meta-model level, the series of formal changes applied to source sub-models is called grammar [12].

In this paper we propose an approach and a tool for transforming sequence diagram models to their equivalent Labeled Generalized Stochastic Petri Net models using Java. The obtained models will be exploited by verification tools.

We have defined meta-models for UML sequence diagrams and LGSPN as Java classes, and for each instantiation, the compiler generate a model according to the selected meta-model class. The process of translation is performed by a set of rules that constitute the grammar.

This paper is organized as follow: Section 1 outlines the major related work and differences between their multiple approaches. In section 2 we recall some basic concepts about UML sequence diagrams, Labeled Generalized Stochastic Petri Nets and graph transformations. In section 3 we describe our approach of transforming sequence diagrams to Labeled Generalized Stochastic Petri Nets, it consists on proposing two meta-models associated respectively to the sequence diagram model and LGSPN model and a grammar that deals with the transformation. The meta-models and the grammar are implemented in Java. In section 4 we illustrate our approach through an example; we give a sequence diagram and execute the tool. The final section concludes the paper and gives some perspectives of future works.

2 Related Work

The most closely topics related to this work are generally dealing with model transformations and especially graph transformations for analysis purposes; using meta-modeling concepts and visual tools like Generic Modeling environment (GME) [16] ATOM^3 [3], and other tools from the Eclipse Generative Modeling tools (GMT) project such as Eclipse Modeling Framework (EMF) [8],Graphical Editing Framework (GEF) [14] and Graphical Modeling Framework (GMF) [15]. In most of this, model transformations have to be described textually. In [7] the authors performed a translation of Act-One to Miranda. There are also similar tools which manipulate models by means of graph grammars, such as PROGRES [23], GreAT [13], FUJABA [10], and AGG [1]. The translation is performed by means of meta-modeling concepts for allowing the reuse of formalisms working on other transformations. However, none of these has its own meta-modeling layer. In [5] a similar work to this one has been developed for obtaining analyzable Petri Net models from UML sequence diagrams and statecharts. The translation into Petri Nets is based on the abstract syntax of UML collaborations and of the state machines packages. In [19] [20], they treat the transformation between UML statecharts and collaboration diagrams to Colored Petri Net models using ATOM[3] since the approach is based on graph transformation and the input and output models are both graphs. It produces graphical models that facilitate early detection of errors. This work was a step in a project that is exploring means to exploit the INA [17] analyzer tool.

3 Background

Our objective is to propose an automatic generation of Labeled Generalized Stochastic Petri Nets from Sequence Diagrams using graph transformation. The abstract syntax of formalism is described by means of a meta-model. The transformation process is performed by a graph grammar that takes the source model (Sequence Diagram) as an input, execute the rules of the grammar, and generate the target model (Labeled Generalized Stochastic Petri Net) as output.

In the following we recall some basic notions about sequence diagrams, Labeled Generalized Stochastic Petri Nets and graph transformations.

Sequence Diagrams

UML [9][21] is a visual language for the object oriented analysis and design of systems defined by the Object Management Group (OMG). It is based on diagrams. UML 2.3 is the last version of UML released in may 2010 and it provides thirteen diagrams for specifying and modeling systems from different views as use cases, logical view, implementation, deployment and processes, even if it doesn't justify the strategy of the choices. The behavioral aspect of a system is defined by how objects communicate together and exchange messages. UML propose multiple views to show interaction between objects, one of them is the sequence diagram [4]. The main role of those diagrams is to illustrate systems use cases and show the temporal execution of communication. A sequence diagram is composed of a set of objects followed by lines that describe their lifetimes in a vertical dimension. Messages between objects sent sequentially are represented as arrows from the sender objects to the receiver ones. Messages may be synchronous or asynchronous. Every message is related to an action performed by its sender. When the message is asynchronous, the termination of the action is validated automatically when the message is sent. But when the message is synchronous, this means that the process has been interrupted and the action will terminate after the resumption of the sender. Messages can be delayed or not.

To illustrate the principle of sequence diagrams, let's consider the example of 4 objects and 4 messages in figure 1.

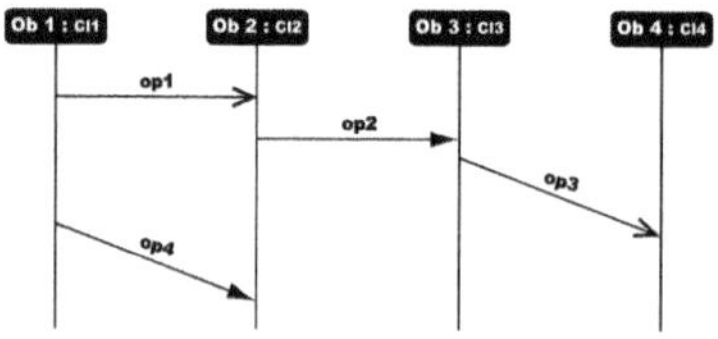

Fig. 1. Sequence diagram

We have 4 objects Ob1, Ob2, Ob3, Ob4. Every object is an instance from the corresponding class Cl1, Cl2, Cl3, Cl4 respectively. To each object frame, an output vertical line describe the lifetime of the object. Messages are call for operations and in the figure they are ordered in time from the top to the bottom op1, op2, op3 and op4. op1 is considered older than op2, and op2 older than op3 and so on.

Every message in the figure has a sender and a receiver, and every message is synchronous or not, delayed or not. Message op1 comes from Ob1:Cl1 (sender) to Ob2:Cl2 (receiver), this message is asynchronous (stick arrowhead) and not delayed. Also op2 isn't delayed but synchronous (solid arrowhead). Op3 is asynchronous but delayed. The last message op4 is synchronous and delayed.

The figure 1 shows the interaction about 4 objects exchanging different messages at different fractions of time, and also giving information on how these messages are send and received, times and delays everything in a graphical manner. This easiness and intuitive aspect is the main power of the unified modeling language (UML).

Labeled Generalized Stochastic Petri Nets

Petri Nets [2] are mathematical models for the formal description of complex systems. A Petri net is a graph, a set of places and transitions linked by directed arcs. The resulting paradigm from the introduction of temporal concept into classical PN is a sub model called stochastic Petri nets (SPN) [2]. When stochastic timing is mixed with deterministic null delays, we obtain a Generalized stochastic Petri net (GSPN) models where each transition is labeled (LGSPN) [2]. A place in an LGSPN graph represents a system state, a situation or a condition. A transition in an LGSPN graph represent actions that when done, change the state of the system (the transition fires).

Arcs specify the relation between states and actions, they link places to transitions and vice-versa. Tokens are markers that reside in places used to specify the LGSPN states and different configurations. The place represents a condition; it contains only one token as a Boolean indicator. In addition, when it represents a situation, it contains as tokens a requisite to express the state. Formally, a GSPN model is defined as follow:

LGSPN = (P, T, $M\pi$, I, O, H, W, PAR, P RED, M P)
where :
$M\pi$ = (P, T, π, I, O, H, PAR, P RED, M P) is a PN model
P: a set of places.
T: a set of transitions, $T \cap P = \Phi$;
I, O, H: the input, output and inhibition functions, respectively.
P AR: a set of parameters.
PRED: a set of predicates.
M P : parametric initial marking .
W : T $\rightarrow$ I is a function defined on the set of transitions that are timed or immediate.
To illustrate the principle of an LGSPN models, let's consider this example (Adapted from [2]).

The LGSPN bellow illustrates timed and immediate transitions, execution of parallel processes, synchronization and free choice conflict.

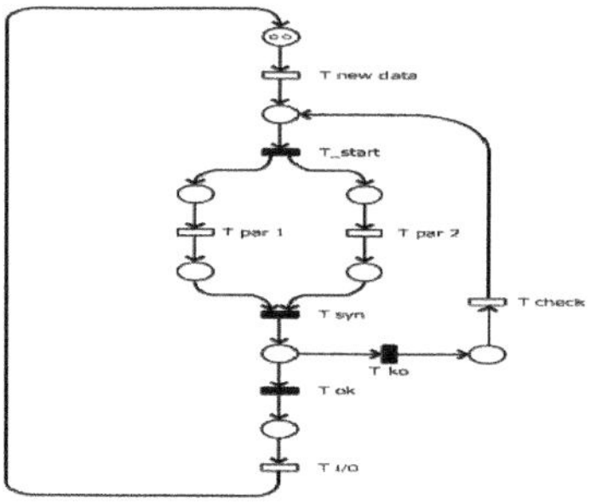

Fig. 2. LGSPN Example

There is 9 transitions: Tnewdata, Tpar1, Tpar2, TI/O, Tcheck are timed and tstart , tsyn , tOK, tKO are immediate.

Every state in this example has a transition in output, and every transition is followed by at least one state.

Tnew_data is the first transition after the initial state that contains two tokens. After the validation of a data, the timed transition Tnewdata fires and the system is automatically switched to a new state. After that, a parallel process starts when the immediate transition T_starts firing. When the parallel processes (Tpar1 and Tpar2) complete; synchronization takes effect at T syn transition. Transitions Tok and Tko describe a free choice conflict case depending on the distribution of weights and tokens in places.

Graph transformation

The transformation between models is a process that converts a model to another model. This task requires a set of rules that define how the source model has to be analyzed and transformed into other elements of the target model. The transformation engine takes the source model in input; execute the rules of transformation and finally generate the target model in output.

Graph grammars [24] are used for model transformation. They are composed of production rules; each having graph in their left and right sides. Rules are compared with an input graph called host graph. If a matching is found between the left hand side of a rule and a subgraph in the host graph, then the rule can be applied and the matching subgraph of the host graph is replaced by the right hand side of the rule. Furthermore, rules may also have a condition that must be satisfied in order for the rule to be applied, as well as actions to be performed when the rule is executed. A rewriting system iteratively applies matching rules in the grammar to the host graph, until no more rules are applicable. In this work, we use Java.

4 Our Approach

In our approach, we propose two meta-models associated respectively to the SD model and the LGSPN model. Then we propose a grammar for the transformation. Meta-models and grammar are implemented in Java since the main purpose of UML is to create object oriented models.

SD meta-model

A sequence diagram consists of objects and messages in time. Our meta-model of SD is composed mainly of three classes (Sequence Diagram, Object, Message).

SequenceDiagram: this class associates objects to messages and build the final model.

Object: this class represents the SD objects that messages send or receive. Every object has a name.

Message: it represents the messages between objects; every message is labeled by an operation, its order in time and boolean attributes to test if it is asynchronous or delayed.

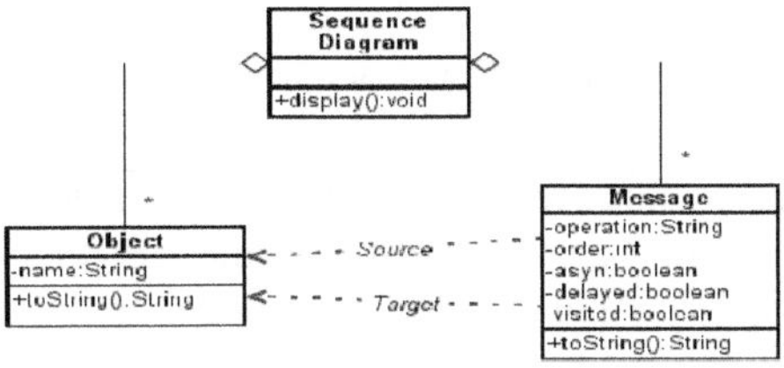

Fig. 3. SD Meta-Model

LGSPN meta-model

In this section, we propose a meta-model for LGSPN, it consists of states and transitions. So our meta-model of LGSPN is composed mainly of three classes (LGSPN, place, transitions).

Place: this class describes the places of the LGSPN, every place has a name.

Transition: is a superclass of two classes: transition_i for immediate transitions and transition_d for delayed transitions. Every transition is labeled by an action.

LGSPN: it builds the final LGSPN model from places and transitions using arcs.

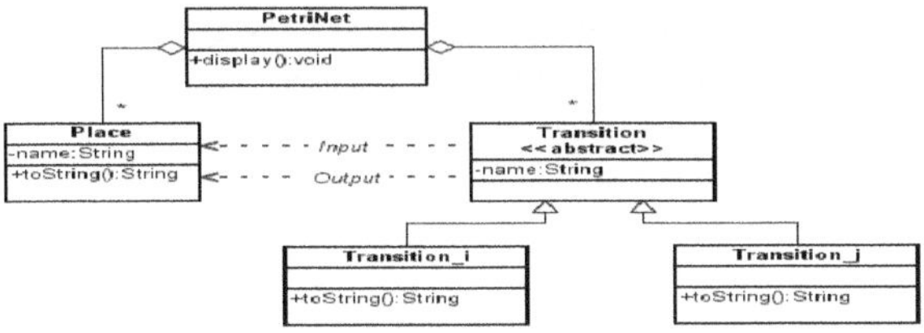

Fig. 4. LGSPN Meta-Model

Our grammar

We have implemented a graph grammar that contains 4 rules such that each rule represents one kind of messages (See figure 5).

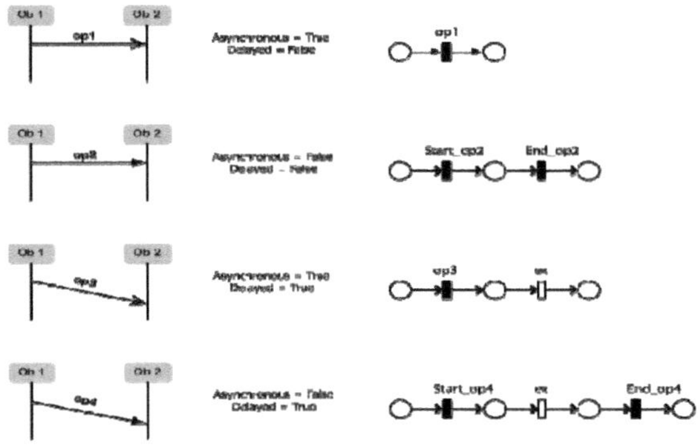

Fig. 5. Graph Grammar rules

The first Rule concerns the asynchronous messages (Asynchronous=True) with no-delay (Delayed=False). When this rule is applied on this kind of messages, it generates an LGSPN sub diagram of two states and one immediate transition.

The second Rule concerns the synchronous messages (Asynchronous=False) with no-delay (Delayed=False). When this rule is applied, it generates two immediate transitions (Start_op and End_op) for the start and the end of the synchronous message.

The third Rule concerns the asynchronous messages (Asynchronous=True) with delay (Delayed=True). When applied, this rule processes to the generation of two different types of transitions. The first one for the operation sent with the message and it is immediate. The second one is a timed transition for the exception.

The fourth Rule is for synchronous and delayed messages (Asynchronous=False and Delayed=True). This rule creates three transitions. Two immediate transitions for the start and the end of the message's operation respectively, and the other timed transition is for the exception.

Every rule has a priority and an order. The execution of the grammar starts from the top of the life-lines of the objects until the last message in the bottom.

In this grammar we apply only one rule on each message.

5 Example

We have tested our approach on several examples. For lack of space, we illustrate our approach using the sequence diagram of figure 6 describing the interaction between a student and an E-learning website server. When the student visits the website, he selects one of the proposed trainings. The system sends an authentification form and the user enters his identity and the system will validate the authentification and send information's form. Then, the user will transmit information and finally the system confirms the operation.

The corresponding sequence diagram consists of 2 objects which are the visitor of the website and the server and 6 messages exchanged between them.

- M1 : Select_Training , Asynchronous, Not delayed
- M2 : Transmit_Authent_Data, Not delayed
- M3 : Authentification_Form, Asynchronous, Not delayed
- M4 : Authentification, Synchronous, Delayed
- M5 : Informations_Form, Asynchronous, Not delayed
- M6 : Transmit_Informations, Asynchronous, Not delayed
- M7 : Validate_Operation, Asynchronous, Not delayed

The application of our approach consists of the following steps:

a) We have first described the sequence diagram of figure 6 in java as shown in figure 7.

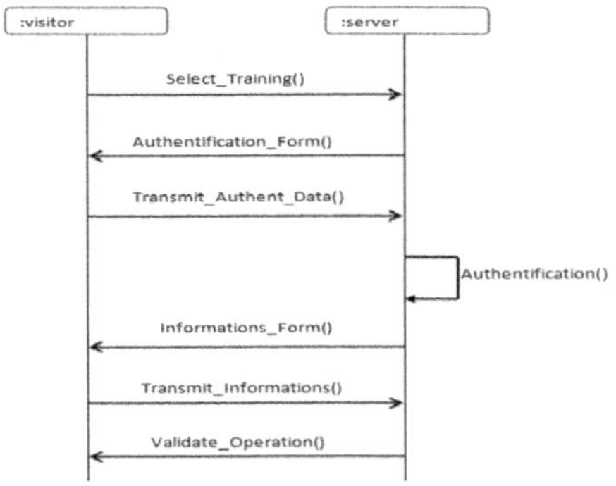

Fig. 6. Sequence diagram of an E-Learning Website

```
<terminated> Main (1) [Java Application] C:\Program Files\Java\jre6\bin\javaw.exe (6 avr. 2011
Sequence Diagram :
==================
Objects :
=========
:Visitor
:Server
Messages :
==========
1 :Visitor---Select_Training()-->:Server
2 :Server---Authentification_Form()-->:Visitor
3 :Visitor---Transmit_Authentification_Data()-->:Server
4 :Server---Authentification()-->:Server
5 :Server---Informations_Form()-->:Visitor
6 :Visitor---Transmit_Informations()-->:Server
7 :Server---Validate_Operations()-->:Visitor
*******************
```

Fig. 7. Sequence diagram of an E-Learning Website in Java

b) Then, we have applied our grammar as shown in figure 8 and obtained the LGSPN of figure 9.

```
******************
Running the Grammar
******************
Rule1is applicable
Rule2is applicable
Rule3is applicable
Rule1is applicable
Rule2is applicable
Rule3is applicable
Rule1is applicable
Rule2is applicable
Rule3is applicable
Rule1is applicable
Rule2is applicable
Rule3is applicable
Rule1is applicable
Rule3is applicable
Rule1is applicable
Rule1is applicable
```

Fig. 8. Graph Grammar execution in Java

```
Petri Net :
***********
Places :
********
(0)
(1)
(2)
(3)
(4)
(5)
(6)
(7)
(8)
(9)
Transitions :
*************
(0)-->|Select_Training()|-->(1)
(1)-->|Authentification_Form()|-->(2)
(2)-->|Transmit_Authentification_Data()|-->(3)
(3)-->|startAuthentification()|-->(4)
(4)-->|endAuthentification()|-->(5)
(5)-->|Informations_Form()|-->(6)
(6)-->[exepInformations_Form()]-->(7)
(7)-->|Transmit_Informations()|-->(8)
(8)-->|Validate_Operations()|-->(9)
```

Fig. 9. Generated LGSPN Model

6 Conclusion

In this paper, we have proposed and approach and a tool for transforming sequence diagrams models to labeled generalized stochastic Petri net models using graph grammar since the input and output models are graphs. To perform this transformation, we have proposer two meta-models; one for the input model and the other for the output model. Then based on these two meta-models, we have proposed a graph grammar that deals with the transformation process implemented in java. We have used java as a programming language for implementing our meta-models and grammar instead of all other tools because java is simple, object-oriented, interpreted, robust, secure, architecture neutral, portable, high performance, multithreaded and dynamic. This design we made allow some flexibility when needs of readjustment or add other classes both in meta-models or grammar. We have illustrated our approach through an example. This work is concerned only with the transformation of SD models to LGSPN models.

In a future work we plan to perform this transformation using graph transformation visual tools like AGG and transform other UML diagrams. We can also use the well known reduction technique on the obtained models before performing the analysis in order to optimize the models, and then use them with INA analyzer. Another way of implementing the transformation is to use the standard exchange format for diagrams of UML.

References

1. AGG home page, `http://tfs.cs.tu-berlin.de/agg/`
2. Ajmone, M.M., Balbo, G., Conte, G., Donatelli, S., Franceschinis, G.: An Introduction to generalized stochastic Petri nets. International Journal of Microelectronics Ans Reliability: Special Issue on Petri nets and Related Graph Models 31(4), 699–725 (1991)
3. ATOM3 home page, `http://atom3.cs.mcgill.ca/`
4. Barbier, F.: UML 2 ET MDE Ingénierie des modèles avec études de cas (2005)
5. Bernardi, S., Donatelli, S., Merseguer, J.: From UML sequence diagrams and statecharts to analyzable petri net models. In: Proceedings of the 3rd International Workshop on Software and Performance, WOSP (2002)
6. Bernot, G., Gaudel, M.C., Marre, B.: Software testing based on formal specifications: a theory and a tool. Software Engineering Journal 6(6), 387–405 (1991)
7. Charles, N., Bowman, H., Thompso, S.: From Act-one to Miranda, a Translation Experiment. Computer Standards and Interfaces Journal 19(1) (May 1997)
8. EMF home page, `http://www.eclipse.org/emf/`
9. Fowler, M.: UML distilled third edition, a brief guide to the standard object modeling language (2004)
10. FUJABA home page, `http://www.fujaba.de`
11. Genrich, H.J., Lautenbach, K.: System Modelling with High-Level Petri Nets. Theoretical Computer Science Journal 13 (1981)
12. Graph transformation and graph grammars, `http://www.gratra.org/`
13. GreAT home page, `http://www.escherinstitute.org/Plone/tools/`
14. GEF home page, `http://www.eclipse.org/gef/`
15. GMF home page, `http://www.eclipse.org/gmf`

16. GME home page, `http://www.isis.vanderbilt.edu/gme`
17. INA home page,
`http://www2.informatik.hu-berlin.de/~starke/ina.html`
18. Kelly, S., Lyytinen, K., Rossi, M.: MetaEdit+: A fully configurable Multi-User and Multi-Tool CASE and CAME Environment. In: Advanced Information System Engineering. LNCS, vol. 1080, Berlin (1996)
19. Kerkouche, E., Chaoui, A., Khalfaoui, K.: Transforming UML models to colored Petri nets models using graph grammars. In: Proceedings of ISCC, pp. 230–236 (2009)
20. Kerkouche, E., Chaoui, A., Bourennane, E., Labbani, O.: A UML and Colored Petri Nets Integrated Modeling and Analysis Approach using Graph Transformation". Journal of Objetc Technology 9(4), 25–43 (2010)
21. OMG Unified Modeling Language Specification: version 1.4. Object Management Group Inc. (September 2001), `http://www.omg.org`
22. OMG: MDA Guide Version 1.0.1. Retrieved from Object Management Group (June 12, 2003), `http://www.omg.org/mda`
23. PROGRES Applications of Graph Transformations with Industrial Relevance. LNCS, vol. 5088 (2008)
24. Rozengerg, G.: Handbook of Graph Grammar and computing Graph Transformation. World Scientific, Singapore (1999)
25. Varró, D., Pataricza, A.: A visual, precise and multilevel metamodeling framework for describing mathematical domains and uml (the mathematics of metamodeling is metamodeling mathematics). Software and System Modeling Journal 2(3), 187–210 (2003)
26. Wing, J.M.: A Specifier's Introduction to Formal Methods. Computer Journal 23(9), 8–23 (1990)

Differentiation Intra Traffic in the IPTV over IMS Context

D. Leghroudi[1], M. Belfkih[1], N. Moumkine[2], and M. Ramdani[2]

[1] Networks Laboratory, Institut National des Postes et Télécommunications, Rabat, Maroc
[2] Department of computer science, Faculté des Sciences et Techniques Mohamedia, Morocco
{Leghroudi,eghoudi}@yahoo.fr

Abstract. On the horizon to distribute a real-time multimedia traffic over an IP infrastructure, the provider must meet several QoS constraint particularly Packet Loss and latency of transmission. With the aim to meet these expectations, we must establish a platform for control and improvement of QoS of the IPTV traffic.The main objective of this paper is to study, by critical point if view, the current QoS mechanisms by analyzing the composition of IPTV traffic in the context of IMS with the performance evaluation of current tools for improving service quality of IPTV in IMS, then we propose a solution that that aims to differentiate the IPTV traffic with prioritization the broadcasting one under other based on DSCP values.

Keywords: Next Generation Networks, Fixed-Mobile Convergence, IMS, IPTV services, BC, VoD, PVR, nPVR, Multimedia Delivery Architecture, QoS, IntServ, DiffServ.

1 Introduction

IPTV technology provides one of the main applications most requested by the market of telecommunication that provides an opportunity for service providers to use IP to carry the various IPTV traffic.However, the composition of the IPTV stream namely Traffic in broadcasting (BC), video on demand (VoD), Personal Video Recorder (PVR) and the QoS Mechanisms that are currently deployed which are based on DiffServ limit of its quality of service.

This standard (DiffServ) assumes that the IPTV stream are of the same priority high compared to other service, however the packets accordingly BC, PVR, and VoD as well video streaming will be treated as best effort among them. In reality there is a major difference between these packages in their sensitivity to delay and other parameters. In this work we propose a mechanism which provides the delivery of IPTV traffic with different service level-based sensitivity to QoS parameters. With an experimental implementation in IMS wired network, we demonstrate the efficacy of mechanism to optimize the quality of service of BC traffic among different other video streaming.

This paper is structured as follows: Section 2 presents the architecture of IPTV. In section 3 we discuss the QoS in IMS, our suggestion and framework are detailed in section 4, The paper closes with a conclusion.

J.J. Yonazi et al. (Eds.): ICeND 2011, CCIS 171, pp. 329–336, 2011.

2 IPTV Architecture

In the IPTV architecture we perceive two types: dedicated IPTV systems and IMS-based systems.

The first system features by a dedicated subsystem within an NGN platform which used to provide all required IPTV functionality to all subscribers [4].service control and user profile management are the main functions. The main advantage of these systems is the dedicated resources, resulting in reliability and performance [5]. But they suffer from the complexity of process to connect with other NGN elements in order to provide convergence's services. The second type that integrates the components of IMS to provide IPTV service. This architecture considers the IPTV

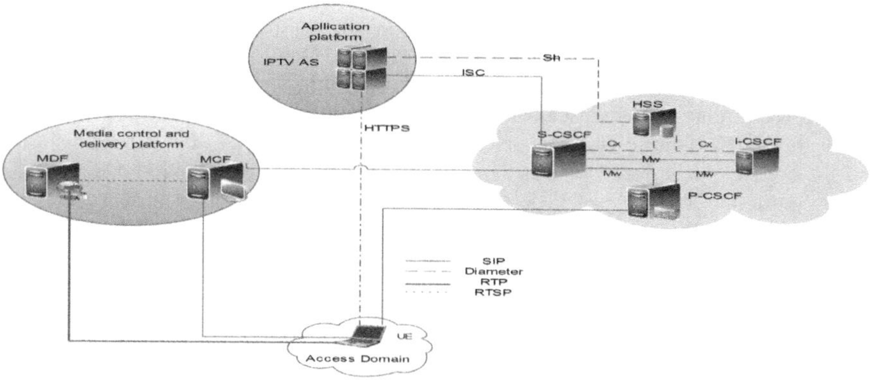

Fig. 1. ETSI TISPAN IMS-based IPTV architecture

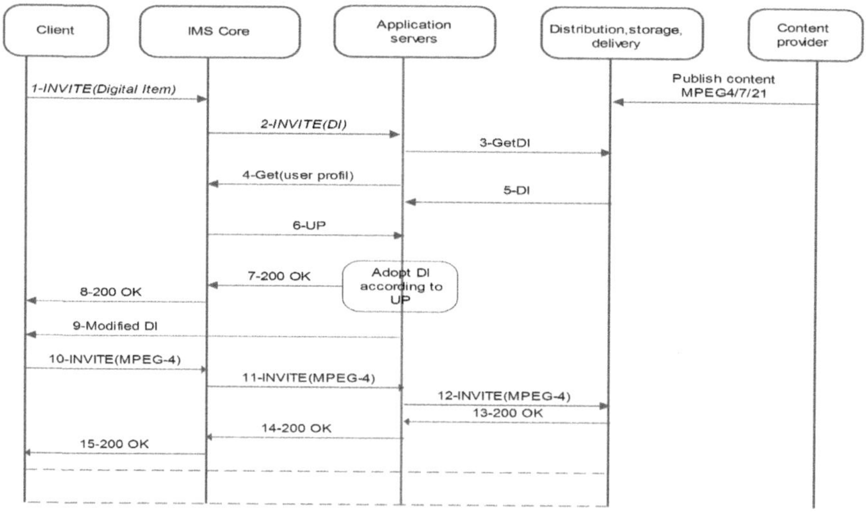

Fig. 2. IMS-based IPTV session

client as an IMS one; its authentication, authorisation and accounting must be made by the IMS functionality [5].the system provides also the support f mobility, interaction with NGN service enabler, service personalisation, adaptation of media [4].over IMS-based IPTV the IPTV stream can be adapted to suit the available network resources and different user terminals. The most concrete framework of this system is the ETSI TISPAN IMS-based IPTV architecture [6] since it is the most widely adopted IMS-based framework in evolving standards and research. Figure 1 shows a simplified IPTV architecture and its operations.

The figure 2 illustrates an example of the interaction between all the entities involved when the user selects a video/channel (the methodology is the same for live and on demand content) for an IMS-based IPTV session.

3 QoS Control in IMS

Quality of Service means the capacity of a network to offer better services for a selected part of the traffic. A policy-based solution is passed by the 3GPP with an objective to satisfy the big challenge by: ensuring that sufficient QoS resources are provided to authorize users in the access network. Before the user can start an IMS session, the UE has to negotiate the media flows for the session with the peering UE according to the service subscription. This is assured with the SIP based signaling in the application-layer signaling plane and the signaling goal is that only those negotiated media flows are allowed to be transmitted in the transport-layer. The policy is applied using a set of policy rules, being each policy rules a set of conditions and a set of actions. The policy rule is stored in the policy repository from which the Policy Decision Point (PDP) retrieves the appropriate policy rules in response to policy events that are triggered by the contracted IP QoS. [14].

4 Our Contribution

IPTV has different video traffic (Broadcast, video on demand, PVR, nPVR) wich has variable data rate due to the dynamic nature of the captured scene and the Encoding process. These types of traffic are different in their sensitivity to latency, if we use an EF behavior[1] to video stream in the DiffServ network there will be a problem because Broadcast video can't support latency compared with VoD/PVR one , and due to the fact that multiple IPTV streams are placed into the same flow aggregate (FA), it is hard to design a maximum limit for traffic policing at the ingress router of a DiffServ domain. if à lot of EF traffic enter into the DiffServ domaine, the core router can cause latency to broadcast packets by serving continuously EF packets at the highest priority, this behavior increases delay. Excessive EF traffic in the core network will therefore lead very fast to full queues and large packet drops [8].

To ovoid this limitation we propose a list of PHBs called IF(IPTV flows) whose classify the packets by priority on based on their sensitivity to latency .we use 3 DSCP bits to recognise the IPTV packets by sensitivity to latency in the same stream.

For IPTV traffic, we will set the three first DSCP bits for all packets, to differentiate between BC, VoD, PVR we will change the other three bits (101xxx), mapping these DSCP values to corresponding PHBs can prioritize BC packets for report those of PVR and VoD.

Our PHBs is defined for high-priority; low latency/loss and jitter traffic is similar to EF.if the resource become insufficient the DiffServ core router will eliminate a packet with precedence from its queue. This way, important packets (broadcast one) have better chances to survive the end-to-end journey. In the case of saturation of the queue, the router proceeds to eliminate packages in the following order: 1← VoD 2←PVR , 3←BC.

To perform DiffServ Code Point (DSCP) markings on the IP packets sent towards the UE, we have implemented the following scenario:Using a modified Linux crtmpserver, which is capable of h.264 video coding and streaming, we analyse each NALU and we set the S_PR value for the current packet depending on the value of NRI field. In the source node (media server), the generation of DSCP values, by translation of S_PR ones, as their association with the corresponding PHB is done by the DSMARK tool which is a queuing discipline. It Is in charge of packet marking in The Linux implementation.

Our test benchmark (Fig 5) consists of the following:

1. Core Router-Linux containing the various components of the IMS (P, I, S-CSCF, HSS) via the solution OpenIMS.
2. One-Edge Linux router that will allow us to connect the application server and the clients to the media Application server. on this router we have installed DSMARK for traffic policing
3. IPTV client.
4. One Linux router that will allow the client to connect to IMS proxy (P-CSCF)
5. Application server that provides services (IPTV_server): BC, PVR, and VoD.
6. A camera as a source of broadcasting traffic.
7. CrtmpServer for encoding in h.264 the flow coming from the camera and stream it to the IPTV client.

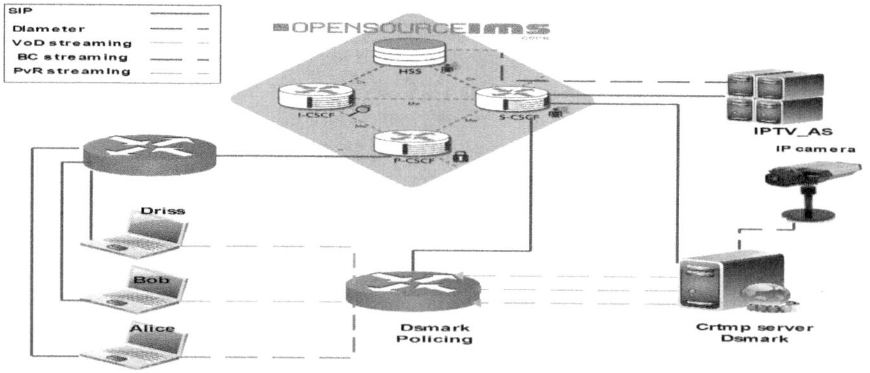

Fig. 3. Our Testbed

To evaluate the importance of policing based on dropping packet, a DiffServ edge router was configured using Linux QoS mechanisms to police traffic according to the DSCP value of each packet. We set the value of DSCP in the video source these values will be used by the edge router to discard excess packet.

4.1 Scenario

Simulation circumstance: we have set up an IP TV CP (Content Provider) system, its inputs contain a movie stored on the disk of the media server (media_AS), a space dedicated to the storage of video recorded by the client through a PvR session, a camera(which filming a movie projected on another PC with a better quality) to provide video that represents the raw material for the sessions BC, its output is H.264.using crtmpserver which can encode the A/V (Audio/Video) signal into H.264.media server receives a video stream in flv, this traffic will undergo encoding in H.264 to give a traffic which will be broadcast to the user alice. the users Bob and driss, successively receiving a stream VoD and PVR using as a source a video stored on the media server.

To identify the traffic, we implemented a Java agent, hosted on the IPTV server, it detects the port and IP address of the client, it communicates this information to the media server to identify packets affected by our policy of marking.

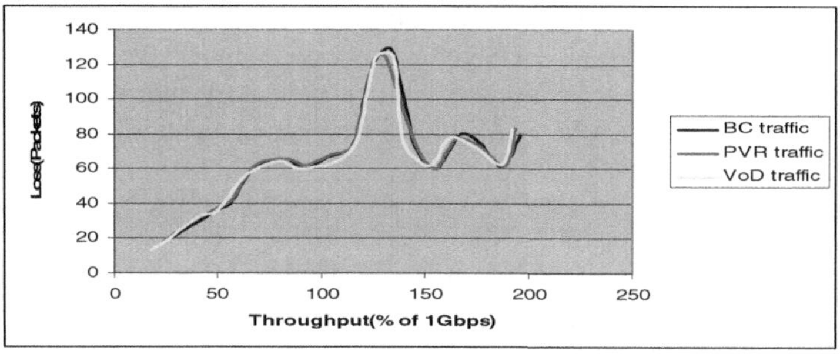

Fig. 4. Latency of BC, PVR and VoD traffics before the change of DSCP values

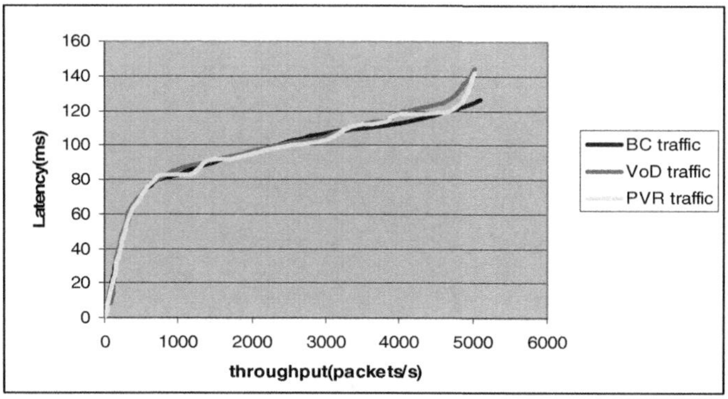

Fig. 5. Loss of BC, PVR and VoD traffics before the change of DSCP values

Fig. 6. Snapshot of the received video (BC video) before the change of DSCP values

Before starting the streaming, the media server must know the state of the router connected to the IPTV client through an XML file sent by the IPTV server to the media one. The parameters sent by the java agent triggered DSMARK at the media server, and the latter (DSMARK), based on the values sent by the socket S_PR, define the DSCP of the packet stream and therefore a corresponding PHB.

The marking done at the media server must be maintained after passing through the Edge router. to do it, DSMARK was installed on this router and it works based on the same filters used by the media server.

These schemes shows the change in latency (Fig 4), Loss(Fig 5) depending on the throughput of the different traffics flow up the IPTV one before applying the new DSCP values. The figure 6 shows the quality of video in this stat.

4.2 Results

After the implementation of our policy of parts marking, we obtained the results shown in Figures 7, 8, and 9.

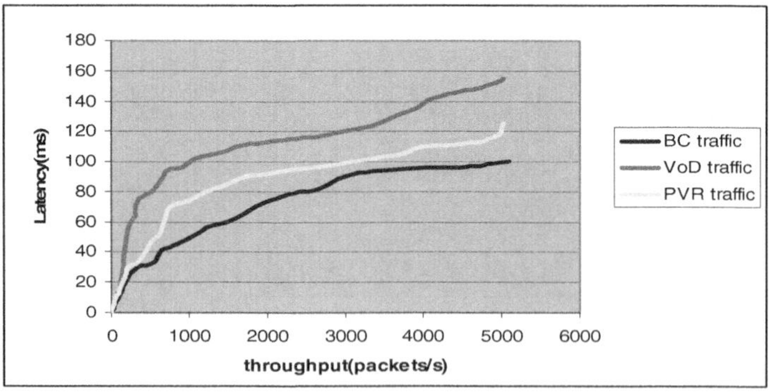

Fig. 7. Latency of BC, PVR and VoD traffics After the change of DSCP values

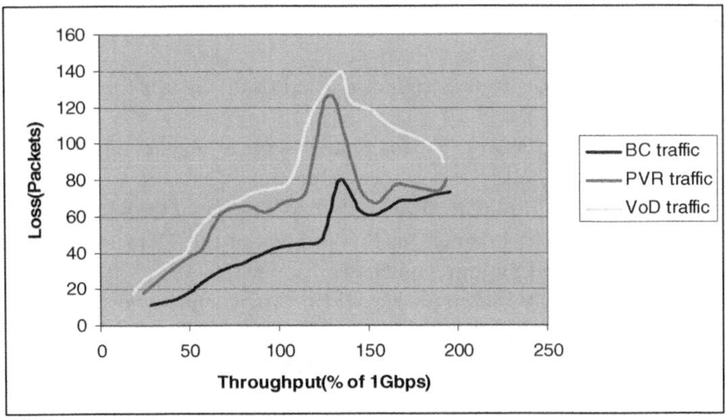

Fig. 8. Loss of BC, PVR and VoD traffics after the change of DSCP values

Fig. 9. Snapshot of the received video (BC video) after the change of DSCP values

5 Conclusions

In this paper, we address a main problem: non differentiation between the BC, VoD, PvR packets. using the new values of DSCP we define new PHB that classifies IPTV packets by their sensitivity to delay, with this solution we improved the Qos of BC traffic in the IMS session, and this improvement can be applied to other traffic based on the charging system.

Reducing the switching time, between the different IPTV sub traffics, is a critical problem to resolve. In general, traffic change times depend on several traffic: command time, network delay time, and MPEG decoder time. For a future work, we focus on optimizing the switching time between broadcast TV, VoD and PVR.

References

1. Grossman, D.: RFC 3260 - New Terminology and Clarifications for DiffServ. IETF (April 2002)
2. Braden, R., Clark, D., Shenker, S.: Integrated Services in the Internet Architecture: an Overview. IETF (June 1994)
3. Ponnappan, A., Yang, L., Pillai, R., Braun, P.: A policy based QoS management system for the IntServ/DiffServ based Internet. In: Proceedings of the Third International Workshop on Policies for Distributed Systems and Networks, pp. 159–168 (2002)
4. Mikoczy, E., et al.: IPTV Services over IMS: Architecture and Standardization. IEEE Comm. Mag. 46, 128–135 (2008)
5. Más, I., et al.: IMS-TV: An IMS-Based Architecture for Interactive, Personalized IPTV. IEEE Comm. 52, 156–163 (2008)
6. ETSI, NGN Functional Architecture Release 1, ES 282 001 V1.1.1. TISPAN (December 2005)
7. Aptixia IxLoad: Video- IGMP, MPEG, RTSP and RTP. Ixia (2007)
8. Armitage, G.: Quality of Service in IP Networks. New Riders Publishing, Indianapolis (2000)
9. IETF, SDP: Session Description Protocol, RFC 4566 (July 2006), http://www.ietf.org/rfc/rfc2327.txt
10. IETF, SIP: Session Initiation Protocol. RFC 3261 (June 2002), http://www.ietf.org/rfc/rfc3621.txt
11. SLA Management Handbook: Document Number: G045. TMF reference GB917 (2004) ISBN: 1-931624-51-8
12. 3588 Diameter Base Protocol (September 2003), http://www.ietf.org/rfc/rfc2748.txt
13. Policy and charging control over Rx reference point (Release 9) 3GPP TS 29.214 V9.0.0 (September 2009), http://www.3gpp.org
14. Ferrus, R., Gelonch, A., Casadevall, F., Pérez, J., Sallent, O., Agusti, R., Nafisi, N.: End-to-end QoS architecture for multi-domain and wireless. Heterogeneous Access Network: the EVEREST Approach (March 2004)
15. Kim, J., Kim, S., Lee, B., Choi, J.: policy-based-control QoS Control for open Service in BcN (February 2005)
16. http://lartc.org/howto/lartc.adv-qdisc.dsmark.html

Seabed Image Texture Analysis Using Subsampled Contourlet Transform

Reza Javidan

Dep. of Computer Engineering and IT, Shiraz University of Technology, Shiraz, Iran
reza.javidan@gmail.com

Abstract. In this paper, a new split and merge algorithm based on the concept of subsampled contourlet transform for automatic segmentation and classification of seafloor images is presented. Contourlet transform is a new extension of the two-dimensional wavelet transform using multiscale and directional filter banks. The subsampled contourlet transform which is introduced by the author is a new version of the contourlet transform that allows analysis of images in square-size coefficients with various resolution levels and directions. It allows analysis of images at various scales as well as directions, which effectively capture smooth contours that are the dominant features in seabed images. The proposed method provides a fast tool with enough accuracy that can be implemented in a parallel structure for real-time processing. In addition, the simulation results are compared with the results of wavelet-based methods as well as other known techniques to show the effectiveness of our proposed algorithm.

Keywords: Seabed, subsampled contourlet transform, texture, segmentation, classification.

1 Introduction

Sonar [1] is a kind of underwater remote sensing system that is used extensively for detecting underwater environment and tracking of different targets using sound signals. Underwater exploration has many applications in different fields such as archaeology, biology, geophysics, cultural resource management, and so on. Today, sonar systems provide near-photographic images of underwater areas, even in zero visibility water [2]. One of the most important applications of sonar systems is the automatic segmentation and classification of the sea bottom area [3]. The segmentation of seafloor sonar images aims to partition the acoustic image into homogeneous regions with respect to certain physical properties or geological characteristics. The goal of the classification task is to assign these different geo-acoustic regions to seafloor types as rocks, sand, pebbles, and etc.

In recent years, for automatic seabed classification, special kinds of sonar systems, i.e., automatic acoustic ground discrimination systems, such as RoxAnn, QTC-View and EchoPlus have been developed [4]; but because of different classification methods, they produce different results for the same region. Some of these systems are susceptible to noise and ship speed. In a large extent, the quality of classification results depends on the skill and experience of the human expert and the intended use of

J.J. Yonazi et al. (Eds.): ICeND 2011, CCIS 171, pp. 337–348, 2011.

the system. In addition, usually sea bottoms having similar acoustic signatures for a particular classification system are not necessarily geologically similar. Therefore, most of acoustic seabed classification systems are essentially empirical devices, which are more or less application oriented and work well for particular cases. In addition, they require intensive calibration (ground truth) when are used to discriminate seabed types [5].

Due to highly textured appearance of sonar images, texture analysis techniques are a common choice for seafloor acoustic images and many researches have been done in this subject [3], [6]-[9]. It has been shown that different transforms, like Fourier and wavelet are valuable for seabed texture analysis. However, the major drawback in the frequency domain is that the time information is lost [10]. On the other hand; one major advantage of wavelet analysis [11] is its ability to perform local analysis for revealing various aspects of data like trends, breakdown points, discontinuities in higher derivatives, and self-similarities .

While seabed images like more natural images contain intrinsic geometrical structures that are key features in image analysis, one major drawback for two-dimensional wavelet is their limited capability in capturing directional information. To overcome this deficiency, researchers have recently come up with a new family of wavelet methods that can capture the intrinsic geometrical structures such as smooth contours in natural images [12]. Some examples include, complex wavelets [13], curvelet transform [14] and contourlet transform [15]. Curvelets are very successful in detecting image activities along curves, while analyzing images at multiple scales, locations, and orientations. While wavelet decomposition captures point discontinuities, directional decomposition links point discontinuities into linear structures. Contourlet transform overcomes directionality lack of 2-D wavelets by geometrically representing smoothness of contours. Contourlet transform allows having different and flexible number of directions at each scale, which makes it a suitable tool for seabed image analysis. In addition, the contourlet transform uses iterated filter banks with computational efficiency. Specifically, it requires $O(N)$ operations for an n-pixel image. Finally, unlike other approaches such as curvelets, contourlet transform starts with discrete-domain construction and then studies its convergence in the continuous domain. The nonsubsampled contourlet transform [16] is a redundant version of contourlet transform which is shift invariant and brings more flexibility, simplicity and accuracy for feature calculation. The subsampled contourlet transform introduced in this paper, is like nonsubsampled contourlet transform, except that it avoids coefficient redundancy at various resolution levels. Unlike standard contourlet transform which does not have square shape coefficients, the subsampled contourlet transform allows practical processing on square-size directional sub-bands that brings more flexibility, simplicity and accuracy for feature calculation. In addition, its multiresolution approach provides capability of using single-sensor system instead of multi-sensor system to distinguish different seabed types which texturally may be very similar but are composed from different sediments.

Common classification algorithms assign each pattern to one and only one cluster. This means that patterns are partitioned into disjoint sets. These algorithms perform well for compact and well-separated classes. However, in most realistic cases, especially in seabed classification, the distributions of two clusters usually overlap in feature space. The boundaries between different classes cannot be defined in specified directions in a clear-cut fashion. One reason is that the feature vector is computed over windows which might simultaneously cover different seafloor types, resulting a mixture of classes. Another reason is the ambiguity that exists between the definitions of for example, rocks and pebbles [17].

In this paper, a modified split and merge algorithm based on the concept of the subsampled contourlet transform for segmentation and classification of the seabed images is presented. We also show that energies of the transformed coefficients are significant features for our application. The classification is done directly on the blocks of the image and the boundaries produced between known classes (coarse segmentation) are refined to enhance the results. We aim to develop a fast algorithm with enough accuracy for real-time processing of textural images of huge size. The main contribution of this work is that the presented method can be used to construct a new seabed ground discrimination system. The novelty of this approach is demonstrated by comparing the results with the results obtained in wavelet domain as well as other well-known methods.

The content of this paper is organized as follows: In Section 2, the subsampled contourlet transform is briefly explained. Our new approach for automatic segmentation and classification of sea bottom based on the subsampled contourlet transform is presented in Section 3. Experimental results are given and discussed in Section 4. Finally, Section 5 will complete this paper by presenting remarks and conclusions.references.

2 The Subsampled Contourlet Transform

The contourlet transform is a new two-dimensional extension of the wavelet transform proposed by Do and Vetterli [15] using multiscale and directional filter banks with critical down-sampling operation. The contourlet expansion is composed of basis images oriented at various directions in multiple scales, with flexible aspect ratio that could effectively capture smooth contours of images. The contourlet transform, , as illustrated in Fig. 1(a), employs an efficient tree structured implementation, which is an iterated combination of the Laplacian Pyramid (LP) [18], for capturing the point discontinuities, and the Directional Filter Bank (DFB) [19], to gather the nearby basis functions and link point discontinuities into linear structures. Since the DFB was designed to capture the high frequency directionality of the input image and it is poor on handling low frequency content, hence the DFB is combined with the LP, where the low frequencies of the input image is removed before applying DFB. It has been shown that the discrete contourlet transform is shift variant, and achieves perfect reconstruction and has a redundancy ratio that is less than 4/3 [12].

This transform uses a structure similar to that of curvelets [14], except at discrete domain. To mathematically define this transform, let us define a curvelet as being indexed by three parameters: a scale parameter a; $0<a<1$; an orientation $\theta, \theta \in [-\pi/2, \pi/2]$, and a location parameter b; $b \in R^2$. At scale a, the family of curvelets is generated by translation and rotation of a basic element φ_a:

$$\varphi_{a,b,\theta}(x) = \varphi_a(R_\theta - b)) \tag{1}$$

where R_θ is a rotation by θ radians and φ_a is a type of directional wavelet with spatial width a, spatial length $\sqrt{a}$, and with minor axis pointing towards the horizontal direction:

$$\varphi_a(x) \approx \varphi(D_a x)$$
$$D_a = \begin{bmatrix} 1/a & 0 \\ 0 & 1/\sqrt{a} \end{bmatrix} \tag{2}$$

where D_a is a parabolic scaling matrix.

The nonsubsampled contourlet transform [16] is a redundant expansion of the contourlet transform to allow practical processing on equal-sized directional sub-bands. The redundancy is achieved by discarding any down-sampling operation in the Laplacian pyramid scheme. We modified this transform by doing down-sampling at each scale to have the chance of multiresolution analysis on square-size directional sub-bands. We can imagine that the subsampled contourlet transform is similar to the standard contourlet transform without using shearing operator and coefficient re-arrangement. Fig. 1 (b) displays an overview of the proposed subsampled contourlet transform while Fig. 1 (c) shows the frequency division of the subsampled contourlet decomposition, where the whole spectrum is divided both angularly and radially and the number of directions is increased with frequency. Fig. 2 shows an example of a real seabed image and its corresponding three levels pyramidal nonsubsampled contourlet transform with 12 directional bandpass sub-bands.

3 The Proposed Approach

The task of a seabed recognition system is to assign class labels to each of the image pixels, efficiently and accurately. Seabed images usually cover a large extent of area and may contain different types of textures. Therefore, they should be segmented into different classified regions. Fig. 3 illustrates block diagram of the proposed algorithm. Three levels nonsubsampled contourlet transform with 12 directional sub-bands are applied to the original image. Three-level subsampled contourlet transform with 12 directional sub-bands is applied to the original image. The transform coefficients in different sub-bands are used for texture analysis. For an original image of size $N \times N$, the coefficients are divided into $M \times M$ $(2 < M < N/4)$ blocks and energy value of each block is calculated to construct the feature vector. Euclidean distance classifier [20] is used for classification of each block. Following block classification, a coarse segmented image is produced. The process is repeated for each of three subsampled contourlet transform coefficients to construct three segmented images with three different resolutions. Finally, three segmented images are merged and the boundaries are refined to produce the final result. The details of the proposed scheme are discussed in the following subsections.

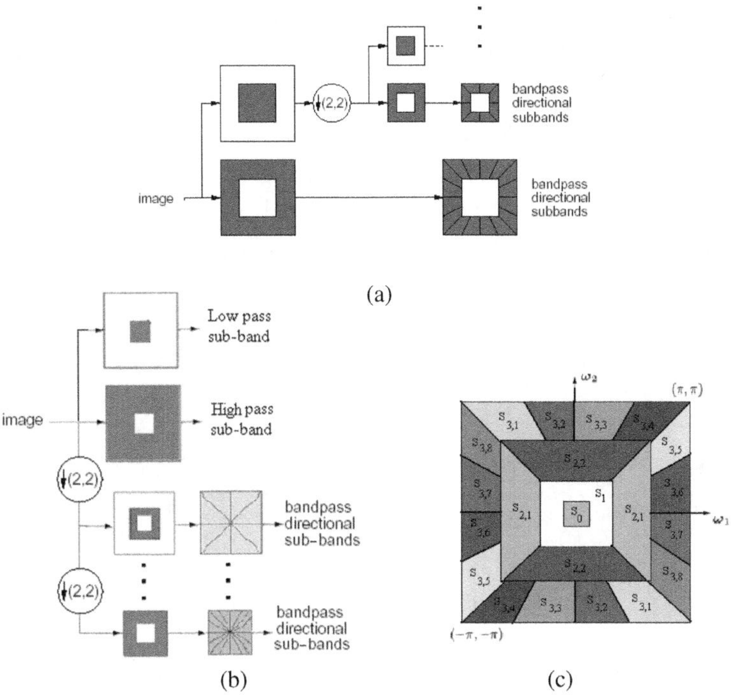

Fig. 1. (a) The block diagram of the standard contourlet transform. (b) Subsampled filter bank structure of the subsampled contourlet transform. (c) The idealized frequency partitioned for for 3 levels with 12 directional bandpass sub-bands of the subsampled contourlet transform.

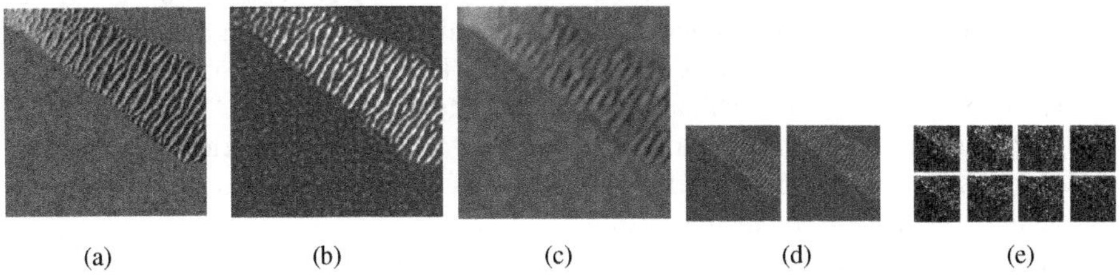

Fig. 2. (a) Original real seabed image. The result of three-level subsampled contourlet transform with 12 directional bandpass sub-bands: (b) s_1 . (c) s_0. (d) s_{21}, s_{22}. (e) $s_{31} \ldots s_{38}$.

3.1 Methodology

Following the block diagram of Fig. 3, the seabed image acquired from a sonar system is first transformed. To completely perform the transformation, several parameters must be precisely selected. The number of levels of Laplacian pyramid decomposition, the number of directional decompositions to perform on each pyramid level, and the filters to use in each of these analyses must be chosen. In this research three levels of decomposition are considered using maxflat filters [16]. Three directional decompositions are performed in the lowest pyramid level, using dmaxflat7 filters [16]. Therefore, based on Fig. 1 (c), we obtain 12 directional bandpass sub-bands (8 at level 3, 2 at level 2, 1 at level 1, and 1 at level 0). Let $S_{0,0}$ be the low-pass sub-band, and $S_{1,1}$, $S_{2,1} \cdots S_{2,2}$, and $S_{3,1} \cdots S_{3,8}$ be bandpass directional sub-bands at the first, second, and third level of decomposition, respectively. Since $S_{0,0}$ and $S_{1,1}$ have the same resolution size, we use them together to construct the highest resolution segmented image. On the other hand, $S_{2,1} \cdots S_{2,2}$ and $S_{3,1} \cdots S_{3,8}$ are used to construct the segmented image with medium and lowest resolution, respectively.

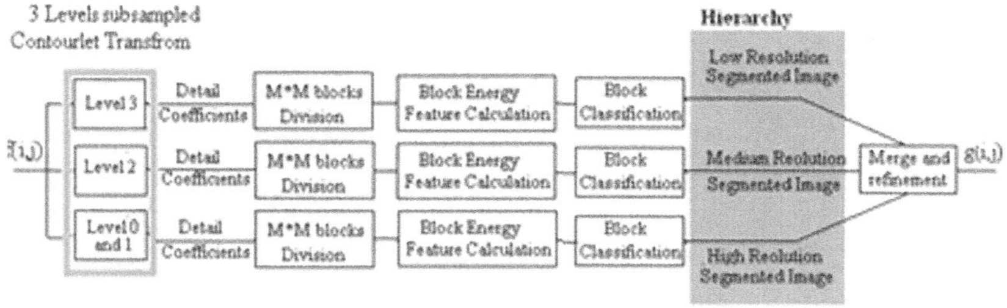

Fig. 3. Block diagram of the proposed method

A general pattern recognition paradigm achieves this task in two stages: first feature extraction and then, classification. We experimentally observed that local energy of the nonsubsampled contourlet coefficients provide good separated feature space. Since the energy of natural textures is mainly concentrated in the mid-frequencies, contourlet transform can preserve most of the original signal energy and can provide more reliable description of the texture [10]. Hence different textures have different energy in the detail sub-bands and this energy can be seen as a magnitude of oscillation of contourlet coefficients for each sub-band. This can also be observed from the compression property of the nonsubsampled contourlet transform, where the transform of a given image consists of small number of large coefficients (high energy) and a large number of small coefficients (low energy). Then, the distribution of energy can be selected as a valuable feature.

The coefficients of all sub-bands are partitioned into non-overlapping blocks of size $M \times M$. The choice of block size used to estimate the local energy feature provides a trade-off in terms of the computational complexity and the accuracy of the results. Using small block size, we can estimate the energy more accurately near the borders and in the small regions, but we have higher energy variability compared with the use of a large window size. On the other hand, using large block size provides enough information in the large regions, but performs poorly near the borders between the textures and in the small regions. The size M also depends on the resolution of seabed textures. The finer the texture is, the smaller the size M should be selected. In this research and due to the type of images obtained from our sonar system, M is chosen to be 4.

Squared root of average energy of the nonsubsampled contourlet coefficients of the $M \times M$ block on each sub-band is calculated as:

$$E_{u,v}(x,y)=\sqrt{\frac{\sum_{i=x}^{x+M-1}\sum_{j=y}^{y+M-1} S_{u,v}^{\;2}(i,j)}{M^2}} \tag{3}$$

The process starts from top left corner of each sub-band and continuing in raster scan manner to form the feature vector $\underline{E}_{u,v}$ with size $N/_M \times N/_M$, where the original image is of size $N \times N$. For three levels of decomposition, the resulting nonsubsampled contourlet feature vector $\underline{\theta}$ consists of 12 energy feature vector, is given by (4).

$$\underline{\theta}=[\underline{E}_{0,0},\underline{E}_{,11},\underline{E}_{2,1}..\underline{E}_{2,2},\underline{E}_{3,1}...,\underline{E}_{3,8}] \tag{4}$$

Euclidean distance [20] of feature block values is used for the block classification. Our experiments show that using other types of distance measurements such as Mahabolis distance [20] did not improve the result much better, except increasing the simulation time. If $\underline{\theta}_p$ and $\underline{\theta}_q$ are the feature vectors of a given image under classification *(p)*, and a known image class *(q)*, respectively, the Euclidean distance between them is given by (5).

$$d_{Euclidean}(\underline{\theta}_p,\underline{\theta}_q)=\sqrt{\frac{1}{r}\sum_{u,v}(E^p{}_{u,v}-E^q{}_{u,v})^2} \tag{5}$$

where r=12 is the number of feature values and $E^p{}_{u,v}$ and $E^q{}_{u,v}$ denote the corresponding feature vector values for image *p* and *q* respectively. .

Each block is classified according to the (5) and the classification process should be repeated for all blocks of the input image. It can also be done in parallel to save time in a real-time environment. After block classification, the input image is segmented block-wise, which is called "crisp segmentation".

3.2 Boundary Refinement

Crisp segmentation algorithms assign each pattern to one and only one cluster. This means that patterns are partitioned into disjoint sets. These algorithms perform well for compact and well-separated classes. However, in most realistic cases, especially in seabed classification, the distributions of two clusters usually overlap in feature space and the boundaries between different classes in the feature space cannot be defined explicitly. Therefore, it is necessary to refine the crisp segmentation result. Since different textures are revealed at different scales, the hierarchy composed of three coarse segmented images obtained from three-level subsampled contourlet decomposition should be merged and the boundaries between classified regions must be refined. To do this, the following algorithm, originally presented by Javidan in [3], with some minor modifications is used. This modified algorithm is another contribution of this paper since it gives good results for the subsampled contourlet decomposition as well.

a. Block refinement: The main purpose of this part is to compare the class label of a block with the labels of its neighbors and modify it if necessary. At this point, block refinement is performed on each of three segmented images of the hierarchy, separately. Consider each $M \times M$ non-overlapping block in any of the segmented images. Again *M* is chosen to be 4 as the same value as considered previously. Like a major vote system, if the block's class label is identical to that of the all four-connected block neighbors, do nothing. Otherwise, if all four-connected neighborhood blocks or at least three of them have the same class label, replace the class label of centered block with the class label of its major neighbors. This process should be done block-wise in a raster scan fashion, from top left corner of the image.

b. Image size expansion: Because of the decimated (down sampling) property of the subsampled contourlet decomposition, the size (dimension) of the segmented image of level three of the decomposition is one quarter of the size of the segmented image at level one and the level two is one half of the size of the level one as well. As a result, the level three and level two must be expanded to the size of level one before merging. Remember that the size of the segmented image obtained from level one of the decomposition is equal to the size of the original image.

c. Merging of three segmented images: Following dimension expansion, scan all pixels (points) of the three segmented images simultaneously from top left corner to the bottom right corner in a raster scan form. For each point of the new constructed image assign a class label that exists in the corresponding points of at least two images of the three segmented images. Otherwise, select the class label of the corresponding point of the lowest resolution segmented image obtained from level two of the subsampled contourlet decomposition. In other words, in cases of no agreement between finer segmentation results obtained from level one and level two (i.e. there are differences between details of regions of the image under segmentation), the coarser segmentation obtained from level 3 which contains less details, gives the most discriminate.

d. Boundary pixel refinement: Scan all points of the resulted image obtained in previous part from top left corner in raster scan form. Consider the pixels of boundaries of adjacent texture regions and test to see if they are similar with all 4-connected neighbors. If any point on the boundary (edge) is evaluated to be of different class label from at least one of its 4-connected neighbors, the class label of that point in the new constructed image should be changed. This change should be based on the equivalent class label of the corresponding point in the original fine segmented image obtained from level one of the subsampled contourlet transform (because it contains detail information of the regions). Otherwise, leave the class label of the new constructed image to be the same as the class label of that point of the merged image.

e. Deleting disconnected islands: The isolated regions with small area should be deleted from the merged image obtained in previous part. Discard any disconnected region which has area less than a known threshold by replacing it with its neighbors. This threshold relates to the sonar image resolution.

4 Experimental Results

To validate our method of automatic seabed classification, the experiments carried out with real sonar images, which were provided by a sidescan sonar, namely the DUBM41, whose frequency is around 500 KHz [17]. A sample image of this sonar system shown in Fig. 2 is used for evaluation of the proposed algorithm and the results are shown in Fig. 4. Using a standard Sobel operator, pure edge of segmentation results is extracted and the final superimposed results are shown in Fig. 4. Fig. 4 (a) and 4 (b) show the segmentation results using energy features of the subsampled contourlet coefficients with Euclidean distance, and the energy feature of the redundant wavelet transform coefficients with Euclidean distance classifier respectively.

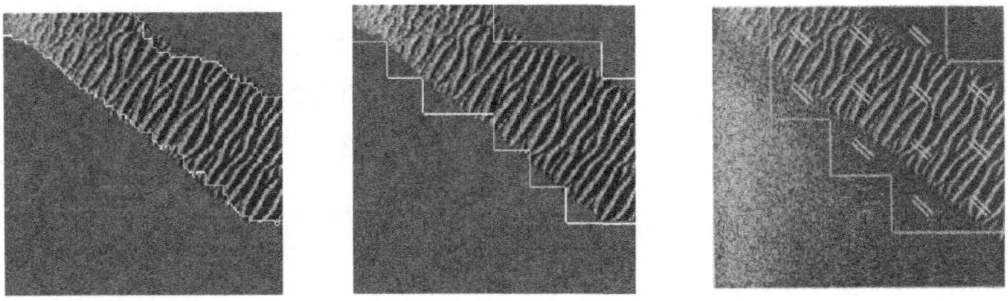

(a) (b) (c)

Fig. 4. (a) Segmentation results of Fig. 2 (a) using energy features of the nonsubsampled contourlet coefficients with Euclidean distance classifier. (b) The segmentation result using energy feature of the redundant wavelet transform coefficients with Euclidean distance classifier. (c) The result of Mignotte method [17].

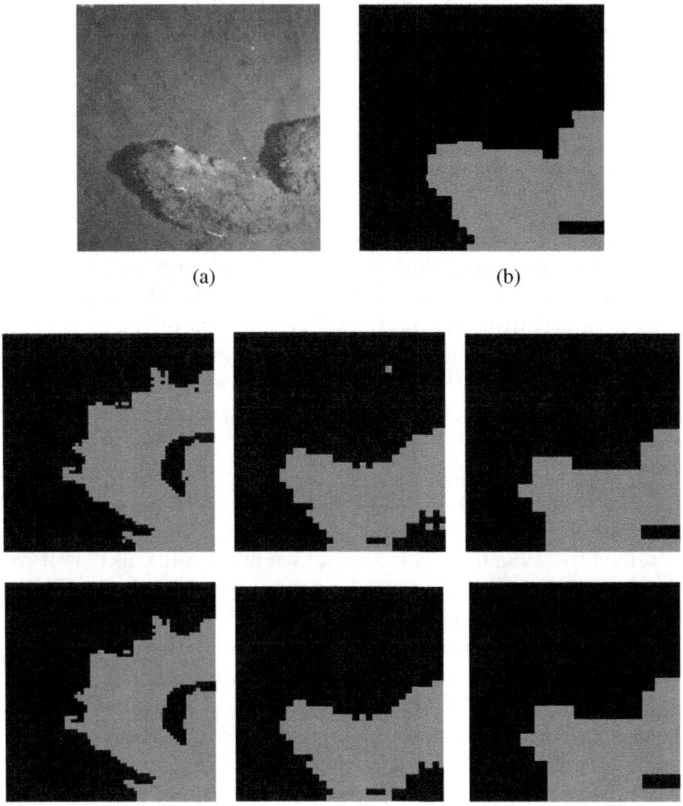

(a) (b)

(c) (d) (e)

Fig. 5. (a) Original seabed image. (b) The final segmentation result where classified regions are shown with different gray levels. (c),(d) and (e) The intermediate segmentation results of level one, level two and level three of subsampled contourlet coefficients, respectively. Upper: the original segmentation result; lower: the segmentation result after applying the refinement algorithm and before merging.

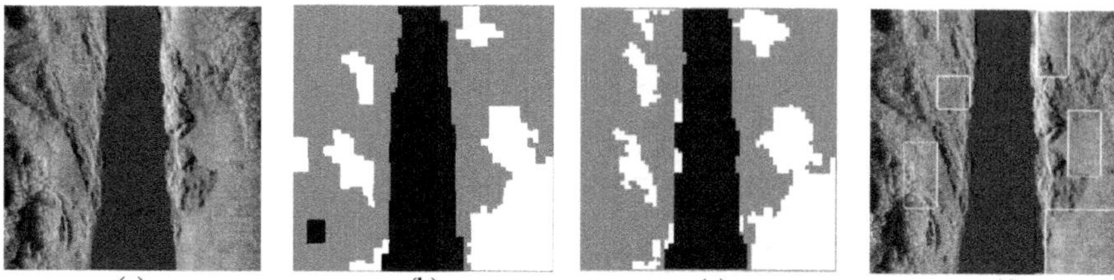

(a) (b) (c) (d)

Fig. 6. A real sidescan sonar image: (a) Original image. (b) The final segmentation result using the proposed method based on subsampled contourlet transform. (c) The segmentation result using energy features of the wavelet transform coefficients with fuzzy approach [21]. (d) The segmentation result based on block by block classification of the original image using two-level standard wavelet transform with energy features and Euclidean classifier.

Mignotte and Collet [17] proposed a method for classification of seabed using high resolution sidescan sonar images. Their method consists of four stages: extracting shadows, shape parameter vectors computation, classification with a fuzzy classifier, and finally, refining the result using Markov random field model. For comparison, their result for the same seabed image is shown in Fig. 4 (c). It can be seen that our proposed segmentation method, is more accurate with extracting better boundaries from perceptual point of view.

As one more example, another seabed image and its corresponding segmentation results are shown in Fig. 5. The image of Fig. 5(a) is composed of boulders (right side) and rippled muddy sand (left side). The final segmentation result is shown in Fig. 5(b). For better understanding of the proposed method, the intermediate segmentation results obtained from the three-level resolutions of the subsampled contourlet coefficients are also depicted above Fig. 5(c), 5(d) and 5(e), respectively. The results after the refinement process (Section 3.2) and before merging are shown below the same figures. The final segmentation result shows acceptable accuracy especially on the boundaries.

Figure 6(a) shows a real sidescan sonar image from seabed. The segmentation result using the proposed method based on energy features of the subsampled contourlet coefficients is shown in Fig. 6(b). For comparison, the segmentation result using another method presented by Javidan in [3] is also shown in Fig. 6(c). Its classification approach is based on energy features of the standard wavelet transform coefficients with fuzzy approach. In addition, the usual segmentation result based on block by block classification of the original image using two-level standard wavelet transform with energy features and Euclidean distance classifier is shown in Fig. 6(d). It is cleared that the segmentation result obtained in subsampled contourlet domain is more accurate than that of the wavelet domain, while the same feature set and distance metric are used.

The structure of the proposed algorithm as shown in Fig. 1 is parallel and it can be used in a real time acoustic ground discrimination system. However, the algorithm is fast enough to be implemented on a personnel computer (PC). In a typical PC with 3 GHz AMD 64 CPU and 1 GB RAM and 128 MB PCIX graphic card, a block of size 32×32 will be classified in less than 0.0104 seconds and the average elapsed time for segmentation of an image of size 512×512 is 7.0204 seconds. This time includes the time required for the classification as well as extracting both feature sets of the contourlet coefficients.

5 Conclusions

In this paper, a new split and merge algorithm based on the concept of subsampled contourlet transform for segmentation and classification of the seabed images is presented. The contourlet transform appears to be a suitable tool for this task, because it allows analysis of images at various levels of scales as well as directions.

It was shown that subsampled contourlet transform derived energy features, are effective tools for texture separation. Most of examined pairs of textures could be separated by this feature with acceptable classification error. The post processing performance that relies on refinement approach has been demonstrated to be able to enhance contourlet crisp segmentation and give better results than other well known techniques from the point of view of speed of execution, complexity of calculations and the final accuracy. The main advantage of the proposed method is a relatively small vector of features, which is sufficient for texture classification. In addition, it is fast enough to be implemented for real time analysis in a new acoustic seabed ground discrimination system.

References

1. Reza, J., Jones Ian, S.F.: High Resolution Acoustic Imaging of Archaeological Artifacts in Fluid Mu. In: International Congress on the Application of Recent Advances in Underwater Detection and Survey Techniques to Underwater Archeology, Turkey, May 3-7 (2004)
2. Reza, J., Eghbali Hasan, J.: Seabed Textural Image restoration and Noise Removal Using Genetic Programming. In: 5th International Conference on Marine Researches and Transportation, Italy, September 19-21 (2005)
3. Reza, J., Eghbali Hasan, J.: Automatic Seabed Texture Segmentation and Classification Based on Wavelet Transform and Fuzzy Approach. International Journal of the Society for Underwater Technology 27(2), 51–55 (2007)
4. Loncarevic, B.D., Courtney, R.C., Fader, G.B.J., Piper, D.J.W., Williamson Costello, A.: Use of acoustics in remote sensing of the seabed. Hydro International 2(3) (1998)
5. Hamilton, L.J., Mulhearn, P.J., Poeckert, R.: A comparison of RoxAnn and QTC-view acoustic bottom classification system performance for the Carins area; Great Barrier Reef; Australia. Continental Shelf Research 19(12), 1577–1597 (1999)
6. Reza, J., Masnadi-Shirazi, M.A., Azimifar, Z.: Contourlet-Based Acoustic Sea-bed Ground Discrimination System. In: Proceedings of IEEE International Conference on Information & Communication Technologies: from Theory to Applications, April 7-11 (2008)
7. Reza, J.: Wavelet-Based Acoustic Seabed Ground Discrimination System. In: Proceedings of IEEE International Conference on Information & Communication Technologies: from Theory to Applications, Paris, July 7-10 (2010)
8. Reza, J., Masnadi-Shirazi, M.A., Azimifar, Z.: Seabed Image Texture Segmentation and Classification Based on Nonsubsampled Contourlet Transfrom. In: 13th Int'l CSI Computer Conference (CSICC 2008), March 9-11. Springer, Heidelberg (2008)
9. Xiaoou, T.: Optical and sonar image classification: wavelet packet trasform vs. Fourier transform. Computer Vision and Image Undersanding 79, 25–46 (2000)
10. Arivazhagan, S., Ganesan, L.: Texture Classification Using Wavelet Transform. Pattern Recognition Letters 24, 1513–1521, 3197–3203 (2003)

11. Stephane, M.: A wavelet Tour of Signal Processing, 2nd edn. Academic Press, London (1999)
12. Po Duncan, D.-Y., Do Minh, N.: Directional Multiscale Modeling of Images using the Contourlet Transform. IEEE Trans. on Image Proc. 15(6), 1610–1620 (2006)
13. Kingsbury, N.: Complex wavelets for shift invariant analysis and filtering of signals. Journal of Appl. and Comput. Harmonic Analysis 10, 234–253 (2001)
14. Candès, E.J., Donoho, D.L.: Curvelets – a surprisingly effective nonadaptive representation for objects with edges. In: Cohen, A., Rabut, C., Schumaker, L.L. (eds.) Curve and Surface Fitting. Vanderbilt University Press, Saint-Malo (2000)
15. Do Minh, N., Martin, V.: The contourlet transform: an efficient directional multiresolution image representation. IEEE Transactions on Image Processing 14(12), 2091–2106 (2005)
16. Cunha Arthur, L., Jianping, Z., Do Minh, N.: The Nonsubsampled Contourlet Transform: Theory, Design, and Applications. IEEE Transaction on Image Processing (May 2005)
17. Mignotte, M., Collet, C., Perez, P., Bouthemy, P.: Markov Random Field and Fuzzy Logic Modeling in Sonar Imagery: Application to the classification of underwater floor. Computer Vision and Image Understanding 79, 4–24 (2000)
18. Burt, P.J., Adelson, E.H.: The Laplacian pyramid as a compact image code. IEEE Transaction on Communication 31(4), 532–540 (1983)
19. Bamberger, R.H., Smith, M.J.T.: A filter bank for the directional decomposition of images: theory and design. IEEE Transaction on Signal Processing 40, 882–893 (1992)
20. Duda Richard, O., Hart Peter, E., Stork David, G.: Pattern Classification. John Wiley and Sones Inc., Chichester (1998)

Secure Interleaving– Physical Layer Security Enhancement of OFDM Based System

Muhammad Asif Khan, Varun Jeoti, and Rana Shahid Manzoor

Department of Electrical and Electronic Engineering,
Universiti Teknologi, PETRONAS, Malaysia
asf_kh@yahoo.com, shahid432001@yahoo.com,
varun_jeoti@petronas.com.my

Abstract. Interleavers are typically used to distribute burst of errors, so they appear as simple random errors. Alternatively, if interleaving patterns are kept secure, then these patterns can be introduced as a physical (PHY) layer security device. In this paper, an efficient technique to introduce security at physical (PHY) layer is proposed to enhance the security of 802.11i, which is designed to improve the security at medium access control. Since it does not emphasize on availability therefore several denial of service (DoS) attacks are possible. The DoS attacks are easy to mount because management and control frames are unprotected and so are MAC headers. This paper proposes a secure seed based random interleaving technique to scramble the OFDM constellation symbols to encrypt data transmission to resist these malicious attacks. In order to analyze the suitability of proposed technique as PHY layer security device key-sensitivity analysis is carried out. The scrambling is completely reversible with the use of appropriate key. However, use of a wrong initial condition even at 4th decimal point produces entirely different sequence resulting in erroneous constellations with equal probability. To analyze the effectiveness of proposed technique various security attacks are analyzed in detail.

1 Introduction

The exponentially growing popularity of wireless communication and its wide deployment in homes, small office/home office (SOHO) and enterprises is due to its mobility, flexibility, ease of use and low cost. As the Wireless LAN is not physically connected as wired LAN (is,) and (since) wireless signals can be intercepted with moderate equipment available to the attacker for manipulation, hence it demands greater security for WLAN. For connection establishment between access point (AP) and client the transmitted frames contain unprotected information for ease of both AP and client. Attacker manipulates these unprotected frames to mount number of crypto and denial of service attacks (DoS). The DoS attacks include flooding the network with authentication request/respond, association request/respond and in response it can jam the network for traffic [11, 12]. Much of the research and publications are being done on DoS attacks due to an increased reputation of WLAN usage [10, 12-19].

Encryption is usually done on MAC layer, where encryption is applied only at bit stream level to protect only data frames. The services or building blocks of PHY layer

J.J. Yonazi et al. (Eds.): ICeND 2011, CCIS 171, pp. 349–361, 2011.

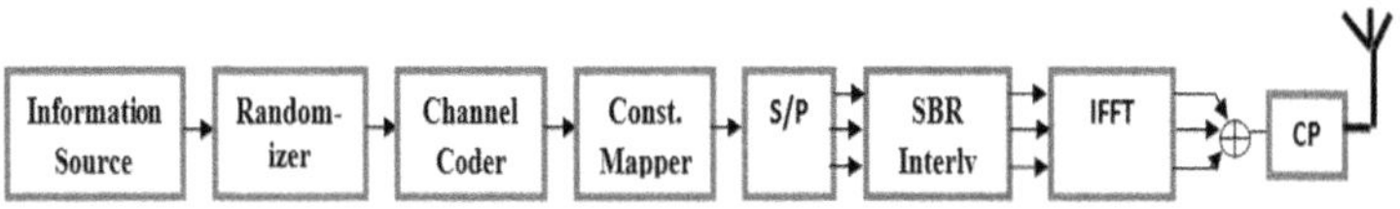

Fig. 1. Block diagram of proposed SBR Interleaver as a PHY layer security device for OFDM system

include coding, interleaving patterns and modulation schemes which are kept unprotected for the purpose to recover the transmitted information correctly at the receiver. The unprotected PHY layer information such as interleaving patterns, modulation and coding is an open invitation for an attacker to sneak into the system.

The future of WLAN is coming up with new standards like 802.11r, 802.11k, 802.11n, which burden up management and control frames by extending the functionality with sensitive information including radio resource data, location based identifier and fast roaming information. Meanwhile the task group of 802.11w is also working to strengthen the security of management and control frames at PHY layer against DoS attacks [20]. Moreover researchers are contributing with ideas to improve 802.11w [1] and securing management frames to avoid DoS attacks.

For reliable and secure data transmission in wireless communication systems interleaver is exploited. Interleaving is the process of rearranging the ordering of data sequence. The basic premise of interleaver is to decorrelate the adjacent bits/symbols so that burst of errors should appear as random as possible. Furthermore, techniques employed to interleaver the input data should be known at receiver side to efficiently restore the original data/sequence. Alternatively, interleaver can be introduced as a PHY layer security device if interleaving patterns are kept secure. Interleaving methods are based on one function or seed based design to interleave the transmitted data. The analysis of various interleavers in terms of their design and complexity has been discussed in detail in [3]. In seed based or pseudo random design, changing input seed can generate different interleaving patterns. Pseudo random source is based on initial conditions/seeds which are used as a key to generate random sequences. For secure interleaving two points should be considered. First, choice of random source that should generates good random sequences. Secondly the interleaving methods should exploit these sequences in such a way that it should retain unpredictability after interleaving. Interleaver should have inherent properties, such as spread and dispersion, to retain good interleaving sequences [9]. By combining both points, one can generate near optimal and secure interleaving sequence which is considered as a strong candidate to introduce as a PHY layer security device. Input seed can be used as a key to initialize interleaving patterns therefore with a different key at the receiver side de-interleaving becomes infeasible.

Wireless LAN (WLAN) is vulnerable to number of passive and active attacks [4]. All these attacks disrupt data transmission of WLAN. IEEE 802.11i, the security standard for wireless LAN, provides effective data confidentiality, mutual authentication and integrity to secure against active and passive attacks. However, it is still susceptible to DoS attacks because, at MAC layer, some of the information are left unprotected i.e., the MAC header, management frames and control frames. The attacker eavesdrop these frames to initialize attacks. Most of the work reported in the literature is focused on enhancing the security at MAC layer [5, 6]. As security is a function of higher layers, PHY layer is also vulnerable to DoS attacks. An adversary can snoop through transmitted frames to disrupt the network and/or can jam the traffic passing through the network. Hence, it is appropriate to introduce PHY security in order to make WLAN robust, to some extent, against such attacks.

In this paper, seed based random (SBR) interleaver is designed and introduced as a PHY layer security device. The proposed SBR interleaver is exploited after the constellation mapper to scramble OFDM constellation symbols. The inherent logic to design SBR interleaver is based on two building blocks. First is to generate random sequences and second is to design scrambling matrix. The proposed interleaver is designed in such a way that it has inherent properties to generate secure unpredictable sequences with any random source. All interleaving patterns are reversible using the same key at receiver end. For our proposed design, external secret key is obtained using 802.11i key management protocol. The distortion in air medium cannot affect the scrambling, small changes in initial condition that generate scrambled matrixes, as decoding and synchronization techniques are used to recover the data accurately. For comparison, random sequences are generated using RAND function in MATLAB and chaotic logistic map (CLM). Chaotic sequences are used to generate the SBR Interleaver in the later part of this study.

This paper is organized in 4 sections which are as follows: Section 2 describes the design of proposed seed based random interleaver. Section 3 describes security analysis and the last section concludes the paper.

2 Seed Based Random Interleaver

In order to design proposed SBR Interleaver, scrambling matrix is designed. The scrambler makes use of random sequences uniquely generated by using an input seed to initialize proposed technique. The SBR Interleaver design method has inherent properties for near optimal performance. The design allows us to use a unique random sequence. As mentioned earlier, this can be generated by using either a RAND function of MATLAB or by using chaotic logistic map (CLM).

The proposed SBRS was first designed using RAND function of MATLAB®. MATLAB® employs three generator algorithms using RAND function to generate random number. The syntax to use random generator is *RAND ('method', S).* The random sequences generated are based on given *'method'* in MATLAB®, and initialized by the state of the generator. In MATLAB® the *'method'* uses *State*, *Seed* and *Twister* to generate sequences.

The chaotic logistic map (CLM) is a well known 1-D chaotic map. Since the chaotic logistic map is convenient to implement, we have selected it for demonstrating our scrambling algorithm. However, it should be noted that even other 1-D chaotic maps can be employed for scrambling purposes – maps which have uniform probability distribution functions such as piecewise linear chaotic maps [7].

The chaotic logistic map is given by (3)

$$x_{n+1} = rx_n(1 - x_n) \tag{3}$$

where $0 < x_n < 1$ and $3.57 < r < 4$

By iterating the chaotic logistic map with a unique initial value $0 < x_0 < 1$ one can generate a unique sequence of random real numbers whose values lie between 0 and 1.

Our proposed SBR Interleaver has same performance using both pseudo random and chaotic sequences. For demonstration, the SBR Interleaver algorithm uses chaotic logistic map to generate scrambling matrix.

2.1 The Algorithm

In simple terms, scrambling is a technique to change the positions of input data elements. In our proposed scheme, each input data element is scrambled. Our aim is to generate scrambling matrix, *S*, of size $N \times N$ where *N* denotes the number of input data elements to be scrambled:

$$S = \{S_i, S_{i+1}, \cdots, S_N\}^T \tag{4}$$

where '*S*' denotes the scrambling matrix, and S_i is a row vector with $N-1$ zeros and only one 1. The position of '1' in row vector S_i denotes the position of ith input element after scrambling.

$$S_i(P_i) = 1 \tag{5}$$

where P_i, a position vector denotes the position of '1' in row vector S_i .The position vector P_i is generated by iterating chaotic logistic map.

The design methodology to get the position vector in order to generate the scrambling matrix is as follows [8].

a) Divide the output range [0.1, 0.9] into *N* equal length subintervals, where '*N*' denotes the number of input data elements to be scrambled. Hence, during the iteration of chaotic map, the output of CLM that occurs outside of considered range will be neglected.

b) Label each region sequentially from $0,\dots, N$. Let the length of each region be denoted by ΔL. Now, let us denote the first region by $R_0 = [0.1, \Delta L]$, second region by $R_1 = (0.1+\Delta L, 0.1+2\Delta L]$, 3rd region by $R_2 = (0.1+2\Delta L, 0.1+3\Delta L]$, and last region by $R_N = (0.1+N\Delta L-\Delta L, 0.1+N\Delta L]$. Now, label each region sequentially, i.e., $R_0 \rightarrow 0$, $R_1 \rightarrow 1$, $R_2 \rightarrow 2$, and $R_N \rightarrow N$

c) Iterate the CLM using selected initial conditions *IC* and fixed value of *r*. Chaotic map is iterated until all the positions in position vector is filled as

$$P = \{P_i, P_{i+1}, \cdots, P_N\} \tag{6}$$

Where *P* denotes the position vector and P_i to P_N signifies the position of '1' in scrambling matrix. During the course of iteration, whenever chaotic map falls in the specific subdomain, the number assigned to that subdomain is stored in position vector *P*. If the chaotic map has already traversed the specific subdomain or interval, then the position corresponding to that subdomain is ignored. Hence, iterations will continue until the chaotic map has traversed all the subdomains. For example

$[x0, \; x1 \; x3 \; \cdots \; x_N]$ are the input elements which may fall in the subintervals indexed as $[P45, \; P5, \; P13 \; P2 \; \cdots \; P_1]$.

d) Stop iterating the chaotic map when it has finished traversing all regions.

e) Finally, the scrambling matrix S of size $N \times N$ is generated by using position matrix generated by the above mentioned methodology. The complete scrambling matrix after assigning each position is written as

$$S_{i,k} = \begin{bmatrix} S_{i,k} & S_{i,k+1} & \cdots & S_{i,N} \\ S_{i+1,k} & S_{i+1,k+1} & \cdots & S_{i+1,N} \\ \vdots & \vdots & \ddots & \vdots \\ S_{N,k} & S_{N,k+1} & \cdots & S_{N,N} \end{bmatrix} \tag{7}$$

The above matrix can be written as

$$S = \{S_i, S_{i+1}, \cdots, S_N\}^T \tag{8}$$

where S_i is the row vector.

The algorithm works in such a way that each row vector in scrambling matrix contains "1" as in (9)

$$S_i \oplus S_j = 0, \qquad i \neq j \tag{9}$$

where j is any other row vector of scrambling matrix $S \in [i, N]$ and "$\oplus$" stands for exclusive OR (XOR) operation.

This scrambling matrix is reversible to correctly recover the data with symmetric key.

2.2 Proposed OFDM System

The proposed OFDM System shown in Figure. 1 can be easily implemented. The scrambling matrix is multiplied with N randomly generated symbols as,

$$X_e = X_N \times S \tag{10}$$

where X_N, S are input symbols and scrambling matrix of size $N \times 1$ and $N \times N$ respectively. We obtain the OFDM baseband signal by applying the IFFT,

$$X_n = IFFT\{X_e\} \tag{11}$$

where, X_n is the frequency domain vector signal respectively. At receiver same procedure follows to descramble the constellation symbols.

3 Security Analysis

Wireless LANs are highly susceptible to numerous malicious attacks. In wireless systems layer abstraction is very important concept, requiring each layer to provide independent functionality separately to strengthen the security of the system. At link layer and higher layers security mechanisms are used to protect the transmission data in order to prevent attacker to manipulate useful information. Even if the strong confidentiality and mutual authentication protocols are used at MAC layer, it still leaves many weak spots for attackers to explore. At MAC layer only data frames are encrypted while leaving management and control frames unprotected. In addition, MAC headers are also left unencrypted. In what follows, it is shown that by providing the security at the physical layer by the proposed SBR Interleaver, which scrambles the complete MPDU (MAC Protocol Data Unit) frame, how a Wireless LAN can be made secure against some of the current prevailing threats.

3.1 Traffic Analysis / Passive Eavesdropping

The security mechanism in WLAN aims to achieve the security level comparable to that of the wired LANs. However due to the characteristics of WLANs, the attacker can sniff and store all the traffic passing through WLAN. Hence it is very important to analyze whether the attacker may learn any meaningful information from the stored traffic of the WLAN.

To provide security at physical layers with proposed SBR Interleaver scheme each transmitting frame is encrypted/ scrambled with a unique key. In order to strengthen the security mechanism, master key/primary key is generated that will serve to initiate our proposed SBR Interleaver algorithm [9]. To analyze the strength of key against passive eavesdropping, key sensitivity and positional significance of each character in external secret key has been discussed in section 3.1.1 and 3.1.2 respectively.

Let this primary key be IC_1 that is used to encrypt/scramble the first frame. Let the frame to be scramble is denoted by F. It can be shown by:

$$S_1 = SBRI\ (F_1, IC_1) \tag{12}$$

where S_1 is the first scrambled frame. To generate the new key to encrypt the second frame $F2$, the next output of $RSNG$ after scrambling the first frame serve as a key to encrypt F_2 is IC_2. The remaining keys from IC_3 to IC_N for encrypting the frames F_3 to F_N respectively can be generated in the same way. The encrypted/scrambled frames S_2 to S_N each with a unique key can be written as:

$$S_1 = SBRI\ (F_2, IC_2) \tag{13}$$

$$\vdots$$

$$S_1 = SBRI\ (F_N, IC_N) \tag{14}$$

where S_N is the total number of scrambled frames.

In our proposed SBR Interleaver each frame scrambled/interleaved contains 64 symbols, so there are 64! possible symbols combinations. We transmit 1000 random OFDM frames which lead to 64000! or 2^{64000} possible combinations. Hence it is infeasible to exhaustively search all the probable secret positions as each frame is encrypted/scrambled by the proposed SBR Interleaver with the different initial conditions. However when more than one frame is encrypted with the same initial conditions, the security of the proposed scheme will be low against the chosen plaintext attack which is evaluated later. From the above discussion, it is evident that encrypting each frame with the distinct initial condition makes it infeasible for the attacker to break the proposed SBR Interleaver through exhaustive searching technique.

The proposed SBR Interleaver helps to increase the entry barrier to break in, since it will take time and cost to break the key in real time. Moreover, attacker needs to check all possible combinations which are infeasible in real time. Finally, our proposed SBR Interleaver is used to scramble constellation symbols. and with the wrong key the values of constellation symbols are still equally likely. These scrambled constellation symbols entail no useful information to the attacker. After the transmission, only scrambled waveform is available which in fact is not useful information. Moreover, it is really challenging to first extract the correct bit level information from waveform and then to manipulate it to sneak through WLAN.

In conclusion, our proposed technique helps to prevent attacks on PHY layer and provides security by avoiding correct recording and snooping of MAC Protocol Data Unit (MPDU). Furthermore, PHY layer headers are also protected using SBR Interleaver. It contains Forward Error Correction (FEC), interleaving pattern, coding, phase offset etc. that are available for the receiver to obtain transmitted data. Encrypting PHY layer information further enhances the security of WLAN.

3.1.1 Key Sensitivity Analysis

Since a cryptosystem cannot exist without a key, it must be clearly defined what parameters serve as a key. Once the key has been defined, it is equally important to analyze the strength of the key depth.

To evaluate the performance of key sensitivity of our proposed SBR Interleaver, randomly generated symbols are scrambled. Simulation in MATLAB® has been performed in order to evaluate the performance of the proposed algorithm. For the modulation of randomly generated data, we consider QPSK, 4-QAM and 8-QAM for N=64, 128 and 256 carriers for 1000 OFDM frames.

At receiver when descrambled with same initial conditions, all constellation symbols are recovered with zero error. However, when the same data is recovered with slightly different initial conditions, almost all the constellation symbols are in error. The probability of error is uniformly distributed in symbols. The probability of occurrence of each constellation symbols when decrypted with slightly different initial conditions is shown in Fig. 2. The X-axis presents the QPSK constellation symbols and Y-axis shows the probability of frequency of occurrence of each constellation symbol. The number of differing positions, in the two scrambling matrices generated with two slightly different initial conditions, is almost 98%. How efficiently our proposed technique will generate difference positions with slightly change in initial conditions is tabulated in Table 1 and initial conditions differ only at 4th decimal digit. The generation of difference position is not dependent on random source; rather it depends on inherent properties of SBR Interleaver. The comparison of probability of error of differencing positions is also carried out using RAND function in MATLAB and chaotic sequence using CLM which is tabulated in Table 2. Results show that both have nearly same performance. It confirms that with the slightly different initial conditions it is not feasible to recover the data.

Table 1. ICs for Typical External Secret Keys

External Secret Key-*K*	R	IC
{'a' 'b' 'c' 'd' 'e' 'f' 'g' 'h' 'i' 'j' 'k' 'l' 'm' 'n' 'o' 'p'}	9.8458	0.8458
{'b' 'a' 'c' 'd' 'e' 'f' 'g' 'h' 'i' 'j' 'k' 'l' 'm' 'n' 'o' 'p'}	9.4438	0.4438
{'a' 'b' 'd' 'c' 'e' 'f' 'g' 'h' 'i' 'j' 'k' 'l' 'm' 'n' 'o' 'p'}	10.0774	0.0774
{'a' 'b' 'c' 'd' 'f' 'e' 'g' 'h' 'i' 'j' 'k' 'l' 'm' 'n' 'o' 'p'}	8.9865	0.9865
{'a' 'b' 'c' 'd' 'e' 'f' 'h' 'g' 'i' 'j' 'k' 'l' 'm' 'n' 'o' 'p'}	8.8735	0.8735
{'a' 'b' 'c' 'd' 'e' 'f' 'g' 'h' 'j' 'i' 'k' 'l' 'm' 'n' 'o' 'p'}	8.8053	0.8053
{'a' 'b' 'c' 'd' 'e' 'f' 'g' 'h' 'i' 'j' 'l' 'k' 'm' 'n' 'o' 'p'}	9.6060	0.6060
{'a' 'b' 'c' 'd' 'e' 'f' 'g' 'h' 'i' 'j' 'k' 'l' 'n' 'm' 'o' 'p'}	10.4678	0.4678
{'a' 'b' 'c' 'd' 'e' 'f' 'g' 'h' 'i' 'j' 'k' 'l' 'm' 'n' 'p' 'o'}	9.8739	0.8739
{'p' 'b' 'c' 'd' 'e' 'f' 'g' 'h' 'i' 'j' 'k' 'l' 'm' 'n' 'o' 'a'}	10.0333	0.0333
{'a' 'o' 'c' 'd' 'e' 'f' 'g' 'h' 'i' 'j' 'k' 'l' 'm' 'n' 'b' 'p'}	9.1932	0.1932
{'a' 'b' 'n' 'd' 'e' 'f' 'g' 'h' 'i' 'j' 'k' 'l' 'm' 'c' 'o' 'p'}	9.4743	0.4743
{'a' 'b' 'c' 'm' 'e' 'f' 'g' 'h' 'i' 'j' 'k' 'l' 'd' 'n' 'o' 'p'}	9.9999	0.9999
{'a' 'b' 'c' 'd' 'l' 'f' 'g' 'h' 'i' 'j' 'k' 'e' 'm' 'n' 'o' 'p'}	9.0108	0.0108
{'a' 'b' 'c' 'd' 'e' 'k' 'g' 'h' 'i' 'j' 'f' 'l' 'm' 'n' 'o' 'p'}	8.5547	0.5547
{'a' 'b' 'c' 'd' 'e' 'f' 'j' 'h' 'i' 'g' 'k' 'l' 'm' 'n' 'o' 'p'}	8.4095	0.4095
{'a' 'b' 'c' 'd' 'e' 'f' 'g' 'i' 'h' 'j' 'k' 'l' 'm' 'n' 'o' 'p'}	7.7317	0.7317
{'o' 'p' 'c' 'd' 'e' 'f' 'g' 'h' 'I' 'j' 'k' 'l' 'm' 'n' 'a' 'b'}	7.2468	0.2468
{'i' 'j' 'k' 'l' 'm' 'n' 'o' 'p' 'a' 'b' 'c' 'd' 'e' 'f' 'g' 'h'}	6.7497	0.7497
{'e' 'f' 'g' 'h' 'm' 'n' 'o' 'p' 'a' 'b' 'c' 'd' 'I' 'j' 'k' 'l'}	8.2779	0.2779
{'a' 'b' 'c' 'd' 'I' 'j' 'k' 'l' 'e' 'f' 'g' 'h' 'm' 'n' 'o' 'p'}	8.68	0.68
{'m' 'n' 'o' 'p' 'i' 'j' 'k' 'l' 'a' 'b' 'c' 'd' 'e' 'f' 'g' 'h'}	9.0319	0.0107
{'a' 'b' 'c' 'd' 'e' 'f' 'g' 'h' 'm' 'n' 'o' 'p' 'I' 'j' 'k' 'l'}	6.7246	0.8041
{'d' 'e' 'f' 'g' 'h' 'a' 'b' 'c' 'm' 'n' 'o' 'p' 'i' 'j' 'k' 'l'}	9.2388	0.1288
{'d' 'e' 'f' 'g' 'h' 'n' 'o' 'p' 'i' 'j' 'k' 'a' 'b' 'c' 'm' 'l'}	6.6594	0.4584
{'j' 'k' 'a' 'b' 'c' 'm' 'l' 'd' 'e' 'f' 'g' 'h' 'n' 'o' 'p' 'i'}	7.6044	0.7049
{'m' 'l' 'd' 'e' 'f' 'g' 'h' 'n' 'o' 'j' 'k' 'a' 'b' 'c' 'p' 'i'}	10.0153	0.0957
{'m' 'l' 'd' 'e' 'f' 'g' 'h' 'n' 'o' 'j' 'I' 'a' 'b' 'c' 'p' 'k'}	9.1755	0.9731
{'m' 'l' 'd' 'e' 'f' 'g' 'h' 'n' 'k' 'a' 'b' 'c' 'p' 'I' 'o' 'j'}	7.4701	0.5209
{'m' 'l' 'h' 'n' 'o' 'i' 'k' 'a' 'b' 'c' 'p' 'I' 'd' 'e' 'f' 'g'}	8.5193	0.6373

3.1.2 Positional Significance of Each Character in the External Secret Key

The simulation parameters to analyze the positional significance in external secret key are same as described in section 4.2.The analysis of master/primary key generation has been discussed in [9]. During the mapping process of the external secret key to some intermediate variables in proposed SBR Interleaver, the positional significance of each character is retained. The sub-algorithm used for mapping the external secret key to IC, is contained in the equations (15-18), which are given as:

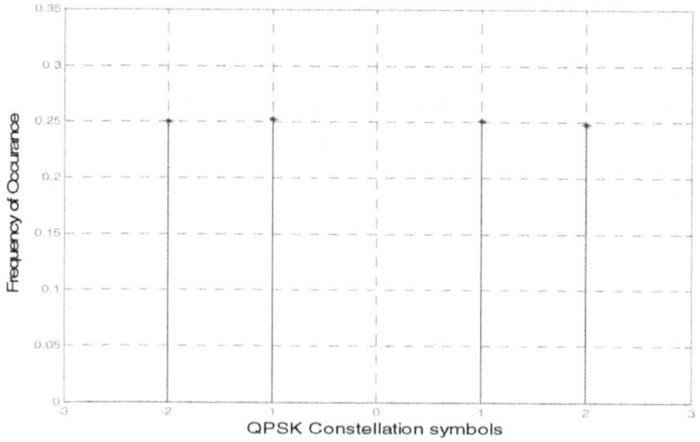

Fig. 2. Probability of occurrence of constellation points with slightly different initial condition

$$K = K_1 K_2 K_3 \cdots K_{16} \tag{15}$$

$$IC_i = K_i / 256 \tag{16}$$

$$R = \sum_{i=1}^{16} RSGF_i^{K_i}(IC_i, p_i) \tag{17}$$

$$IC = R \bmod 1 \tag{18}$$

The random sequences can be generated using any random source, so that *RSGF* in above equations stand for random sequence generator function. Equation (12) represents external secret key that consists of 16-characters. In equation (13), each character is uniformly mapped to a real number in the interval $(0, 1)$, that is represented by IC_i which serves as the initial condition for i^{th} RSGF. In equation (14), i^{th} RSGF with initial condition IC_i, is iterated K_i times to derive 16 random numbers that are summed together resulting in the intermediate variable S.

During the mapping process to the intermediate variable S, the positional significance of each character in the secret key is retained. From equation (13), it is evident that the ith character in the secret key serves as initial condition for the ith RSGF and it is iterated K_i times, where K_i is the ASCII value of the corresponding i^{th} character. Hence different combinations of the secret key consisting of the same characters will result in different random numbers that are summed together, resulting in different values for the intermediate variable S which are shown in Table 1.

3.2 Data Forgery Attacks

The MAC frames which are not encrypted, can serve as starting points to initialize different forgery attacks. The attacker eavesdrop the unprotected information and masquerades as access point (AP) to initialize de-authentication and disassociation attacks. The unprotected information available in MAC frame gives a chance for an attacker to sneak in and disrupts the transmission. The information in MAC header gives source and destination addresses, controlling parameters and MAC address, which are there to determine correct destination. But, attacker uses this information and initializes session-hijacking attacks to disconnect devices. Typically an intruder forces a legitimate user to terminate its connection to an access point.

By snooping unprotected frames at MAC layer, intruder initializes Man-in-the-Middle attack to snoop their credentials by inserting himself between legitimate client and AP. By doing this the attacker forges the unprotected frames, modifies the frames and forwards it to the recipient. Intruder pretends to be authorized AP to client and authorized client to AP and fool them both.

All these attacks are prevented by our proposed SBR Interleaver.. The unprotected frames at MAC layer and MAC header are protected so the data recorded at MAC layer is completely wrong, and wrong frame format does not give any information to intruder. For attacker, there is no information at all, since the transmitted data is encrypted at PHY layer. Data insertion attacks are also not possible because the data is encrypted and intruder needs to break the key to get the correct datafor which he needs to check all possible key combinations to get the correct key.

3.3 Denial of Service Attacks

One of the active attacks in WLAN is Denial of Service attacks (DoS). Typical DoS attacks involve flooding the network and preventing legitimate user to access the network resources. By using the characteristics of WLAN, attacker can launch DoS attack to disrupt the network traffic. At link layer, one type of attack is to forge the

Table 2. Comparison of Probability of Wrong Input Elements with Diff. Key using Chaotic Sequence and RAND based sequence

IC with	Chaotic Sequence		RAND based Sequence	
Slight Diff.	Diff Position/512	%age Diff. position	Diff Position/512	%age Diff. position
0.1534,0.1535	511	99.80	511	99.80
0.2411,0.2412	508	99.21	509	99.41
0.3855,0.3856	510	99.60	511	99.80
0.4882,0.4883	508	99.21	510	99.60
0.5371,0.5372	512	100.00	511	99.80
0.6981,0.6982	509	99.67	511	99.80
0.7191,0.7192	511	99.80	511	99.80
0.8323,0.8324	510	99.60	511	99.80
0.9167,0.9168	511	99.80	512	100.00

unprotected management frame to de-authenticate and disassociate frames to prevent the legitimate clients to use the network resources. The adversary forges the control frame to initialize attack to disrupt the virtual carrier sense mechanism [10]. Hence the introduction of SBR Interleaver at PHY layer secures such information which are left unprotected at link layer. The DoS attacks cannot be eliminated completely but can be minimized. Therefore, PHY layer security could help to prevent attacker to exploit the protocol weaknesses and resist against DoS attacks.

Since, PHY is secured with SBR Interleaver; therefore to initialize DoS attacks requires reasonable efforts by the attacker. With the proposed technique any insertion attack can be filtered out because it needs to break the key to get in. The worst de-authentication and disassociation attacks can be minimized and eliminated.

3.4 Known Plaintext Attack

It is an attempt to decode the current plaintext using the current ciphertext and previous samples of plaintext and their corresponding ciphertext. This attack is more likely to succeed than the ciphertext-only attack. In this type of attack the unauthorized receiver knows what the plaintext was for some previous messages, however he cannot choose those plaintext samples. Therefore the samples he has may or may not enable him to decode the current message and recover the secret key.

Generally permutation-only schemes are considered to be insecure if the same secret key (initial conditions /control parameters) is used for the encryption of more than one sets of data (let's say more than one frames). One way to break permutation only schemes with only one known frame or set of data would be to see the effect of the permutation on the corresponding input and output differentials $(\Delta x_i, \Delta y_i)$ in two frames since permutation with same secret key will map the corresponding bytes (i^{th} bytes) within the frames to same location j. As permutation-only schemes do not change the value of the input data, hence input differential Δx_i will be equal to the corresponding output differential Δy_i. Now assume that the adversary has access to one known set of the data- P_1, then the second set of data P_2, which has the same length as P_1, can be recovered as: $P_2 = P_1 \oplus C_m$, where $C_m = C_1^{'} \oplus C_2^{'}$ and $C_1^{'}$, $C_2^{'}$ are the encrypted form of P_1 and P_2, respectively. Here C_m servers as equivalent to the secret key and can be called as mask frame.

However, if the frames are being encrypted (permuted) by the encryption algorithm using different secret keys (initial conditions/control parameters), then the corresponding input differential Δx_i will not be equal to the corresponding output differential Δy_i. Hence the adversary will not be able to recover the second frame (or set of data) P_2 using C_m even if he has the access to P_1. From the above discussion, it is obvious that it is not possible to break SBR Interleaver using known plaintext attack if the frames are scrambled using different secret keys.

4 Conclusion

In this paper, securing OFDM system at PHY Layer is reported. A novel security mechanism is proposed for OFDM based systems, where constellation symbols are dynamically scrambled. In order to do so, a novel seed based random interleaver is designed for secure interleaving. It will generate secure unpredictable sequences to interleave constellation symbols. The analysis of proposed technique as a PHY layer security device has been carried out. Results show that proposed SBR Interleaver can be used to secure PHY layer data. The proposed method is extremely sensitive to the initial conditions, therefore a slight difference in initial conditions result in almost completely different position matrix. Furthermore, it is shown that recovering constellation symbols with a wrong key is not feasible because attacker has only waveform information. Hence, the attacker needs to break into t waveform level first, which is not possible in real time, and then only he can try to sneak into bit level information for further breaking in. Our proposed secure interleaving technique has inherent properties to generate unpredictable sequences with any random source, so that the key sensitivity analysis gives nearly same results with both RAND based and chaotic sequences. It is also shown that by scrambling the transmission data helps in resisting DoS attacks. Securing PHY layer enhances the security at MAC layer.. Data privacy and data forgery attacks can be prevented. PHY layer security by our proposed scheme substantially increases the entry barrier for breaking in.

References

[1] Liu, C., Yu, J.: A Solution to WLAN Authentication and Association DoS Attacks. IAENG International Journal of Computer Science 34(1) (2007)

[2] Malekzadeh, M., Abdul Ghani, A.A., Ahmad Zulkarnain, Z., Muda, Z.: Security Improvement for Management Frames in IEEE 802.11 Wireless Networks. IJCSNS International Journal of Computer Science and Network Security 7(6) (June 2007)

[3] Asif Khan, M., Asim, M., Jeoti, V.: Chaos Based Constellation Scrambling: Security and Interleaving Issues. In: ITSIM 2008, pp. 1–7 (August 26-28, 2008) ISBN: 978-1-4244-2327-9

[4] Hiltunen, K.: WLAN attacks and risks, http://www.comlab.hut.fi/opetus/333/2004slides/topic30.pdf

[5] Xiao, Y., Pan, Y., Du, X., Bandela, C., Dass, K.: Security mechanism, attacks, and security enhancements for the IEEE 802.11 WLANs. International Journal of Wireless and Mobile Computing, special issue on Medium Access Control for WLANs, PANs and Sensor Network 1(3/4), 276–288 (2005)

[6] He, C., Mitchell, J.C.: Security analysis and improvements for 802.11i. In: The 12th Annual Network and Distributed System Security Symposium, NDSS 2005, pp. 90–110 (February 2005)

[7] Baranovsky, A., Daems, D.: The design of one dimensional chaotic maps with prescribed statistical properties. International Journal of Bifurcation of Chaos & Fractals 5(6) (1995)

[8] Asim, M., Jeoti, V.: Hybrid chaotic image encryption scheme based on S-box and ciphertext feedback. In: IEEE International Conference on Intelligent and Advanced Systems, pp. 736–741 (November 2007) ISBN: 978-1-4244-1355-3

[9] Asif Khan, M.: A Novel Seed Based Random Interleaver Design for OFDM System and its PHY layer Security Issues, Master's Thesis, Universiti Teknologi PETRONAS (2009)

[10] Bellardo, J., Savage, S.: 802.11 Denial-of-Service attacks: Real vulnerabilities and practical solution. In: Usenix Security Symposium, pp. 15–28 (August 4-8, 2003)

[11] Liu, C., Yu, J.T.: Review and Analysis of Wireless LAN Security Attacks and Solutions. Journal of International Engineering Consortium 59, 539–554 (2006) ISBN: 978-1-931695-53-4

[12] Liu, C., Yu, J.T.: An Analysis of DoS Attacks on Wireless LAN. In: IASTED International Conferences on Wireless Networks and Emerging Technologies (WNET 2006), Banff, Canada (2006)

[13] Ding, P., Holliday, J., Celik, A.: Improving the Security of Wireless LANs by Managing 802.1X Disassociaion. In: Proceedings of the IEEE Consumer Communications and Networking Conference, Las Vegas, NV, pp. 53–58 (2004)

[14] Grech, S., Nikkanen, J.: A Security Analysis of Wi-Fi Protected Access. In: The 9th Nordic Workshop on Secure IT-systems. Helsinki University of Technology, Finland (2004)

[15] Ge, W., Sampalli, S.: A Novel Scheme For Prevention of Management Frame Attacks on Wireless LANs (2005)

[16] Chen, D., Deng, J., Varshney, P.K.: Protecting Wireless Networks against a Denial of Service Attack Based on Virtual Jamming. In: ACM MobiCom 2003, Poster, San Diego, CA, USA (2003)

[17] Gupta, V., Krishnamurthy, S., Faloutsos, M.: Denial of Service Attacks at the MAC Layer in Wireless Ad Hoc Networks. In: Proceedings of 2002 MILCOM Conference, vol. 2 (2002)

[18] Vladimirov, A.A., Gavrilenko, K.V., Mikhailovsky, A.A., Wi-Foo: The Secrets of Wireless Hacking, pp. 159–195. Pearson/Addison Wesley (June 2004)

[19] Mishra, A., Arbaugh, W.A.: An Initial Security Analysis of the 802.1X Standard. University of Maryland, CS-TR-4328, UMIACS-TR-2002-10 (February 2002)

[20] Walker, J.: Status of Project IEEE 802.11 Task Group w, Protected Management Frames (2007), http://grouper.ieee.org/groups/802/11/Reports/tgw_update.htm

Author Index

GPSR Compliance

The European Union's (EU) General Product Safety Regulation (GPSR) is a set of rules that requires consumer products to be safe and our obligations to ensure this.

If you have any concerns about our products, you can contact us on ProductSafety@springernature.com

In case Publisher is established outside the EU, the EU authorized representative is:

Springer Nature Customer Service Center GmbH
Europaplatz 3
69115 Heidelberg, Germany

Batch number: 10844619

Printed by Printforce, the Netherlands